A HISTORY OF
THE UNITED NATIONS

Volume 1: The Years of
Western Domination, 1945–1955

A HISTORY OF
THE UNITED NATIONS

Volume 1: The Years of
Western Domination, 1945–1955

Evan Luard

St. Martin's Press   New York

ISBN 0-312-38654-0

Library of Congress Cataloging in Publication Data

Luard, Evan, 1926–
  A history of the United Nations.

  Bibliography: v. 1, p.
  Includes index.
  Contents: v. 1. The years of western domination,
1945–1955—
    1. United Nations—History. I. Title.
JX1977.L79 1982   341.23′09   81–16701
ISBN 0-312-38654-0 (v. 1)

Contents

Preface

This study does not purport to be a comprehensive, still less a definitive, history of the United Nations. It is not comprehensive since it is concerned almost exclusively with the central responsibility of the organisation, the maintenance of international peace and security, and deals only briefly, and almost in passing, with other important areas of the UN's work – for example with its activities in the economic field and its human rights work – and barely mentions the multifarious activities of the specialised agencies (which are part of the UN 'system', but not of the UN itself, having separate memberships and assemblies).[1] It is not definitive because some of the evidence necessary for final judgements, including all the internal documents of the UN Secretariat, are not available.

Quite apart from these problems, there is a major difficulty of scale in writing a history of this kind. To give a detailed account of the way the UN has handled every problem which has come before it would have required a history of even more ample proportions than this has assumed. Even on its present scale, the book confines discussion of major events in international history – such as the Korean war and the Suez episode – to a single chapter, with all the dangers of oversimplification which this involves. Yet to have provided still more detailed accounts, of the kind which may well be required to afford a full understanding of such issues, and of the standpoint of each individual party to them, would have involved writing something like a history of the world over the last 30 or 40 years, a quite different task which I am in no way competent to undertake. I have, therefore, sought to confine my account of the background to each conflict to a brief description of the main events, usually at the beginning of each chapter; and to concentrate primarily on describing the action which the UN has taken in seeking to confront each dispute or threat to peace. The eventual aim will be to seek to draw conclusions about the effectiveness of the organisation in fulfilling the responsibilities which have been laid upon it, and to consider whether the use of alternative responses and procedures might enable it to play a more significant role.

I should like to express my gratitude to the Social Science Research Council for the award of a grant which enabled me to embark on this history; to the Institute for the Study of International Organisations (now defunct but formerly attached to Sussex University), and especially to its former director, Mr Robert Rhodes James, for much valuable assistance and support while this volume was being written; to St Antony's College, Oxford, for providing a home for me during the time I was engaged on the work; to many international officials and some former ambassadors who have kindly provided information for me on individual points; and last, but not least, to Mrs Toni Tattersall for her invaluable secretarial assistance over many years, which has made the task of bringing this history to publication very much easier than it would otherwise have been.

E.L.

Part I

The Birth of the New Organisation

1 The Lessons of the League

Those who want peace, it is said, prepare for war. Those who are already at war prepare for peace. So, before the Second World War was even halfway through, debate began about the new organisation which was to be established at its end.

Both among the general public and among governments there were varying views about the form the new organisation should take. But about one thing there was general agreement: the new organisation, whatever its powers and functions, must be an improvement on the one which had gone before. All those involved in the deliberations had lived through the painful and disillusioning history of the League. All had shared, at least in some measure, the hope that that institution, revolutionary in its original conception, would be a means of abolishing war from the earth and substituting the saner procedures of international conciliation. Instead they had seen that brief and inglorious organisation prove totally ineffectual.

The League's record in fact, even in matters of peace and war, was not altogether bad. Once or twice in its very early years, when the incident was small and the nation to be withstood was weak, the League had begun to live up to its promises. It resolved a frontier dispute between Finland and Sweden; defended the sovereignty of infant Albania when she was threatened by Greek and Yugoslav forces; secured the withdrawal of Greek forces from Bulgaria in 1925 and the payment of compensation by Greece after an incident between the two countries; resolved a territorial dispute between Turkey and Iraq over Mosul; and even, in 1934, sent a small peace-keeping force to occupy an area disputed between Colombia and Peru, which secured the withdrawal of Peruvian forces. All of these, though relatively trivial, could be regarded by optimists as the successful application of the principles the League was created to uphold. But in almost

3

every case the success, such as it was, was achieved by the relatively easy course of passing resolutions and exerting pressures, never through the more onerous burden of despatching troops and tanks to defend a threatened member, as the Covenant of the League presupposed. And so, when, later, more powerful threats to the peace appeared – the Japanese incursion into Manchuria, the Italian attack on Ethiopia, the successive German annexations of the Rhineland, Austria and Czechoslovakia – the League proved incapable of putting into effect the main principle to which it was committed.

The determination to learn from this experience was among the most important influences affecting those who sought to establish a new and better organisation. So important was this influence that it is worth examining in some detail the main lessons that were drawn from the history of the previous twenty years.

THE NEED FOR CLEAR-CUT OBLIGATIONS

The League had been designed to implement, in the most explicit and concrete form, the principle of 'collective security', to which lip-service at the time was everywhere paid. This was the principle of each for all and all for each: the rule that, wherever an act of 'aggression' occurred, the whole international community would combine to defend the victim. In so doing, it would defend not only the particular country concerned, but peace itself. In place of the partial and mutually conflicting alliances of the pre-1914 war, a new, universal alliance would be created, a permanent coalition of the vast majority against any state that dared threaten the peace. So the Covenant declared, in Article 11, that 'any war or threat of war, whether immediately affecting any of the members of the League or not, is hereby declared a matter of concern to the whole League'; and in Article 10 it laid down that 'therefore the members of the League undertake to respect and preserve as against external aggression the territorial integrity and existing political independence of all members of the League'. To achieve this object, when an act of aggression took place, the League's Council was to 'advise upon the means by which this obligation should be fulfilled'.

In theory this system should have been foolproof. If the principle had been fully implemented, in both the spirit and the letter, on every occasion when peace was threatened, no nation would ever have dared to take action to breach the peace, certain in the knowledge that this would unite against it the combined forces of the rest of the world. Japan would not have invaded Manchuria, Italy would not have attacked Ethiopia, Germany would not have invaded the Rhineland, Czechoslovakia or Poland. If, therefore, these things had none the less happened, there was something wrong with the theory. What this was was plain. It was that, while nations would readily subscribe to the abstract theory of 'collective security', they were not usually willing, in concrete situations, to undergo the strenuous sacrifices involved in going to war to fulfil it. They would not feel that an aggression on the other side of the world, or even on the other side of Europe, was so immediately a 'matter of concern' as to make involvement in war to defeat it obligatory. Aggression by one state against another was more common in the League's life than at any time in the preceding century. Yet on no occasion, for all their undertakings, did any member of the League 'take up arms to respect and preserve, as against aggression, the territorial integrity and existing political independence' of another member-state. The principle of collective security (except possibly in the self-interested action of Britain and France in going to war over Poland in 1939) was never put into effect.

Part of the problem was that the Covenant never really demanded this. Under Article 16 members were under an absolute obligation to apply economic and communications sanctions against another member which had gone to war in disregard of its covenant. But they were under no obligation to take any stronger action. If economic sanctions were to fail the Council might 'recommend' armed action to defend the victim. But no member was automatically obliged to respond. And in fact no such recommendation was ever even made by the League Council.

This, in the eyes of its successors, was one of the major weaknesses of the League system. Despite the fine sentiments contained in the Covenant, there was no total obligation on the part of members to fulfil its principles. In fact, the textual weakness might not have mattered so much if the spirit had been strong. But the spirit was far from strong. And, given that most members were only too glad of any justification for avoiding unpleasant action where possible, the lack of any absolute obligation provided a heaven-sent justification to members for escaping all unwelcome responsibilities.

The lesson was clear. A purely voluntary commitment to go to the defence of other states if they were attacked was far too feeble to be of any value. It in practice enabled each member to interpret its obligations to suit its own tastes and interests. Each member did so in a way which minimised obligations and nullified effective deterrence. Clearly a far more specific obligation, based on collective and not individual judgement, would be required. The theory of all for each and each for all had been exploded. The fact was that each was not for all, but only for each. Only all might act effectively for all.

THE NEED FOR TEETH

There was another lesson that was equally widely drawn. Many felt that the reason for the League's failure lay not so much in the weakness of the Covenant's obligations, or the pusillanimity of its members, as in the deficiency of power available to it. The League had collapsed because it had no 'teeth'.

The idea that the League should possess and control forces of its own had been too revolutionary to be seriously entertained at the time of its foundation. France alone at that time favoured the idea: the League should possess substantial forces under its control to uphold the Versailles settlement. But this was because the League was, in France's eyes, merely a legalised form of the victorious alliance and should so enforce the peace on its victim, Germany. Virtually no other nation supported such a proposal. In general the prerogatives of national sovereignty were still far too deeply cherished at the time the League was founded. And it was almost everywhere taken for granted that national governments must retain control of their own forces and themselves determine whether or not they should be committed to any particular collective action to defeat aggression.

The only substitutes were the non-military collective measures which were supposed to be the first response. If a member resorted to war in disregard of its covenants, other members would 'immediately . . . subject it to the severance of all trade and financial relations, the prohibition of all intercourse between the nationals of the covenant-breaking state and the nationals of any other state, whether members of the League or not'. In other words, the proposal was for a blockade, as well as a boycott, in the first place. Only if these measures failed would the Council 'recommend to the several governments concerned what effective military, naval or air forces the members of the League should severally contribute to the armed forces that were used to protect the Covenant of the League'. But such a recommendation, as we saw, would not be binding in effect.[1] And it was inevitably assumed that, even if used for that purpose, such forces would remain solely under national control.

Nor did the actual experiences of the League give much confidence in the type of sanctions with which it had been provided. Only once, and all too briefly, were even economic sanctions employed, against Italy after an especially brazen assault on a fellow member of the League. They were applied in a way that was likely to rob them of all effect. Most of Italy's immediate neighbours and chief trading partners refused to apply them. Oil, the only commodity an embargo on which was likely to have much effect, was explicitly excluded. And most non-members of the League continued to supply the products that were partially cut off from elsewhere. After less than a year, and with Italy still in control of much of Ethiopia, the measure had been withdrawn.

Still less did the League ever call for the use of collective military force, as Article 16 proposed. It was never once suggested that member-states should 'severally contribute' the forces needed for effective resistance to aggressions; nor even that they should mobilise or threaten such resistance. Japan, Italy and Germany were enabled to get away with their successive aggressions without any serious suggestion that the League should call for the use of force against them.

Thus the application of sanctions by the League was a disastrous failure. Without the will to fight, its members comforted themselves with the thought that this was because the League never had the means to fight. It was thus almost universally concluded that, to be effective, any subsequent organisation must be equipped with some more substantial military power to implement its decisions.

THE NEED FOR NEW PROCEDURES

There was a third lesson that was drawn by some. The League inherited from the world before 1914 the tradition that what was really required to resolve the conflicts of states were legal procedures, comparable to those used to resolve disputes within states.

Mediation and arbitration had been used since the time of ancient Greece. They had been refined and developed during the nineteenth century in Europe. Foreign sovereigns or governments had often been asked to resolve disputes over frontiers or other questions between states. And the Hague conferences of 1899 and 1907 had sought to develop further the use of such procedures: for example, by setting up a permanent court of arbitration.

In the League there had been an attempt to carry these methods to their logical conclusion. On the one hand, still more legal bodies were established. A Permanent International Court of Justice was now set up which, it was hoped, would resolve some of the conflicts about which nations had formerly gone to war. A new procedure of 'conciliation', a more informal method of mediation, was developed. And, under the Optional Protocol of the Court, it was even laid down that states might accept the 'compulsory' or automatic jurisdiction of the Court in a dispute involving another state which had accepted this. If widely adopted, this would indeed have established a form of jurisdiction not unlike that exercised by law-courts within states: one which governments would have been legally bound to accept. In fact, the effect was largely nullified because few states ratified the Optional Protocol; and those that did in many cases made substantial reservations, excluding all the most important types of conflict from its provisions.

But the use of legal procedures was not confined to the tribunals set up for the purpose. Even the normal procedures of the League resembled a legal hearing. The issues between states were everywhere conceived as 'disputes' between two states. Members were obliged under the Covenant to submit all such questions to the Council for decision if they had not been submitted to legal procedures. The Council would hear the pleas of the parties, would retire to consider its verdict, and finally issue its judgement. The parties would be under an obligation not to go to war until this process had been completed, nor to make war against any other party which accepted the judgement. Only if the Council failed to reach a unanimous judgement would the parties be relieved from this pledge: they could then take what action they considered necessary 'for the maintenance of right and justice'.[2] Even in this case they were pledged not to go to war during the six months allowed to the Council for reaching its judgement, nor for three months after publication of the judgement.

There were many who had hoped that procedures of this kind might provide, like law-courts within states, a way of securing the peaceful adjustment of disputes. Disputes between states should be as capable of resolution by legal means as those between individuals. Even where no substantive law existed, from treaties, international conventions or customary law, the courts could establish new law based on principles of natural justice, just as domestic courts might create the law through their judgements. Thus it could always be shown which of the parties was in the 'right' and which in the 'wrong'. Those in the wrong must then be forced by the international community to accept the solution the legal procedures declared right. An objective test would in this way be provided for the rest of the international community to judge between states. If a nation rejected a judgement, whether of the Court or of the League Council, or resorted to war in defiance of that judgement, other members would be under obligation to take up arms to defend the country attacked.

There was an attractive simplicity about this formula for maintaining world peace. But in practice the experience of the interwar years scarcely provided a strong recommendation of its efficacy. For the important sources of conflict in that period were not of a kind which could have been resolved through the type of legal procedures then set up. The resentments of Germany against the provisions of the Treaty of Versailles, the demands of Italy and Hungary for further territorial gains, the expansionist ambitions of Japan, or the many other conflicts between *status quo* and revisionist powers, could never have been decided through elaborate procedures which must by definition support the *status quo*. The whole complaint of the revisionist powers was against the existing legal order and the legal principles which it embodied. Thus they would never accept procedures which depended on applying those principles.

There were, besides, no ultimate sanctions by which judgements could be imposed. Even if there had been, legal procedures must depend on some general consensus on what represented a 'just' legal system. At the very least it demanded respect for 'law' and some agreement as to its content. And none of these existed.

Here was another conclusion which had become part of the conventional wisdom by the time the UN was being planned. Most of the disputes of the time were essentially political rather than legal in character; and it was political procedures rather than legal which were required to resolve them effectively. International law, and the legal procedures which applied it, might have their part to play in resolving certain kinds of international dispute, though not usually the major ones. But they were unlikely to be able to maintain for long a peaceful and harmonious order unless they were supplemented by procedures which were political rather than legal in style.

OTHER LESSONS

These were the three most important lessons drawn from the experience of the League. But there were other conclusions, which may be mentioned more briefly.

A more universal body was needed. The League had always been limited in its membership and so robbed of the authority which many hoped it would have as a representative world body. The United States had never belonged. Germany belonged only for a brief period between 1926 and 1933. The Soviet Union belonged for a still shorter time, between 1934 and her expulsion in 1939. Italy and Japan left in the early 'thirties. And huge areas of the world, then still under colonial rule, possessed no voice at all in the organisation. To a large extent the League was run and controlled by Europe. There was a general demand that any new organisation should be in a much more real sense a world body. Above all, the great powers should all be members and play a dominant role if it was to carry influence. The United States and Soviet Union in particular must this time be accommodated within it. And the unity between the established powers in the wartime alliance must be carried into the peace that followed.

Many felt too that the rule of unanimity which had prevailed in the League must be abandoned. This had been inherited from the conference system of the nineteenth century: decisions could take effect only if they were unanimous. This was applied equally within the League's Assembly and its Council. Whatever the merits of such a system when applied to conferences which often had only five or six participants, each of them great powers whose assent was often essential to a decision becoming effective, it obviously produced far greater difficulties in an organisation of forty or fifty members. Here only a single, small and insignificant power needed to raise an objection to prevent a decision which all others might support from taking effect. In many cases this had prevented or deterred a decision that was essential if the organisation was to act effectively. For example, over Manchuria in 1931, Japan was able to prevent the adoption of a resolution against her, by her own contrary vote.[3] There was a general demand that this weakness should be rectified in any future organisation.

Next, there was a general desire that the new organisation should have wider responsibilities in the economic and social field than its predecessor. Even the League itself had come to the conclusion in its final years that it should expand its activities in this area. It had from the beginning had some duties of the sort. It held tenuously within its embrace the International Labour Organisation (ILO), which, however, had won for itself an increasingly independent existence. It established in addition a 'health organisation', concerned with the notification of diseases and the control of epidemics; but this was on a tiny scale and had at first a budget of only £20,000 a year. It had a number of committees and commissions concerned with economic and financial affairs, communications, trade and other questions. And it acquired a growing but still tiny range of human-rights responsibilities in seeking to cope with slavery, white slavery, narcotic drugs and similar questions. But all this was on a very small scale. It undertook no economic-development assistance (though it helped several East European countries restore their tottering finances). In 1938, therefore, the League had decided to consider a substantial expansion of work in this field; and on the eve of the Second World War the Bruce Committee had recommended a large-scale expansion of economic and social work, under a new central committee for economic and social questions (not unlike what ECOSOC was to become in the UN). Thus, when a successor organisation was being planned a few years later, the need for it to be given substantial responsibilities in this field was widely accepted.

Again, there were some who felt that, if the new organisation to be created was to be more powerful in relation to member-states and more independent in its judgements than its predecessor, a larger role would have to be given within it to the international officials who ran it. Sir Eric Drummond, the first secretary-general of the League, had brought to his job all the traditions of faceless anonymity of the British Civil Service. He made few personal initiatives. He would advise if consulted (and because his advice was good he was increasingly consulted), but he would not offer it uninvited. In this he performed the role not only as he himself visualised it, but also as most of the members demanded it. His successor was little different in this respect: he certainly made no effort to galvanise the organisation into action during the successive aggressions of the late 'thirties. The result was that many concluded that there was scope for a secretary-general of much wider and stronger authority. President Roosevelt wanted a well-known and powerful political personality to act as 'the world's moderator', who would play an active role on the world's stage, perhaps indeed be the dominant figure of world politics. Though others had a somewhat less exalted conception of the new secretary-general's role, all were agreed that he should be a significantly different figure, more active and less discreet, more independent and less invisible, than the chief official of the unhappy League had been. If the world organisation was itself to become a powerful force in the world, then its chief executive too must become a more powerful figure, able to inject an international viewpoint into the bickerings of national governments; to arouse the conscience of the world when international action was urgently needed; and to act as a watchdog always on the alert for situations where the peace could be threatened.

Besides these awful *warnings* derived from the League's experiences, there were also some lessons of a more heartening kind: ways in which the League had pointed the way. One of the major innovations of that organisation had been the introduction of the mandate system. The former colonies and possessions of defeated powers were not, as after previous wars, simply annexed by the victorious states, but given a more respectable status by being placed, even if somewhat theoretically, under the general oversight of the new organisation. The difference from the traditional colonial system was only marginal. Though the administering power made regular reports to the League, in practice it did very much as it liked within its own mandated territories. Few believed that the mandatory power could easily be dispossessed of its new charges by the League, even if the League so declared, or that their policies were significantly influenced by the League's injunctions. But at least the principle of accountability to an international body was established. This principle was seen as an example to be followed by those who planned a new organisation to replace the League.

Again, the example of the ILO, the largely autonomous organisation set up under the League, was one which many felt should be followed by any future organisation. Designed to promote better labour standards throughout the world, the ILO had originally been very much a part of the League itself, and was throughout financed from its budget. But it had in practice won for itself almost total independence, partly because of the energetic and effective empire-building of Albert Thomas, its first director-general, and partly because its membership was distinct from that of the League: the United States, for example, had been a member of the ILO without joining the League. Many held that its independence, strengthened in the war years, should now be recognised and further increased. In two senses, therefore, the ILO served as a model for the future. Its success within the specialised field allotted to it encouraged the notion of establishing other agencies which might be able to perform similar services in specialised fields, unencumbered by political interference (an idea elaborated by writers of the 'functionalist' school, such as David Mitrany). Secondly, the *de facto* independence which the ILO had acquired, and the benefits which many believed had been gained by it, encouraged the notion that any such agencies to be created in the future should also be endowed with a considerable measure of autonomy, to enable them to go about their business untroubled by the rivalries and dissensions of more political bodies.

Finally, perhaps the most important way in which the League served as a model for the future was the simplest: in influencing the basic structure of the organisation. The League was formed on a simple foundation: an assembly, a council, a secretariat and an international court. There was little disposition to improve on this. It provided a reasonably efficient division of labour. The only modification demanded by some was that in future responsibility in the field of security should be more exclusively concentrated in the Council, where the great powers would dominate. So the delays and political unpredictability of the League's Assembly would be avoided.

All these conclusions were present to some extent in the minds of those that came after. But a consideration of the League's record posed a wider problem. It was only too easy to fall into an elementary fallacy. The League had been founded to keep the peace, and after twenty years the world was in ruins. But was this because of the League itself, or was it because of the governments which operated it? Could any other kind of organisation have fared any better? Was it as a result of the League or in spite of it? If the latter was the case, then the new organisation did not have to be wholly different from that which came before: it was the governments and their policies that must be different. If the former was the case, a wholly different type of organisation was now required.

There was something to be said for both views. It was not the Covenant which made the League weak: the provisions of Articles 10, 11 and 15 gave it authority not merely to consider and pronounce on every international issue of the day, but also to demand particular settlements, to impose sanctions against governments that refused to accept the settlements, and, if these failed, even to call for the joint use of force against a defaulter. These were not weak powers – in their own day they were revolutionary. But their effectiveness depended utterly on a willingness to use them: that is, on the policies and attitudes of individual members. If these lacked resolution to resist aggression, no organisation, whatever its constitutional structure, could preserve the peace.

But this was not the whole truth. For the willingness of members to respond to a call for action, the willingness of the decision-making bodies to demand that action, and the authority they possess to demand it must depend in part on the constitution of the organisation concerned. And, even if governments should take the major blame for the breakdown of the previous order, it did not follow that a new constitutional structure could not produce better results in the future.

This was especially true on one point. Any collective security system would always come up against one overriding difficulty: that of securing a willingness among the rank and file of the membership to undergo the costs and pains of joining in armed action against an aggressor, over issues whose rights might be obscure and ambiguous, and in areas wholly remote from the interests of the state concerned. The constitution of an international organisation is important because it may affect this willingness. The League had attempted to establish a trigger-mechanism that would auto matically identify a transgressor: if a party in dispute refused to accept the solution which the Council laid down, then the procedure for collective enforcement would be automatically brought into play. But the system's weakness was that aggressions sometimes occurred independently of those procedures. And it remained in the final resort at the discretion of the individual member-state what action it should take in such a situation, even in response to a clear call to the Council to take action.

These were the failings that were most apparent to those that came after. A more effective security organisation, it was widely held, would need to leave less scope for individual discretion in response to an act of aggression; less opportunity for a small minority to prevent a call for action by their veto power; and less chance of delay and procrastination because of the non-availability of international forces.

Not all drew the same conclusions, nor were the attitudes of governments by any means united. But these were the common-sense lessons of the League. They were widely held in the early war years. And they were the lessons applied when plans for a new organisation to replace it began to be made from 1942 onwards.

2 The Planning of the Charter

THE FIRST DISCUSSIONS

From the beginning of the Second World War it was taken for granted in most countries that a new international organisation would be required at its end. There was little disposition to revive the League, whose manifest failures were so universally deplored, and which was anyway already almost defunct by the time the war began (though it still maintained a lame-duck existence in Geneva). A new organisation would symbolise the birth of a new world, in which peace would now at last be more effectively safeguarded.

In the early years of the war, however, there was little time to consider the form a new organisation would take, or even the principles on which it would be based. Statesmen were far too busy fighting the existing conflict to think about the means of preventing those of the future. This did not prevent a few grandiloquent references to the new world that was to come. The Atlantic Charter, issued on 14 August 1941, spoke of the creation of a 'wider and permanent system of general security', which would 'afford to all nations the means of dwelling in safety within their own boundaries' at the war's end. On 1 January 1942, the twenty-six states which after the entry of the United States and other countries into the war had established the alliance against the Axis, reaffirmed this declaration and now named themselves the United Nations. And the speeches of statesmen increasingly frequently referred in general terms to the new world order to be created at the war's conclusion.

Only during 1943 did more explicit discussion begin to be devoted to the subject. Random ideas had been formulated within foreign-offices before this. In the United States as early as April 1940, long before US involvement in the war, State Department officials sketched out the form of possible new international machinery. These ideas in some ways foreshadowed what finally came into existence: the general rule of unanimity would be abandoned; the great powers would be accorded a special position in a new executive committee; and this body would have armed forces at its disposal to maintain the peace.[1] In a public speech in July 1942, Cordell Hull, the US Secretary of State, listed among the essential requirements for the postwar world some international agency capable of using force when necessary. In Britain too there were many advocates of a new and more powerful international organisation, better equipped to defeat aggression by force if necessary, in which the leading role would be played by the great powers. In August 1942, Foreign Office officials, after some consultation with the State Department, produced a document, the *Four Power Plan*, running to 11,000 words, describing and analysing a system in which the primary responsibility for maintaining peace in the postwar world would be held by the United States, the Soviet Union, Britain and China. This was submitted in October to the War Cabinet, but received there a somewhat mixed reception. Churchill himself apparently was too preoccupied to read the document, even when it was presented to him in a shortened version.[2]

In both countries, thinking aloud at this comparatively junior level was of little significance unless it received endorsement from the men at the top. Both Roosevelt and Churchill were concerned to keep a personal eye on any proposals made for the postwar organisation of the world. Both had strong personal views of their own on the subject. But for long neither found the time to give any significant amount of thought to the matter, which they felt of little urgency in relation to the more pressing problem of winning the war.

There was one view which both leaders shared. It could be represented, like those described in the last chapter, as a lesson of the interwar years. But, perhaps more significantly, it was one which corresponded with the interests of both powers. The League had failed partly because some of the big powers played no role. If the UN was to succeed there must be a dominant place within it for the great powers.

Roosevelt had, even before US entry into the war, thought in terms of the policing of the world by a small group of big powers. Before Pearl Harbor he thought that the United States and Britain alone should be involved in this task.[3] Later he was prepared to include the Soviet Union and China, but still felt that this policing role should be kept in the hands of a few powerful states, and that most of the rest of the world should be disarmed altogether. Thus the former enemy states – which he regarded as the only true danger to future world peace – would be prevented from becoming once more a menace, and the small states would be able to go about their business in peace. Such a system was explicitly proposed to the Soviet Union in May 1942, when Molotov visited Washington. This would be the main mechanism needed (possibly with a watchdog committee of neutrals to report on violations of the disarmament arrangements) to maintain the peace; but in addition the League, or something similar, might be re-established in Geneva to promote economic and social co-operation.

Churchill distrusted the idea that the new international organisation should depend on co-operation between the Big Four, which, he realised, might not choose to co-operate. He was dubious about the status proposed for China, at that time prostrate under Japanese occupation, in some of the plans going around. And he foresaw special difficulties in working with Russia. He correctly recognised the major difficulty of any collective security system: that of securing a sufficient commitment to the defence of other states by distant powers whose security was not closely involved. He felt that 'it was only the countries whose interests were directly affected by a dispute who could be expected to apply themselves with sufficient vigour to secure a settlement'.[4] And, unlike Roosevelt, he thought the smaller powers had an important role to play in any future peace-keeping system. He believed that Britain's own interests lay largely in Europe. Thus then, as later, he favoured giving a larger role to regional organisations. 'I must admit' he wrote to Eden,

> that my thoughts rest primarily in Europe. . . . I trust that
> the European family may act unitedly as one under a

Council of Europe.... I hope to see a Council consisting of perhaps 10 units, including the former Great Powers with several confederations – Scandinavia, Danubian, Balkan etc. – which would possess an international police and be charged with keeping Prussia disarmed. Of course, we shall have to work with the Americans in many ways, and in the greatest ways, but Europe is our prime care, and we certainly do not wish to be shut up with the Russians and the Chinese, when Swedes, Norwegians, Danes, Dutch, Frenchmen, Spaniards, Poles, Czechs, and Turks will have their burning questions, their desire for our aid and their very great power of making their voices heard.[5]

In February 1943 Churchill jotted down some 'Morning Thoughts on Postwar Security' and sent them to President Roosevelt. These incorporated his conception of separate regional bodies. He proposed a UN declaration to the effect that

it is the intention of the chiefs of the United Nations to create a world organisation for the preservation of peace, based upon the conception of justice and the revival of prosperity. As a part of this organisation an instrument of European government will be established, which will embody the spirit, but not be subject to the weakness, of the former League of Nations. The units forming this body will not only be the great nations of Europe and Asia Minor, as long established, but a number of Confederations formed among the smaller states, among which a Scandinavian bloc, a Danubian bloc, and a Balkan bloc appear to be obvious. A similar instrument will be formed in the Far East with different membership and the whole will be held together by the fact that the victorious powers intend to continue fully armed, especially in the air, while imposing complete disarmament upon the guilty.[6]

In any case there must be every effort to maintain the wartime coalition of great powers in being after the war to act together against aggression.

In a broadcast in March 1943 Churchill declared that he favoured the establishment after the war of a 'world institution', representing the United Nations, and some day all nations, under which should be a 'Council of Europe and a Council of Asia'. The European Council could be formed even while the war continued in the Far East, and could bring about a settlement on the European continent and provide for enduring security there. This Council of Europe should be 'made into a really effective League, with all the strongest forces concerned woven into its texture, with a High Court to adjust disputes and with armed forces, national or international or both, held ready to enforce these decisions and prevent renewed aggression and the preparation of future war'. Later on, during a visit to Washington in May 1943, Churchill modified this proposal in talking of *three* regional councils, beneath a world council: one for the Western Hemisphere, as well as those for Europe and the Far East. But he thought that some of the great powers could be represented in more than one council, the United States perhaps in all three; and there would always be recourse to the world council if the regional organisations failed to secure a settlement.

Roosevelt moved very slightly towards Churchill's position. On 10 April 1943 an article written by Forrest Davies but published with the President's approval and describing his views appeared in the *Saturday Evening Post*. The proposal was now that there should be two security commissions: one, including the United States, Britain and Russia, looking after the affairs of Europe; another, including China, for Asia. These countries would have a monopoly of armed force, and there would thus be no need for international forces or international bases. The rest of the world was apparently to be content with this four-power dictatorship: the smaller nations, confident in its effectiveness and impartiality, would thus easily, it was suggested, be 'brought to disarmament'.

Thus both Churchill and Roosevelt at first favoured the idea of a postwar system in which power would be wielded mainly, or exclusively, by the great powers, and in which part of the responsibility would be accorded to regional bodies. This was not a view that was shared by foreign-offices in either country. They believed neither that other states, such as France and other West European countries, could be kept in a state of disarmament or at least general impotence; nor that the new organisation should be primarily regional in structure. In the United States, perhaps because Roosevelt had little time to devote to the question, the regional approach largely disappeared. A committee under Sumner Welles proposed in the summer of 1943 an interim UN authority, with an executive committee consisting of the four great powers and a few others, which should take over responsibility for world security, even while the war was still on, pending the establishment of a more comprehensive organisation. Though this was intended in the first place as a temporary measure, it probably represented the kind of organisation that many in the US government would have liked to see emerge in the long term as well.

Britain too formulated proposals for the period before a permanent body could be established. Unlike Roosevelt with the US Government, Churchill for some time still imposed his regional concept onto the official British position. British ideas were put forward in an *aide-mémoire* sent by the UK Government to the United States on 14 July 1943. This proposed the setting up of a United Nations Commission for Europe, to be composed of the United States, Britain, the Soviet Union, France and other European allies, and of the Commonwealth dominions if they so desired. This would, as Churchill had earlier proposed, supervise the action of the armistice commissions and deal with all the problems, political, economic and military, that would arise in the immediate postwar period. It would be led by a special committee of the Big Three, to be joined by France later when she was restored. There would also be organisations concerned with refugees, shipping, inland transport, telecommunications, reparations and other problems. It is likely that Churchill saw this machinery as persisting for a considerable time, so establishing the decentralised structure he favoured. But the United States was by this time by no means so favourable to the regional idea, nor to the total domination of the Big Three envisaged by Churchill (who constantly dismissed the idea that China should be regarded as an equal with the other great powers). Thus Churchill's proposals were never explored in any detail. All that emerged was that at the Moscow Conference in October of that year it was agreed to establish the European Advisory Commission to consider problems arising in Europe, occupation policies, control machinery and so on.

But its functions were limited. And it was henceforth never seen as the embryo of some more permanent peace-keeping organisation.

The United States was by this time far more interested in a permanent postwar organisation and in the procedure for establishing it. In her view the time for desultory suggestions or separate planning exercises was now over. But she wanted the initiative to remain firmly with the big powers. She therefore proposed that the first step should be to secure agreement between the four great powers on a declaration about postwar intentions generally, and that the Big Three should then proceed to negotiate a protocol for a provisional world organisation of the kind they had in mind. At the Quebec Conference in August 1943, the United States and Britain agreed on the text of a declaration of this kind which it was hoped the Soviet Union and China would also endorse. In this the four governments would 'recognise the necessity of establishing at the earliest practicable date a general international organisation, based on the principle of the sovereign equality of all nations and open to membership by all nations, large and small, for the maintenance of international peace and security'. At the Moscow Conference of foreign ministers in October of that year, the Soviet Union agreed to the proposed text, which was amended only by the insertion of 'peace-loving' between 'all' and 'states', so ensuring that former enemy countries would not automatically qualify for membership. At the same time, the three countries agreed privately among themselves to begin joint consultations 'on questions connected with the establishment of an international organisation for the maintenance of peace and security, the intention being that this work should be carried out in Washington, London and Moscow'.[7]

A new and more intensive phase of negotiations for the postwar world organisation was to begin.

THE THREE BEGIN TO GET TOGETHER

There were a few further exchanges before the detailed discussions began.

At the Teheran Conference at the end of November 1943,

Roosevelt described to Stalin his concept of the Four Police-men, who would undertake the main, or even the sole, re-sponsibility for keeping the peace after the war. He felt there should be, first, an assembly that would be worldwide and include the united nations, meeting in different places throughout the world, to discuss international problems and make recommendations. Next, there would be an executive committee consisting of the four major states, together with representatives of other groups of countries. This would deal mainly with non-military problems, food, health and economics. It would only have the power to make recommen-dations, including recommendations for the peaceful settle-ment of disputes. Finally, there would be the Four Policemen, the chief enforcement body, with the power to deal with any threat to the peace in any sudden emergency.[8]

Stalin objected that such a concentration of power among the Big Four would be resisted by the smaller states; and, in any case, China would not be of sufficient power after the war to be a generally acceptable member of a body having en-forcement powers in Europe. He proposed a system more like that favoured by Churchill: a committee for Europe, includ-ing Britain, Russia, the United States and perhaps one other state, together with a similar body for the Far East. But Roosevelt doubted whether Congress would agree to the United States taking part in a primarily European body which could involve the commitment of US troops.[9] On these grounds Stalin eventually appeared to accept that a single worldwide organisation might be better than one divided on regional lines.

At the beginning of 1944 the governments of the three powers began, as they had agreed at Moscow, to 'draw up a more detailed and comprehensive document' on the form of a postwar organisation. Eden believed that the United States should take the initiative in this process. The Soviet Union, which showed no signs of having formulated any definite views of her own at this stage, did not object. The result was that, throughout the discussions which followed, the United States took the initiative, formulating proposals to which the others reacted. And the UN Charter, as it finally emerged, was an only slightly modified form of the original US plan.

Between December 1943 and February 1944 the US State

Department prepared a relatively detailed plan for the new organisation. In February President Roosevelt gave preliminary approval to the ideas set out. But the US administration wanted time for further consultation, with Congressional leaders and with service chiefs, and for any further revision which might be necessary, before they could be discussed with other governments. Discussion between the three powers at the first stage, therefore, was only about procedure, the agenda, and the time and place for the conference that was to take place between them. Eventually, after a long Soviet silence lasting several months, it was agreed that the conference should take place at Dumbarton Oaks, near Washington, in August 1944. Because of the poor state of Sino-Soviet relations (the Soviet Union was still officially in alliance with Japan, while China was at war with her), it was agreed that the two powers should not be present together: the Soviet Union would take part in the first part of the conference and China in the second.

It was not till July that the US Government completed its 'Tentative Proposals for an International Organisation'. These were transmitted to the other powers on 18 July. In return, Britain sent to the others five memoranda, setting out her views on different aspects of the new system. The Soviet Union sent a single 'Memorandum on the International Security Organisation', which the others received only on 21 August, the day the conference was to open. China was even later with her proposals, submitting her 'Essential Points in the Charter of an International Organization' only on 22 August. But all the documents other than those submitted by the United States were in general terms. None included, like that of the US, a skeleton plan for the organisation as a whole. It was thus the US proposals which, to a large extent, formed the basis for discussions at the subsequent conference.

The proposals revealed a considerable measure of agreement from the start. This was partly because all were quite prepared to follow, in a fairly general way, the pattern already set by the League. Thus all accepted that there would be an assembly, in which every member state would be represented. There would be a council, sometimes named the 'executive committee' or 'executive council', consisting, as in the League, of four, or possibly five, permanent members as well as several other members, which would have the main responsibility for considering questions of peace and security. There would be an international secretariat, under a chief official variously named as 'director-general' or 'secretary-general'. And there would be an international court of justice, perhaps set up afresh to determine all legal issues arising between states. The four even agreed to some extent on the way the organisation would differ from the League. It should be equipped with a greater degree of armed force to maintain the peace. There would be a more dominant role for the major powers (that is, themselves) in exercising enforcement authority. And the veto power would be abolished, for all except the permanent members (again mainly themselves).

But there were still differences between them. The British had somewhat weakened on their insistence on a regional system, but had not altogether abandoned that view. The Russians were also inclined this way, being reluctant to concede China a recognised place of influence over the affairs of Europe. The Chinese, on the other hand, wanted a more centralised system, which would enhance their own role, and believed that any regional arrangements could be established only with the authority of the Security Council. The US proposals, despite the Monroe Doctrine and the traditional US desire for predominance in Latin America, at first made no proposals at all for special regional arrangements.

There were also, predictably, differences between the Soviet Union and all the rest. These particularly concerned the powers of the new organisation in the economic and social field. The non-communist powers, recalling the conclusions reached by the League (see p. 12 above), wanted the new organisation to be equipped with considerable responsibilities in these fields; the Soviet Union wanted an organisation restricted to the area of peace and security. This divergence of views has left traces until the present day. But there were some differences among the Western powers too in this respect. Britain and China proposed that the executive council (what became the Security Council) should be the body mainly responsible for action on economic and social affairs, while the United States wanted a separate body created to perform this role. Here, as on much else, it was the US view which ultimately prevailed.

Most of the other differences were on points of detail: the composition of particular bodies or their powers. It was only at the conference itself that more important divergencies of conception and viewpoint came out into the open.

THE DUMBARTON OAKS CONFERENCE

The Dumbarton Oaks Conference opened on 21 August, at the elegant and spacious country house outside Washington which was made available to the US Government for the purpose. The discussions were intended to be informal and exploratory. They were undertaken among officials, and in theory did not commit their governments finally. The proposals agreed were subsequently to be put to the world as a whole as the united view of the Big Four. The assumption was that, if the Four could reach substantial agreement among themselves, the objections of other powers would not count for very much.

The chief participants were Stettinius, Under-Secretary in the State Department, Cadogan, British ambassador in Washington, and Gromyko, then Soviet ambassador in Washington. The US proposals were quickly accepted as a basis for discussion. There was little inclination among any of the other states to challenge the general structure which they described, including a general assembly, an 'executive council', a secretariat, and an international court of justice; nor the proposal for separate procedures to deal with the 'pacific settlement of disputes' and for 'threats to the peace or breaches of the peace' (these separate parts of the US paper eventually became Chapters VI and VII in the final Charter).

Under the US proposals member-states would agree, in settling 'disputes', to use various bilateral procedures: negotiation, conciliation, mediation and so on. If this failed, they would be obliged to refer them to the Council. At Dumbarton Oaks it was agreed that the Council could then, as the Soviet Union demanded, call on the parties to reach a settlement, or even recommend procedures or 'methods of adjustment'.

Where force had been used or seemed likely to be used, the Council could 'take any measures necessary for the maintenance of international peace and security'. In the first place, it could use measures not involving force, such as sanctions or breaking off communications (as in the League); and, if these failed, it would take action by air, naval or land forces, including demonstrations or blockade. Every member of the organisation would 'obligate' themselves to accept and carry out the decisions of the Council. The Soviet Union submitted proposals calling for a carefully graduated escalation of such measures, beginning with an appeal to the parties and ending with naval, air and land operations against the aggressor. This was not adopted. But it was accepted that, as the US plan suggested, states should make available to the Council, by agreement, forces that would be used in operations of this kind. The United States had proposed that there should be a 'security and enforcements commission', of unspecified composition, which would provide the Council with expert military advice and assistance. At Dumbarton Oaks this was replaced by a proposed military staff committee, consisting of the chiefs-of-staff of the five permanent members,[10] who would advise on such matters. In general, all these provisions, the central element of the proposed postwar system, were reproduced virtually unchanged in the final UN Charter.

There were, however, some differences at this stage. The Soviet Union suggested that states not able to provide forces to the Council should offer bases instead. This was turned down by the United States and Britain. They said it might be seen as a means by which the big powers stationed their forces on the territories of smaller powers (this was almost the exact opposite of the positions taken by the three states three or four years later, when negotiations for Security Council forces took place).[11] Both the Soviet Union and China proposed that fully international air forces (rather than national forces offered for the purpose) should be available to the Council, and the British suggested that at least this idea should be examined in depth after the Conference. This, however, was rejected by the United States, which held that the holding of national air-force contributions 'immediately available' for emergency use by the Council was the most that could be realistically envisaged: since the United States had by far the most powerful air forces to provide; this position, though perhaps realistic, also kept a greater degree of control in her own hands.

The most important point of controversy concerned the scope of the veto which would be available to the great powers. There was never at any stage any dissension about the general principle of the veto. All four governments had no difficulty in agreeing that they themselves (together with possibly one other state) should enjoy the privilege of permanent member- ship of the Council. They also agreed that with this they would enjoy the right to prevent any decision unacceptable to them. The differences concerned only the way the system would operate when one such power was itself involved in a dispute or a complaint. At this time the assumption was made, as in the League, that most issues would arise in the form of 'disputes' between one state and another. When the dispute was between smaller states it was hoped the Big Four would usually be able to agree on the action or settlement required so that a decision could be reached. But it was always foreseen that in some cases these powers themselves might be involved in disputes or even accused of breaches of the peace: in this case, it was felt by the Western powers, that the state, as a party to the dispute, should, as in the League, be unable to vote and therefore unable to veto. Early in the Dumbarton Oaks Conference Britain made a proposal to this effect. The United States generally supported this position, but was ready to consider a compromise under which, even in such cases, the veto could be used to prevent *enforcement* action being taken against the permanent member concerned. But even this was not enough for the Soviet Union. She held that a great power should be able to prevent any action by the Council, even including measures of peaceful settlement, when it was itself involved. This became a key issue. Cordell Hull personally urged Gromyko to accept the US compromise. Roosevelt sent a personal message to Stalin on the matter. But the Soviet Union refused to budge. And this was the most important point which, at the end of the Conference, remained unre- solved.

There was a smaller controversy, concerning the majority required to pass a Council resolution. Britain and China wanted a two-thirds majority. Both the Soviet Union and the United States at first favoured a simple majority. But this would have meant (with a Council of eleven members) that a resolution could be passed with only one vote other than those of the great powers. Since it was feared that the organisation would in any case be regarded as under the domination of those powers, Britain and China argued that it would be better to provide for a larger majority, so giving a bigger voice to smaller powers. Eventually this point too was left undecided.

The United States proposed for a time that, to provide a wider geographical distribution, Brazil should be a permanent member of the Council. But this was not well received by other members, who felt that it would produce pressures for similar concessions elsewhere, and eventually the United States withdrew the proposal. All agreed, however, that France should be offered a permanent seat on the Council. This would then consist of five permanent and six non-permanent members. Unlike the League Council, it should be in a position to function continuously, so each state in the Council should send permanent representatives to the seat of the organisation. In addition, there could if necessary be periodic meetings at which members of governments or some other special representative would attend.

A more substantial difference concerned the provision for 'regional arrangements'. The British were still anxious to leave open the possibility that local disputes could be considered in the first place by regional bodies. This question was not covered at all in the US draft, which seemed to suppose that the world organisation would take all conflict situations under its care. During the Dumbarton Oaks Conference the British, while they accepted that the world organisation should have overriding responsibility, again proposed that provision should be made for regional bodies, perhaps as part of the enforcement machinery. The United States felt that, if such bodies had a role, it was rather as part of the machinery for peaceful settlement. Eventually a compromise was reached. It was agreed that the Council would 'encourage' the settlement of local disputes by regional agencies, and use them also for enforcement action 'where appropriate'. But in the latter case the regional bodies would act only with the authorisation of the Council. This was quite a significant change in the original plan: a change which was carried further, as we shall see, at San Francisco.

The United States had originally wanted a system of weighted voting to be used in the Assembly in decisions on financial questions (somewhat on the lines of the system of voting adopted at about the same time for the World Bank). But this was unacceptable to the others (it would have given a large proportion of the votes to the United States); and eventually there was general agreement that a simple majority would apply for most questions in the Assembly, with a two-thirds majority needed only for 'important' questions, including budgetary matters. The United States had wanted the Secretary-General to be elected by the Assembly with the concurrence of the Council, so leaving the initiative with the Assembly; but the Soviet Union, supported by the others, thought that the Security Council, having first reached agreement, should recommend a name to the Assembly, and this was finally accepted. From the very beginning the Soviet Union was pursuing the policy she has followed ever since: of concentrating authority in the Security Council, where she holds a veto. Britain and China both wanted the Secretary-General to have the power to bring before the Council any matter which he considered a threat to the peace (a right which the chief official had not had in the League): the United States and the Soviet Union accepted this, and the provision eventually became Article 99 of the Charter.

There were also disputes about membership. First, there was no agreement whether the 'associated states' not formally at war with the Axis powers but committed to the Allied cause (mainly Latin American states) should be members from the start and be invited to the conference to establish the organisation. But there was a much more important issue than this: Gromyko caused consternation in demanding that all sixteen Soviet republics should be admitted as separate members of the organisation. No doubt only too aware that communist states would be in a tiny minority in the new organisation, the Soviet Union adopted this device to redress the balance a little. The proposal was firmly rejected by the other powers. But the Soviet Union held firmly to it, and Stalin sent a telegram to Roosevelt, claiming the republics enjoyed autonomy under the new Soviet constitution just adopted and that some were far larger in population than many independent states. Here too it was agreed to shelve the matter for the moment.

Another source of disagreement was the proposal in the US

draft that the Assembly should be able to make recommendations 'for the promotion of the observance of basic human
rights'. This was a substantial advance on anything that
existed in the League. Both the Soviet and British representatives objected that this might give the organisation powers to
intervene in the domestic affairs of member-states and so
violate national sovereignty. They even resisted a revised
draft which merely referred to the responsibility of each state
'to respect the human rights and fundamental freedoms of all
its people', arguing that this too related to the domestic
policies of states, in which the organisation should not be
concerned. Stettinius, however, was insistent on the question.
Eventually the Soviet representative received instructions to
make a concession on the point; and this induced the British
representative to do likewise. It was agreed that it should be
provided that the organisation would 'promote respect for
human rights and fundamental freedoms': a fairly innocuous
undertaking which was, however, to have increasing importance in the future.

The conference with the Russians took over five weeks. The
Chinese phase lasted only just over a week. This was partly
because they disagreed less; partly because they were thought
less important. They accepted what the other powers proposed almost without a murmur.

On 9 October it was thus possible to publish the 'Proposals
for the Establishment of a General International Organisation'. There was still disagreement on a number of important
points. The most important were the degree to which a
permanent member could use its veto to prevent a decision
from being reached in a dispute to which it was itself a party,
and the demand for separate representation for the sixteen
Soviet republics. There were other points of difference which
stemmed from the disagreement about the veto. There were
also a few questions which had not been discussed at all:
particularly the trusteeship system, on which the United
States had not made up its own mind, and the reconstitu-
tion of the International Court of Justice. But at least the
general outline of a possible future organisation had been
agreed. The first task, before other nations were brought in,
was to try to resolve the remaining differences between the
three powers.

BETWEEN DUMBARTON OAKS AND SAN FRANCISCO

Some of the disputed points were followed up fairly quickly. The US Government produced a new formula to overcome the difficulty about voting rights for the permanent members. It proposed that such a member would be able to veto enforcement action proposed against it in the Council, but could not veto 'judicial or quasi-judicial' proceedings when the Council was merely considering and pronouncing on a dispute. President Roosevelt personally pressed Stalin to accept this formula in early December.

The effect would be that, in decisions relating to the peaceful settlement of disputes or the use of regional agencies, a party to a dispute, even if a permanent member, would have to abstain from voting. This formula would have safeguarded the Soviet Union's essential interests, since a mere declaration by the Council could not seriously damage her. But the Soviet leaders, knowing that their country would be in a permanent minority within the Council, were unwilling to see it assailed by successive resolutions. Thus on 26 December Molotov again turned down the proposal. On the following day Stalin telegraphed Roosevelt justifying this on the grounds that, if a great power could be arraigned against its will in this way, the effect would be to destroy great-power unity, on which the future peace of the world depended – an argument he knew must appeal to Roosevelt.

On the question of separate membership for the sixteen Soviet republics, neither Roosevelt nor Churchill was disposed to give way. Roosevelt declared to members of the Senate Committee on Foreign Relations that, if Stalin insisted on separate membership for the sixteen republics, he would demand seats for each of the forty-eight American states. Gromyko insisted, in conversations with US officials, that most of the Soviet republics were 'much more important than say Liberia or Guatemala' and, he maintained, effectively independent in foreign affairs: an assertion received with understandable scepticism. It was thus agreed to leave the matter over until the leaders of the Big Three should meet.

Both questions were therefore discussed between the three heads of government at the Yalta Conference in February 1945. On the question of the veto, Churchill, like Roosevelt, had had some doubt whether it was advisable to press the Russians too hard, and in so doing to prejudice great-power unity, on which the future depended. He had, however, been persuaded by Eden to stand firm, and he vigorously supported the pleas of Stettinius, now US Secretary of State, on the point. If a great power could veto even the discussion of peaceful means of resolving disputes, they argued, some of the most important postwar issues might be excluded altogether from the authority of the new organisation. Small states would feel aggrieved if the great powers were uniquely protected in this way, and might decline to join the organisation altogether. Eventually, this combined pressure seemed to have some effect. On the following day Molotov announced that the Soviet Union was now satisfied with the latest US formula, which demanded that there should be no veto in such cases if peaceful settlement of a dispute only was under discussion. This seemed an important step forward.

But he immediately proceeded to raise the issue of membership for each of the sixteen Soviet republics. The close juxtaposition seemed to imply that there was a linkage between the two issues. Using the analogy of the British Commonwealth countries, which had successively acquired independence and separate voting rights, he went on to announce that the Soviet government would be prepared to accept, as a first step, that only two or three of the republics should be given separate membership. Roosevelt was still cool to the proposal, substantially though the Soviet demands had been scaled down, and proposed that the matter should be left to the founding conference. to decide. But Stalin, in a remarkably frank private discussion with him, told him that his position in the Ukraine was a weak one, that there was controversy among the Soviet leadership as a whole on the whole question of Soviet membership of the new organisation, and that he needed a concession if he was to bring them round.[12] This seems to have carried some weight with Roosevelt. Stettinius the next day informed Molotov that, though the founding conference should be confined to existing signatories of the United Nations declaration, the United States accepted that the proposal for 'multiple membership' for the Soviet Union should be given sympathetic consideration at the opening conference. Churchill too was prepared to accept Stalin's proposal of three seats for the Soviet Union, feeling that this was a small price to pay for Soviet agreement on Security Council voting and the prospect of having general agreement among the Big Three on the shape of the organisation.[13]

But other members of the US delegation were unhappy at the President's concessions on this point. They felt that public opinion in the United States would feel aggrieved. Not only was Russia expected to be given three seats, but Britain too would have several, because of the separate representation of the dominions (a somewhat extraordinary estimate of the degree of influence Britain had over those countries). Roosevelt was therefore prevailed on, while the Conference still continued, to write to the other two leaders to ask them to support a proposal to give the United States parity in seats with the Soviet Union. Churchill agreed that the US should 'propose the form in which her undoubted equality with every other member state should be expressed' (a somewhat ambiguous assent), while Stalin accepted that the number of votes for the USA might be increased to three to match those agreed for the Soviet Union. In the event, before the San Francisco Conference the US Government decided not to press any claim of this kind.

There was also a general agreement in principle at Yalta that the Charter should include a system of trusteeship. Even this was at first rejected by Churchill, who was fearful that the system might be extended to the whole of the British empire (this is indeed what Roosevelt personally would have liked to see). When it was explained that the system was designed only to cover former enemy territories, territories that were already mandates and those voluntarily offered, Churchill relented. He was prepared to accept a general reference in the communiqué to the need for such a system. There was some discussion between Roosevelt and Stalin of a possible trusteeship system for Korea (to be held perhaps by the Soviet Union, the US and China) and for Indo-China. But, like much else discussed at Yalta, this was all very vague and undefined.

It was agreed to go ahead with the establishment of the new organisation as soon as possible – that is, before the war was ended – even if this meant that it was made to appear like a glorified alliance of the victorious powers. 'This time we shall not make the mistake', Roosevelt told Congress, 'of waiting until the end of the war to set up the machinery of peace. This time, as we fight together to get the war over quickly, we work together to keep it from happening again.' One of the main advantages of this procedure was that it was much less likely that, while the momentum of the war was still at its height, US opinion would again seek a withdrawal from wider commitments and reject membership of the new organisation. So invitations would be sent out by the Big Five for a conference to found the new organisation, probably in San Francisco, within the next month or two. This would recommend that the basis for the Charter should be the Dumbarton Oaks proposals, as amplified by the Yalta Agreement.

It was only now, therefore, that most of the nations of the world were to be given any opportunity to have a say in the type of international organisation to be established. By this time, a relatively detailed draft had already been prepared, setting out in detail the form that was favoured by the major governments of the world, and major points of principle agreed between the great powers. It still remained to be seen how far that draft would be acceptable to other states.

3 The San Francisco Conference

Even before San Francisco, while the war was raging, new international organisations had been formed for particular purposes. It was hoped these would eventually form part of a wider United Nations system. Already in 1943 the United Nations Relief and Rehabilitation Administration (UNRRA) had been established to help restore and supply the devastated areas of Europe occupied by the advancing Allied armies. In the same year, a United Nations conference on food and agriculture was held at Hot Springs, Virginia, and led to the establishment of the Food and Agriculture Organisation (FAO) in the following year. In July 1944, the Bretton Woods Conference on monetary and financial questions bought about the establishment of the International Monetary Fund (IMF) and the World Bank (IBRD), to promote international action in the field of monetary affairs and development, respectively. In November 1944 a new International Civil Aviation Organisation (ICAO), to replace the moribund and incomplete organisation which had existed for the same purpose between the wars, was set up. And by the beginning of 1945 the ILO, which had emigrated from Geneva to Canada during the war, was beginning to agitate with some success for its re-establishment in a still more independent form in the postwar world.

No decision had been reached about the precise relationship of such bodies with the future world organisation. It was generally felt that they should be associated with the new organisation, but should not be part of it, still less directly under it and subject to its orders. Some of these agencies had already existed for many years – the Universal Postal Union (UPU) and the International Telecommunication Union (ITU), for example – and there was no means, short of

37

concerted action by all their members, for bringing them
compulsorily under the authority of a new world body. To
place all international bodies within the same structure would
in any case have created a bureaucratic monstrosity of a kind
most people wished to avoid. The idea of separate and largely
autonomous agencies anyway fulfilled the view, at that time
being expounded by the 'functionalists', that there was a better
chance of inducing and strengthening international co-
operation through separate agencies with a clearly defined
functional purpose of their own.

This meant that it began to be accepted that the UN was not
going to be an all-purpose organisation with powers in every
field. Although it might be given some responsibilities in the
economic and social field, it was never envisaged as being the
only, or even the chief, international body active even in those
areas. Nor was it even anticipated that it would exercise direct
control over the whole new family of agencies now coming
into being. On the contrary, each of these were endowed with
a considerable degree of independence. It came to be accepted that the new world body might have a general role in
'co-ordinating' the activity of this family of agencies, but it
would not be in a position to issue direct commands to them.

It would be wrong to suggest that all this represented the
fulfilment of a deliberate policy for the international organisations of the future, a policy which had been agreed among the
great powers and was subsequently implemented by them. To
a considerable extent the specialised agencies came into
existence, as the British Empire is supposed to have done, in a
fit of absence of mind. Unlike the British colonies, the
agencies were given dominion status from the beginning;
they became autonomous and self-governing agencies which
largely went their own way, with only the most fitful obeisance
to their mother country. This was to present many problems
for the United Nations in the future. But it was not a question
which most of the delegates who assembled at San Francisco in
April 1945 thought much about, or could now have effectively
influenced if they had.

At Yalta it had been envisaged that invitations to the San
Francisco Conference should be sent out by the Big Five: the
four Dumbarton Oaks powers plus France. But the French
had been deeply offended at the failure to invite De Gaulle to

Yalta. And on 24 February the French Government replied to the invitations to co-sponsorship rejecting the offer unless France's suggested amendments to the Dumbarton Oaks proposals were used as a basis for the conference on an equal footing with those proposals themselves. The Four were unwilling to agree to this: it could have provoked demands from other countries to put forward suggestions of their own which should receive similar treatment. Besides, the full text of the invitation to be issued had been carefully agreed among the Three at Yalta, so that the French proposal, involving a significant change, could not have been accepted without further discussion and delay. The result was that France did not become one of the sponsoring powers. Soon after the opening of the Conference, however, she was treated on an equal footing by the other four for the purposes of consultation.

There were a number of questions about participation in the conference which had to be decided before it began. At Yalta it had been agreed that existing signatories of the UN Declaration (all those at war with the Axis powers) were qualified to take part, together with any powers that became so before 1 March: the United States was especially concerned to give this opportunity to six Latin American powers which had so far only broken off relations with the Axis states. By 1 March not only these six states (Chile, Ecuador, Paraguay, Peru, Uruguay and Venezuela) but also Turkey, Egypt, the Lebanon, Syria and Saudi Arabia had all declared war, and so became eligible to receive invitations. Iceland, on the other hand, which decided not to declare war, was not invited. Nor at first was Denmark, which, unlike most West European countries, had no government-in-exile. But, when, during the Conference, Denmark was liberated, she was immediately admitted. About the participation of some other countries, there were much more serious disputes, which were only to be resolved at the Conference itself.

Only ten days before the Conference was due to begin, on 12 April, President Roosevelt, after a short illness, suddenly died. Roosevelt had been so intimately concerned with the preliminary drafting of the Charter, and had done so much to inspire enthusiasm for the new organisation among Congressional and public opinion in the United States, that there was a momentary fear that his death might weaken the impetus which had been built up. But, within an hour of formally taking office, President Truman declared that the Conference would go ahead as planned, and that US support for the project was undiminished. The fears of a new growth of US isolationism declined once more.

The Conference opened at the Opera House in San Francisco on 25 April. Stettinius, the US Secretary of State, was in the chair at the opening meeting and welcomed the delegates on behalf of the US Government. But there almost immediately arose an East–West battle, ominous for the future course of the Conference, on the question of the presidency. In the Steering Committee, Molotov immediately objected to Stettinius remaining in the chair for the whole conference, demanding that the presidency should be held in rotation by each of the four sponsoring powers. This request had already been put forward by the Soviet Union in preliminary discussions about the Conference. Traditionally the presidency of international conferences goes to the host state, but it may also in some cases go to the initiating country or countries. In substance, therefore, the Soviet demand had some justification, since, in a matter as important as the preparation of a new world organisation, there clearly could exist a significant national advantage for the country occupying the presidency. It was the brusque and uncompromising way the demand was presented which aroused apprehension. The episode scarcely exhibited to the world the united front between the sponsoring powers which many had hoped to see. Eventually a compromise proposed by Eden was accepted. The presidency of the public sessions was to rotate among the four sponsoring powers, while in the steering and executive committees, and in meetings of the four presidents themselves, Stettinius was to be in the chair.

Almost as soon as this was out of the way, another procedural question was raised which proved even more contentious: this time over participation in the Conference. There were four countries about which disagreements had not been resolved before the Conference began: Argentina, Poland and the two Soviet republics (Ukraine and Byelorussia). It had been agreed at Yalta by the United States and Britain that the last two should be accepted ultimately as members of the organisation. But their participation in the *Conference* had been left open. In subsequent discussion among the Four, the Soviet Union had continued to insist that they should take part. When the Conference began, the Soviet delegate proposed that they should be accepted immediately as original members of the organisation. This was supported by the three other sponsors, and was quickly accepted; and the Soviet Union then went on to propose that the two should be immediately invited to the Conference. Latin American delegates, however, anxious to use this as a lever to ensure the admission of Argentina, managed to ensure that this latter proposal was for the moment remitted to the Executive Committee.

The next question concerned Poland. The character and composition of the future government of Poland had been one of the main subjects of dispute at Yalta. Eventually it had been agreed there that a new Polish government would be formed which would be seen as representative of the Polish people as a whole: this implied that it should be neither the Lublin Committee, established on Russian soil and under Soviet auspices, nor the government-in-exile which had existed in London throughout most of the war, but a new and more broadly based government. There had been continued dissension on the matter in the period since Yalta, without coming any nearer to agreement, and it had become probably the main point at issue between the Allies as the war drew to its end. The British Government had even been prepared to see the San Francisco Conference postponed unless the Polish issue was satisfactorily resolved beforehand. It did not feel that an organisation supposed to be based on great-power agreement could be satisfactorily launched when an issue of this magnitude had not been resolved. President Truman, on the other hand, was determined to go ahead with the Conference, but was prepared for a mighty battle over the Polish issue. Then, on 22 April, three days before the Conference was to begin, it was announced that the Soviet Union had entered into a treaty of mutual assistance with the Lublin government. On the following day there was still more dramatic news: emissaries of the London Polish government had been arrested in Moscow by the Soviet authorities. This lent a new bitterness and intensity to the discussion of Polish participation at San Francisco. When the Conference began, the Soviet Union demanded the admission of representatives of the Lublin government as those of Poland. This was of course opposed by the United States and Britain and by many others. There was angry debate for a few days and it seemed for a time as if breaking-point had been reached. Eventually Molotov, seeing that there was no hope of representatives of the Lublin government being accepted by the majority at San Francisco, agreed to a compromise Belgian motion. This expressed the hope that the new and representative Polish government of which the Yalta Agreement spoke should be formed as soon as possible, and should send delegates to San Francisco before the Conference adjourned.

This left the question of Argentina. While the Argentine Government of Peron was by no means universally loved in Latin America at this time, it had been admitted to the conference of Latin American states which met shortly before San Francisco and Latin American delegates now felt obliged to act as its sponsor. These therefore tried to link agreement to the representation of the two Soviet republics with that of Argentina. The Soviet Union, on the other hand, sought to link the representation of Argentina with the settlement of the Polish issue. No Argentina without Poland. Again there was deadlock. To help resolve the issue a special meeting was arranged between representatives of the Latin American states and those of the sponsoring powers. When this failed, the matter was put to the Executive Committee of the Conference. The proposal to invite the Soviet republics was first discussed. When this was approved, the Latin Americans argued that, on these grounds, Argentina should be invited too. This was accepted, even by the Soviet Union now; but the Soviet Union then argued that, on these grounds, Poland should be invited too. This attempt to revive the Polish issue, which was thought to have been resolved, annoyed other delegates and the suggestion was turned down. So, finally, it was agreed that invitations should be sent to the two Soviet republics and to Argentina but not to Poland.

At last the Conference was able to get down to its serious work. Discussions were divided among four main commissions: on general provisions, on the General Assembly, on the Security Council and on judicial organisation. These were

committees of the whole, on which every state was represented, and they did much of the substantive work of the
Conference. There was also a steering committee, consisting
of the heads of all delegations, which decided all major
questions of procedure and organisation. There was a smaller
executive committee, including the heads of fourteen delegations, which dealt with more immediate and detailed questions of organisation and made recommendations to the
Steering Committee. Finally there was a co-ordination committee, which (with the assistance of an advisory committee of
jurists) examined the texts proposed by each committee to
secure uniform terminology.

But much more important than these official bodies were
the frequent meetings between the great powers, to which all
the major differences were remitted, and which indeed
effectively controlled the Conference – for the smaller states
knew that in the final resort the organisation could not come
into existence against the expressed views of the great powers.
At first these meetings brought together only 'the sponsors' –
the United States, the Soviet Union, Britain and China. But
on 4 May France was invited to join the group as well. This
group considered all the main proposals and amendments of
other delegates, announced whether they could be accepted,
and even proposed their own amendments to the original
Dumbarton Oaks draft.

It was agreed almost from the beginning, at a meeting of
the heads of delegations on 27 April, that the agenda would be
the Dumbarton Oaks proposals, as supplemented by the
Crimea Conference and by the Chinese proposals agreed to
by the sponsoring governments, and the comments thereon
submitted by the participating countries. On 5 May the
sponsoring countries put down a series of new amendments to
Dumbarton Oaks which were also added to the agenda, and
on 11 May the sponsors proposed two more amendments.
This procedure represented a huge advantage to the sponsoring countries. It meant in effect that a two-thirds majority was
required to *change* the proposals of the great powers. The
result was that some features of the Charter were accepted
which would never have come into being if the Conference
had started from scratch. Because discussion began from the
Dumbarton Oaks plan, the Charter emerged rather as a

variation of this theme than as an independently conceived creation.

The surprising feature of the Conference is not that the Charter as it finally emerged was so close to the Dumbarton Oaks draft – for in the final resort, the Big Four, if only they kept united, had only to dig in their heels and threaten non-co-operation to make this inevitable – it is that, with a few notable exceptions, all the essential features of that draft were accepted almost without resistance, even without serious challenge, from the rest. Many of those features which most emphasised the dominance to be enjoyed by the Big Five – permanent membership of the Council, the veto power they wielded there, the primary role given to the Security Council on all matters of security, the absolute obligation of all members to obey decisions of the Council and to provide forces for the implementations of these decisions, the authority of the Council to recommend the terms of a settlement in disputes between other members, the establishment of a military advisory body confined to the great powers – all these, which represented in effect a revolutionary transformation of the existing international system in favour of the great, were accepted by the majority of the middle and small powers at San Francisco virtually without question. Some of the points on which major disputes did arise – the circumstances in which the great-power veto could be exercised on questions affecting one of those powers, the right of nations to be represented on the Security Council when their own forces were being used, the distinction between the Security Council's powers in dealing with 'situations' and 'disputes' – were in practice, as subsequent history proved, of minimal importance. The essential features of the system as it actually emerged were accepted with little discussion or dispute.

THE SECURITY SYSTEM

It was scarcely surprising that the most intensive discussions at San Francisco concerned the system of security proposed in the Dumbarton Oaks proposals. The unique prerogatives which the great powers had reserved for themselves in this were scarcely calculated to endear themselves to the lesser states deprived of those privileges, but in fact were generally meekly accepted by them. But what particularly aroused concern was the point that had been raised by the United States and Britain at Dumbarton Oaks and had supposedly been resolved at Yalta: the danger that the permanent members might be in a position to prevent the organisation from operating in any dispute concerning themselves. These were precisely those situations which, in the eyes of others, were most likely to represent serious threats to the peace in the future.

At Yalta, as we have seen, the Big Three had secured agreement on a formula which at least limited the use of the veto by great powers in their own defence. The formula provided that procedural questions, including the decision to place a matter on the agenda, could be reached by a vote of seven members of the Council, with no veto. The veto would normally apply to subsequent decisions of the Council. But a permanent member who was a party to a dispute could not vote to veto any decision to institute peaceful settlement procedures, including decisions concerning regional arrangements, relating to that dispute. The effect of that formula seemed to be that the veto could not be used to prevent any question involving a permanent member from being *discussed* by the Council, but it might be used to prevent enforcement action from being taken against such a member.

This formula was widely challenged at San Francisco. It was held to be unclear and imprecise. And it was feared that in practice it might still enable a permanent member to prevent a subject from being discussed at all. A sub-committee was set up to examine the matter, and eventually, on 22 May, the majority on this sub-committee directed a series of twenty-three searching questions to the sponsoring powers on the meaning of the Yalta voting formula.

The Soviet Union had seemed up to this point to maintain the position held at Yalta: that is, her representative did not maintain that a permanent member could prevent *any* subject from being discussed at all, nor that the Yalta formula would give this right. At this point, however, the Soviet representative at San Francisco seemed to repudiate this interpretation. When the Big Five began to discuss among themselves the agreed statement they were to make in reply to the questionnaire, the Soviet representative refused to endorse a declaration that, 'since the Council has the right by a procedural vote to decide its own rules of procedure, it follows that no individual member of the Council can alone prevent a consideration and discussion by the Council of a dispute or situation brought to its attention'. The reason for the Russians' objection on this point may have been generally misinterpreted. There is every probability that it was the first part of the statement to which they objected. For, if maintained, it would have deprived them of the right, to which they subsequently attached importance, of the 'double veto': that is, the right for the Council to decide itself, in a vote subject to veto, which questions were or were not procedural. It was, however, generally taken that it was the final point to which the Soviet Union objected and that the object was to maintain the right of a permanent member to prevent even discussion of questions brought to the Council. When the question was put to Moscow, the initial answer certainly justified this fear. The Soviet government supported its delegate's position, and used the reasoning, which was later partially accepted, that a 'chain of events' culminating in enforcement action might follow from any initial Council action on such a dispute; and so maintained that even the decision to *discuss* was subject to veto. The United States, Britain and France categorically rejected this interpretation and were determined to maintain their position at all costs. They were indeed prepared even to risk the breakdown of the entire conference rather than give way.

By chance, at this moment Harry Hopkins, President Truman's special emissary, was in Moscow to try to resolve the very serious difficulties that had arisen with the Soviet Union concerning Poland. He was instructed to see Stalin personally about the veto question, and to warn him that this was regarded as a breaking-point in the West and could bring the collapse of the entire conference if it was not resolved. When Hopkins and the US ambassador saw Stalin on 6 June, it seemed to them that he was not well informed on the matter. In any case, he said he regarded the question as trivial and immediately accepted the Western position that the veto could not be used to prevent all discussion. The Soviet delegate was instructed to accept the passage in the joint five-power statement making this point clear. The same statement did, however, include, with the consent of the Western delegates, a provision that 'the decision regarding the preliminary questions as to whether or not such a matter is procedural must be taken by a vote, including the concurring votes of the permanent members'. In other words the veto did apply to the decision whether or not a matter was procedural. On this crucial point, which was of great importance to the Soviet Union, since it determined the scope of the veto, the Soviet Union got her way.

But to accept that the veto could not be used to prevent a question from being discussed at all was in fact little enough. Many delegates wanted to go much further. There was a group led by Australia demanding that, even if a permanent member could prevent enforcement action against itself, it should not be able to block resolutions proposing *peaceful* settlement procedures, even concerning itself. Some of the permanent members had originally felt the same and were prepared to go some way to meet this demand. The British delegate said he saw no reason why any proposal for the Council to investigate whether a dispute was a threat to the peace, or a call on the parties to settle by peaceful means, should be subject to veto. The US delegation would have been prepared to see all peaceful settlement procedures used free of veto. But the Soviet Union was adamantly against this interpretation. And the Western powers, now somewhat exhausted by their tussle with the Russian on the question of free discussion (and possibly aware that a more restrictive interpretation of the veto power might on occasion suit their own interests), made a substantial concession to the Russians. They agreed on an interpretation which would sharply restrict the Council's right to propose even measures of peaceful settlement where a great power was involved. They accepted an agreed five-power statement on the veto which stated that

> no individual member of the Council can alone prevent consideration and discussion by the Council of a dispute or situation. . . . Beyond this point decisions and actions by the Security Council may well have major political consequences and may even initiate a chain of events which might in the end require the Council under its responsibilities to invoke measures of enforcement. . . . This chain of events

begins when the Council decides to make an investigation,
or determines that the time has come to call upon states to
settle their differences, or makes recommendations to the
parties. It is to such decisions that unanimity of the permanent members applies, with the important proviso . . . for
abstention from voting by parties to a dispute.

In other words, at least in cases where a permanent member
was not a party to a dispute, the veto could be used even to
prevent peaceful settlement measures.

This statement did not satisfy most delegates. The Austra-
lians in particular repeated their demand that decisions for
peaceful settlement should be universally free of veto. There
was considerable support for this view, but most delegates
were not prepared to force the issue in the face of the united
front being maintained by the Big Five. The result was that,
for all the objections, the Yalta formula, as interpreted by the
great-power statement, was maintained intact. Much of the
discussion was in fact largely irrelevant. Delegates continued
to think of international issues arising as a series of 'disputes',
to which some countries were parties and some were not. At
the best of times it would have been extremely difficult to state
with certainty which countries were parties to any of the
disputes that arose in subsequent years: for instance, would
the United States and the Soviet Union have been held to be
parties to the conflict in the Middle East over the next
twenty-five years; or would China and the Soviet Union have
been parties to the 'dispute' in Vietnam? For this reason the
Council in practice soon ceased to define issues as 'disputes', or
to exclude interested parties from voting. But, even if such
judgements could have been objectively made, the effect of
the decision was the reverse of the logical one. There would
have been some case for saying that, since the veto power was
accorded to permanent members to enable them to defend
their own vital interests, it was precisely over the disputes to
which they were parties that they most needed to be able to
make use of it. But there could be no justification whatever for
their using the veto to prevent measures of peaceful settlement (or indeed enforcement) in areas and conflicts in which
they were *not* directly interested; and the history of the subsequent fifteen or twenty years showed that it was precisely in

such cases that the veto was to be most frequently abused.

Again, the contention of the big powers that even an initial decision to investigate could finally lead to a decision for enforcement action was quite without foundation. It simply was not true that one type of decision could not easily be distinguished from the other. This was indeed a fundamental distinction that the Charter itself strongly underlined, in treating the two types of resolution in separate chapters. And there was therefore no reason at all why the Council should not be able to make enquiries on particular situations or to make recommendations about them, while being prevented from deciding on any enforcement action in such cases.

There was a particular aspect of the veto power which came in for heavy criticism at the Conference. This was the provision under the Dumbarton Oaks proposals that the permanent members should be able to veto amendments to the Charter. This was another special privilege of the great, of a kind that was highly unpopular with many smaller states. But it was not one which was likely to be easily relinquished. There would be little point in the permanent members' bitterly debating every article of the Charter if it could be easily amended later to their disadvantage. The Big Five therefore stood firm on this. The most they were willing to allow was that a special conference to review the Charter might be called, free of veto, if demanded by a two-thirds majority. It was agreed that after ten years the possibility of holding such a conference should be considered, but a Canadian proposal that a conference would anyway be held at that time was turned down.

The dominant role accorded to the Council at Dumbarton Oaks was maintained. The powers of the Security Council in securing the peaceful settlement of disputes were even strengthened. The Dumbarton Oaks proposals described a series of procedures (negotiation, mediation, conciliation, arbitration and judicial settlement) which were to be used in the first place in resolving a dispute. The Security Council would if necessary call on the parties to make use of these procedures. At San Francisco, besides adding 'inquiry' and 'resort to regional agencies or arrangements' to the proposed procedures, the Conference decided that the Security Council should itself 'investigate' such disputes to decide if they endangered peace and security, and recommend appropriate procedures or methods of adjustment. Later a more drastic addition was proposed. Britain suggested, and the sponsoring powers later together demanded, that the Council might in such cases not merely propose procedures of this kind, but actually recommend the terms on which the dispute might be settled. This was a substantial power to accord the Council, and it was accepted only with some misgivings by other representatives. It was, for example, carefully provided in the official committee interpretation that such a Council recommendation 'possessed no obligatory effect for the parties'. None the less, this represented a considerable strengthening of the powers of the Council, proposed by the permanent members but not opposed elsewhere.

For dealing with more serious situations – threats to the peace, breaches of the peace and acts of aggression – the Council already had ample powers in the Dumbarton Oaks proposals. It could issue orders which every member would be obliged to obey; it could decide on enforcement action against a member state; and it could make use, for this purpose, of forces already made available to it by members under special agreements. All of this – a revolutionary relinquishment of sovereignty – was accepted without question by the smaller states. If anything, the Council's powers were reinforced. It was authorised, for example, to take 'provisional' measures to deal with a threat to the peace before reaching a final decision on enforcement action (a suggestion made by China in memory of the year-long delay by the League in deciding what to do about Japanese aggression in Manchuria). Other proposals, which would have amplified but not significantly changed the system for enforcement – suggestions to include a definition of aggression, or an undertaking by each member to preserve the territorial integrity and political independence of other states – failed to obtain the necessary majority. But there was included a general prohibition of the 'use or threat of force', which was eventually placed in Article 2(4) of the Charter.

The concern of the small powers indeed was not so much to weaken the Council as to secure a greater influence over its decisions. The Latin American countries, for example, wanted another permanent seat for a Latin American state, or at least three non-permanent seats for their continent. Others, including the Philippines, wanted a fixed regional distribution of seats (as was later agreed). Liberia wanted an alphabetical rotation among the non-permanent members, so that small states would have an equal chance of election with the large ones – a proposal happily rejected. The Netherlands, on the contrary, wanted a special role specified for the middle powers in the Council. India, not surprisingly, wanted special account taken of population as well as economic resources. Many other states wanted an increase in the size of the Council and the number of non-permanent members. None of these proposals was adopted. The Dumbarton Oaks proposal for an eleven-state Council with five permanent members was retained. But a small step was taken to meet the concern of the Netherlands by including a provision (in Article 23 of the Charter) that in electing members of the Council the Assembly should pay special regard to 'the contribution of members ... towards the maintenance of international peace and security and towards the other purposes of the organisation, and also to equitable geographical distribution'. This could be taken to imply paying some regard to size in electing members of the Council, though it has not always been interpreted in this sense by the regional groups which make the elections.

However, non-members of the Council were given improved rights in other ways. The Dumbarton Oaks proposals already envisaged that a non-member should have the right to appear when any dispute to which it was a party was being discussed. It was now proposed that, in these circumstances, such a member should sit as a member of the Council with full voting rights or even with rights equal to that of any other party to the dispute (i.e. would have a veto if a permanent member was also involved). Neither of these was accepted, but a Canadian proposal that any member providing forces for a Security Council operation should be able to sit as a member of the Council when it discussed the use to be made of such forces was adopted in a modified form: any member called on to provide forces was enabled to send a representative at its request to take part in decisions concerning the use of its contingents (Article 44 of the Charter).

The most important change in the security arrangements envisaged at Dumbarton Oaks resulted from the decisions concerning 'regional arrangements'. The Dumbarton Oaks proposals provided that the Security Council should use and encourage the use of regional agencies, both for peaceful settlement and for enforcement when appropriate, but that the regional agencies should not be used for enforcement without express authority from the Security Council. This represented some concession to the original British view about the role of regional organisations, but kept primary responsibility entirely in the hands of the Security Council. But the provision came under sustained attack at San Francisco, from the Latin Americans in particular. These states had only recently joined in setting up their own regional system under the Act of Chapultepec, under which each member undertook to defend others which were under attack. The whole tradition of the area favoured the settlement of local disputes on a local basis, without interference from outside nations or bodies. In her traditional diplomacy the United States too had strongly supported this view. The League Covenant had even, in deference to this tradition, expressly made an exception of its normal rules to allow the Monroe Doctrine to operate in the Western hemisphere if so desired. But the US Government was torn at San Francisco (and its delegation itself divided) between the desire to maintain the tradition of the Monroe Doctrine and the aim of establishing an integrated and effective world security system. The difference of view in the delegation could only be finally resolved by a decision of President Truman in favour of a compromise proposal.

The desire for a wider role for regional arrangements did not only stem from Latin American sources. A number of European countries were concerned at the possibility of a renewed threat from Germany or other former enemy countries. These felt that the right of immediate retaliation against such countries, even without prior approval by the Security Council, should be retained. Thus amendments were proposed by Turkey, Belgium and Czechoslovakia permitting immediate action by states in 'cases of immediate danger where suspension of any coercive action until the intervention of the Security Council may cause irremediable delays'; and the Soviet Union also proposed an amendment allowing unilateral action in an emergency in conformity with treaties (such as the Franco-Soviet Treaty) against renewed aggression by a former enemy state. France demanded a similar exception. The United States and Britain were anxious that any such exception should cover only an interim period – until such time as the organisation was strong enough to deal with such a situation itself. The issue was thrashed out mainly among the Big Five, and they finally adopted a compromise. This proposed that no action should be taken by regional organisations without the consent of the Security Council; but, it added, 'with the exception of measures against enemy states' taken as a result of the Second World War, or 'regional arrangements directed against a renewal of aggressive policy on the part of any such state, until such time as the organisation may, on request of the government concerned, be charged with the responsibility for preventing further aggressions by such a state'. Since no time-limit was placed on the clause, this represented a fairly sweeping qualification of the normal rights of the Council in cases involving former enemy states; and one which, more than twenty years later, West Germany still feared might be invoked against her (though some held it helped to support the four-power position in West Berlin).

This special exception to the general subordination of regional operations intensified the demand by the Latin Americans that their own regional arrangements should be similarly treated. The US delegation finally resolved its own internal dispute. It rejected the notion of adding another specific exception to the prior authority of the Security Council. It proposed instead an entirely new article which would reaffirm the 'inherent' right to take necessary measures for self-defence, whether undertaken by a state or by a group, in arrangements 'like those embodied in the Act of Chapultepec', if the Security Council should fail to prevent aggression. In that form this was not acceptable to others of the Big Five, who claimed it would lead to regional organisations taking action independently of the UN. But the British then proposed a rather less general exception, without specific reference to the Latin American case: 'nothing in this Charter shall invalidate the right of self-defence against armed attack, either individual or collective, in the event of the Security Council failing to take the necessary steps to maintain or restore international peace and security'.[1] Any such steps should be reported immediately to the Security Council and would not affect the responsibility of the Security Council 'at any time' to take the action it felt necessary. This reserved a rather more general responsibility for the Security Council but was none the less finally acceptable to the US delegation.

The Latin Americans at first still wanted a specific recognition of their own regional system. Only when the United States undertook to proceed rapidly to convene an inter-American conference which would draw up a binding treaty implementing the commitments of the Act of Chapultepec would they agree to accept the proposed new wording.

It is arguable that these changes brought a significant alteration in the emphasis of the Charter taken as a whole. Instead of a system in which the Security Council was the only body responsible for dealing with breaches of the peace all over the world (even if it might authorise action on its behalf by a regional organisation), it might now become a system in which breaches of the peace were met in the first place by action taken by individual states or groups of states, while only at some subsequent stage would the Security Council be called on to take action if necessary. In other words, it made it substantially less likely that the new UN enforcement machine would ever come into use, and more likely that conflict situations would be dealt with in the traditional way, as for hundreds of years before.[2] This may have reflected a realistic recognition of the world as it was likely to be. But it also removed something of the revolutionary significance of the Charter as originally proposed.

THE ASSEMBLY AND ITS POWERS

Complementary to the effort to reduce great-power domination of the security arrangements were the efforts made at San Francisco by the smaller powers to enhance the role of the Assembly. Not surprisingly, the assembled multitudes at San Francisco, which would constitute the bulk of the future Assembly, were anxious to see that body's powers strengthened, especially in the security field. In that area the Assembly had been given, under the Dumbarton Oaks plans, virtually no powers at all. It could consider general principles of co-operation in maintaining the peace, but any questions on which action was necessary were to be referred to the Security Council. 'The General Assembly should not on its own initiative make any arrangements on any matter relating to the maintenance of international peace and security which is being dealt with by the Security Council.' It was here above all that the delegates at San Francisco sought changes. While in general they accepted and approved the proposals for a strong Security Council, they sought to ensure that the Assembly would at least have some concurrent powers in this field.

The most sweeping proposal was that made by New Zealand, that the Assembly's consent would be required to any proposal by the Security Council to undertake enforcement action. This would have had the major disadvantage that it would have made decisions on such matters far slower and more uncertain: one of the main advantages of using the Council was that it was a relatively small body which could quickly reach decisions in times of emergency. The proposal was thus quickly rejected by the great powers. They pointed to the need for speedy action and to the ineffectiveness of the League Assembly in this field. But the small powers remained insistent that the Assembly should have a wider authority to discuss matters of peace and security. New Zealand demanded that the Assembly should be able to consider 'any matter within the sphere of international relations'. Eventually, and somewhat unwillingly, the Five relented. A new article was introduced by the United States, declaring that the Assembly could recommend measures for the peaceful adjustment of any situation, regardless of origin, 'which it deems likely to impair the general welfare or friendly relations among nations'. But this was still subject to the exception concerning matters before the Security Council – an exception on which the Five insisted, to prevent a division of authority within the organisation.

But the smaller powers wanted wider powers to discuss other questions. New Zealand and Australia held out for the very general statement of the Assembly's powers already proposed by New Zealand, which asserted the Assembly's right to discuss anything under the sun. The Soviet Union was strongly opposed to this statement, apparently foreseeing

Assembly discussion of the world communist movement or domestic matters in the Soviet Union. She therefore wanted the phrase limited to cover only matters which 'affect the maintenance of peace and security'. Though this limitation was voted down by a large majority, the Soviet Union maintained its view in discussions with the rest of the Five. These eventually accepted that Assembly recommendations should be limited in the way the Soviet Union suggested. Again the assembled smaller states refused to budge. The matter became a critical one. Gromyko informed Stettinius that he had received instructions to refuse to sign the Charter unless his objections were met. Eventually a sub-committee of Stettinius, Gromyko and Evatt, the Australian Foreign Minister (who played a prominent part as the champion of Assembly powers), was set up to find an acceptable compromise. After various disagreements, Evatt and Stettinius proposed that the Assembly's competence should be defined as extending to any question within the 'sphere of the Charter' or the 'scope of the Charter' or the 'sphere of action of the organisation'. Again the matter had to go to Moscow, and Harriman, the US ambassador, was instructed to warn the Soviet Government that, if none of these was accepted, the United States would reserve its 'freedom of action' for the future. By this time the Conference was almost over and the Charter due for signature in a few days. Finally the Soviet Government relented. It was thus provided, in Article 10 of the Charter, that the Assembly could discuss 'any questions or any matters within the scope of the present Charter'; but the exception of matters under consideration by the Council remained.

There was one other attempt to strengthen the powers of the Assembly. This took the form of demands that the Security Council should report to it on every measure it took in the field of peace and security, and that the Assembly would then submit recommendations 'with a view to ensuring complete observance of the duties of the Security Council'. This would have made the Council almost the servant of the Assembly, and the idea was resisted strongly by the Soviet Union, and to a lesser extent by the rest of the Five. Somewhat reluctantly, the smaller powers again had to give way. A much more innocuous text was finally approved: 'the General

Assembly shall receive and consider annual and special reports from the Security Council; these reports should include a report of measures the Security Council had decided upon or taken to maintain international peace and security'. This made clear that there was no question of the Security Council taking orders from the Assembly, and in practice the Security Council's reports have been barely debated or discussed by the Assembly.

There were a few areas where the Assembly's powers were reaffirmed or even enlarged. Even under the Dumbarton Oaks proposals the Assembly was to have the sole right to discuss economic and social questions, and would supervise a special economic and social council (ECOSOC) which would meet between sessions of the Assembly. The smaller states welcomed the role envisaged for the Assembly in this field, which many regarded as one of the most important areas of the new organisation's responsibilities. To draw added attention to that importance, they demanded, and obtained, the recognition of ECOSOC as one of the 'principal organs' of the organisation, so specified under Article 7 of the Charter. Secondly, they tried, but failed, to get the membership of ECOSOC increased, and to lay down arrangements for election which would ensure increased representation for small and developing countries. Thirdly, the Five themselves added 'promoting and encouraging respect for human rights' and cultural co-operation to the purposes of the organisation and placed these two among the responsibilites of ECOSOC. Fourthly, it was decided to establish a UN commission on human rights in addition to the other commissions already provided for at Dumbarton Oaks. Finally, ECOSOC was made the body responsible, and over it the Assembly, for securing co-ordination of the whole UN family of agencies: it was laid down that it could make recommendations to the specialised agencies, call for reports on the implementation of these recommendations, and, if necessary, create new agencies.

In a number of ways, therefore, the powers of the Assembly had been marginally increased. It was given wider powers of discussion, even in the area of security, and slightly increased responsibilities in the economic and social fields. But none of this altered the basic structure, or the general subordination

of the Assembly in matters of peace and security which the
Dumbarton Oaks powers had ordained.

OTHER PROVISIONS OF THE CHARTER

There were a number of other ways in which the Dumbarton
Oaks proposals were amended or supplemented at San
Francisco.

Perhaps the most important concerned the system of
trusteeship. This was one of the only features of the Charter
which had not been fairly clearly sketched out in the proposals
of the great powers. A section had been designated to deal
with the matter, but, largely because of disagreements within
the US Government, this had not been filled in, and was barely
discussed among the powers until the San Francisco Conference began.

Roosevelt had cherished the hope that the new organisation
could be given special responsibilities, not merely for taking
over the League's mandated territories, but for exercising a
watch over all dependent territories, and assisting their
progress towards independence. The first State Department
proposals had, however, run into strong opposition from the
US service departments. These were anxious to maintain
unfettered US control of conquered Japanese Pacific territories, which in their eyes were essential to US security. None
the less, Roosevelt at Yalta discussed possible trusteeship
arrangements for captured Far East territories. During these
discussions Stettinius spoke in a general way of UN machinery
for dealing with 'trusteeship and dependent areas'. Churchill
exploded at this idea, declaring that 'he did not agree with a
single word of this report on trusteeship' and would not
consider any suggestion 'that the British Empire is to be put
into the dock and examined by everybody'.[3] As a result the
Yalta communiqué referred to the possibility of trusteeship
only for existing mandates, for conquered territories and any
other territory voluntarily offered as a trust territory. Meanwhile it was agreed that representatives of the three powers
would get together to work out acceptable trusteeship proposals before the San Francisco Conference.

These discussions, however, did not take place until the eve of the Conference. Meanwhile there had continued to be an acrimonious debate within the US Government, with the service departments continuing to resist any proposal which would mean that the United States would have to be internationally accountable for any territories she took from Japan in the Pacific. As a result US officials conceived the idea of establishing two types of trust territory, the normal type, similar to mandates, to be supervised by a new trusteeship council; and 'strategic trust territories', which would not come under that council but which would be supervised, if at all, by the Security Council, where each permanent member would exercise a veto. The power exercising physical control of each territory would say to which kind of trusteeship it would commit it. The main trusteeship arrangements, providing for investigations in the trust territories, the acceptance of petitions from local inhabitants, and so on, would apply only to the non-strategic territories.

These proposals were put by the US Government to the rest of the Five at the opening of the San Francisco Conference. Britain strongly opposed the idea of a special status for strategic trust territories. She felt that the general aim of protecting the interests of the inhabitants through international supervision applied just as much to the strategic territories as to others; and that it should be possible for the controlling power to protect any special strategic interests there without a wholly separate scheme. 'The US idea would remove from the purview of the trusteeship council many of the matters for which the trusteeship system was primarily designed . . . .' In such areas, therefore, the administering power should still report to the Trusteeship Council on most matters, and to the Security Council only on security questions. The Soviet Union thought that the occupying power should not be able to take unilateral decisions on how each territory should be treated, it was for the Security Council, she said, to decide which territories should be designated as security areas. This view was supported by China.

The United States maintained its view that there should be wholly separated 'strategic trust territories', and that these should be designated by the controlling power. Eventually this was reluctantly accepted by the Five, and transmitted to the Conference. The Conference committee concerned was not disposed to challenge the US view, but it was proposed by Egypt, and accepted by the United States, that, 'subject to the provisions of the trusteeship agreements', the Security Council would 'avail itself of the assistance of the Trusteeship Council to perform those functions . . . under the trusteeship system, relating to political, economic, social and such matters'. No specific provision was included in the Charter to this effect, however. And in practice the Trusteeship Council for long took little notice of the single strategic territory (that of Micronesia in the Pacific) to be designated. Still less has the Security Council made any attempt to exercise its responsibilities in relation to the territory, which perhaps for this reason remained the last to be brought to independence (and then no longer as a single unit, a part remaining with the US).

On the other trust territories Britain and France were anxious to protect the administering power from undue interference by the Trusteeship Council. The United States, on the other hand, wanted to prevent the establishment of new preferences like those given in colonies; the United States demanded, on these grounds, that there should be a general non-discrimination undertaking.

For the rest, the Five fairly quickly reached agreement on the system to be applied. The Trusteeship Council would exercise a general overview of the administration by the metropolitan power, and could send visiting missions as well as receive regular reports. Within the Conference there was some attempt to extend the scope of the system. Australia and the Philippines proposed that all dependent territories should be made into trust territories, but did not pursue this idea far. An Australian proposal that the General Assembly could decide which territories came under the system was not even considered. On the contrary, the Conference accepted a proposal of the Five that any designation of a trust territory would be subject to a subsequent agreement, so making clear that it was for each occupying power to make the decision on the question. The prohibition of all military uses of the territories contained in the mandate system was abandoned: it was arranged that the administering power could 'ensure that the trust territory shall play its part in the maintenance of international peace and security and could make use of volunteer forces, facilities and assistance' from the territory for this purpose, or for local defence and law and order. It was also laid down that no alteration or amendment of the agreements could be made without the consent of the administering authority; which implied that they could not be deprived of their responsibilities against their will.[4] And, when Egypt proposed an amendment under which the Assembly would be given the power both to transfer a territory to another administering authority in the event of violation of the arrangements, or to terminate the trusteeship agreement and declare a territory independent, this was turned down by the great powers and was not even further discussed. Britain and France also ensured that the Council would consider petitions from the territories only 'in consultation with' the administering authority; and that investigations on the spot would take place 'at times agreed with the administering state'.[5] By these arrangements all effective control in such territories was firmly kept in the hands of the administering powers.

These arrangements for trusteeship were to be accompanied by another section of the Charter concerning all non-self-governing territories. Britain, having accepted the idea that there should be some general declaration of this kind, in which the colonial powers would undertake to protect the interests of the inhabitants of such territories and to promote their political, economic and social advance, presented her own proposals for this to the Five. These then incorporated much of this in a proposed statement of principles governing dependent territories which they included in their working paper on trusteeship. This accepted that it was a 'sacred trust of civilisation' to promote to the utmost the well-being of dependent territories and to 'develop self-government in forms appropriate to the varying circumstances of each territory'. Nothing was said about leading the territories to independence, though both the Soviet Union and China had demanded that this should be included in the list of responsibilities. This demand was particularly unacceptable to France, which at this time did not accept independence as the ultimate goal for her dependent territories. The point was taken up vociferously in the Conference. Even the Covenant, it was pointed out, had referred to the aim of independence, at least for mandates: to drop it now would be a step backwards. China, the Soviet Union, the Philippines, Egypt and Iraq argued strongly in this sense. The traditional colonial powers, backed by the United States, resisted the demand. The United States finally proposed, as a compromise, that the declaration on non-self-governing territories would refer only to the goal of 'self-government', but the objective of the trusteeship system should be broadened to refer to independence, the protection of human rights and the wishes of the people concerned. This compromise was, somewhat reluctantly, finally accepted. Thus, the Declaration Regarding Non-Self-Governing Territories, eventually incorporated into Chapter XI of the Charter, while it committed the administering power to irreproachable but ill-defined goals, such as political, economic, social, and educational advancement, 'just treatment', 'progressive development of free political institutions', 'constructive measures of development', and so on, did not refer, even as an alternative, to the aim of independence, which most delegates regarded as the most important goal of all. Included with the Declaration, however, was a commitment, unspectacular but potentially important, to 'transmit regularly to the Secretary-General . . . information relating to economic, social and educational conditions in the territories'. It was this undertaking which finally became the basis of the extensive discussion of colonial questions which, quite against the wishes of the colonial powers, came to be so regularly and vociferously undertaken by the Assembly at a later date.

Another important controversy concerned the question of domestic jurisdiction. Most states wished to include in the Charter some kind of prohibition of discussion of questions held to be within the jurisdiction of member-states. The Covenant of the League had excluded from consideration any 'matter which by international law is solely within the domestic jurisdiction of a member'. The Dumbarton Oaks proposals included a reservation with similar wording. At San Francisco the United States had second thoughts on this. The US Congress had traditionally been, even more than most other similar bodies, intensely jealous in reserving to the nation absolute sovereignty over matters within domestic jurisdiction. Before the San Francisco Conference began, therefore, the United States had decided to propose a broader and vaguer reservation which would refer to matters 'essentially', rather than 'solely', within a state's own jurisdiction; and would omit the reference to 'international law', always unpredictable in determining what was or was not within domestic jurisdiction. In this she was, inevitably, supported by the Soviet Union, if anything even more determined to protect sovereign rights and more concerned to prevent interference by the UN in her own affairs. China and Britain, on the other hand, together with a majority of states in the Conference, wanted at least some reference to international law as determining what was domestic and what was not. Indeed, there were many states, especially Latin American, which wanted the International Court to be able to decide on such questions. The United States declared that, if such provisions were included, she might not ratify the Charter. The Latin American proposal in fact received a majority within the Conference, but not the two-thirds majority that was required to amend the proposal of the Big Five. This stated simply, 'nothing contained in the Charter shall authorise the Organisation to intervene in matters which are essentially within the jurisdiction of a member-state'. It was this which was finally incorporated in the Charter in Article 2(7). As the Belgian delegate pointed out, the vagueness of the wording in fact presented the risk that 'each country would finally be the judge of its exclusive jurisdiction'. This was indeed the danger: it had of course been the whole idea.

There was also conflict about membership of the organisation. The Dumbarton Oaks proposals, as we saw, had said that membership should be open to all 'peace-loving states'. But some countries, especially the Latin Americans, wanted the UN to be more expressly committed to the principle of universality. Against this, others wanted membership to be clearly denied to certain states: for example, the former enemy countries, or, as Mexico demanded, Franco's Spain. Thus, eventually, a rather ambiguous compromise was accepted. The Dumbarton Oaks formula was expanded to read, 'Membership of the UN is open to all . . . peace-loving states which accept the obligations contained in the present Charter and, in the judgement of the Organisation, are able and willing to carry out these obligations.' This gave a spurious impression of universality while in fact providing a ready-made justification for denying membership to any state which might be for any reason disapproved of by a majority at any one time.

This raised the question of how admission should be decided. At Dumbarton Oaks it had been agreed that admission would be on the recommendation of the Security Council, so ensuring that the great-power veto would apply. But at San Francisco many states wanted admission to be by the Assembly alone and free of veto. Once again, however, the great powers held together. The United States, which at one time had herself favoured admission free of veto, now supported the Dumbarton Oaks formula. Thus it was finally decided that admission would be 'by a decision of the General Assembly upon a recommendation of the Security Council': a provision that was to lead to many bitter conflicts in the first ten years of the organisation's life.

It was generally agreed that the Charter should (unlike the Covenant) contain no explicit reference to withdrawal. The advocates of universality claimed that this implied that it should be made impossible. Thus the grand gestures, such as those made by Germany and Italy in flouncing out of the League and repudiating its obligations, would be made impossible. The United States and other great powers resisted this interpretation. Withdrawal could only be prohibited, it was argued, if some sanctions against it were provided. Few countries would be willing to use force against such a state, and therefore it would be better to say nothing at all about the question. Moreover, it would be unfair to prevent any state withdrawing in any circumstances – for example, if amendments to the Charter might be subsequently made which it did not accept. These arguments prevailed, and no reference to withdrawal was made in the Charter.[6]

A commitment to universality also implied opposition to expulsion. Thus the proposal of the sponsors that the Assembly could expel a member which persistently violated the principles of the Charter was opposed by Belgium and other states, which said that suspension should be sufficient in such a case. The Soviet Union, however, insisted that the right to expel was essential and in this was backed up by the other great powers. The committee concerned reluctantly agreed to reverse its initial decision. Both expulsion and suspension of membership (for example, when an enforcement action was being taken against a state) were to be on the recommendation of the Security Council and so subject to veto.

There was also controversy about the election of the Secretary-General. Many states wanted him to be elected directly by the Assembly. This was strongly opposed by the permanent members, however, and was not pursued. It was next suggested that the Security Council should propose a list of three names to the Assembly, which would elect one from this list; but this too failed. Finally it was agreed that the recommendation of the Council in such cases should be made by a majority of seven votes. But it was argued that there should be no great-power veto. This was resisted by the Five; and, once it had been decided that the veto applied to all non-procedural questions, they were able to point out that the election of a Secretary-General was not a procedural matter. This was eventually somewhat reluctantly accepted, and so the Charter finally provided that the Secretary-General should 'be appointed by the General Assembly upon the recommendation of the Security Council'. In theory the Assembly could reject the nominee of the Security Council, but this was not a step which it was normally likely to wish to take; and in practice so far every nominee of the Council has been overwhelmingly endorsed by the Assembly.

There was an accompanying discussion about the appointment of deputy secretary-generals. The Soviet Union proposed that the Secretary-General should be elected for only two years, and would not be immediately eligible for re-election, while four deputies would be elected in the same way. All should be nationals of the major powers, and each deputy would expect to become Secretary-General eventually. The effect would be that within a decade a national of each of the great powers would serve as Secretary-General. The other big powers wanted the term of office extended to three years; and, though they were willing to see deputies appointed, did not demand that they should be nationals of the big powers. The Conference decided against naming any term of office for the Secretary-General (the first Assembly eventually decided on a five-year term). It also decided against electing deputies. It was held that this would reduce the independence of the Secretary-General, who should be free to appoint his own senior staff. The United States and Britain were prepared to accept this, but the Soviet Union held out for the election of deputies, even though she no longer held that they need be nationals of the great powers. In this she was eventually supported by the rest of the Five. But the rest of the Conference, who had already had to give way on the method of election of the Secretary-General, were not prepared to make another concession. Proposals for five, four or an indefinite number of deputies were successively voted down. It was left to the future Secretary-General to appoint his own deputies if necessary.

There was less controversy about the functions of the Secretary-General. Like his predecessor in the League, he was to be 'the chief administrative officer of the Organisation'. He was to perform secretarial and organisational functions for all organs of the UN, and report annually to the Assembly. He was, however, given wider responsibilities than the League's secretary-general. As the Five had proposed, he was given the right, under Article 99, to bring to the attention of the Security Council any matter 'which in his opinion may threaten the maintenance of international peace and security': a right which, as we shall see, was used by later secretaries-general as a means of expanding their own role. General guidelines ensuring the international character of the Secretariat and forbidding its members to seek or receive instructions from any government or any external authority were included. Criteria for recruitment were laid down which, though apparently innocuous, led to perpetual difficulty and controversy in later years. The paramount consideration in securing staff, it was decided, was to be the necessity of 'securing the highest standards of efficiency, competence and integrity'. But at the same time due regard was to be paid to the 'importance of recruiting the staff on as wide a geographical basis as possible'. The real problem was to know which of these considerations carried greater weight; and in subsequent years it was the latter rather than the former which, in the eyes of many, became the 'paramount consideration'.

Finally, various points arose concerning the renewal of the International Court of Justice. The great powers, as we saw, had finally proposed the establishment of a new court with a new statute, to which all members of the organisation would automatically be parties. Immediately before the San Francisco Conference a wider meeting had been called in Washington to consider the revision of the old statute. This had approved a number of technical amendments but had left the most difficult points to be decided at San Francisco, where it was eventually confirmed, after considerable discussion, that a new court should be established. It would be continuous with the old one and references in earlier treaties to the Permanent Court would now be applied to the new court. The old and complicated system of elections to the Court, first by the Council and then by the Assembly, was maintained, despite some pleas that election should be by the Assembly only.

A more controversial point was the proposal that every UN member should accept the compulsory jurisdiction of the Court. This was rejected by both the Soviet Union and the United States. New Zealand then proposed a compromise whereby every state would accept the compulsory jurisdiction of the Court, but subject to general and uniform reservations. The US and Soviet delegates made it clear that, even in this form, the proposal would prevent their countries from ratifying the statute. The effect of these clear warnings was that, even though a majority of states favoured compulsory jurisdiction, they also found discretion the better part of valour and refrained from pressing their view to the limits. Once again the united front of the great powers prevailed. There was much dissatisfaction with the position taken by the two super-powers, but reluctance to cause a rejection of the statute on these grounds.

The other important point concerned how the verdicts of the Court were to be enforced. The Covenant had given the League Council authority to 'propose what steps should be taken to give effect to a decision of the Court' when a member failed to comply with it. The Committee of Jurists, meeting before San Francisco, had been concerned that some effective means for enforcing Court decisions should be found, and decided that the question was so important it should be left to the Conference. Everybody was agreed that the Charter should lay down a general obligation on all members to comply with Court decisions. China proposed that, over and above this, the Charter should provide that, where a party failed to comply with a judgement of the Court, 'the Security

Council may . . . take such action as it may deem necessary to give effect to the judgement'. Norway wanted a still stronger wording, demanding that the Council should do this. Both proposals were opposed by the United States and the Soviet Union, and were viewed with misgiving by Britain. Within the Conference, however, opinion in favour of some such provision was overwhelming. Eventually it adopted, by a two-thirds majority, wording very similar to that proposed by the Chinese. The Soviet Union pointed out that this would radically change the Security Council's powers, by empowering it to deal with matters which had nothing to do with security. Eventually, despite some misgivings among the great powers, it was accepted that, where a Court judgement had not been complied with, the aggrieved party could apply to the Security Council, 'which may, *if it deems necessary*, make recommendations or decide upon measures to be taken to give effect to the judgement'. It was agreed by the permanent members that the italicised words would justify the Council in calling for enforcement action only if peace and security were threatened: therefore its effective powers were not really changed.

There were a large number of smaller points on which disagreements of various kinds emerged, and small modifications of the original draft were introduced. None of these made any difference to the basic structure and powers of the organisation. In all its essentials the proposed organisation remained the body which the United States, Britain, the Soviet Union and China had conceived at Dumbarton Oaks.

For all the long discussions and bitter debates at San Francisco, the new United Nations remained an organisation conceived and created by the great powers. Its form and structure clearly reflected this birth. That is, it was an organisation in which the great powers of the world would have the dominant say: in which they could, in particular, prevent any positive action of which they disapproved. Some held that this meant that the organisation could be sure of retaining the support of these powers, and so would deal more effectively with the crises which arose. Others feared that it might be helpless in dealing with precisely the most threatening situations likely to arise.

4 The Setting up of the New Organisation

Immediately after signing the Charter, the delegates at San Francisco approved an agreement on 'Interim Arrangements'. This established a preparatory commission representing all who signed the Charter. This was to begin making preparations for the new organisation, even before it was formally established (which would occur only when the necessary ratifications had been received). It would start setting up the Secretariat; establish the new International Court; and make arrangements for the first meetings of the Assembly and other UN bodies. It would also recommend a permanent location for the new organisation – the responsibility that proved the most lengthy and intractable of its tasks.

Apart from one brief meeting in San Francisco, the Commission did not meet again until the autumn. Meanwhile its work was performed by an executive committee, composed of the same fourteen states which had formed the Executive Committee of the San Francisco Conference. This held its first meetings in London in the middle of August. Gladwyn Jebb, a member of the British delegation at San Francisco, was appointed Executive Secretary. He began immediately to assemble the staff necessary to service the meetings.

The establishment of a smaller body to do much of the donkey work seemed a practical arrangement. But in practice it proved cumbersome and time-consuming. The Executive Committee itself established ten subordinate committees to consider the main individual points to be decided. These then made recommendations to the Executive Committee, which reconsidered the same points. The Preparatory Commission, when it met in November, set up eight main committees to consider many of the same subjects again. The final decisions on each point had to be made by the Preparatory Commission itself. Even then this could only make recommendations to the Assembly. This meant that every point had to be considered at least four times.

Some points could be agreed relatively quickly, and with little controversy. The Executive Committee proposed, and the Preparatory Commission agreed, that the first General Assembly should meet as soon as possible, in a divided session. The first part of the session would be devoted mainly to organisational questions; the second, to be held some months later, would be a normal session devoted to discussing the main issues of the day. The Preparatory Commission, again following the Executive Committee, proposed a structure of six Assembly committees, based on that used in the League. These would, again as in the League, be committees of the whole: in other words, each would have a representative of every member-state. Discussion of most issues would take place in the first place in these committees. There would be a political and security committee; an economic and financial committee; a social, humanitarian and cultural committee; a trusteeship committee; an administrative and budgetary committee; and a legal committee. This structure was finally accepted by the opening Assembly, and became the basic structure to the present day. The only significant change was the subsequent addition of a 'special political committee', a kind of 1½ committee, to consider certain political issues for which there was not time in the First Committee.

It was also decided that the Assembly should have an advisory committee on administrative and budgetary questions (ACABQ). This, corresponding roughly to the Supervisory Committee which had been set up in the League, would have a considerable influence in scrutinising the budget of the organisation and generally advising on all financial matters. A proposal that there should be a nominations committee, to receive and assess nominations to UN bodies and consider the suitability of candidates, a proposal much favoured by the Soviet Union, was turned down. It would clearly have been merely a means by which great powers would veto, or at least influence, nominations by smaller states, and would have interfered with the free electoral process within the organisation. There was also to be a general committee, a kind of steering committee, which would adopt the agenda and manage the business for each Assembly session. This would consist of the officers of the Assembly, committee chairmen, the permanent members, and a few others. There would also be a credentials committee, to examine the credentials of delegates.

The most important point of controversy concerned the Secretariat. The Soviet Union proposed that, instead of an integrated secretariat covering the whole of the organisation, there should be separate secretariats for each of the main organs – Security Council, General Assembly, and so on. Like the proposal for deputy secretaries-general made at San Francisco, this was probably designed to ensure that one of the proposed secretariats should have a Soviet national as its head. At least it would have the effect of dividing and weakening the influence of international officials generally (as much an object of Soviet policy then as fifteen years later, when the Russians proposed the comparable troika idea). The proposal received support only from Yugoslavia and Czechoslovakia. It was strongly opposed by most others. And it was rejected by both the Executive Committee and the Preparatory Commission.

Again, the Soviet Union objected to the proposal that the existing specialised agencies should be 'brought into relationship' with the UN as soon as possible. Russian hostility was directed primarily at the ILO, of which the Soviet Union had never been a member, and which was particularly suspect as seeking to interfere in the internal affairs of member-states. But here again the object may partly have been to weaken the influence of international organisations generally, by keeping them in separate compartments, each quite independent of the other. Thus Gromyko demanded that the ILO should be reconstituted before it was brought into relationship with the UN; while other prewar agencies, which he regarded as Western-governed, should be liquidated altogether. For the same reason, the Soviet Union opposed the recommendation that the League's economic and social activities, based in Geneva, should be transferred to the UN. This may have been partly a relic of the Soviet Union's hostility to the League, which had expelled her. But it was probably mainly an expression of her general opposition to the UN's undertaking any responsibilities in this wider field. In any case, on both points she was overruled.

Arrangements had to be made for the dissolution of the League of Nations. The League had been virtually defunct for several years, but it was to have a final Assembly meeting to wind up its affairs. The old Permanent International Court of Justice could only be dissolved by the League; so the Preparatory Commission passed a resolution saying that it would 'welcome' steps by the League to do this. In addition, arrangements were made for the transfer of the 'social, technical and non-political' functions of the League to the UN. The UN took over the League's property. Thus the old League building, the Palais des Nations in Geneva, was made an important centre for UN meetings: more meetings are in fact held there today than in New York, and it has had to be much expanded over the years.

THE ASSEMBLY MEETS

The Preparatory Commission, in recommending that the first session should be divided into two parts, had suggested that the first should be devoted mainly to organisation and procedure, and the second, in the spring, to substantive political questions. There would then be another normal session in the following September. Soon after the first session began, however, it was decided not to hold any meeting in the spring. There would be simply one meeting in September, which would become the second part of the 1946 session.

The first meeting of the Assembly was held in Central Hall, Westminster, on 10 January 1946. Almost its first act was to elect a president for the session. This proved a controversial matter. As soon as the proceedings began, Gromyko, the Soviet chief delegate, strode to the rostrum and declared immediately that he favoured the election of the Norwegian Foreign Minister, Trygve Lie, as president. Lie had once been the US candidate for president, having been approached by Stettinius the previous August, and again by Stevenson, the US delegate to the Preparatory Commission in December. A day or two before the Assembly session began, however, the United States withdrew its support for him, and transferred it to Spaak, the Belgian Foreign Minister, a staunchly pro-Western and anti-communist statesman, who was also supported by Britain and other countries. Spaak was, however, by no means acceptable to the Soviet Union, because of his robustly uncompromising political views. The Russians, alarmed at the nomination, were eventually able at the last minute, to persuade the US delegation to revert to their support for Lie. Thus the Ukrainian delegate, supporting Gromyko, proposed that Lie should be elected by acclamation without a ballot. This was turned down by the Assembly. The US delegation, now in two minds, made no declaration of its support for Lie. Thus in the event Spaak, despite strong Soviet opposition, was elected president by 28 votes to 23. This was generally regarded as a considerable political defeat for the Russians, who were known to dislike Spaak. The whole affair lent an ominous tone to the first day's proceedings of the Assembly.

Far more important was the election of the organisation's secretary-general which was to follow. This had been discussed informally for some time. In this case the veto operated, so the first essential was that the candidate should be acceptable to all the permanent members. Many names had been tentatively discussed, ranging from Anthony Eden to General Eisenhower. It came, however, to be generally agreed that the post should not go to a national of one of the major powers. The US Government actively discouraged suggestions of an American secretary-general, especially after the United States had been selected as the site of the organisation's headquarters.

Instead the first choice of the United States became Lester Pearson of Canada. He, however, was regarded by the Russians as too pro-Western. They countered by proposing a Yugoslav, Simic, previously a member of the Yugoslav government-in-exile, but now Foreign Minister in Tito's government. He, as the Russians must have known, was equally unacceptable to the United States and other Western countries. A number of other names were mentioned, including van Kleffens of the Netherlands, and Rzymoski of Poland.

But at this point attention turned increasingly to Lie. He had always been second on the US list of suitable candidates. He was strongly supported by Australia, New Zealand and some other small countries. He was clearly not unacceptable to the Russians, because they had supported him for president of the Assembly. On 28 January, at a meeting of foreign ministers of the permanent members, Stettinius formally proposed Lie to the rest. Most agreed fairly readily. The most reluctant, surprisingly, was Ernest Bevin of Britain, who might have been expected to welcome a fellow socialist, especially one who had spent the war years in London, in Norway's government-in-exile. But Britain was reluctant to relinquish the hope that Pearson might get the job. Eventually, twenty-four hours later, when this was clearly shown to be impossible, Britain too agreed to the nomination of Lie. On 29 January he was formally recommended by the Security Council to the Assembly. On 1 February, by a vote of 46 to 3, he was appointed by the Assembly as the first secretary-general of the UN.

Trygve Lie had a number of advantages for the post. The Secretary-General, it was generally accepted at this time, should not be a mere administrator and backroom boy, but should be a forceful figure who would bang together the heads of fractious statesmen, and play a prominent part on the world scene, demanding action by the world body when necessary. Trygve Lie, unlike his successors, was a politician by training and experience. He was robust and outspoken in style, a quality then regarded as an asset, though it ultimately proved a heavy liability for Lie. As Norwegian Foreign Minister he had had dealings with the Russians and had won their respect. His government's policies at this time were not so pro-Western as to rule him out as a possible candidate in Soviet eyes. In his own words, Moscow wanted a 'man who, without being committed to the East, was not hostile to it; and it felt that the Norwegian foreign minister was such a man'.[1]

Most of the rest of the business of the opening session passed without controversy. In theory the Assembly was to consider only questions of organisation and procedure, but in practice the session did discuss a number of political matters of immediate concern. One of its first actions was to pass a resolution on the question of atomic energy, in the minds of most people the most immediate danger to mankind at that time. On 24 January a resolution was passed setting up an atomic energy commission, consisting of the members of the

Security Council plus Canada (which had acquired some knowledge and capability in nuclear matters), to examine the problems of the control of atomic energy and the peaceful exchange of atomic information. The Assembly also endorsed the declaration of the San Francisco and Potsdam conferences that Spain was not qualified to become a member of the UN, and recommended member-states to 'act in accordance with the letter and spirit of these statements in the conduct of their future relations with Spain'. It remained to be seen exactly what this meant (see p. 363 below).

For the rest, the Assembly in this opening session contented itself with tidying up and confirming the organisational arrangements proposed by the Preparatory Commission. It established most of the subordinate committees and commissions which that body had proposed. There were pressures from some of the smaller nations for increased representation on some committees. This was turned down in the case of the General Committee, but the Committee on Contributions, which was to assess how much each member-state was to pay to the organisation, was increased from seven to ten members and the ACABQ from seven to nine. Elections were held without controversy for the first Security Council, for ECOSOC and for the International Court of Justice. Arrangements were made for the participation of non-governmental organisations in the work of the organisation.

The general feeling was that the new body had now finally found its feet.

SETTING UP OF THE NEW SECRETARIAT

One of the first tasks of the new secretary-general was to build up the Secretariat. Some staff had already been taken on, in many cases former League employees, to service the meetings of the Preparatory Commission and its Executive Committee. But when the first session of the Assembly met, a fairly large number of new employees had to be recruited rather quickly.

The first task was to appoint the assistant secretaries-general (as they were then called), who would be the heads of the main departments and become in effect the inner cabinet of the Secretary-General. Here Lie was to some extent limited by previous understandings reached among the great powers. At San Francisco, as we have seen, the Soviet Union's proposal for four deputies to the Secretary-General, who would be nationals of the great powers, had not been accepted. Neither the Charter nor the Preparatory Commission had laid down any stipulation about deputies.[2] The appointment of staff, including the most senior, and the organisation of the Secretariat were to be left to the Secretary-General himself. During the first Assembly, however, the representatives of the permanent members had got together and agreed among themselves a kind of share-out of the most senior posts. They had agreed that among the assistant secretaries-general a national of each of the five permanent members should be appointed. The Soviet Union demanded that in the first instance the post of assistant secretary-general for Political and Security Council affairs should go to a Soviet national. This was apparently believed by the Soviet Union to be the most important and influential post, since whoever was appointed would be dealing mainly with the important questions considered by the Security Council itself. The others eventually agreed to this. The post, though it has continued to be occupied by a national of the Soviet Union, has in fact secured for her no great political influence.

Lie was therefore approached, soon after his appointment, by Vyshinsky, the Soviet Foreign Minister, with a demand that he should comply with this great-power understanding. Lie confirmed with the other four foreign ministers that such an agreement had indeed been made, though Stettinius, for the United States, insisted that it referred only to the initial appointments to these posts, and it was not recognised that the Soviet Union had any permanent lien on the job. This placed Lie in something of a quandary. The understanding among the big powers was in fact quite unconstitutional. The Secretary-General was supposed to be responsible for all appointments and he was strictly enjoined to take no account of political factors in making them. Under the letter of the Charter he would therefore be fully justified in refusing to take any account of great-power views.[3] He decided, however (as have all his successors), that discretion was here the better part of valour, and that it would be foolish to ignore the claims of the most important supporters of the organisation to some senior posts within the Secretariat: above all since the Secretary-General himself was by general consent always likely to be a national of a smaller power. Nor did he seek to overrule the distribution of posts which they had agreed among themselves, a liberty he might well have allowed himself. In fact he went still further. He not merely consulted the five governments about the individuals to be appointed, but in practice accepted their nominations in each case.

Thus the Soviet nominee was appointed Assistant Secretary-General for Political and Security Council Affairs; a nominee of the US Government was appointed to take charge of administrative and financial services; and a Frenchman was appointed from among two or three names suggested as head of the Department of Social Affairs. A Chinese proposed by the nationalist government was appointed to look after trusteeship and non-self-governing territories. The British Government was somewhat diffident in making suggestions, and eventually Lie appointed his own executive assistant, David Owen, to run the Department of Economic Affairs. To these he added a Chilean to take charge of information work, a Czech to run the legal department, and a Dutchman to look after conference and general services.[4]

The task of engaging more junior staff then began. The first Assembly had approved the general structure of the Secretariat proposed by the Preparatory Commission. The Commission had recommended that eight departments should be organised, to correspond with the main bodies of the UN – the Assembly, the Security Council and the Trustee ship Council – and with the committees of the Assembly. In addition there would be a department of public information, serving all the others, and two general administrative departments for conference and general services and for administration and financial services. This organisation of departments, which was accepted by Lie when he became Secretary-General, has remained the basic structure ever since, with the single exception that the departments of economic and social affairs, though they served two separate assembly committees, were ten years later merged by Hammarskjöld into a single department.

Provisional staff regulations had also been drawn up by the Preparatory Commission. The establishment of an international civil-service commission had been recommended to advise the Secretary-General on methods of recruitment. The Preparatory Commission had also approved a set of principles and standards governing recruitment: it had, for example, firmly turned down a proposal that the consent of an individual's government would be required before he was appointed to the Secretariat, a proposal that had been strongly supported by the Soviet Union.

Much of this was accepted by the Assembly, and therefore by Lie on his appointment. He set about undertaking recruitment according to the principles clearly laid down in the Charter. A wide range of staff was required: specialists, such as lawyers, economists, statisticians, social scientists and so on; general administrators of a high calibre; translators, interpreters, reporters and researchers. People of the right quality, if possible with two or three languages, are not easily come by at the best of times. But the difficulty was greater because, so far as possible, they were to be recruited on 'as wide a geographical basis as possible'. There was obviously a greater number of qualified people, and even more of applicants, in some countries than in others: there were 10,000 applicants from the United States even before the UN had set up its offices in New York. Staff were taken on a temporary basis at first, and from the areas where qualified staff could most easily be found, which meant primarily Western Europe and North America. They were only re-engaged permanently later when there had been more time to assess their abilities, and when a more prolonged effort had been made to recruit elsewhere and so secure the desired geographical balance.

The delay in securing a permanent site of course increased the problems of organisation. Meetings of both the Assembly and the Council were held for the first three or four months in London. From May onwards both the Security Council and ECOSOC began to meet in New York. At first everything there was improvised. The Assembly that year had to take place in a converted skating rink at Flushing Meadows on Long Island, in buildings which had once been part of the World's Fair. From the end of 1946 both the Secretariat and the Assembly moved to Lake Success, outside New York, camping in the buildings of a disused gyroscope factory.

It was several years later before the organisation found a permanent home.

THE LOCATION OF THE HEADQUARTERS

By far the most controversial question discussed at the Assembly's first session was the question of a site for the permanent headquarters of the organisation. This was not to be decided until many months later.

The matter was first discussed in the Preparatory Commission and its executive committee. From the beginning there were strongly conflicting views on the point.

Many were influenced by traditional loyalties. Thus most Europeans demanded a site in Europe, either in Geneva, like the League, or in some other suitable spot, away from the territory of a great power: possibly the Hague, Vienna or Prague.

These countries argued that Europe was the centre and source of many of the world's political problems and disputes; it was therefore necessary to site the new organisation near to the troubles with which it would be dealing. They pointed out that a considerable number of existing members of the organisation were either European, or had close traditional ties with Europe. Europe was a natural centre of communications and the cultural centre of much of the world. It was held that the Soviet Union and other communist states would more easily be induced to play an active and positive part in the new organisation if it was based close at hand. For all these rationalisations, the prime, though unspoken, motive was no doubt the desire to keep Europe's century-old position as the political centre of the world.

Against this, many others believed that there was a strong case for a change. The failure of the League made necessary a new start in some other centre, remote not only from Geneva but from the world's traditional trouble-spot in Europe. The new organisation should be a worldwide body, as the League had never been, and should thus no longer be dominated by the old powers of Europe. Above all, to succeed it was essential that the new organisation should secure the wholehearted support of the United States, to prevent her from relapsing into isolationism. The best way to assure this was to set up the organisation within her own borders. As Trygve Lie, the first secretary-general, was to put it later,

> It was of paramount importance that the nerve-centre be located as close as possible to the new economic and political centre. . . . The challenging question of the future was how to secure the fullest possible US participation in whatever international organisations might emerge. A repitition of the tragedy of the League of Nations, stemming not least from the US's refusal to join, could not be permitted.[5]

A US site would be midway between the twenty-odd countries of Latin America and the similar number of European states, between them representing at this time about four-fifths of the membership.

These conflicting views were held by people of all states, partly regardless of national interest. Many individual Europeans, like Lie, favoured a US site, while many non-Europeans favoured a European one. But, among governments, it was mainly the Europeans, led by Britain, France and the Netherlands, which wanted a European headquarters; the non-Europeans which favoured the United States. Paradoxically, the two super-powers adopted opposite positions. The Soviet Union, despite the arguments sometimes put forward on her behalf, almost from the beginning wanted a site in the United States, provided it was on the east coast. The United States, conversely, at no time pushed the claim for a site in North America; indeed, the United States and Canada were the only two countries which abstained on the issue when a vote was first taken.

The most obvious European site was Geneva. Large and imposing buildings had been purpose-built for the League. There would have been a clear financial saving in using these, rather than building new ones (it was not then widely realised that the League's would be required anyway). But the chances that a Swiss site would be chosen were weakened by the ambiguous position taken up by the Swiss Government, which was even more cautious towards the new organisation than it had been to the League. The experiences of the Second World War had made clear to the Swiss the manifest advantages of their neutral status. They were somewhat alarmed at the concept of the new organisation as a body which might quickly find itself making war to keep the peace, using its own armed forces against an errant member-state. Even to be host to such an organisation, it was believed, could threaten Switzerland's neutral status. So the Swiss Government declared that, while they would be willing to see a new organisation set up on Swiss soil if this was generally desired, any decision by the Security Council involving the use of force would have to be taken outside Swiss territory: a somewhat absurd position which effectively excluded Switzerland as the site for the headquarters.

Within the Executive Committee of the Preparatory Commission, the West European states strongly advocated a European site. Nearly all the rest, including the Soviet Union, China, Australia, Czechoslovakia and the Latin American countries, wanted a site in the United States. The United States and Canada remained neutral. Accordingly a US site was recommended to the Preparatory Commission, though no exact location was suggested.

By the time the Preparatory Commission began to discuss the question, at the end of November 1945, the issue had become a public one. This stimulated a flood of offers of sites in a number of cities and areas of the United States, on a large number of well-meaning grounds. Delegations from all over North America flocked to London to preach the merits of their own particular city, anxious to acquire celebrity or commerce as the site of the new organisation. The places offered included Hyde Park, the estate of the late President Roosevelt in New York State; a place on the border between the United States and Canada, which it was proposed should become international; an area of the Wild West in the Black Hills, on the border between South Dakota, Nebraska and Wyoming; the estate of Abraham Lincoln; an island in Niagara Falls; a place in Hawaii; and other picturesque spots, together with a dozen US cities, including San Francisco, New York, Denver, Boston and Philadelphia. There was active lobbying by the various delegations on behalf of these different localities. The governors of Massachusetts and California, the mayors of San Francisco, Chicago and Atlantic City, and committees of distinguished citizens argued the special attractions of their states and cities. Altogether, twenty-two sites had been offered – nineteen in the United States and three in Canada – by the time the Preparatory Commission met at the end of November.

Within the Commission, Adlai Stevenson, the US delegate, expressly stated that his country made no special claims, but that, if the United States were the general choice, the UN would be welcomed there. France and Britain continued to claim it was essential to choose a seat in Europe. The initial vote came down against a European site, but only by the barest majority (25–23, with 2 abstentions). But, once this had been rejected, the main resolution favouring a US site was carried by a substantial majority. Later it was decided overwhelmingly that the seat should be in the eastern part of the United States.

An interim committee of twelve members was then established to inspect the main alternatives offered and report to the Assembly. The sites to be considered were one in the Boston area and three others east of the Hudson River: in New York, Connecticut and near Princeton in New Jersey. At this time, the general view was that the headquarters should be in a rural area, where a whole new international city could be established. After inspecting various sites, the Committee came up with a recommendation for somewhere in the region around North Stamford and Greenwich, not far from New York City. The Assembly accepted this in a modified form, proposing two particular areas. It set up a new headquarters committee to make a final choice.

But the residents in the area recommended had different views. Unlike the mayors and other dignatories who had flocked to London a few months earlier to tout their own state or city, they had altogether no desire to see the headquaters of an international organisation despoiling the countryside where they lived. They did not relish the prospect of having a huge cosmopolitan colony of international bureaucrats and politicians dumped down in their midst. And they therefore protested in loud and unflattering terms. The result was that the Headquarters Committee, intimidated by this outcry, rejected the recommendation of the previous committee in favour of the Greenwich area. Instead it came down in favour of an alternative site close to New York, either in Westchester County, or in Fairfield, Connecticut.

But once again the local residents took a hand. The reaction was quite as hostile as it had been in Greenwich – and the extremely wealthy residents even more influential. By the time the Assembly met again in the autumn of 1946, this protest movement had become loud and articulate. To impose the new headquarters on a bitterly hostile population, it seemed to suggest, would be to land the new organisation in trouble for years ahead, and trouble of a totally unnecessary kind, since there were many localities clamouring to receive the new organisation. As a result a number of delegations felt that the whole question should be looked at afresh; and the restriction to a site in the New York area should be abandoned.

This triggered off a further round of offers, from other areas. Consideration began to revert to a city site: it was the big cities, conscious of the commercial benefits, as well as civic honour, that had always been the most welcoming. New York City, where a temporary headquarters had already been provided, and San Francisco, still somewhat resentful of having been given no serious consideration despite having hosted the founding conference, renewed their invitations in pressing terms. Each offered specific sites within their cities. The US Government, no doubt hard pressed by both cities (as well as by the irate residents of Westchester County), called for a new look, including consideration of San Francisco once more.

So the whole issue had to be considered afresh. The Soviet Union announced itself as implacably opposed to a west coast site, and even for a time talked of reverting to the idea of a European headquarters. But the United States by this time favoured a site on its own territory, and resisted any reopening of that possibility. Britain too opposed any site on the west coast, and demanded that, if San Francisco was again to be considered, so too should alternative US cities less far afield. So in the end yet another committee was set up, authorised to consider sites in New York, San Francisco, Philadelphia and Boston. This rashly recommended in favour of Philadelphia or San Francisco. Of these, San Francisco was the most widely supported, especially by Latin American and Asian states, and the US President offered to provide a site there free of charge. But the Europeans were mainly hostile; and the Soviet Union threatened to boycott any meetings held in that city (though closer to Soviet territory than New York, it was of course far further from Moscow and, in Soviet eyes, on the far side of the globe). The US Government now again changed course and announced that it favoured an east coast site. Britain preferred Philadelphia.

The disagreement, after months of argument, was thus as great as ever. On 9 December, at a meeting of the Headquarters Committee, the United States proposed that the whole matter should be shelved until the next session of the Assembly. Others were strongly opposed to further delay. In any case, many wanted to make sure that San Francisco was among the possibilities considered.

At this point J. D. Rockefeller Jr made a dramatic offer. He announced he was ready to give $8.5 million to purchase a derelict site on the East River of New York, between 42nd and 48th Streets, in the area known as Turtle Bay.[6] It was made a condition that the gift should not be taxed by the US Government, that New York City should make over the streets included in the site, and that the offer should be accepted within thirty days. The United States immediately proposed the appointment of a new sub-committee to consider the site and report back. Despite some grumblings from states supporting other cities, this was accepted. Within a day (the Assembly was now drawing to its close) the sub-committee reported that it had visited the site, had had discussions with New York City officials and had concluded that the site would be excellent for the construction of a headquarters building. The Headquarters Committee, followed by the Assembly, accepted the recommendation by a large majority.

So the Rockefeller gift was accepted. The Secretary-General was called on to prepare plans for financial estimates for the construction of a permanent headquarters in New York.

Early the next year a headquarters planning office was established, with Wallace Harrison, the distinguished US architect, designer of the Rockefeller Centre, as director of planning. He appointed an international staff and a distinguished board of architectural consultants, including some of the world's most well-known architects, such as Le Corbusier and Oscar Niemeyer. Arrangements were made with New York City for clearing the site, acquiring the necessary roads and property, and rehousing remaining residents. The City donated $20 million for improving and beautifying the adjoining area. A plan for the building was agreed between Wallace Harrison and his team of consultants in May 1947. The US Government agreed to lend the sum required to construct the building, $68 million. Work began on the site in September 1948 and construction was finally completed in October 1952.

The building is generally accepted as an architectural masterpiece, which not only slashes a striking and individual silhouette against the New York skyline but also admirably meets the functional requirements of the world organisation. So, finally, seven years after it had been founded, the new organisation had acquired a permanent home of its own. It only remained to be seen whether it would perform its functions in a way that would match its bold and spectacular setting.

5 The Birth of a New Security System

So a new organisation had come into existence. A totally new security system had now been established, very much on the lines the great powers had originally planned.

The system that had been set up appeared in many important ways an advance over that established in the League. It should be far easier for the new organisation to call on the use of force to resist aggression, since all members were now clearly pledged to obey a demand for this made by the Security Council with the necessary majority. The universal veto available within the League, which had weakened its effectiveness in a number of crises (above all in dealing with the Japanese attack on Manchuria), was now replaced by a far more limited veto power, restricted to the permanent members alone, which even in their case allowed them to prevent only positive action, not discussion, by the Council: a restriction which seemed likely to be essential if the organisation was not to be torn apart by conflicts between the great powers themselves. More varied and more flexible procedures for the discussion of disputes and threats to the peace had been established, less formal and strictly juridical in character than those provided for in the League, and more suitable for the discussion of conflicts that were political rather than legal in nature. The organisation was given powers in a wider range of affairs than the League: it was made capable of at least discussing economic affairs and human rights questions, both of which were believed by some to lie at the root of many important disputes between states. Finally, all the great powers were this time members from the beginning and were pledged to work together in maintaining the peace of the world; this 'great power unity' too, to which all at least paid lip-service, should make it easier for the organisation to fulfil its tasks effectively.

All of these represented significant advantages which the new system held over its predecessor. They were, however, counterbalanced by a number of defects in the system, none of them adequately perceived at the time, which were in practice to prevent the new organisation from working in the way the blueprint laid down in the Charter suggested.

First, that blueprint presupposed that all disputes which arose among states could be neatly subdivided into the minority in which the great powers were 'parties', which the organisation would not be equipped to deal with (or, at least, could not employ enforcement powers to meet), and the great majority effecting the mass of smaller states, over which the organisation *could* act effectively – led, it was hoped, by the five permanent members, which, having no direct interest in the affair, could agree on the solution required. But no means was laid down for determining whether or not a great power was a 'party' to a dispute in a particular case. In any case, the distinction proposed altogether underestimated the contraction of the world that had taken place over the previous decade or two and the extent to which, therefore, the great powers would normally be parties to all disputes occurring. The League had been called on to deal with number of 'disputes' between lesser powers – Greece and Bulgaria, Lithuania and Poland, Colombia and Peru, Bolivia and Paraguay – in which the major powers had little interest or influence; and so had been able to act without arousing the concern of those powers for their strategic or political interests. But after the Second World War this was no longer possible. Every dispute that arose, in whatever part of the world, was of direct concern to the great powers and would be judged by them in the light of their own political interests and ideological views. To that extent they were always parties to each dispute. This made a nonsense of the idea suggested in the Charter that the Big Five, while unable to act in disputes among themselves, could easily get together to keep the peace in the wide open spaces beyond their own back doors. From now on the entire world adjoined their own back doors and every issue which arose was of direct concern to them.

Secondly, and for this reason, the idea that the veto power could be carefully restricted, as the Charter proposed, so that great powers would employ it only when their own interests

were directly involved, proved equally fallacious. In the new
and much smaller world which emerged, the great powers
believed that there were no issues which did not affect their
interests in some degree; and they thus felt constrained to
exercise their veto powers over issues arising far from their
own borders which others might well have considered of only
marginal interest to them (the fact that it was the Soviet Union
which was mainly to use her veto for this purpose was not the
effect of a special malevolence or original sin: it was only the
Soviet Union which *required* to use its veto for this purpose,
since the other governments were in a majority anyway). And
they proceeded therefore systematically to restrict the category of issues named as 'disputes', where their veto power
might be limited. Even in the first two months of the organisation's life, over Azerbaijan and the Levant, the great powers
concerned, the Soviet Union, Britain and France, all denied
that the cases in question represented 'disputes' to which they
were parties. And increasingly, from this point on, the organisation ceased even to attempt to determine whether a particular issue represented a 'dispute', or therefore to apply the
provisions of Article 27(3) limiting the veto for parties to a
dispute. So the veto became freely available in every case.

Thirdly, though it was true that on paper the new system,
containing the clear obligation of all members to obey a Council decision, should make the mobilisation of armed force
easier to achieve, in practice the difference was only marginal.
This time a force, in the form of earmarked units made
available by member-states, was to be permanently available to
the Council for that purpose. But the exact shape and nature of
that force had never been spelled out in the Charter. It was
never intended, even in theory, to be a separate and integrated international force, but was expected to be a collection
of national units; and, as we shall see shortly, the negotiations
to define the way the force should be established and maintained were quickly to break down. The failure to create such
a force need not in itself have made it impossible for the
organisation to call for enforcement action where necessary,
since it would still have been possible for the Council to 'decide' that member-states should employ their own forces to
defend a state under attack. But psychologically the failure
to establish the force was important; and in practice the power to

call for force, held by many to be the supreme advance of the new system over its predecessor, was never to be used. In practice no case of 'aggression' was ever so clear-cut (not even the relatively straightforward case of Korea) that different interpretations of its outbreak might not be put forward, and there would thus inevitably be a reluctance on the part of many members to respond to a call to send forces in such circumstances. For this reason it was held wiser not to strain the loyalty of members too far even by calling for such assistance. So the mobilisation of force proved no easier under the new system than it had under the preceding one.

Fourthly, the proposed new order totally failed to anticipate the political conditions of the postwar world. Even at the best of times, the five most powerful nations of the world might have found it difficult to co-operate in keeping the peace. But such a goal must inevitably prove particularly difficult in a world of intense and bitter political warfare such as was soon to emerge. The effect of this was that the UN, instead of becoming the instrument by which the great powers would act together to keep the peace, became instead the instrument with which they fought their own political warfare against each other: for winning voting victories rather than securing settlements; for confrontation rather than co-operation. Within this climate it was never likely to be able to reach the joint decisions which the founders of the Charter envisaged.

Finally, and in consequence, the organisation did nothing, at least in its first twenty years, to develop the machinery for *negotiation* among states, which alone could give a body without the sanction of force any effective influence. To a large extent, at first it operated entirely by public debate rather than by private discussion. There was little previous consultation even about the terms of resolutions. Even among members of the same bloc, consultation was at first minimal: in many cases the United States would introduce a resolution of her own drafting and expect her allies immediately to support her. And when, in the late fifties and the sixties, there did begin eventually to be more consultation, first among allies and then between the groups as well, this was still mainly confined to the texts of resolutions, rather than concerned with the substance of the issues discussed. The resolutions were, on most subjects, designed to secure the support of the majority, not to win an overall consensus. They were designed to achieve legitimation and endorsement for one point of view rather than a reconciliation between two. Only twenty years later, in the famous Resolution 242 over the Middle East, did a resolution emerge, which was designed to secure through prolonged negotiation, unanimous support and so to represent an international consensus on a major political issue. And that remained a quite exceptional case. Until that time the system of majority voting which many regarded as a huge advance of the UN over the League, in practice encouraged the attempt to secure voting victories, to mobilise majorities for partisan solutions, rather than the negotiation of settlements with which all important groups could live.

The world the new organisation encountered, therefore, showed itself in many ways different from that which its founders had anticipated when they drafted the Charter. Many of the provisions of the Charter which had been so laboriously negotiated proved unworkable or fell into disuse. It was many years before the organisation began to develop new procedures and traditions to replace the theoretical framework laid down. Meanwhile, to a large extent, it simply had to improvise.

Part II
The Era of Confrontation

6 The Negotiations for a Security Council Force

The UN, it is said, is always a mirror reflecting the world without. As the world changes, so too does the reflection in the mirror.

For the first ten years of the UN's life the world reflected was above all a world of cold war. This political reality dominated and shaped the UN throughout this period. It brought indeed a whole new peace-keeping system into operation.

The issues that arose in the organisation were not all cold-war problems in origin. Some did arise directly from the confrontation between East and West: Azerbaijan, Greece, East European questions, above all Korea. Others had different causes, arising in quite other areas of the world from the centre of East–West confrontation: Indonesia, Palestine, Kashmir. Yet all, whatever their origin, came to be seen in the UN through cold-war eyes. All were fought and manoeuvred over, partly at least, as episodes within the wider struggle between the two great ideological camps. The UN, continually in the glare of the spotlight, provided the perfect, highly publicised forum for this, where the machinations of antagonists could be denounced, appeals for justice proclaimed, the righteousness of one's own cause declared to the world.

Strategies were adopted by each side accordingly. The UN had within it, and in all its constituent bodies, a clear majority supporting Western positions. Early in its history, the Security Council arrived at a 'gentleman's agreement' governing the distribution of seats within it. This provided two seats for Latin America, one for Western Europe, one for Eastern Europe, one for the Commonwealth and one for Asia, besides the five permanent members. This normally secured a predominance for the West of at least eight seats to two; and in practice from 1948 this became at least nine to one, since from that year the majority ensured that the East European seat ceased to be given to a communist country for the next ten years. The proportions in the Assembly, where there were, at the beginning, five communist states out of fifty-one, were little different.

The Western powers, therefore, could normally expect to win each vote. They had no need to negotiate compromise solutions: they had only to mobilise the majority permanently available for their own view. On most issues they would support strong action by the UN, since they knew they could control the action the UN took. And they could thus proudly present themselves, almost tautologically, as the supporters and upholders of the organisation, and of its declared views; for to support the UN was to support themselves and their decisions.

The communist countries, on the other hand, knowing they could always be outvoted, sought on the contrary to play down UN legitimacy, to restrict UN activities and power, which were always likely to be unfavourable to them. They too sought to organise an equally, indeed even more, partisan group, however exiguous, to contest every sentence in every resolution proposed. And they could, if necessary, in the final resort, use the veto to frustrate action, even to prevent judgements, by the Security Council that the Western majorities would otherwise impose: a course which cold-war confrontation made far more frequent than those who framed the Charter had ever envisaged.

This in turn provoked another strategy by the West. Because effective action by the Security Council could be so easily frustrated through the Soviet veto, the Western countries, above all the United States, sought to transfer discussion from the Council to the Assembly. First they established an interim, or 'little', assembly, which could be called at short notice to consider any international issue on which the Security Council had not been able to act. Secondly, special assemblies were called on occasion, such as those set up to deal with Palestine in 1947 and 1948. Thirdly, and above all, in the Uniting for Peace resolution of 1950 (p. 253 below), a procedure was laid down whereby not only could the General Assembly be recalled at short notice when the Security

Council was deadlocked by veto (emergency Assembly sessions were already provided for under the Charter), but the Assembly could call for the use of force in such situations—a provision that was emphatically not contained in the Charter.

This elevation of the Assembly, in conjunction with the failure of the negotiations for a force to be established under the Security Council (p. 103 below), soon brought a considerable transformation of the security system as it had been laid down in the Charter. This, as we saw, had provided that the Security Council should be the main peace-keeping agency; and that within it the big powers would play together the dominant role in maintaining world peace. This concept was not, as is sometimes suggested, based on the belief that peace would be kept through 'unity' among the great powers. Statesmen and officials were not so naïvely unrealistic as to be unaware that the great powers might not always be united: acute conflicts between East and West had broken out well before the Charter was signed. But the system was based on the idea that, when the great powers were totally divided, the UN would not (and should not) be able to act. The veto was thus accorded as a kind of safety valve: to prevent the organisation from disintegrating in attempting to act against the will of a great power in such situations.

When discussion of security issues was shifted to the Assembly, with the avowed purpose of by-passing the veto, this assumption was destroyed. Instead of being an organisation run by the big powers to make the small behave, it became one in which the small were called in to keep the great (or some of them) in order. And the safety valve provided for the great powers was destroyed. For the West this did not matter, since they could rely on their majority anyway. But for the Soviet Union it removed the essential safeguard she had carefully secured for herself and threatened the assumptions on which her co-operation had been promised.

This created in turn the danger that the organisation might be destroyed by internal dissension: a danger which seemed about to be realised with the withdrawal of the Soviet Union from all active participation in the organisation for six months in 1950. The threat to the organisation was brought partly by the Soviet Union herself, through her continual abuse of the veto; not merely to prevent action against her vital interests, but to prevent *any* action or judgement of which she disapproved, whether or not it genuinely threatened her interests. But it was brought partly by the Western powers, seeking to win their way by mobilising majorities rather than serious negotiation, confrontation rather than consensus. Whoever was responsible, the focus and shape of the organisation was changed, almost unrecognisably, from its original conception.

For the shift in authority to the Assembly meant that any attempt to *negotiate* solutions or compromise courses among the permanent members, scarcely attempted even in the Council, was now totally abandoned. This in any case had been made difficult by the passions of the cold war, which forbade any communication with the enemy, and demanded total victory in every encounter. But it was made more so by the shift to the Assembly. Since, in the vetoless Assembly, majority views could be pushed through anyway, there was no need to discuss or take account of minority opinions. Thus one of the main objects of the veto – to create the need to negotiate mutually acceptable courses of action among the great powers (a need universally accepted in the successful system of the nineteenth century) – was now frustrated.

So, uninhibited by the inconvenient veto power, inevitably Western views prevailed over the great majority of issues. This was not, of course, how the Western countries themselves viewed the matter. In their eyes it was the majority within the UN whose views prevailed; and, if these happened to coincide with those of leading Western governments, this was a happy coincidence, but not necessarily anything of which they need feel ashamed. This no doubt was factually true (though it left out of account why the policies of the twenty or so Latin American states tended to resemble so much those of the leading Western power, let alone how far they really reflected the views of their populations). But it ignored the wider question of how successfully the UN could operate if a majority of members forced through resolutions favouring their own viewpoint, however numerous its adherents: a problem that was to arise in a new form in the sixties and seventies when a different majority dominated.

Few bothered to consider whether the proper object should not have been, as in the Concert of Europe, to secure the maximum possible *consensus*, taking account of minority opinions, rather than always to win a victory for those then in command.

Admittedly, consensus would not have been easy to achieve. Given the passions and prejudices of this ideological age, any attempt at compromise was precarious. On occasion, it is true, it was possible to arrive at resolutions that secured common consent: as over Palestine and Indonesia. But, for the most part, the mood of the times, especially the intransigent attitude of the communist countries, did not encourage agreed positions, even if they had been sought. The trouble was that the habit of attempting to negotiate agreed texts which even political adversaries would support had not evolved in the UN at this period at all. Most resolutions were proposed, almost unheralded, by individual states: they were supported by those which chose to do so, and opposed by those which did not. The procedures for backstage negotiation were undeveloped. The concept of the Council as a forum for negotiating agreed solutions had not begun to emerge.

The use of the Assembly as an arena for confrontation was encouraged by another fact. At this time the third world scarcely existed. India, almost alone, with two or three other Asian states, might be placed in this category. By far the greater proportion of all UN members, including all the Latin American, the only two black African, and three or four Asian states, were ranged firmly within the Western camp. The most significant fact of later years, the emergence of a large and ultimately dominant middle group, committed neither to West nor to East, had now scarcely begun. Nearly every speech made in the organisation was uttered by a representative belonging to one or other of the great ideological camps, and conditioned by their special vision. Thus the important role of third-party states in mediating between the two main blocs remained largely unperformed.

It was not a propitious environment for an emerging international organisation. It promoted acrimony and antagonism. It caused the whole organisation to take a shape utterly different from the envisaged for it, and without the peace-keeping mechanism the Charter prescribed. The mutual understanding among the great powers, which some expected to be the organisation's main bulwark, never existed. Nor, still worse, did the willingness to compromise. As a result, from the wreckage of the system so recently devised a quite different type of peace-keeping mechanism began to emerge.

One of the first effects of the new confrontation was that within a year or so of the new organisation's foundation, one of the major features of the system which had supposedly been created had collapsed.

Under the Charter the Security Council was to have at its disposal a force which would be formed from contingents contributed by each member-state. This would be its main weapon for maintaining the peace. It would represent the 'teeth' which the League had so conspicuously lacked and which the UN, it was believed, would require if it were to be an effective agent for peace-enforcement.

Arrangements for establishing the force were to be made by the Military Staff Committee, representing the five permanent members, under the general auspices of the Security Council. In theory this committee was to consist of the chiefs-of-staff of the permanent members. But it was quickly accepted that these august personages would not normally attend themselves, but would appoint their representatives to the Committee.

The Security Council, at its second meeting, in January 1946, asked the five governments to appoint their representatives. This was quickly done. The Committee came together first briefly in February in London, and then more regularly from March onwards in New York.

Two sub-committees were appointed: one to consider the general principles which would govern the organisation of the proposed force; another to consider a standard form of agreement with member-states concerning their contribution of forces. Each of the permanent members then submitted their views to these two bodies.

The negotiations immediately showed that, though all the five powers had agreed, at Dumbarton Oaks and San Francisco, to the establishment of a standby force, they had given little thought to the form this should take or the way it should be organised, still less considered how far their ideas coincided. On a number of relatively uncontroversial questions some common ground was reached. There was agreement, for example, that the force would be composed of units which were normally a part of the armed forces of each member-state: that is, there would be no fully international and directly recruited force. The contingents provided should be among the best trained and equipped units of each force. Every member-state would have the opportunity to contribute, though in the first place the permanent members would provide 'the major portion' of the force. No member would be asked to expand its normal armed forces to help make its contribution to the UN force. The contingents would be used only by a decision of the Council, and only for the period necessary for the fulfilment of the tasks laid down in Article 42 of the Charter. Members would provide the necessary supplies, transport and replacements for their own forces. The force would, while being employed by Security Council, be under the strategic direction of the Military Staff Committee, but each contingent would even then retain its own commander and national character, and be subject to the discipline and regulations of its national armed forces.

However, on a number of important points differences of view soon showed themselves. These were not all between East and West. China and France, for example, both felt that there should be an escape clause by which, at a time of 'national emergency', a member should be enabled temporarily to withdraw its forces from Security Council control to use them for national defence. This was opposed by all the other three members, on the ground that national emergency was difficult to define, that there was no provision in the Charter for exceptions and that the effectiveness of the UN force would be weakened if contingents could be withdrawn at short notice. Britain and France wanted provision for the appointment not only of a supreme commander for the force, as the others agreed, but for separate commanders of the land, sea and air contingents (possibly hoping that one of their own nationals would be appointed to these posts): this was opposed by all the others. There were also considerable differences among the Western powers concerning the size and balance of the forces which would be required.

But the more important differences were between East and West. One of these concerned where the forces should be stationed. The Western powers held that the UN forces would be stationed, even when not in use by the Security Council, in any territory to which the contributing state had 'legal right' of access. It would thus be for the contributing states themselves to decide, if necessary by agreement with the receiving country, where they placed their forces. They felt indeed that the UN should have a series of 'bases', offered by member-states scattered across the world: in the words of the French paper, 'bases are a vitally important factor in the employment of armed forces'. Thus the bases available should be clearly known in advance and listed in the special agreements. The Soviet Union, on the other hand, demanded that the earmarked forces should be held only in the territory of the contributing state. Experience had shown 'that the presence of foreign troops in the territories of other member nations without sufficient grounds does not facilitate ... the development of good neighbourly relations', but led to a 'feeling of anxiety among member nations for their national independence'. There is little doubt that the Soviet Union feared a kind of 'capitalist encirclement', brought about under the cloak of the UN, which might enable Western forces to be stationed in UN bases around the world, possibly close to the Soviet borders (this was before the days when US forces were anyway established in such areas). Soviet concern was to keep such forces as far from the Soviet Union as possible.

For similar reasons the Soviet Union objected to the Western proposal that one country might give assistance to another in the equipping and supply of the earmarked forces. She argued that the Western powers were in this way 'seeking to occupy a dominant position with regard to the armed forces to be placed at the disposal of the Security Council'. The Western powers argued that some countries might be unable adequately to equip the forces they contributed; and it was only reasonable that in these cases the smaller nation should be able to count on the help of friends elsewhere. Again, it seems, the Russians were afraid that what were nominally UN forces might become in effect a close-knit alliance among countries that were hostile to her.

More important was the question of the length of time after the completion of a security operation that a force could be kept in existence. Again the Russians seemed to fear that a Western-dominated force, though established for a given emergency, might be kept in being indefinitely, and so represent a threat to herself or her allies. She therefore proposed a strict time-limit of thirty to ninety days, after which the forces would need to be withdrawn to their own territories. This time-limit would be laid down in the special agreements for the supply of the forces. It would, she claimed, prevent their being used for political purposes unconnected with the security operation itself. The Western powers held that there need be no time-limit laid down, and that it was impossible to foresee in advance the situation which might arise in such circumstances, or the reasons why a longer period of occupation or peace-keeping might be necessary. A decision to end the operation should be a matter for the Security Council at the time, and should not be rigidly prescribed in advance by the Military Staff Committee.

By far the most important difference, however, concerned the size of the force, and the relative size of the contribution of each permanent member. On the total size there was almost as much difference among the Western powers as between East and West. The United States wanted a substantial force of twenty divisions, nearly 4000 aircraft, three battleships, fifteen cruisers, six carriers and eighty-four destroyers. France wanted a rather smaller, but still very substantial, establishment of sixteen divisions, 1275 aircraft, three battleships, six carriers, and so on. Britain, supported by China, wanted a smaller force of eight to twelve divisions, 1200 aircraft, two battleships, four carriers and six cruisers. But the Soviet Union, knowing that political control of the force would for the foreseeable future always be in Western hands (since these had a majority within the UN), favoured a much smaller force. She did not specify the exact size she wanted, being more concerned about the balance of contributions between the permanent members, but she challenged the ambitious nature of the Western proposals, indicating that a more modest force should be sufficient. And, indeed, since the force could never be used against one of the permanent members themselves, some of the ideas put forward by the Western nations certainly seemed somewhat extravagant.

The difference concerning the overall size of the force might not itself have been decisive. But it was accompanied by a much more serious conflict over the contribution which would be made by each permanent member. The Soviet

Union held that all the permanent members should make contributions of equal size to the force. This was an understandable view, given the fact that the Western powers, at this time virtually in control of the organisation, could, at least in theory, have built up a huge force consisting predominantly of their own contributions, including the US strategic air force (equipped with atomic bombs). The force might then have been used to promote Western political interests all over the world, even if presenting itself as a UN force. Whether or not for this reason, the Soviet Union held out strongly for contributions of exactly equal size. The proposals of the Western countries would, she declared,

> promote a situation where certain of the five states may, for instance, contribute the major portion of the armed force, chiefly in air forces, others chiefly in sea forces and a third group chiefly in land forces, and so on. That would lead to advantages in the position of certain states in the contribution of forces and therefore would be in contradiction to the equal status of these states as permanent members of the Security Council.

It could easily 'lead to the organisation of the armed forces being used in the interests of individual powerful states and to the detriment of the legitimate interests of other countries'.[1]

The four Western powers, on the other hand, demanded that the forces need only be 'comparable'. They could 'differ widely as to the strength of the separate components, land, sea and air'.[2] The French delegate accepted that there should be a 'comparable overall strength of the contingents'; and the British that there 'should be equality of sacrifice among the permanent members'. But they thought it unnecessary that there should be equality in the contributions made in each particular arm – land, sea or air. The United States went further: she held that every member 'should have the right to offer in its own contribution such forces as it considers reasonable and proper'. A permanent member should have the theoretical right to contribute forces equal to those contributed by another, but this would be limited by their capacity to do so. Although it might be desirable for the contributions of the permanent members to be 'not greatly disproportionate', this 'should not jeopardise the all-important goal of effective UN armed forces'.

It was impossible to reconcile these differences. In every case they reflected the sharp conflict of interest between a nation which expected to be in a small minority within the organisation, and which therefore wished to limit its armed power and to ensure equality of influence, and those countries in a majority within the organisation, which wished the organisation, which was largely under their control, to have at its disposal a strong force, much of which would consist of contingents they themselves provided.

The report of the Committee recorded these differences. It was later debated in the Security Council. But identical differences emerged there too. The Western powers continued to argue for a larger force, with contributions from the major powers that were not necessarily identical; which could be maintained in existence for considerable periods even after the end of a particular operation; and which could be held in bases scattered all over the world. The Soviet Union, unwilling to see powers of this order placed in the hands of the UN (or of the group controlling it) resisted on all these points.

That was the end of the matter. The Security Council was unable to reconcile these fundamental differences. So the agreements that were to be reached with individual member states on the contributions they were to make could not be concluded. The Security Council had to report its failure to agree; and the Security Council force, which was to have been the centre-piece of the new UN system, never came into existence at all.

One of the ironic features of these negotiations is that they never really reached the heart of the matter. It is quite possible that, if such negotiations were to be reopened today, the Western powers might be willing to accept something close to the Soviet position on almost all the items discussed. They might well, after the experience of the past twenty-five years, be somewhat less ambitious in their ideas of the kind of force which could be created. They might be willing to settle for one limited in size, to which the permanent members made identical contributions (if any), which would have no permanent bases, and which would be used only for authorised operations of strictly limited duration. Any permanent force at all, even of earmarked contributions, would, it would be accepted, represent a bold initiative (indeed, the fact that the Western powers no longer control a majority in the organisation might well make them reluctant to contemplate even a limited force of this type).

But the fact is that, even if agreement had been reached upon all these points – and it is not altogether inconceivable that in a better political climate some compromise might have been found – it does not follow that it would have been possible to establish the kind of force that the Charter envisaged. For the most important and difficult questions to be decided were not those then debated at all. These were the principles for the command and control of the force, for authorising each operation and for arranging its financing (all of which were to create difficulties when peace-keeping forces were eventually set up). Far more than the size of the force or the balance between contributions, these fatally determine how far each particular operation may come to be used for political purposes which are unacceptable to one or another of the permanent members. Agreement on them would have been difficult, as subsequent discussions proved, at the best of times; but almost certainly quite beyond the range of the possible in the bitter political climate of 1946–7.

So the force which the Charter had contemplated never came into being. It was recognised that this need not necessarily make the UN totally ineffective, nor without any capacity to wield force at all. It could still call on member-states to use their own forces in particular situations (as the organisation subsequently did in Korea). All the non-military sanctions laid down in Chapter VII of the Charter could still be used if the will to use them existed. If both these courses have virtually never been adopted, it is not because of the failure of the negotiations of 1946–7. It is because the majority in the organisation, and in the Council, have not been ready to subject the loyalty of member-states to the substantial strain involved in calling on them to take strenuous action to meet threats to the peace which they may themselves not see as serious dangers to their own individual security.

In other words, the provisions of the Charter had not basically resolved the age-old problem of collective security: how to induce member-states to join in collective action when their own individual judgement does not drive them to do so. The failure of the Military Staff Committee negotiations merely stripped bare the pretence that the paper obligations of the Charter had finally resolved that problem. It made it the more necessary for the infant organisation to consider alternative means by which it could make its authority effective when the peace was threatened: to develop political skills rather than military enforcement power.

It had no lack of opportunity to try its skills in this direction over the coming years.

7 Azerbaijan and the Levant

AZERBAIJAN

As soon as it came into existence the Security Council found itself deep in ideological conflict.

On 19 January 1946, before the first Security Council had even met, the Iranian ambassador addressed to it a letter complaining about the failure of Soviet troops to evacuate Azerbaijan, Iran's northern province.

In 1942, to prevent Iran from coming under German occupation and control, British and Soviet troops had moved in to occupy, respectively, the southern and northern parts of Iran. Shortly afterwards they concluded with the Shah of Iran a tripartite treaty of alliance, under which the two powers were authorised to maintain land, sea and air forces in Iranian territory 'in such numbers as they consider necessary'. The treaty provided that 'the presence of these forces on Iranian territory does not constitute a military occupation and will disturb as little as possible the administration and the security forces of Iran, the economic life of the country, the normal movements of the population and the application of Iranian laws and regulations'. Despite this provision, under the protection of the Soviet occupying forces, a local Azerbaijan government of left-wing persuasion had been established which increasingly disputed the authority of the Iranian Government.

Under the Tripartite Treaty the occupying forces were to be evacuated within six months of the end of the war – that is, by 2 March 1946. On 18 November 1945, the Iranian Government had sent its forces to reoccupy Azerbaijan. The Soviet army authorities had prevented passage of this force, declaring it would cause disturbances. The Iranian Government had then sent two notes to the Soviet Government, demanding that the Soviet army authorities in Iran should be instructed to cease intervening in Iran's internal affairs and to allow free passage to the Iranian forces, as the Treaty provided. The Soviet Government denied any interference in the affairs of the province, but declared that the passage of the Iranian government forces would result in armed conflict with the existing authorities in the area. The Iranian Goverment then declared that, from the Soviet Government's declaration that it did not wish to interfere in the affairs of the region, it assumed that Iranian forces would now be allowed to proceed. No further reply was received.

In its note of 19 January 1946 to the acting Secretary-General, the Iranian delegate declared that Soviet interference in Iranian affairs had led to a situation that could 'lead to friction'. Direct negotiations had failed. The Iranian Government therefore wished to raise the matter under Article 35(1) of the Charter. Under this article the Council could investigate the situation and recommend the terms of a settlement.

An accusation levelled against one of the permanent members was not a happy opening to the Council's proceedings. It is open to question whether Iran was well advised to bring public charges against the Soviet Union there before bilateral negotiations had been thoroughly exhausted or before other means of pressure had been given a chance to work. It was particularly unwelcome to the Soviet Union, which had never concealed its fear that she might find herself placed in the dock by other members of the Security Council. She may well have believed that in this case Iran was acting with the encouragement of Britain, with whom she had long competed for influence there, or of the United States, her main antagonist. Since the UN, in her eyes, was an organisation whose success depended on great-power unity, she could claim that to open the Council's affairs with a charge against herself was to betray the spirit that lay behind the organisation's creation.

She immediately proceeded to retaliate by bringing to the Council charges of an exactly comparable kind against Britain. Within two days she too addressed a communication to the acting Secretary-General complaining about the interference in Greek affairs of British troops remaining in that country (pp. 118–20 below); while the Ukrainian delegate raised a similar charge about the presence of British forces in Indonesia (pp. 132–3 below). So, already, in the very first days of the Council's life, the fire and counter-fire of cold war had erupted there.

The Soviet representative also sent a letter replying to Iran's charges. The situation in Azerbaijan, he maintained, resulted from the actions of popular forces in that province seeking 'some sort of national autonomy', and had nothing at all to do with the presence of Soviet forces. The Soviet Union had negotiated with Iran on the question in November and the Iranian government had given every impression of being satisfied. There was therefore nothing now for the Council to consider. After the item was placed, without objection, on the Council's agenda, Vyshinsky, sent from Moscow to London, repeated these arguments. He denied that Article 35 or any other article of the Charter concerning peaceful settlement was relevant to the situation. The Charter called on members to settle their disputes by direct negotiation and the Soviet Union was perfectly willing to do this. The Iranian delegate repeated the charge of Soviet interference, but replied that Iran too was willing to negotiate on the matter. Meanwhile the question should remain on the agenda, and regular reports on the progress of the negotiations should be made.

The Council accepted a solution somewhat on these lines. On 30 January a resolution was passed which merely recorded the stated willingness of both parties to negotiate, and requested them to keep the Council informed of any results achieved. In this way some kind of pressure was to be maintained on the Soviet Union while the negotiations progressed. No more was heard of the subject at the UN for another two months.

Negotiations between the two countries began soon afterwards; but they soon proved inconclusive. On 18 February the Iranian Prime Minister flew to Moscow and asked for a quick evacuation and an end to interference. The Soviet Government, it was reported, asked for recognition of the autonomy of Azerbaijan, for a discussion of oil concessions for the Soviet Union in Iran and even for an agreement to station Soviet troops in northern Iran for an indefinite period. But it did give renewed assurances of its intention to evacuate all its forces by 2 March, six months after the end of the war.

None the less, when 2 March came and went, Soviet forces remained. On 18 March the Iranian ambassador therefore addressed a further note to the president of the Council. He accused the Soviet Union of retaining troops in Iran after the date due for withdrawal, and for continuing to interfere in Iran's affairs. The Soviet delegate rejected these charges. He said that negotiations were continuing and asked that consideration of the item be deferred until 10 April.

When the Council none the less met on 26 March, the Soviet delegate declared that there was nothing to discuss. Evacuation of Soviet forces generally had begun on 2 March; withdrawal of those stationed in Azerbaijan had started on 24 March, two days earlier, and would be completed in five or six weeks. At the following meeting the Soviet delegate therefore again proposed postponement until 10 April. When this was defeated, the Soviet delegate declared that he could not participate in the discussion and left the chamber.

Everything therefore hinged on what the Russians were really doing and what concessions they were demanding in return. On 29 March it was agreed in the Council that the Secretary-General should discover from the two parties the existing state of negotiations and whether, as the Iranian delegate had reported, the withdrawal of Soviet troops was being made conditional on agreement on other questions. In reply to these enquiries the Soviet delegate declared that a firm agreement had already been reached between the two governments and that withdrawal would be completed early in May. Other matters, such as the Soviet proposal for an oil concession or a joint stock company, had been raised entirely independently and had in fact been under discussion since 1944. They were thus not intended as preconditions for withdrawal. The Iranian ambassador quoted earlier conversations in Tehran in which the Soviet ambassador had raised the question of autonomy for Azerbaijan and the formation of a joint Soviet–Iranian oil corporation at the same time as discussions about withdrawal. But he confirmed that the Soviet ambassador there had now confirmed the promise to evaucate Iran 'provided no unforeseen circumstances occur'. At the following Council meeting, on 4 April, the US

Government proposed, and the Council accepted, a resolution that, in the light of the Soviet Government's declared intention of withdrawing its forces in five or six weeks, discussion should be deferred until 6 May, when the Council would consider what, 'if any, further proceedings on the Iranian appeal was required'. So some form of external pressure was maintained.

The same day a general understanding was reached between the Soviet and Iranian governments; and two days later the Soviet representatives requested that the item should be removed altogether from the Council's agenda. This request was at first resisted by the Iranian ambassador. A week or so later, however, on 15 April, the Iranian Government formally requested that her complaint should be withdrawn from the Council, saying they had complete confidence in the pledges of the Soviet Government.[1]

There followed a long and complicated legal wrangle concerning whether a complaint, once considered by the Council, could be simply withdrawn at the request of the original complainant. This seemed the common-sense conclusion. The item had been inscribed originally as a 'dispute' under Article 35, and it was arguable that, if both parties held the dispute to be at an end, the Council had no more to do with the matter. On the other hand, it was held by Western delegates that, so long as any threat to the peace persisted, it was a legitimate subject for the Council's attention. The matter was discussed in a long memorandum put forward by the Secretary-General (drafted by his legal counsel). In somewhat ambiguous language he found that, in the case of a 'dispute' that had been resolved, the Security Council might have no grounds for continuing to consider the matter once the complaint had been withdrawn: in these circumstances 'it might well be that there was no way in which it could remain seized of the matter'. A committee of experts was established by the Council to consider the question. But this consisted only of the legal advisers of each Council member, and it divided, not surprisingly, in exactly the same way as the Council itself: eight for retention of the item and three (the Soviet Union, Poland and France) for deletion. A French resolution which in effect withdrew the matter from the agenda was lost; and in these circumstances the Soviet delegate again announced his intention to withdraw from all further discussion of the matter.

On 6 May, the deadline which had been set by the Council in its resolution of 4 April, the Iranian ambassador reported on the situation. Although Soviet forces had been withdrawn from certain areas of Iran, the Iranian Government was not at that time able to say definitely whether evacuation of Azerbaijan had been completed. The Council therefore asked the Iranian Government to provide a further report as soon as possible, and in any case by 20 May. On 20 May the ambassador announced that he had not been able to discover whether or not Soviet troops had left, because of interference by Soviet forces. But the next day he declared that a commission of investigation had now reported that there was no trace of Soviet troops, which had apparently left on 6 May. On the following day the Council resolved, with the Soviet representative again absent, that discussion should be adjourned until a date in the near future, but that the Council should remain seized of the question.

The matter was not discussed again until the following December. The Iranian representative then reported to the Council that 'those in control of affairs in Azerbaijan' (presumably the government established in the province when Soviet forces left) had objected to the entry of Iranian forces there and that the Soviet ambassador in Tehran had again warned that the movement of Iranian forces could cause disturbances, advising that these plans should be abandoned. He did not ask that the Council should reconsider the matter – indeed, unless he could have shown active interference from outside the borders, it is doubtful whether he had the grounds to do so. But he said it was his duty to provide the information, so that the Council could 'better interpret the course of events'.

The issue was not discussed again. Not long afterwards the Iranian Government regained full control of Azerbaijan and set up a new administration more in accordance with its own political ideas. Even then the Council kept the question on its agenda and did so for many years. 'The Iranian question' continued to head the list which the Security Council must submit to the Assembly of subjects still under discussion in the Council. The theory behind the list is that it shows the

Assembly which issues it is not able to discuss because they are receiving attention in the Council. In practice, however, most of the items have not been discussed for many years; and even those which have are not necessarily avoided in the discussions of the Assembly either. But like much of the rest of the discussion, the decision to retain the item on the list reflected the cold-war political aims then everywhere prevailing.

LEBANON AND SYRIA

Only three weeks after the Azerbaijan issue, another question was raised at the UN, also concerning the presence of foreign forces, this time Western, on the territory of another state requesting their withdrawal. Though not one of those raised by the Soviet Union in retaliation for the discussion of Azerbaijan (probably because it was French rather than British forces that were mainly concerned), it represented none the less a very close parallel.

After the fall of France in 1940, Lebanon and Syria were for a year controlled by Vichy forces. In 1941 they were invaded by the British and the Free French. The Free French general, Catroux, thereupon proclaimed the future independence of the two states, a promise that was underwritten by the British Government. In 1943, after disturbances and political crises in both countries, the French commander, under pressure from the British, was compelled to transfer power to local governments in both countries. By early 1945 the two governments had secured diplomatic recognition from a number of Allied powers. They declared war on the Axis in February 1945, and were represented at the San Francisco Conference.

Negotiations then began between the two states and the French Government now re-established in Paris. In May 1945, while these were proceeding, fresh French forces were landed in Beirut. At the same time France called for new agreements satisfying French strategic and cultural interests in the area. This demand provoked disturbances in Syria. French guns proceeded to shell Damascus. At this point the British Government asked the French authorities to withdraw their forces to barracks, and British forces intervened to restrain the French. The governments of Lebanon and Syria, regarding Britain as their supporter, then asked Britain not to evacuate her own forces so long as 'other foreign forces' remained.

During the rest of 1945 little progress was made in the negotiations between the two states and France. Meanwhile French forces remained and were regarded by the governments of Lebanon and Syria, even though inactive, as a form of tacit pressure on the negotiations. In December Britain arranged with France a meeting of military experts, which discussed a date for the withdrawal of forces from the region. When this produced no change, the governments of Lebanon and Syria in February the following year brought the question to the newly established Security Council.

The continued presence of foreign forces in their territory against their will, they said, represented a threat to international peace and security. The agreement reached between Britain and France, concluded without their participation or consent, was a breach of their sovereignty which was not justified by any existing danger in the area. The charge fitted neatly into the pattern already established by the Azerbaijan, Greek and Indonesian issues: all concerned the continued presence of foreign forces in another territory many months after the war was over. French representatives held that French forces were in the area only as a temporary measure resulting from the war. France had expressed her willingness to withdraw and was willing now to negotiate on the method of achieving this. The British delegate said Britain sympathised with the demand for withdrawal, but recalled that Britain had been asked not to remove her forces so long as others remained.

Resolutions were put forward by Mexico and Egypt calling for the forces of both Western powers to be withdrawn and demanding negotiations to bring this about. Both resolutions were defeated, as too strong, by a combination of Western powers. The Netherlands and the United States then each proposed resolutions expressing 'confidence' that foreign troops would be withdrawn 'as soon as practicable' and that negotiations for this purpose would be undertaken shortly. Syria and Lebanon proposed amendments to these, to ensure that the resolution spoke of negotiations undertaken 'independently of other issues': their main aim was to ensure that the offer to withdraw was not used to extract concessions on other questions. The Soviet Union demanded that the resolution should explicitly demand that British and French troops should be withdrawn and that negotiations should be begun 'immediately'. These amendments were both defeated. In retaliation the Soviet Union proceeded to veto the US resolution (the Netherlands proposal had now been withdrawn).

This was the first time the veto had been used in the UN and it foreshadowed the reckless way that weapon was to be used in the following years. No essential interest of the Soviet Union was at stake here. Her only criticism was that the resolution was not strong enough. Yet she condemned the Council to impotence, simply because the wording was not to her taste.

Though the resolution was not carried, however, Britain and France announced that, since it had had majority support, they would consider themselves bound by it. This was scarcely an onerous undertaking, since the resolution only asked for them to negotiate, which both had promised to do in any case. The resolution did, however, marginally alter the environment within which these negotiations took place: as with the Soviet Union over Azerbaijan, both powers were put on notice that the world was watching what they were doing and expecting them to announce a withdrawal.

Whether or not for this reason, the issue was fairly quickly resolved. Within two months both France and Britain had come to an agreement for the evacuation of their forces. They would be withdrawn from Lebanon by 30 June in the case of Britain and 31 August in the case of France; and both would have withdrawn from Syria by 30 April. No significant undertakings were made to France on other matters. The agreements were reported to the president of the Security Council by the British and French governments. In due course the final evacuation of the forces was reported by Syria and Lebanon.

So the matter was brought to an end. The Council had perhaps marginally contributed to the pressures being exerted on the French to agree to withdraw their forces without imposing conditions. Like the Soviet Union in Azerbaijan, France had probably been trying it on. Her hope of gaining a long-term strategic position in the area had probably, as with the Russians, never been high; but a show of force in the region during the negotiations might, it had been believed, strengthen her hand. The interest taken in the matter by the Security Council, together with the refusal of Lebanon and Syria to negotiate under duress, perhaps persuaded France, as the Soviet Union was persuaded in the case of Azerbaijan, that it might be better not to push her luck too hard.

As in that case the troops were finally withdrawn, no concessions were made, and the Council was able to abandon discussion of the matter. The only difference was that in this case the built-in Western majority in the Council ensured that the matter was not listed, over the next thirty years or so, as being one among the subjects that still remained on the Council's agenda.

CONCLUSIONS

The first issues in the Council's history revealed, even at this early stage, some of its strengths and weaknesses.

Nobody can be certain that events in the Council had the smallest influence on Soviet actions in Azerbaijan. Probably the Council's discussions did have the effect of magnifying the pressure of outside opinion on the Soviet Union. The Security Council was given a watching brief in a dispute which was primarily negotiated between the parties themselves. By capitalising, in its first resolution, on the expressed desire of both parties to negotiate a solution, and by calling for regular reports on these negotiations, the Council made the Soviet Union publicly accountable for its actions. The question could no longer be regarded as a purely private or local conflict between two neighbouring states. This may well have had some effect.

But it is probable that Soviet policy here, as in many other cases at this time, was experimental and improvised. There was probably never any firm plan to annex, or even to occupy permanently, Azerbaijan, nor perhaps even to obtain any particular concession as the price for withdrawal. But the presence of Soviet forces, and the concern of the Iranian Government to see them withdrawn (not to speak of the undoubted unpopularity of the Iranian Government among many in Azerbaijan), presented a heaven-sent opportunity to seek some political *quid pro quo* – the granting of an oil concession, the accordance of autonomy for the province, even possibly the continued presence of Soviet forces, as an inducement to a transfer of power. As soon as she found she had the Security Council looking over her shoulder at every move, her bargaining power, in what was originally a somewhat unequal confrontation, was weakened, while the moral authority of the Iranian Government in demanding the return of its own territory was correspondingly strengthened.

Even the timing of various Soviet moves supports the thesis that the pressure of publicity in the Council had some impact. The first general undertaking to negotiate for the withdrawal of Soviet forces was given by the Soviet Union shortly after the first Security Council resolution, on 30 January. The first evacuation of forces from Azerbaijan began on 24 March, immediately after the next Iranian complaint to the Council and two days before the Council was to meet. The evacuation was finally completed on or about 6 May, precisely the deadline laid down by the Council, and not long before a subsequent meeting was scheduled. While the Soviet Union would doubtless have liked to secure concessions, she was reluctant openly to defy the Council before the eyes of all the world to achieve that end. So, it would appear, the actions of a powerful member of the organisation had been at least significantly influenced by the actions the Council had decided to take.

But the episode also showed the Council's ultimate weakness in dealing with such situations. It never had the means of compelling the Soviet Union to withdraw if she had chosen to resist. Even the proposed Security Council force, if it had been established, would have been powerless in such a case. If the Council had any influence at all, it was through publicity and moral authority rather than its physical power.

The Azerbaijani issue was scarcely the most momentous in the organisation's history. But it did, in the first months of its life, underline the basic fact of the Security Council's situation: the organisation's primary sanction was not the armed force it was supposed to have at its disposal but the volume of world opinion which it could mobilise on its behalf. By use of that sanction the organisation had been able to cope reasonably well with the first challenge it had confronted: a great power had been persuaded not to use a position of strength to enforce concessions. But it had done so only at the cost of sharpening confrontation among the permanent members. It had evolved no effective procedure for promoting negotiation among the great powers on the question. This basic weakness in its way of handling cold-war issues was seriously to inhibit its capacity to cope with more deep-seated disputes of the same era.

Over Syria and Lebanon, too, though the balance of forces was quite different, a similar strategy was employed. By expressing confidence that a withdrawal would take place, the powers concerned were put on notice that they were under observation. And the fact that the resolution was vetoed did not significantly reduce its moral force. France and Britain were constrained to announce that they felt bound by its terms. So here too the UN could feel it had had some marginal influence. Probably France, like the Soviet Union, was anyway reconciled to withdrawing, but hoped to extract some *quid pro quo* for so doing. The interest taken by the Security Council in the affair inhibited her ability to extract such concessions. As in the other case, the UN's ultimate power was limited: nobody believed that it would give military help against France, least of all the French. But that France, like the Soviet Union, withdrew without having secured any concessions was at least partly because of the moral authority wielded by the new international organisation.

Now that it was clear that the organisation was unlikely ever to have force at its disposal, it would clearly be able to secure law and order only by maximising intangible influence of this kind. Unfortunately, it would not often lead to such rapid results as here.

8 Greece

In retaliation for the Iranian complaint against herself, the Soviet Union raised a complaint about the presence of British forces in Greece.

British troops had been sent to free Greece from German forces in 1944. They had almost immediately become involved in a bitter civil conflict in Greece between right-wing forces supporting the Greek king (who was also supported by the British) and left-wing forces, especially the EAM and ELAS, which were anti-monarchist and anti-British. The monarchist forces had finally prevailed and had welcomed the continued presence of British forces in helping them to maintain their position in the country as a whole.

The Soviet Union had never liked this situation. She had protested about the continued presence of British forces in Greece at the Potsdam Conference in June 1945, at the London meeting of foreign ministers in September, and at the Moscow meeting of foreign ministers in December of the same year. But she was relatively restrained in her protests as a result of the agreement which she had reached with Churchill during the war, under which Greece was regarded as primarily a British sphere of influence. The Iranian complaint against herself gave her the opportunity to raise the matter once again in the newly established Security Council.

Her complaint was heard at a meeting of the Security Council on 1 February. The continued presence of British forces in Greece, she claimed, represented an interference in Greek internal affairs, and a threat to peace and security in the area. British troops were being used to influence the internal political situation in Greece and to support reactionary elements in the country. They should therefore be immediately withdrawn. In reply, Ernest Bevin, the British Foreign Secretary, denied that British troops were being used to influence the political situation in Greece. He pointed out that British forces went to Greece during the war at the request of representatives of almost all elements in Greek political life, and had remained at the request of the Greek Government. Britain had been in a position to instal a government of her own choosing if she had so wished. She had not done so and wanted to see free elections to decide what government should rule. British troops would be withdrawn immediately if the Greek Government so decided. The Greek delegate confirmed that British forces were present in Greece at the request of his government.

The US representative then proposed that no action be taken. He was supported by other Western delegates. Poland, however, proposed that the Council should formally take note of the statements made, and of the assurance by Britain that she would withdraw as soon as possible. This, like the similar action taken over Azerbaijan, might have represented gentle pressure on Britain for the future. The proposal was not carried. And the proceedings were concluded by the first known use of the 'consensus' procedure – the use of an impartial statement by the president to sum up the sense of the meeting. The president said on 6 February that he thought the Council should take note of the declarations made 'by the Soviet Union, Britain and Greece and of other views put forward and would consider the matter closed'. This was accepted, and concluded discussion of the question for the time being.

During the next six months the political conflict in Greece intensified. In March a right-wing government came to power in elections which, though supervised by the United States, Britain and France (the Soviet Union had refused to take part), were widely challenged. The left-wing parties had withdrawn in protest at the way the elections were conducted. Even of those registered only 49 per cent had voted. After the election there had been continuing political conflict, including arrests of the Government's political opponents.

This provoked antagonism with Greece's neighbours. Greece's borders, which had been disputed for over a century, became subject to claim and counter-claim. Yugoslav journals demanded self-determination for 'Aegean Macedonia', including much of northern Greece, where there lived 250,000 Slavs. Bulgaria voiced longstanding historical claims to

Thrace and Macedonia. The new Greek government in turn made public claims to 'northern Epirus' – that is, southern Albania; and at the Paris Peace Conference she demanded an adjustment of Greek borders with Yugoslavia and Bulgaria. These historical conflicts were of course strongly exacerbated by cold-war rivalries. Tension in the area mounted. In August the Ukraine demanded a further meeting of the Security Council to discuss Greece.

Greek forces, she claimed in justifying this call, were provoking incidents on Greece's borders with Albania so that Greece could annex parts of that country. Greece was also persecuting national minorities, while British forces were continuing to interfere in Greek internal affairs on behalf of 'aggressive monarchist elements'. When the Council met on 30 August, Britain questioned whether a series of unsubstantiated allegations of this sort should be placed on the agenda of the Council without question (a somewhat curious objection in the light of the passionate Western concern at Yalta and San Francisco about the absolute right of free discussion in the Council). The United States, rather more consistently, held that the complaint should at least be heard. And the question was in fact placed on the agenda. The Ukrainian delegate then launched a tirade against the Greek Government, denouncing it for its oppression of opposition elements, the dissolution of trades unions, expeditions against national minorities, the setting up of special military courts to try resistance fighters and for provoking incidents against Albania. He accused the British authorities of widespread interference, especially in influencing the plebiscite on the monarchy that had just been held. These accusations were supported by the Soviet Union and Albania, which complained of Greek provocations on her frontier and the persecution of the Albanian minority in Greece.

The Greek delegate rejected as absurd claims that Greece threatened Bulgaria and Yugoslavia, which had far more powerful military forces than Greece. He attacked Yugoslav support for the idea of a Macedonian state as the real source of tension. To raise Greek civil conflicts in the Security Council was an attempt to support rebels against the Government of Greece, and to influence the result of the plebiscite which had just taken place. The British and US delegates favourably compared the admittedly imperfect electoral and plebiscite arrangements in Greece with those existing elsewhere in Eastern Europe (Bulgaria was at that moment organising a similar plebiscite on the future of the monarchy in that country): the very fact that there was a substantial vote against the monarchy in Greece, the US representative pointed out, implied that there was at least some degree of political freedom there (the Bulgarian poll had just shown less than 1 per cent of the electorate as favouring a continuation of the monarchy there, which was held more likely to reveal the absence of political freedom than the absence of support for the monarchy).

It was of course the international aspects of the situation which were of prime concern to the Security Council. Even while it met, incidents were taking place on Greece's frontier with Bulgaria, Yugoslavia and Albania. While the communist states claimed that these resulted from incursions by Greek forces, the Greek Government and its supporters held that they were the result of infiltration by guerrilla bands, who received periodic shelter and support within the borders of neighbouring states. The United States therefore proposed the establishment of an investigating commission of impartial observers, to be nominated by the Security Council, which should proceed to the borders and check the causes of the disturbances. She even suggested, to meet communist complaints, that it should look at the situation of national minorities within the area, in so far as this affected international peace and security (a proposal which Greece might well have complained violated her sovereign rights). Even so, the idea was rejected, on somewhat obscure grounds, by Gromyko, who proceeded to veto the US proposal. A Soviet counter-resolution, placing all responsibility on 'aggressive Greek monarchist elements', and calling on Greece to refrain from persecuting national minorities, was supported only by Poland. As a result no action resulted from the Ukrainian complaint.

Less than three months later the issue was again before the Security Council, this time raised by Greece. By now the situation on Greece's borders had become even worse. In November 1946, the Greek village of Skra was attacked by 700 guerrillas, apparently from across the Yugoslav border: 150 houses were burnt down and nineteen Greek soldiers killed.

Communist parties all over Europe were calling for support for the Greek partisans, struggling against a reactionary government maintained only by Anglo-American support. A situation of civil war was rapidly being reached. The Greek delègate complained to the Council of systematic violations of Greece's frontier by her neighbours, which were said to be supporting guerrilla warfare against her. He called once again for an investigation of the situation on the spot. The Greek Prime Minister, who flew to New York to address the Council, charged Yugoslavia in particular with intensive propaganda in favour of the creation of a Macedonian state to be incorporated in Yugoslavia, and all three neighbours of allowing their territory to be used as a base for operations aimed against Greece. Representatives of the three countries denied these charges and replied with accusations of their own against the Greek Government. The US representative pointed out that the debate itself showed there existed a dispute between Greece and her neighbours and supported the Greek demand for an investigation. The Soviet Union, to the surprise of everybody, this time accepted the proposal; but she demanded that the commission, instead of consisting of three respected neutrals, as the United States had formerly proposed, should include communist representatives. And she ensured that it should be empowered to investigate the 'causes and nature' of the border troubles, so possibly enabling it to examine internal Greek questions as well as border violations.

The Commission was composed of representatives of each member of the Council. It spent just over two months between the end of January and early April 1947 in the Balkans, visiting all four countries and sending investigating teams to particular areas to interview witnesses. From the beginning its proceedings were punctuated by continuing conflict between the communist members and those of the West over the procedure to be employed, the witnesses to be examined, and the whole purpose of the inquiry. The Soviet and Polish members managed to take up 75 per cent of the time spent in questioning witnesses, focusing attention exclusively on the policies of the Greek Government, the activities of British forces in Greece, the imprisonment and execution of resistance fighters, the suppression of Greek trade unions, and Greek frontier claims. The Western representatives sought to direct the inquiry to the activities of guerrilla bands in the northern areas of Greece and the support being given them by the neighbouring countries.

The report finally appeared in June. The majority found that Yugoslavia in particular, and to a lesser extent Bulgaria and Albania, had 'supported the guerrilla warfare in Greece'. In the case of Yugoslavia this included not only the arming but also the training of refugee soldiers, especially at Bulkes, a camp in Yugoslavia which the commission actually visited. Albania, though it no longer trained forces, continued to supply arms, guides, clothing, food and other assistance. Both Yugoslavia and Bulgaria had encouraged a separatist movement among the Slav minority in northern Greece. Although unrest among the people of Macedonia resulted originally from the deliberate promotion of Macedonian nationalism by the Germans in the war, and later partly from the policies of the Greek Government, the Yugoslav and Bulgarian governments had deliberately, by speeches and articles, revived and promoted the separatist movement and so aggravated tensions. The majority report therefore made three main recommendations: that normal good-neighbourly relations between the four countries should be resumed, so that all incidents could be resolved by bilateral exchanges or recourse to the UN; that in future when a government refused to take effective action to halt support for armed bands operating in the territory of another the matter should be considered by the Security Council as a threat to the peace; and, above all, that a permanent commission or commissions should be established in the area to keep the border under observation. In addition refugees sheltering in neighbouring states should be kept well away from the borders of their own country; and consideration should be given to concluding new agreements for the voluntary transfer of minorities.

The minority, the Soviet Union and Poland, of course dissented totally from these conclusions and recommendations. Their judgement was that there was a large-scale civil war in Greece which resulted from the reactionary and dictatorial character of the Greek Government, the discontent that this aroused amongst their own people and the repeated territorial claims against neighbours.[1] Only a transformation of the Greek political system to eliminate the reactionary elements could restore peace.

By the time the Council met to consider the Commission's report at the end of June 1947, there had been some change in Greece's international position. On 24 February the British Government announced that it no longer had the economic resources to maintain its support for Greece. On 12 March the US Government proclaimed the Truman Doctrine, under which the United States would take over the economic and military support of Greece and Turkey. In June, this programme for Greece and Turkey was followed by the still more comprehensive Marshall Plan, providing for US economic assistance for the whole of Western Europe. The effect of all this, and of the refusal of the Soviet Union, with its East European allies (including eventually Czechoslovakia), to take part in the programme was to make the division of Europe even deeper than before.

The United States had become more deeply committed to Greece and its defence than ever before. Within the Council she proposed the endorsement of the commission's proposal to send a permanent body to Greece to observe her borders. But this was condemned by the communist states as a cold-war move. They complained that to set up a permanent body was, in effect, to accept the unproved Greek charges against her neighbours. They refused to undertake to provide facilities for a commission in their own countries. And when the resolution was finally put to the vote, though it obtained nine affirmative votes, it was vetoed by the Soviet Union.

But the Western governments, knowing that they had a majority in support of their position within the organisation, were now no longer prepared to accept that the actions they proposed could be frustrated by the use of the Soviet veto in the Council. Now, in the first of many similar occasions during the next decade, they turned to the Assembly, where no veto operated. In the autumn session of 1947, the United States put before the Assembly an almost identical proposal to that which had been vetoed in the Council. The resolution called on Albania, Bulgaria and Yugoslavia to cease giving assistance to the Greek guerrillas and called on all four countries to seek to settle their disputes peacefully, to establish diplomatic relations among themselves, to consider concluding frontier conventions and to co-operate in solving refugee problems. It proposed the establishment of a permanent committee, of the kind that had been recommended in the Commission's report, to assist in the implementation of the resolution and to 'observe the compliance by the four governments concerned'. Though opposed by the communist states, this was passed by 34 votes to 6, with 11 abstentions.

As a result there was established the UN Special Committee on the Balkans (UNSCOB). Like its predecessor, this was to consist of the representatives of all members of the Security Council. This time the Soviet Union and Poland, though elected, refused to take part. This was no doubt partly because the terms of reference were now carefully defined to apply only to border violations and not to the internal causes of the Greek civil war. The Committee was, moreover, likely to be engaged in a continuing investigation of activities on Greece's borders and could make requests to undertake on-the-spot investigations within the territory of her neighbours: this could obviously prove highly embarrassing to those neighbouring countries. The communist states preferred, by boycotting it, to be in a position to denounce the entire operation as a Western-inspired anti-communist manoeuvre, and so to devalue its effect.

Almost as soon as it was established the new committee had to confront a major development. On 24 December 1947, the Greek guerrilla leader, Marcos, announced the establishment of a Greek provisional government, in rivalry to that established in Athens. There seemed a distinct possibility that this body might secure the recognition of Greece's communist neighbours, and that these might then proceed to give it military and political support. UNSCOB, meeting only five days after the announcement of the government's establishment, passed a resolution declaring that recognition of the new government, even on a *de facto* basis, and the provision of military aid to it, would constitute a grave threat to international peace and security. If it secured evidence of any association between Balkan governments and the new self-styled government, the Committee would call for a special meeting of the General Assembly. The US Government made a similar statement the following day, a juxtaposition of events which was naturally used to demonstrate the Committee's pro-Western bias.

It still seemed likely that recognition of the new authority by Greece's neighbours would follow. Indeed, if the Balkan governments had formed their own policies independently, there is every likelihood it would have been recognised. But Stalin himself had at all times, it seems, kept in mind his understanding with Churchill, reached in 1944, that Greece should be regarded as outside the Russian sphere of interest (Britain had in return recognised a predominant Russian interest in Romania and Bulgaria). At any rate, no recognition of the self-styled government took place. And it seems more likely that it was the Soviet Union's influence, rather than the warning presented by UNSCOB, which deterred Greece's neighbours from making such a move.

The Greek civil war, however, continued. UNSCOB made a succession of reports about evidence of assistance for the guerrillas. It reported that arms and supplies of all kinds were reaching the guerrilla forces from Yugoslavia, Albania and Bulgaria. It discovered a radio transmitter located near Belgrade that was broadcasting propaganda and entertainment for these forces. It found that the Greek guerrillas frequently crossed the border to find refuge in the neighbouring states. Albania, Yugoslavia and Bulgaria, on the other hand, continued to maintain that they gave no assistance to the rebels other than occasional asylum for those who requested it.

In May 1948, the Committee reported a new development. It provided evidence that the Greek Democratic Army, the main guerrilla force, had sent large numbers of Greek children across the border to Bulgaria for care, training and indoctrination. Many of these were no doubt the children of the guerrillas themselves, sent away to avoid the danger of reprisals and warfare in Greece. The communist states described the children as refugees, seeking to escape the repressive policies of the Greek Government, which threatened to use them as hostages for their fathers' guerrilla activities. The Greek Government, however, claimed some were taken away unwillingly, and against the will of their parents, apparently to be used as hostages.

Although Albania, Bulgaria, Yugoslavia and the Soviet

Union had at first refused to recognise the competence of the Committee or to allow it to visit their territory, they did make frequent reports to it of alleged Greek provocations on their own borders. In time they relaxed their refusal to co-operate. In April 1948 Bulgaria even agreed to allow an inspection team into Bulgaria, so that it could interview a Bulgarian officer, Tsouroff, who alleged violations of Bulgaria's borders by Greek forces. The Committee of course welcomed this development and reported the officer's attitude as correct and cordial. It is perfectly possible that, in the fighting in the north, Greek forces had overstepped the border, and the Bulgarian Government was no doubt only too happy to provide evidence of such an incident. The Committee, however, reported more widespread evidence of logistic supply for the Greek guerrillas from Albania and the sheltering of guerrilla forces in Bulgaria and Yugoslavia.

In the autumn of 1948 the General Assembly debated the activities of UNSCOB. The communist delegations complained that the Committee's report was based on rumour or false accounts deliberately circulated by the Greek Government. Its staff were partly US nationals who sought to promote US interests by its activity. The majority, however, felt that the Committee had played a significant part in observing and deterring hostile action on the Greek border. But even among Western delegations there was some concern that the emphasis of the Committee's work was too much on the attribution of blame for incidents rather than on genuine conciliation between the countries concerned. Australia, Pakistan and Brazil, all members of the Committee, expressed this viewpoint. This affected the Assembly's action. The Committee's work was endorsed and its mandate renewed, but at the same time an Australian resolution was carried calling for a meeting of representatives of the countries concerned, together with the UN Secretary-General, the president of the Assembly and other UN officers, to seek a political settlement.

Meetings on these lines took place in Paris in November and December. But there was little meeting of minds. Greece again complained of border violations and assistance to rebels by the others. The others complained of the repressive policies of Greece. In particular, the communist countries demanded from Greece a repudiation of expansionist ambitions and a recognition of her present frontier with Albania. This Greece consistently refused to give, claiming that the frontier remained to be settled through a peace treaty. So Dr Evatt, the president of the Assembly, had to report that attempts at mediation had failed, at least for the moment. They were renewed briefly the following year with a broader representation. This time representatives of the United States, Britain and the Soviet Union took part, as well as those of the Balkan countries and the UN officers. But the result was the same. With the failure of these meetings, all attempts by the UN at mediation, as opposed to observation, came to an end.

During 1949 a major change affected the Greek situation, one that ultimately proved crucial. This was the break between Yugoslavia and the Soviet Union. Very shortly after, Yugoslavia decided to reduce her commitment to the guerrillas in Greece. She formally closed her borders with Greece and stopped altogether the traffic of guerrillas between Greece and Yugoslavia. This change was reflected in the activity and reports of UNSCOB. During 1949 it reported fewer violations. While Yugoslavia had in the early part of that year still been aiding the rebels, this had subsequently abated and might now have ceased. But Albania and Bulgaria had continued to give assistance to the guerrilla movement's attempts to overthrow the Greek Government and had now been joined by Romania in this effort. The 1949 Assembly declared that this activity was contrary to the Charter and a threat to the peace; if it went on it would justify a special meeting of the Assembly. This was perhaps the toughest language yet used by the Assembly about any international situation, and partly reflected the intensification of the cold war in the previous year. Ironically, it came at a time when, with the closing of the Yugoslav border, the Greek civil war was rapidly coming to an end.

But UNSCOB remained in existence for another two years. In 1950 its reports were briefer and rather less severely worded than before. It noted the reduction in the scale of fighting and infiltration. But it still concluded that there remained a threat to Greece's political independence; and the Assembly accordingly kept it in existence for a further year. In the following year the incidents declined to a trickle. But the Committee's report still held that, though changed in character, a threat to Greece continued. There had been a decline in guerrilla activity and a withdrawal of forces over the borders, but the number of countries said to be assisting rebel activity had increased yet again, now including Hungary, Poland and Czechoslovakia. Yugoslavia, now finally divorced from the Soviet camp, was omitted altogether. So, it was said, UN vigilance in the area must be maintained.

By this time, however, a majority in the Assembly recognised that the Committee's task was done. To renew it yet again would be a purely political act. It was therefore decided to discontinue UNSCOB, and in its place to set up a Balkan sub-committee of the recently established Peace Observation Commission (p. 000 below). This sub-committee was largely inactive. In January of the following year, at the request of Greece, it undertook observations of the Greek borders with Bulgaria and with Albania. But it had little of substance to report, and it made no recommendations to the Peace Observation Committee. In 1954 it was disbanded altogether. The Greek episode was at an end.

This was, in a sense, the UN's first attempt at peace-keeping; the first time it had despatched a body to observe military activities along a frontier, and to issue regular reports on the situation. This was the type of activity which, many felt, should be the main function of the UN. And it was one which it was to undertake many times in the future. Some felt the episode on these grounds alone represented a significant advance in the organisation's history. It had in this case not merely discussed the issue and passed resolutions: it had taken practical action to halt warlike activity on Greece's borders.

In a sense, certainly, UN action here can be said to have succeeded. Public attention was focused on the area, and evidence of activity against Greece's borders publicised. This probably did something to deter such activity, or at least its more overt forms. The capture and identification of Bulgarian or Albanian forces, even the proof of military support, by a UN body would have been embarrassing to those countries. The fact that Greece's neighbours denied giving active support to the guerrillas suggests that they themselves were reluctant to appear to flout too blatantly the current norms of international behaviour. Within two or three years, active support for the guerrillas, in the sense of equipping, training and sheltering them, had almost come to an end. And at the very least the UN had provided a forum for publicly ventilating the issue.

It was possible, however, to judge the record less favourably. Under this view, the handling of the question from the beginning was rancorous and partisan, and had brought no genuine reconciliation between the parties. Action was entirely one-sided, in the sense that it had been largely at the instigation of the West, and had been mainly boycotted or opposed by the Eastern countries. The reports issued by UNSCOB largely endorsed the version of events put out by the Greek Government, and took little account of the versions proffered by the communist states. Little importance was attached to the Greek Government's claims to the territory of its neighbours, nor to the oppressive domestic measures taken by it within its own territory, as factors contributing to the conflict. For this reason the reports of the Committee, it could be held, had little influence. The war was not brought to an end by anything done by the UN; but by the change in Yugoslavia's political situation and the subsequent closure of her border with Greece.

The truth perhaps lies between these two judgements. The majority in the UN, both in the Assembly and the Council, were undoubtedly pro-Western in their views. In the intensifying cold war, they were not disposed to be conciliatory or charitable in their method of handling the matter. They were not willing to confine membership of UNSCOB to genuine neutrals. They were not inclined to pull their punches in denouncing the actions of Greece's neighbours or to balance their judgements with criticisms of Greece. But UN action was not wholly partisan or politically motivated. At this time the organisation was still considered to be concerned wholly with *external* threats to the peace. Deficiencies in Greek domestic policy, it was held, were not the responsibility of the UN. The concern of the organisation was thus with action from across the borders to assist one side in a civil conflict. In this sense the Greek civil war foreshadowed the type of situation which the UN was to be increasingly involved in over the years (for example, in Lebanon, Yemen, the Congo, Cyprus, the Dominican Republic, Vietnam and other parts of Indo-China, El Salvador and elsewhere), conflicts that were primarily civil rather than international, yet in which there was a considerable measure of external involvement. By making a start in Greece in developing the machinery for observing and deterring such external assistance the new organisation took the first tentative steps along a path it was to tread much more firmly over the years to come.

But, like the Azerbaijani issue, the episode showed the difficulty the organisation had in this period in dealing with cold-war issues. In a sense this was not surprising. The organisation had not been equipped to deal with such questions. Disputes between two or more of the permanent members were those it had always been recognised that the UN might not be able to solve: the veto power had almost been designed to ensure this. What the Greek affair began to make clear was that almost any issue in any part of the world might fall into this category. The great powers felt their interests to be engaged everywhere; so the UN must equip itself for dealing with those disputes which involved the great powers not directly but indirectly.

The other main lesson of the episode was that in such cases the organisation might do better to seek to promote negotiations among the permanent members. Throughout the Greek civil war, there was never any serious attempt to settle it through bilateral negotiations between the Soviet Union and the United States. The UN did nothing to encourage this. The desultory talks in Paris in the autumn of 1948 were too unwieldly and too widely publicised to serve this purpose. The age of super-power politics had not yet begun. If UN bodies had been more disposed to promote or demand confidential negotiations of this kind, even within the UN buildings, rather than public confrontation, it might have had a more visible and immediate impact on the Greek civil war, and have made itself better able to influence similar situations in the future.

9 Indonesia

Not every issue which emerged in this period originated directly from the conflict between East and West. The external reality which the UN mirrored was not only an age of cold war, but an age of colonial revolution. And, for more than twenty years after it was born, many of the threats to the peace that the UN considered arose directly or indirectly from this source.

But unhappily even questions of this type were viewed by the two blocs in cold-war terms. Each would use discussion of the item as the opportunity for a propaganda victory against the other. So it was, at first at least, with the question of Indonesia. This was originally raised at the UN, in the organisation's earliest days, as a direct result of cold-war rivalries. It was the second of the two items raised in the Security Council by the Soviet Union in retaliation for the discussion of Azerbaijan. And as that item had been concerned primarily with the presence of Soviet Union forces on Iranian territory, so the Soviet item was directed at the continuing presence of British forces in Indonesia.

British forces had originally landed in Java in September 1945. They had been sent on the orders of the Supreme Allied Commander to arrange the Japanese surrender and re-establish law and order. The Netherlands Government held that this should lead to the return of the territories to Dutch rule. But over a month before, on 17 August, Indonesian republican leaders had declared Indonesian independence. Sukarno had been made President. And an Indonesian republican government had taken over control of most departments of government from the Japanese.

The British Government decided that its forces, which in any case were limited, should not be used to reimpose Dutch rule. They would merely secure the surrender of Japanese forces, release about 100,000 prisoners and internees, mainly

Dutch, previously held by the Japanese, and occupy a few key areas around Batavia and Surabaja. Mountbatten, the Allied Commander-in-Chief, while he recognised that the Netherlands was legally the sovereign power, urged the Dutch to come to a settlement with the republicans. In response to protests by the Indonesian authorities, he halted the landing of Dutch troops in Java and Sumatra in October. But British forces sought to win control of two or three main cities and came into conflict there with Indonesian forces seeking to resist this. In Surabaja there were casualties on both sides and a British brigadier and other British forces were killed.

The British Government announced that it had no wish to remain in Indonesia, but that it felt bound to keep its troops there for the moment, in fulfilment of Allied war aims and the orders of the Allied Supreme Command. It said it hoped for a settlement between the Dutch and the Indonesians, after which Britain would be only too pleased to withdraw. The Dutch still insisted on their legal right, as the sovereign power, to re-establish control, and they published plans for constitutional development in the territory. These plans were unacceptable to the republican government, however, which demanded acknowledgment of its *de facto* authority in Java and Sumatra.

This remained the situation when in January 1946 the Ukrainian delegate, on behalf of the Soviet Union, raised its complaint against Britain in the Security Council. He charged that Britain was interfering in the internal affairs of Indonesia and assisting in the reimposition of Dutch colonial rule. The UN should assist the Indonesians in their just demand for self-determination. He therefore proposed that the Council should set up a special commission to investigate the situation, particularly the behaviour of British forces, and restore peace in the area. Ernest Bevin, the British Foreign Secretary, representing Britain in the Council while it met in London, replied in characteristically blunt terms. He 'gave the lie' to charges that British forces had attacked those of Indonesia. Britain had been merely carrying out Allied policy in accepting the Japanese surrender and making ready to restore the country, by mutual agreement, to the sovereign power. There was no action of British forces which required investigation: they had never provoked hostilities with anybody, though they had in some cases been obliged to defend themselves against Indonesian forces. The job for the UN was to try to secure a settlement between the Indonesians and the Dutch, not to seek to investigate the activities of British troops, which had throughout tried to stay neutral. Britain would indeed be only too pleased to withdraw her forces as soon as possible.

The Netherlands Foreign Minister, van Kleffens, also defended the conduct of British troops and denied that there was any dispute or any threat to the peace which would justify action by the UN. The problem was primarily a domestic one, which the UN had not the competence to investigate (the first of many claims of domestic jurisdiction made by colonial powers over the next twenty years). The Netherlands would therefore not accept any UN commission which was concerned with the future of the territory as a whole. If Britain would accept one to examine the conduct of British forces this was her affair. Other speakers from Western countries – the United States, France and Australia – equally rallied to the support of Britain and the Netherlands. They all either opposed the sending of a commission or said it must depend on Dutch consent. Only Mexico, other than the communist states, favoured to the idea of sending a commission.

None the less, on 13 February the Ukrainian delegate put down a resolution proposing that a commission should be sent to Indonesia, to inquire into the use of British forces against the Indonesian 'national movement of liberation'. This was put to the vote and predictably lost. Thereupon, however, Egypt put down a further resolution, perphaps the first anti-colonial resolution of very many to be debated within the Council. It was no longer concerned only with the conduct of British troops, but called on the Netherlands to reach a settlement, based on the principle of self-determination, with the Indonesians. At a later stage in the UN's history such a resolution would have been regarded as mild in the extreme and passed overwhelmingly, but at this point, with a Western majority still controlling the Council, it failed. There were no further proposals. And so the matter rested for the moment.

So the retaliation which the Soviet Union had attempted for discussion of Azerbaijan, in this case as over Greece, had on the face of it suffered a setback. But the Western majority in the Council was always certain to ensure a defeat in terms of votes. The Soviet Union none the less had succeeded in focusing attention on a significant movement for independence from colonial rule and on actions by colonial powers designed to suppress or resist that movement. She had stimulated an attempt by Egypt to get the Council to demand a settlement based on the principle of self-determination. And in this way she had set in motion the first of a long series of discussions, not only of Indonesia itself but of colonial matters in general, which would prove highly embarrassing to the colonial powers.

The matter was not to be discussed again for more than a year. Meanwhile talks began between the Dutch and the Indonesians. In November 1946, after eight months of negotiations, with the help of a British mediator, they had concluded the Linggadjati Agreement. Under this the two parties were to co-operate in setting up, before 1 January 1949, a sovereign democratic United States of Indonesia, consisting of the Republic, Borneo, and the Great East (the islands of eastern Indonesia). Each part would decide independently whether it wanted to join the union or would prefer an independent relationship with the Netherlands. There would be a Netherlands-Indonesian union joining the two main states under the Netherlands crown.

The Agreement, however, was in very general terms and there was soon sharp disagreement about its interpretation. These concerned the form of government to be established in the period before the union was formed, the status of the Republic in the interim, its right to conduct its own foreign relations (it had already won *de facto* recognition from the United States, Britain, Australia, and other states), the reserve powers to be enjoyed by the Dutch during this time, and the efforts already made by the Dutch to restore their control and influence in areas outside the Republic. In the summer of 1947 the Dutch prepared for a showdown. In May they made new proposals, which represented in many ways a retreat from the Linggadjati Agreement. When this was not immediately accepted, the Netherlands on 20 July invaded the territory of the Republic in the so-called 'first police action'.

Australia and India immediately addressed notes to the Security Council asking for action to end the hostilities. India asked that action should be taken under Chapter VI: in other words, some form of peaceful settlement. Australia, declaring the action a 'breach of the peace' under Article 39, demanded still stronger measures: action under Chapter VII 'to restore international peace and security'. This might mean enforcement action by the Council to bring about a withdrawal of Dutch forces.

When the Council met, Australia proposed a resolution specifically referring to Articles 39–40 of the Charter (Chapter VII) and calling for an end to hostilities and a resort to arbitration. The form of the resolution implied that the UN was dealing with a 'dispute' between two parties of equal status, to be dealt with as if they were two sovereign states. This was a position wholly rejected by the Netherlands. She claimed that the whole of Indonesia was under her sovereignty, and that in these circumstances the UN had no business to intervene. However, virtually no other member would accept the view that the Council could take no action. Other colonial powers had some sympathy for the Dutch position, but would not agree that nothing should be done at all. The French proposed an amendment to the Australian resolution, making clear that its passage would not affect the juridical situation in Indonesia; but this was turned down by the Council. Similarly, the United States proposed deleting the references to Articles 39–40, since this too implied an 'international' situation and the involvement of two sovereign states; which was accepted. But these were details. The main point was that already the Security Council was moving to the position in which it did not accept that a colonial power could exclude UN action simply by pleading domestic jurisdiction.

The Australian resolution now became essentially a call for an immediate cessation of hostilities and for a settlement of the underlying dispute, either by arbitration or by other peaceful means. This was passed overwhelmingly on 1 August. In a sense this was the first ceasefire resolution ever passed by the organisation. The UN was here acting, in the eyes of many, exactly as it was originally intended to do. It had taken a step, largely undeterred by ideological sympathies, simply designed to restore the peace.

It was, however, a somewhat hesitant and ambiguous step. It was widely noted that there was no specific call for a withdrawal by Netherlands forces to the positions occupied before

20 July, as the Soviet Union had demanded. It was feared that negotiations or arbitration might therefore take place under circumstances which were militarily very unfavourable to the Republic. In any case, there was doubt whether the ceasefire call would have much effect, particularly given the Netherlands rejection of UN competence in the affair.

On the surface there was an unexpectedly prompt response. By 4 August – in other words, within three or four days – both parties had accepted the ceasefire, and ordered their forces to comply. This was, however, short-lived. Within two days fighting had broken out again, and there were accusations from both sides that the other was failing to observe the ceasefire. Nor was there any clear line of demarcation between the areas controlled by the two sides. On 6 August the Council met again. This time the republican authorities demanded that they should be heard. This was strongly rejected by the Dutch, who regarded this as acknowledging their status; but to their chagrin the demand was accepted. An invitation was sent to Sjahrir, one of the Indonesian leaders, to state the Indonesian case. A Dutch demand that representatives of West Borneo and Eastern Indonesia (which were largely under Dutch control) should similarly be heard was turned down. Not only, therefore, did the Council refuse to accept that the matter was a purely internal one; it rejected the legitimacy of the Dutch-created states – a double blow to the Dutch.

Australia, which was the Western power least influenced by a sense of solidarity with the Dutch, and the most concerned to show its sympathy for the Indonesian nationalists, called for a commission to be sent to Indonesia to report on the situation in Java and Sumatra; that is, to the chief republican areas. The Netherlands opposed this since it would imply a right of intervention by the Council, which she strongly resisted. She suggested instead that the consuls of the foreign powers in Batavia should send reports on the situation in that area. This was somewhat unwillingly accepted by Australia, which on 22 August put down a resolution, together with China, requesting the six members of the Council which had consuls in the area (Australia, Belgium, China, France, Britain and the United States, all Western powers) to arrange for reports to be sent 'on the observance of the ceasefire orders and the conditions prevailing in areas under military occupation, or from which armed forces now in occupation may be withdrawn by the parties'. The Soviet Union, which had no consul in the area, was unhappy about this monopolisation of the reporting role by the Western powers (one of the main merits of the Dutch proposal in Western eyes). Nor did she accept the Netherlands' rejection of any UN competence in the matter. She therefore proposed instead that a commission to consist of all members of the Council should be sent: this was similar, it will be recalled, to the procedure in the Greek case and similarly ensured that she would have a voice in any report which was made. France, however, which emphatically supported the Dutch position concerning UN rights of intervention, vetoed this resolution; the first non-Soviet veto to be cast.

The Council therefore proceeded to set up its consular commission in Indonesia, which was to report on the fulfilment of the ceasefire resolution. But this was generally felt to be mainly an interim measure. It would have little effect unless there were at the same time steps to bring a settlement of the underlying conflict. Already, soon after the fighting began, the United States had offered her good offices to the two parties. The Indonesian leaders, however, wanted a more formal procedure for arbitration, if possible involving the UN, which might enhance their equal status with the Netherlands. This view was supported not only by the Soviet Union and Poland, but also by Australia, Syria and Colombia. Poland proposed that the Council itself should act in the capacity of mediator and arbitrator (again allowing a communist voice). The Netherlands preferred mediation to any strict form of arbitration or any formal UN role, and she obtained US support for this view. In consequence the United States proposed that the two sides should each appoint a friendly state to act as mediator: these two would then themselves choose a third, neutral arbitrator to assist them. This third party might also supervise the implementation of the ceasefire order and promote the resumption of bilateral negotiations. Australia, now clearly representing the Indonesian viewpoint, proposed a variant of this which would somewhat enhance the UN's responsibility: the third party would be chosen not by the two others but by the Council itself. These three alternative proposals were each voted on on 25 August. The Polish and Australian resolutions obtained only three votes each. The US proposal was then adopted by a large majority (8–0, with 3 abstentions). As a result, there was established a good-offices committee, consisting of Belgium (the nominee of the Netherlands), Australia (that of Indonesia) and the United States (chosen by the other two). Though not the solution most desired by the republicans, the outcome was something of a victory for them. The UN had now become firmly implicated in their dispute with the Netherlands. And, because a form of mediation had in effect been instituted, the Republic had been invested with the status and authority which the Netherlands had long sought to deny it. The Council, as was often to be the case in the future, had refused to be deterred from action because of constitutional niceties – in particular, because of a claim that a colonial problem was one for domestic jurisdiction only. As on almost all subsequent occasions, the Council was flexible in its interpretation of the words of the Charter, not specifying, for example, in this case, whether or not there existed a 'dispute' or a 'breach of the peace'. All it wanted was to be able to deal in some fashion with a critical situation.

THE RENVILLE AGREEMENT

Before the Good Offices Committee had had time to arrive in Indonesia, the Consular Commission began to report on the situation on the ground. By this time the Dutch had acquired a number of towns in Java and Sumatra and continued to occupy and control a large area of the territory formerly under the control of the Republic. There was still sporadic fighting in some areas. The Commission reported on 11 September that casualties and damage were occurring. A month later it reported that the Dutch were still continuing to undertake 'mopping up' operations in the rural areas, which they had bypassed in their initial advance. Republican leaders declared that their own guerrilla operations would continue in these rural areas if the Dutch tried to extend their control there.

On 3 October the Security Council met to consider these reports. The Soviet Union and Poland called for a withdrawal of Dutch forces to the positions occupied before the 'police operation' began. Australia wanted at least a withdrawal to the positions held on 1 August, when the ceasefire resolution was passed. The United States, however, resisted now, as for a year or so to come, any moves likely to create too great difficulties for the Dutch. Her representative held that the Good Offices Committee should be given general discretion to seek a settlement, but no specific line for withdrawal need be laid down. Eventually a compromise was reached. Agreement was found on a resolution which merely declared that the earlier ceasefire resolution of 1 August prohibited either party from altering 'substantially' the territory under its control on 4 August 1947 (when the ceasefire went into effect). This ruled out the Netherlands' contention that 'mopping-up operations' were permissible, but did not call for her forces to give up their gains since these operations had begun. Under the resolution the Good Offices Committee and the Consular Commission were to assist in ensuring observance of it. The two parties were called upon to stop all further hostile action and to consult on the means of implementing the ceasefire. The resolution was passed on 1 November.

The Good Offices Committee arrived in Batavia on 27 October. After some dispute about where the negotiations between the parties should take place (the Dutch favouring Batavia, the Republic a place outside Dutch control), it was agreed that they should be held on board a US ship off the Indonesian coast. Meanwhile, to deal with the immediate issue of disengagement, a number of committees were formed, including representatives of the two sides and of the Commission. But these quickly ran into disagreements, arising from conflicting claims to authority in the rural areas. The Good Offices Committee felt that they were unlikely to be resolved unless the conversations were accompanied by some attempt to settle the underlying political disagreements.

Discussions of the wider issues therefore began on 8 December, on board the US warship *Renville*, off Batavia. After an abortive attempt to secure mutual agreement on the interpretation of the Linggedjati Agreement, the Good Offices Committee decided to put forward its own proposals. It did this in a message broadcast on Christmas Day. Essentially the proposal consisted in making a substantial concession to the Dutch on the military question, in return for concessions to the Republic on the long-term political issues. On the military side they proposed a new truce based on the van Mook line (the line claimed by the Dutch as the limit of their authority), with a demilitarised zone on either side of the line. To balance this, it proposed, as a step towards a long-term political settlement, that Java, Sumatra and Madura would be largely restored to republican control, the Dutch would cease organising new states in these islands, elections would be held within a definite time-limit, a democratically chosen constituent assembly would then draft a constitution for the United States of Indonesia, and Dutch forces would in three months withdraw to their positions of 20 July.

As was to be expected, the Indonesians did not like the military proposals, nor the Dutch the political. After intensive negotiations the Duch produced a variation on the Committee's ideas which drastically reduced the role that would be played by the Republic in the forthcoming period. They then issued an ultimatum demanding acceptance of their own proposals, after which they would resume 'freedom of action'. The Committee would not accept this demand, which would have effectively put an end to negotiations. They proposed six additional principles, effectively modifying the twelve-point proposals of the Dutch, especially in recognising that the Republic would be one of the states of the union, that it would be accorded a reasonable share in the interim government to be established, and that there should be a plebiscite in Java, Sumatra and Madura to confirm the Republic's authority in these islands.

Both parties were eventually willing to accept this compromise. On 17 and 19 January, the so-called Renville Agreement was signed in two separate parts, on board the warship. Although it seemed at the time an important step forward, the Agreement was, like its predecessor, so ambiguous on many of the important points that it could be quoted by both sides to their own advantage. The eighteen principles provided for the eventual establishment of a sovereign independent state which would be joined in a union with the Netherlands under the Dutch crown. The Republic would be a state within this Union, and a plebiscite would be held within a year in Java, Sumatra and Madura, to find out whether the people of those islands wished to be part of the Republic. All states of the area would be accorded 'fair' representation in an interim government to be set up before the United States of Indonesia came into existence. The Good Offices Committee would remain available to assist the constitutional development if either side wanted it (the Netherlands had previously held that the Committee had no role to play except in relation to military disengagement). Until the United States of Indonesia was formed, Indonesia would be under Dutch sovereignty.

But the Agreement said little about the nature of the interim government to be formed before the proposed United States of Indonesia came into existence, nor the degree of influence which the Republic would have within it; nothing about the conduct of foreign relations during this period; nothing about the powers which the Netherlands representative would hold; practically nothing about the nature of the proposed Netherlands–Indonesia union that was eventually to be established: in a word, nothing about most of the subjects that had been in dispute before the first police action took place.

During the following months, therefore, the Good Offices Committee tried to secure agreement on the detailed implementation of the Agreement. To secure a military disengagement, fifty-five observers, operating in teams of three, supervised the withdrawal of 35,000 Indonesian forces from behind the Netherlands lines and freed about 9000 prisoners held by the Dutch. But progress on the political issues proved much harder. The Dutch, meanwhile, on the basis of their military gains, proceeded to strengthen their position in apparent defiance of the Agreement. For example, they caused, or allowed, the formation of new states in eastern Sumatra, western Java, and Madura, though they had undertaken to form no new states. They began to set up a new interim government, in which the Republic was not represented, claiming this was not the 'provisional government' provided for in the Agreement but an interim authority. This then proceeded to give substantial power to the local states which the Dutch had created. Conversely, the Indonesians were, according to the Dutch, responsible for periodic breaches of the ceasefire.

This attempt by the Dutch to strengthen their own position in defiance of the Renville Agreement aroused concern among those members of the Security Council most sympathetic with the Indonesians. Australia, China and Colombia called for a strengthening of the mandate of the Good Offices Committee to enable it to play a more positive role in implementing Renville. In particular it should be able to initiate proposals, as well as respond to those of others. The United States, however, and other states supporting the Dutch, opposed this. So for the moment the Council contented itself with asking the Good Offices Committee to keep it informed of progress towards a settlement.

The Good Offices Committee accordingly became more active in organising new meetings between the parties, to clarify and elaborate the Renville Agreement. These however, brought agreement no nearer. The Dutch called for a rigorous application of the military agreements (which had favoured them), but did nothing to implement the political aspects except on their own highly partisan interpretation. The Republicans insisted that the Dutch should take no political action except in accordance with the Agreement, and should agree to substantial representation for the Republic in the interim government that was to be set up. In May the Dutch, claiming that agreement with the Republic was impossible, proceeded to call a conference of representatives from thirteen areas outside the Republic, to consider the formation of the United States of Indonesia: an act understandably denounced by the Republic as a violation of the Renville Agreement. Military incidents between the two sides began to recur. Dutch-owned estates in Java were destroyed by the republicans. Mutual blockades were maintained.

To help avert a critical breakdown, the US and Australian representatives in the Good Offices Committee decided to put forward their own ideas about the way the Renville Agreement should be implemented. The essence of these proposals (the Critchley–Dubois proposals) was that a constituent assembly should be created in elections held throughout Indonesia, and this should in turn form a provisional government. This would decide on the representation of states in the United States of Indonesia with the help of an expert committee. Each state would then decide whether or not it would join the union. These proposals, though by no means favourable to the Republic (since they made possible the fragmentation of Indonesia into many states), were accepted by her as a basis for discussion. But they were rejected by the Netherlands, whose military position was now a strong one, and which claimed that the Good Offices Committee had no mandate to promote proposals of this kind.

At this point, however, the Security Council again met to consider the situation. The Indonesians complained of the setting up of new states and of the federal conference organised by the Dutch in May. Australia, India and the Philippines wanted the Council to call for the implementation of the Critchley–Dubois proposals. But a Chinese resolution calling for this just failed of adoption. The Indonesians demanded the appointment of a mediator to replace the Good Offices Committee, now increasingly immobilised by the pro-Dutch Belgian representative's disinclination for any positive action. But this also was not proceeded with. A majority in the Council were still reluctant to endorse any too positive interference in what the Dutch claimed to be their own territory. All the Council could manage therefore was a call to the parties to apply strictly the military and economic terms of the truce agreement and the implementation of Renville.

The Netherlands now increasingly felt she held the whip-hand militarily, and should be able to impose her own will in Indonesia. She controlled the richest and most fertile areas in both Java and Sumatra, as well as in the other islands. She was therefore prepared, if necessary, to stick it out until the Republic gave up through economic collapse. New elections in the Netherlands in July 1948 produced a more right-wing government. This produced proposals for a still looser federal structure for the United States of Indonesia, with a direct relationship between the constituent parts and the Netherlands. In August the Dutch accepted proposals put forward by the local governments which they had established for the formation of an interim all-Indonesian federal government. This was likely to establish a highly decentralised political structure, in which the influence of the Netherlands would be greater and that of the Republic less. In talks with Dr Hatta, the republican Prime Minister, they demanded a strong role for the Netherlands representative in the period of interim government, including the right to despatch forces to maintain order.

In the autumn a new set of proposals was made by the US member of the Good Offices Committee (the Cochran Plan). This provided for a timetable for elections and a transfer of power first to an interim government and eventually to the United States of Indonesia, with the republicans to have a third of the seats in the proposed General Council. Once again the Republic, whose military situation was still very weak, accepted the proposals almost immediately. The Netherlands put forward counter-proposals, rejecting elections, and demanding a considerable concentration of power in the Netherlands representative in Indonesia. This constituted in effect a rejection of the Good Offices Committee's proposals.

THE SECOND DUTCH POLICE ACTION

On 18 December 1948, direct talks between the Dutch Foreign Minister and Dr Hatta failed to resolve their differences. Now once more the Netherlands Government issued an ultimatum, demanding acceptance of its own proposals within eighteen hours. In the words of the chairman of the Good Offices Committee, 'this in effect called for a surrender to the position' of the Hague 'on every material point'. It was physically almost impossible for an answer to be given within the time specified.

The Dutch then launched their second police action. They quickly captured most of the Republic's leaders, including Sukarno, Hatta and Sjahrir, and placed then in exile outside Java. They conquered most of the towans of Java and Sumatra, expelling the republican forces into the countryside. The Good Offices Committee (including this time the Belgian representative) declared that no effective notice of termination of the truce agreement had been given and that the Dutch had initiated hostile military action at a time when the obligations of that agreement were still in operation. Its own facilities for negotiation 'had not been exhausted or effectively utilised' and there was no 'legitimate basis upon which a party could forsake the forum of negotiation for that of armed force'.[1]

The strong-arm tactics employed by the Dutch had finally alienated almost all foreign opinion, including that, mainly in North America and Western Europe, which had previously been most indulgent to her. In the United States there were calls for economic sanctions. The Economic Co-operation Administration did in fact cut off aid to the Netherlands in Indonesia.

Within the UN the United States, until this time the member most favourable to the Netherlands, now demanded strong action against her. Together with Australia she called the Security Council into action on 19 December.

When the Council met, the US delegate, Jessup, declared that the 'simple massive fact is that the Council's own order of 1 August 1947, has been contravened'. He submitted a resolution, supported by Colombia and Syria, calling for an immediate withdrawal of forces and asking for the Good Offices Committee to assess responsibility for the outbreak of hostilities. The Soviet Union wanted a still tougher resolution, condemning Dutch 'aggression', calling for the release of the republican leaders and again asking for a commission, representing the Council as a whole, to go to Indonesia. A compromise resolution was eventually agreed, which called for a ceasefire and demanded the release of the republican leaders. It did not, however, include any demand for withdrawal, owing to the inexplicable refusal of the Soviet Union and the Ukraine (together with France and Britain) to support it: another example of how the Soviet Union prevented the UN from acting effectively if it would not act in the way she herself demanded.

The Good Offices Committee transmitted the resolution to the parties. But it made clear to the Council that the resolution, by allowing one party to hold conquered territory, could scarcely be expected to encourage negotiation. On 27 December, therefore, the Council met again. The Soviet Union proposed a resolution calling for an immediate cessation of military operations within twenty-four hours. This failed, but the next day the Council passed two other resolutions. One, proposed by China, called for the release of the republican leaders within twenty-four hours. The other

called for an urgent report on the situation from the Good
Offices Committee. Still no demand for withdrawal was made.
And by now the Dutch representative was able to inform the
Council that the purposes of the police action had been
achieved. All military action would cease on 31 December in
most areas, and three days later in Java.

These meetings had taken place in Paris, where the
Assembly was at that time meeting. On 7 January the Council
met again in New York. The Netherlands Government then
announced that hostilities had ceased a few days earlier in Java
and Sumatra. The republican leaders had been released from
house arrest, but were still confined to the island of Banki.
The Dutch Prime Minister had travelled to Indonesia for
consultations with Indonesians of all views. Later the Dutch
announced plans to establish an interim government and, at a
later stage, to hold elections. These arrangements were
apparently to exclude the Republic and its representatives

This was the final straw. The Dutch attempt to impose by
force a solution in which the republican leaders, the main
representatives of Indonesian nationalism, were to have no
part was quite unacceptable to the majority in the Council.
The Indonesian representative, Palar, pointed out that the
failure of the Council to demand withdrawal had enabled the
Dutch to obtain a position of military power in the towns; yet
action by Indonesian guerrillas in the countryside would now
be regarded as a violation of the ceasefire. The US delegate,
briefed by Cochran, the US chairman of the Good Offices
Committee, now came out still more strongly against the
Dutch. He condemned the long history of Dutch non-co-
operation with the Good Offices Committee, their 'unilateral
attempt to establish governments, and to weaken the republic,
and their current attempt to impose their own will by force'.
He asserted that the Republic was an existing political force
and the heart of Indonesian nationalism. Dates should be
fixed for elections and a transfer of sovereignty, and Dutch
troops should withdraw as soon as possible.

This was a radical change in the US position, far removed
from the rather equivocal statements of US representatives
before. Other members of the Council expressed themselves
in similar terms. Dutch assertions of their intention to
establish an interim government soon (there was no mention

of participation by the Republic), and to hold elections under UN supervision, were treated with scepticism. This was intensified when the Dutch made statements, both in the UN and in Indonesia, showing that they no longer recognised the Republic as exercising even *de facto* authority.

This prompted a new and stronger assertion of the Council's will. On 28 January another resolution was passed by the Security Council, more comprehensive in its impact than any passed before and in effect laying down a timetable for Indonesian independence. It called not only for the release of the republican leaders, but for their reinstatement in Djakarta to 'exercise their appropriate functions in full freedom'. The Good Offices Committee was to be strengthened, and its authority enhanced, by renaming it the UN Commission for Indonesia, which was to 'act as the representatives of the Security Council in Indonesia'. It would consult with all parties in Indonesia, including the federalists (now themselves increasingly disillusioned with the Dutch – two local governments had resigned in protest against the second police action), to find a solution. By this means a representative interim government for Indonesia would be established by 15 March; an elected constituent assembly by 1 October; and a transfer of sovereignty to the United States of Indonesia by 1 July 1950. Meanwhile, the Commission was to supervise the transfer back to the Republic of the territories controlled by it at the time of Renville.

This was by far the most ambitious resolution yet passed by the Council on Indonesia – or, indeed, on any colonial territory. It was no longer simply concerned with calls for a ceasefire, or for mediation. It sought to lay down the constitutional future of the territory. This was something the UN was virtually never again to attempt (except in the case of the Congo) in all its dealings over colonial territories in the years to come. It could be held to represent a significant breach of Article 2(7), prohibiting UN intervention in matters which were essentially within domestic jurisdiction. But the Security Council was no longer in the mood to be deterred by such considerations.

The Dutch were deeply unhappy about the resolution. Militarily, having now successfully completed their operation, they were in a stronger position than they had ever held before. Yet their political position was, weaker than before the action started. Western opinion had been alienated. The United States had deserted them. The Security Council had intervened far more directly in the situation than before, seeking now to lay down the main terms of a settlement. In particular, it had once again recognised the legitimacy and authority of the Republic, which it had been the whole Dutch aim to destroy. And this weakening of their political position finally proved more important than the strengthening of their military power.

While announcing acceptance of the new resolution, the Dutch sought means of evading its terms. They declared it impossible to set up an interim government as quickly as the resolution demanded. They refused to release the republican leaders. Instead on 18 February they offered a round-table conference in the Netherlands, to which all the parties in Indonesia, including the republicans, would be invited, which would arrange for the transfer of sovereignty to an interim government by 1 May. This interim government might include representatives of the Republic, up to perhaps a third of the places, subject to agreement among the Indonesians.

Even this represented a somewhat greater recognition of the rights of the Republic by the Netherlands Government (though it may well have hoped that other parties to the conference would not allow it even one-third representation in the proposed interim government). In any case, the republican leaders refused to accept this proposal as it stood, since it did not conform with the Security Council's demands. Even the federalists were not entirely favourable. The UN Commission for Indonesia had to report to the Security Council that no interim government had been created by 15 February, as it had demanded. It requested instructions on the conference proposed by the Dutch.

The Dutch plan would in fact have transferred sovereignty to Indonesia even earlier than the Council had demanded. But it would have given no authority to the Republic itself, and would provide for no direct negotiations with it. The UN Commission would play only a subsidiary role. The initiative would remain firmly in Dutch hands: they would organise the conference and at a time when they still exerted dominant military power in Indonesia. For this reason most members of the Security Council were unwilling to accept the Dutch response, and particularly their refusal to release the republican leaders and restore the administration in the Djakarta area. But they wished to make use of the Dutch offer of a conference in which the republicans would be represented: for this itself was an advance over any previous position of the Netherlands. Canada accordingly proposed a 'consensus' of the Council, declaring it was the Council's view that the newly established Commission for Indonesia should assist the various parties to reach agreement on an ending of hostilities, restoring the republican authorities to Djakarta, and arranging the conference proposed by the Netherlands.

The Commission accordingly set to work to arrange discussions between representatives of the two sides in Indonesia, even while the Republic's leaders were still under detention. These talks began on 12 April. External pressures on the Dutch built up. The US Senate threatened to cut off all US aid to the Netherlands if she failed to conform with Security Council resolutions. Australia and India put the question down for discussion at the forthcoming, resumed Assembly session. And two Afro-Asian conferences in New Delhi demanded a settlement in accordance with the Council's resolution of 28 January.

Within a month, the Commission had succeeded in securing substantial agreement on the preliminary measures. It was announced on 7 May that the republican leaders had agreed to halt guerrilla activity and to co-operate in the restoration of peace. In return, the Dutch agreed to release all political prisoners captured since 17 December and to return the residency of Jogjakarta to republican control. They would allow republican officials to continue to operate in areas not under Dutch military control and to halt all their military operations. And they would suspend the creation of new local governments in Java and Sumatra. Both sides agreed to take part in a proposed round-table conference at the Hague, to establish a United States of Indonesia to which sovereignty would be quickly transferred. A representatve body for the whole of Indonesia would be established, in which the Republic would have a third of the seats. And no more new states in the outlying territories would be created.

This agreement was a significant turning-point. For the

Dutch now for the first time made concessions which accorded a considerable role in the political evolution of Indonesia to the republicans: the point they had previously fought hardest to prevent. They no doubt still saw the probable outcome of the Conference in entirely different terms from the republicans, believing that most of the individual governments in other parts of Indonesia would agree with them in preferring a decentralised structure, and strong continuing links with the Netherlands. They had, however, at this point made concessions which finally made these goals unattainable. They had been induced to do this mainly by the very strong external pressures brought to bear on them, focused in the demands and resolutions of the Security Council.

THE ROUND TABLE CONFERENCE

The decline in the moral authority of the Dutch was reflected also in the changed attitudes from this point of the federalists – the Dutch-created authorities in other parts of Indonesia. After the May agreement these hastily sought to come to terms with the republicans, realising that they would certainly enjoy a dominant position in any future regime for Indonesia. They became as keen as the republicans to secure the handover of effective power, and were finding the Netherlands authorities almost as reluctant to hand this to them as to the Republic. They were therefore willing to agree with the republican leaders that the sovereignty of the new state would derive partly from the Republic, as well as from the Netherlands. They accepted that the Republic would provide the nucleus for the future federal army and that the individual states would not maintain their own armed forces. The Republic would be restored to the territory it had held at the time of the Renville Agreement. A joint committee would be set up to co-ordinate their activities. The effect of this was that, even though the republicans accepted that they would have only a third of the representatives in the new assembly, from this time the Republic effectively dominated the forces negotiating with the Dutch. The fifteen Dutch-created states were numerically superior to the republicans, and negotiated separately. But there was, from this point, increasingly a similar viewpoint among all the Indonesian representatives.

The Round Table Conference began in the Hague on 23 August 1949. The UN Commission was represented throughout and had a considerable influence on the negotiations. It had no specific instructions from the Security Council on the line it was to take but was guided partly by past UN resolutions, especially that of 28 January, and partly by its own judgement and knowledge derived from the experience of the previous months. All decisions of the Conference were to be taken by unanimous decision, and when there was disagreement the Commission was asked to mediate. The Conference lasted for two and a half months. By 2 November agreement had been reached on almost all points. On a number of the most crucial questions – including New Guinea, the conduct of foreign relations, the transfer of debts to Indonesia, the withdrawal of Dutch forces, the Surabaja naval base, and the issue of currency – the UN Commission was explicitly asked to mediate by the two sides; and it did so successfully.

The two most controversial points were the future of New Guinea, and the debts of Indonesia to the Netherlands. Both were resolved largely through the intervention of the Commission. On West New Guinea the Dutch demanded that the territory should not be included in the general transfer of sovereignty, on the grounds of its different ethnic character and more backward political development. The Indonesians insisted that it should be included, on the grounds of its similar historical background and geographical continuity. The Federalists, representing somewhat comparable territories, were even more insistent on the point than the republicans. The compromise put forward by the UN Commission provided that the issue should remain undecided until further discussions in the following year (which eventually also failed to reach agreement). In effect the Commission suggested that disagreement on this point should not be a barrier to a conclusion of an agreement on the rest. On the debts the Commission proposed a compromise between the hugely differing figures proposed by the two sides. Under its proposal Indonesia was eventually to assume responsibility for 3000 million guilders of internal debt (including, astonishingly, all of the cost of the Dutch military effort against the

Republic) and 1300 million guilders of external debts. Much of this was in fact never paid.

Eventually the various points of disagreement were resolved. The Dutch began to realise that they were not likely to achieve the highly decentralised structure, nor the tight link with the Netherlands crown, which they had originally envisaged. Instead they began to place their hope in a close bilateral relationship in the future. Finally, in December, an agreement was reached. Sovereignty was to be transferred, completely and unconditionally, by 30 December 1949, to a new United States of Indonesia, under a federal government to be formed of the existing Republic and the fifteen political units established by the Dutch. The Republic would hold, within this federation, the territory it had held before the second police action. A federal constitution for the new state was drawn up between the republican and federalist delegations. Dutch troops would be withdrawn in the shortest possible time after the transfer of sovereignty. The Netherlands and Indonesia would then be joined in a union, with the Dutch Queen as head of the union. The two parties would consult each other on matters of common interest, especially at biennial conferences of ministers, but otherwise each would be completely free and independent. There would be a union court of arbitration to settle matters arising out of the union statute, or from the decisions of the ministerial conferences.

The agreement was ratified by both governments on 21 December, and on 27 December sovereignty was finally transferred. A new independent state, with a population of 100 million and huge resources, had come into being. The UN had in this case played a substantial role in creating the new state.

Even now, however, the UN's role was not completed. A majority in the Security Council proposed it should not merely commend the Commission for its success in helping to bring the agreement about, but also ask it to 'continue to carry out its functions in accordance with its terms of reference, and observe in Indonesia the implementation of the agreements reached at the Round Table Conference'. The Soviet Union proceeded to veto this resolution, condemning Sukarno and Hatta, the two principal architects of Indonesia's independence, as 'executors of their own people' (the republican leaders had put down a communist revolt the previous year) and puppets of the Dutch – an action typical of Russian mis-judgement of colonial leaders at this time. The Commission none the less continued its work, since it felt it still had a mandate under previous Security Council resolutions. It therefore returned to Indonesia in December 1949, and stayed there throughout 1950.

During that year the forces favouring the Republic within Indonesia rapidly extended their power. A large number of the local governments were quickly merged voluntarily into the Republic. One of the rest was disbanded by the central government and brought under its control. West Borneo and Macassar were conquered after brief revolts. By April there were only three separate units left within the new state. In May an agreement between the Republic and the federal forces for the establishment of a unitary state was reached; and in July this was implemented. So the decentralisation the Dutch had tried so hard to achieve was finally undone.

The Commission, however, was mainly concerned with conflicts between Indonesia and the Netherlands. One was a dispute about the military provisions of the Round Table Agreement. At the transfer of sovereignty there were still 80,000 Netherlands troops in Indonesia, together with 65,000 Indonesian soldiers of the Royal Netherlands Indonesian Army. The Commission, and the contact committee, including representatives of the Netherlands and Indonesian Governments, that it established, were able to reach an agreement for the establishment of assembly areas, where the Netherlands forces were to be stationed after independence pending their withdrawal. The Commission's military observers supervised the draft implementation of this plan. It also helped to supervise the disbanding of the old Netherlands Royal Indonesian Army. Part of this force came from the south Moluccas, especially Amboina. When a revolt broke out in these islands, in April–May 1950, the Dutch claimed that many of the forces then still under their command who came from the islands wished to join in the revolt against the Federal Government. They accordingly asked the UN Commission to attempt to mediate between the Indonesian Government and the revolting islands. The Commission twice offered its good offices. But these were refused by the Indonesian Government, which claimed that the affair was one under its own domestic jurisdiction. The Commission reported the matter to the Security Council, which did nothing. Eventually Amboina was taken by force, with heavy loss of life. Many Moluccans fled to the Netherlands, the source of future problems there.

The Netherlands also sought the help of the Commission in another way: to promote the independence of the outer islands The Round Table Agreements had provided for the right of self-determination for the individual Indonesian territories This would include for each the choice between remaining within the United States of Indonesia and attaching itself to the Netherlands. In fact the Federal Government, not surprisingly anxious to retain the unity of the Republic, did not encourage any act of choice of this kind. The Netherlands, increasingly dissatisfied with this state of affairs, asked the UN Commission to help secure implementation of the provision for self-determination. But the Indonesian Government declared that each territory was in practice enjoying the right of self-determination, through the arrangements being made to hold general elections throughout the area, and through the creation of autonomous provinces. The Commission decided that this was a matter to be discussed between the parties, who had the main responsibility for implementing the Round Table Agreements. Perhaps encouraged by this assurance of UN detachment, President Sukarno on 15 April declared the Republic of Indonesia a unitary state.

On West New Guinea a long series of meetings failed to resolve the matter. The strains between Indonesia and the Netherlands became more acute. The constitutional links between them grew weaker. The ministerial meetings broke up in disagreement and eventually were discontinued. Eventually, in August 1954, the Netherlands–Indonesian union, which in any case never had much substance, was effectively dissolved by the Indonesian Government.[2] Shortly afterwards, on 18 August 1954, Indonesia raised at the UN the question of West Irian (West New Guinea), asking that it should be placed on the agenda of the forthcoming Assembly. A whole new phase of the Indonesian question began within the organisation.

CONCLUSIONS

The Indonesia affair was an important event in the development of the UN, the first of a large number of comparable issues over the next twenty years. It was essentially a colonial question concerning the conflict between the representatives of an independence movement in a colonial territory and their former rulers. It raised, therefore, in acute form, one of the most fundamental problems facing any international organisation: what is its right of intervention in conflicts that occur exclusively in territory claimed to be under the jurisdiction of a single government?

Partly at the insistence of colonial powers, Article 2(7) of the Charter provided that nothing in the Charter authorised the UN to intervene in 'matters which are essentially within the domestic jurisdiction' of a state, except in carrying out enforcement measures under Chapter VII. The exact meaning of this phrase was much debated during the Indonesian affair, as it has been ever since. The Dutch claimed it meant that the UN had no role; the Indonesians claimed the opposite. The text was of little help, since it was difficult to determine what constituted 'intervention', what matters were 'essentially' within domestic jurisdiction, and even whether or not 'enforcement' measures were being undertaken. As the International Court of Justice was later to observe, 'the question whether a certain matter is or is not solely within the jurisdiction of a state is an essentially relative question. It depends upon the development of international relations.' The Dutch in this case maintained consistently that they still held sovereignty throughout Indonesia, and what they did there was their own affair. The Indonesians insisted that the jurisdiction of the Dutch Government had never been re-established after the Japanese occupation, that the Republic of Indonesia represented a state which was an equal party in a 'dispute' with the Netherlands, and that in any case the Security Council from the beginning had undertaken 'provisional measures' under Chapter VII of the Charter (Article 40), so that the domestic jurisdiction provisions were suspended.

Members of the Security Council were throughout the episode commendably reluctant to become bogged down in theological arguments of this kind. At this period there was more inclination than later to base actions of the Council on specific articles of the Charter. Even so, the majority agreed with the view, first put forward by the United States, that there was little to be lost and much to be gained in not specifying whether action was taken under Chapter VII, or whether the Republic was regarded as a 'party' to a 'dispute' (though this was accepted by implication when it was decided to seat its representative in the Council). Fundamentally, the attitude of the majority was the attitude of the ordinary layman or of common-sense: there was a situation of conflict in which fighting was occurring, and it would be an abnegation of responsibility if the Council was not to make some attempt to deal with the situation. This was, as we shall see, typical of the pragmatic approach of the Council in dealing with conflict situations throughout its later history, even when, as so often, they could be held to be essentially domestic (Korea, Hungary, the Congo, Cyprus, Lebanon, and so on).

The justification found for this was one that was to be used many times in the future: namely, even events that were formally domestic could, in their effects, come to represent 'threats to international peace and security'. Even the other colonial powers, Britain and France, which originally supported the strict constructionist interpretation of the Charter, as the Netherlands demanded, modified their view. Britain abstained on the first resolution passed by the Council, on the grounds that the affair was essentially within Dutch jurisdiction. But she later supported the resolution of January 1949, which represented a far more flagrant interference in domestic affairs (since it laid down a timetable for Indonesian independence and other procedures for settling the problem). As the Dutch representative complained at the time, this resolution could scarcely have been a more drastic and decisive interference in the internal affairs of a state. But by that point such interference is what even the conservatives in the Council accepted as necessary.

The UN could, moreover, in this case pride itself that its action eventually succeeded in bringing about a resolution of the conflict. After each of the two police actions, UN ceasefire orders and follow-up action by UN bodies on the spot succeeded in restoring peace on the ground: the ceasefire calls in July 1947 and December 1948 were twice accepted and, with some delays and isolated breaches, were put into effect, under UN inspection and control. More important, it maintained a continuing interest in the political discussions which followed. The result was that, though by each police action the Netherlands was able to achieve part of her purely military aims, her political objectives were frustrated. As in later comparable situations – for example, the Congo and Cyprus – UN action was increasingly not simply to secure a ceasefire, but actively to promote negotiations and actively to intervene to secure and influence the settlement. It was able in this way to propose compromises and middle courses which were finally accepted. So it finally compelled the Netherlands to come to terms with the existence of the Republic, and to accept it as the core of the newly independent state. Without the UN's intervention, it is unlikely that this would have occurred, and probable that a protracted and bitter war would have ensued.

There were none the less initial hesitations which reduced UN effectiveness in the early stages. The United States was initially cautious in bringing any pressure to bear against the Netherlands, and the US attitude, as always at this time, influenced the response of the Security Council as a whole. The Council's response to the first Dutch police action, for example, included no call for withdrawal, so that the Dutch were allowed to obtain a substantial military advantage in the subsequent negotiations. And, though the Good Offices Committee afterwards seemed to have won a significant success in securing agreement on the Renville terms, these in fact were so imprecise that they had little effect in moderating Dutch ambitions. It was only after the second Dutch police action, when external opinion, especially that in the United States, became much more strongly aroused, that the Security Council decisively influenced the situation, with its demand for the release of the Indonesian leaders and their restoration to Jogjakarta, and its proposals for the general outlines of a settlement. It was this, above all, which finally compelled the Netherlands to treat the republican leaders as valid negotiating partners, and which in turn finally led to their domination of the independent Indonesia. This occurred in spite of the fact that the military dominance of the Netherlands was never so pronounced as at that point. The UN showed here that it could, even without any military presence at all, exercise considerable influence on a settlement through its authority alone.

This occurred partly because of the persistence and skill of members of the Commission. But it was partly because of the ability of the UN to appear, rightly or wrongly, as the focus of world opinion generally. The changes in UN policy, its increasingly anti-Dutch and interventionist bias, reflected changes in world opinion as a whole. As international opinion became more concerned about events in Indonesia, leading members of the UN became more determined it should act effectively to keep the peace, and to prevent the Netherlands from suppresing the Republic by armed force. And success in this was assisted because here, for once, there was no major conflict of opinion between East and West, or, at least, only in degree.

But the other major reason for UN success was that in this case it acted as it in other cases often failed to do: as the spur to effective negotiations between the parties themselves. Those negotiations it was able actively to influence, both through the continuous presence of the UN Commission on the spot and through the passage of resolutions on the objects to be achieved. As a result, the episode represented, above all in the successful mediation undertaken after each police action and at the Round Table Conference itself, one of the most success ful achievements of the UN until this time.

10 Palestine

THE SPECIAL COMMITTEE ON PALESTINE

The Middle East was one of the areas most transformed by the Second World War. Not only had large areas been the scene of prolonged fighting or military interventions, but, in addition, wholly new states had begun to emerge (Syria, Lebanon, Libya). The governments of others had been overthrown or disrupted by military action (Iraq, Iran and the Maghreb). And in the most politically sensitive area of all, Palestine, though little fighting had taken place and British administration remained unchanged throughout, an increasingly tense confrontation between the two main communities had built up, encouraged by the certainty that independence would be granted soon after the war came to an end. Within little more than a year of its birth, this problem was placed in the lap of the UN General Assembly.

Palestine had been administered by Britain as a League Mandate since 1922. Although the majority of the population at that time were Arabs, whose interests under the terms of the Mandate Britain was to protect, she was also, under the agreement, to place 'the country under such political, administrative and economic conditions as will secure the establishment of a Jewish National Home'. These two aims were scarcely easy to reconcile.

The contradiction only reflected the equal inconsistency in the promises made by Britain herself to both Jews and Arabs during the First World War. Her policy became inevitably a compromise which alienated both parties. The heart of the problem concerned immigration: the number of Jews who were to be allowed to share the territory with the existing Arab population. Britain allowed enough Jewish immigration to antagonise the Arabs, but not enough to satisfy the Jews. In 1939 there were about a million Arabs and 400,000 Jews in

Palestine. Even before 1939, there were outbreaks of fighting between the two communities and between them and the British. In that year, just before the outbreak of war, Britain once again restricted immigration and promised independence to a unitary state with an Arab majority: an action which further antagonised the Jews and their supporters, but did not satisfy the Arabs either.

After the Second World War the question became particularly explosive. Jewish immigration was officially frozen at 1500 a month. But in practice the figure was hugely exceeded, because of large numbers of illegal immigrants, seeking to escape the nightmare which their people had experienced in Europe, who landed by boat on the coast. Increasingly the Jews, in Palestine and elsewhere, and their supporters in North America and Europe, saw the creation of a Jewish state in Palestine as the only solution to their age-long woes. Such people became increasingly impatient and dissatisfied with British efforts to control the flow of immigration, efforts that sometimes involved returning to Europe the Jews who were apprehended before they reached the coast of Palestine.

For Arab opinion, however, the rate of immigration was still much too high. As between the wars, therefore, British policy satisfied neither side. Armed action, mainly by Jewish organisations against British forces, became more frequent. Many British soldiers lost their lives seeking to uphold a policy which they did not understand, which was reviled throughout much of the world, and which was quite irrelevant to Britain's own interests. Finally, during the course of 1946, British opinion became weary of the ungrateful responsibility of seeking to solve an apparently insoluble problem, at the cost of the lives of British soldiers for whom the future of Palestine was a matter of profound unconcern. As a result, in the spring of 1947, Britain decided to place the matter in the hands of the UN. Although Palestine had not, like most mandated territories, been converted into a UN trust territory, it was still a mandate and generally felt as a matter of international responsibility. Moreover, since Britain's own policies were so unpopular, and any ultimate decision she might make on the territory's future likely to be more so, there was some advantage in sharing responsibility with other members of the international community.

Accordingly, on 2 April 1947 Sir Alexander Cadogan, the British delegate to the UN, wrote to the acting Secretary-General, asking that the question of Palestine should be put on the agenda for the next regular session in the autumn: the British Government would then submit an account of its administration of the mandate and ask the Assembly to make recommendations for the territory's future. Meanwhile, because the Assembly might find it difficult to make any recommendation without preliminary study of the question, Britain proposed the calling of a special session of the Assembly to look at the question. This might then wish to establish a special committee to study the matter in detail before making a recommendation.

This was a somewhat revolutionary idea. So far the UN had been used mainly, as its founders intended, for discussing threats or attacks by one state against another, together with a few more general subjects, such as disarmament and human rights. But it had never been formally asked to give its judgement on the constitutional future of a particular territory, let alone one as explosive and contentious as Palestine.[1] Even the fate of trust territories was not in practice entrusted to a decision by the UN itself. This British initiative might therefore have become a precedent of huge importance for the future. But Britian herself, although claiming she wished to seek the advice of the UN, remained continuously ambivalent about the UN's role. She never committed herself to abide by a UN decision. When one was made which she felt to be totally unacceptable to one of the main communities involved, she refused to implement it, as did the Security Council. Though, therefore, the initiative was certainly a significant one in UN history, it did not have the effect of enhancing the UN's future role as some optimists at the time had foreseen. On the contrary, it perhaps acted as an awful warning of the dangers of committing to the UN responsibilities it was not equipped to fulfil.

The acting Secretary-General telegraphed all members, informing them of the British proposal for a special assembly and asking whether they agreed. If the majority accepted within thirty days such a session would be called. Forty members answered, and all but one agreed. The session was therefore called for 28 April 1947.

Originally the only item on the agenda was the British proposal for 'constituting and instructing a Special Committee to prepare for the consideration of the question of Palestine at the second regular session'. But the Arab states felt that this mandate was far too vague. It raised the danger, in their eyes, that, under the influence of the United States and other states favouring the Jewish cause, proposals might be made for something other than the normal procedure for a mandate, independence of the entire territory. This could include federation, partition, creation of a separate Jewish state, and so on. Moreover, because of the existing rate of immigration, they wanted the time-scale for independence to be as short as possible. They therefore proposed for the special session an additional item for discussion: 'the termination of the mandate over Palestine and the declaration of its independence'. They argued that there was no need for fact-finding, or for long discussions by a committee or the Assembly. The principle of the ultimate independence of Palestine had long been accepted, in the Covenant of the League of Nations and in declarations by Allied powers. All that the Assembly need do therefore was to apply the principles of the Charter and declare the granting of that independence under democratic rule – a step which would of course have precluded the creation of a Jewish state. The majority felt that this would prejudge the questions which the proposed committee had to decide. The possibility of independence would anyway be one of the questions the committee would discuss, and it should not be imposed on it in advance. For these reasons the proposed Arab agenda item was not adopted.

The Soviet Union, Poland and India none the less wanted a specific reference in the committee's terms of reference to 'the question of establishing without delay the independent democratic state of Palestine'. This was not designed as support for the Arab cause: the Soviet Union and Poland made no secret of their sympathies with the Jewish cause in Palestine, and Poland even made herself the spokesman for this, on the grounds that many Palestinian Jews had originally come from Poland (an ironic position in the light of subsequent Polish policy regarding Jews). It was designed rather as support for the general anti-colonial position that independence should be given as soon as possible to all the dependent territories, and the influence of colonial powers removed from the scene as quickly as possible. But the United States, many Latin American countries and others favouring Jewish claims opposed the proposal for the same reason as they had opposed the Arab agenda item: it would prejudice the conclusions which the committee had to reach. Eventually, therefore, more non-committal terms of reference were agreed. These provided that the committee should prepare a report simply 'on the question of Palestine'. The committee would have wide powers to ascertain and record facts, would conduct investigations in Palestine and anywhere else it thought useful, taking account of the various religious interests in the area. It would then submit proposals 'for the solution of the problem of Palestine' before 1 September.

It was agreed to hear at the start representatives of the Jewish Agency and of the Arab Higher Committee to put the point of view of the Jewish and Arab populations of Palestine. Abba Silver, speaking for the Jewish Agency, set out the case for the creation of a separate Jewish state in Palestine:

> the Jewish people is no less deserving than other peoples whose national freedom and independence have been established and whose representatives are now seated here. The Jews were your allies in the war and joined their sacrifices to yours to achieve a common victory. The representatives of the people which gave to mankind spiritual and ethical values, inspiring human personalities and sacred texts which are your treasured possessions, and which is now rebuilding its national rights in its ancient homeland, will be welcomed before long by you to the noble fellowship of the UN.

Henry Katan, a Palestinian lawyer, speaking on behalf of the Arab Higher Committee, declared that 'no amount of propaganda can change the Arab character of Palestine'. He therefore called for the end of Jewish immigration and a termination of the mandate. Ghoury, Secretary of the Arab Committee, declared 'the right of Palestine to independence as an independent whole'.

There was little disposition to question the proposal to set up a special committee. There were two main questions to be decided: its composition and its terms of reference. On the composition, the main controversy concerned whether the permanent members should be represented, as the Soviet Union (as always) and some others wished, or not. Britain from the start had declared she did not wish to be 'judge in her own case'. The United States and China also declared that they did not wish to put themselves forward, though they would serve if this was generally wished. The majority felt the permanent members should be excluded. It was finally decided that the Special Committee should consist of Australia, Canada, Czechoslovakia, Guatemala, India, Iran, the Netherlands, Peru, Sweden, Uruguay and Yugoslavia.

On the terms of reference the Arab governments protested strongly that all reference to the goal of independence for Palestine had been omitted. Nor was there even a reference, as had been proposed, to the need to consider the interests of all the inhabitants of Palestine. The British proposal, itself vague enough, to consider the 'future government of Palestine' had been replaced by the still vaguer term 'the problem of Palestine'. Finally, they objected to the decision to allow the Special Committee to conduct investigations wherever it wished, on the rather far-fetched grounds that this was intended to enable it to visit camps for refugees in Europe and so mobilise support for increased Jewish immigration to Palestine. For all these reasons the Arab representatives at the Special Assembly reserved their position. The Arab League issued a statement denouncing Zionist influences in the USA for a decision that was inconsistent with the Charter and the mandate. It announced the intention of the Arab governments to raise the demand for independence for Palestine at the Assembly's autumn session. More significant, the Arab Higher Committee, representing the Arabs of Palestine, resolved that Palestinian Arabs should not co-operate in any way with the Special Committee or appear before it.

This was a thoroughly foolish decision and typical of the tendency of the Arab states to cut off their nose to spite their face: to damage their own case by taking an extreme and intransigent position. Whatever they thought of the Committee's terms of reference, Arab interests would obviously have been better served if they were represented there, and so were able to put their own case to it as forcefully as possible. Now, as so often on this issue, Arab governments made the best the enemy of the good. Since they could not have the decision they demanded, they refused to have anything to do with the decision that was actually to be reached. Very different was the reaction of the Jewish Agency and other Jewish organisations. These determined to make use of all their considerable resources to place the Jewish case before the Committee as powerfully as possible. So already there began to emerge, both in the UN and in capitals all over the world, above all in the United States, the effective and high-powered pressure groups that were to serve the Israeli cause so well in subsequent years. The effect on the Committee cannot be accurately judged. But it seems not unlikely that the fact that its ultimate proposals were so favourable to the Jewish cause was not unrelated to the relative efforts made by the two parties to present their case.

The Committee set out at the beginning of June for the Middle East. It visited Palestine, Lebanon, Syria and Transjordan. It continued to be boycotted by the Arabs of Palestine, but evidence was given to it by the Arab governments of the region. These made clear that they would oppose, by all means in their power, the establishment of a Jewish state in the area. The Committee subsequently decided (by 6 votes to 4) to send a sub-committee to visit displaced persons' camps in Germany and Austria. The representatives of the Jews of Palestine, Abba Eban and David Horowitz, put the Jewish case before the Committee with great force. There is little doubt that in the course of its examination of the problem the sympathies of many members became more favourable towards Jewish aspirations. Certainly all members of the Committee, including even the few who were sympathetic to the Arab position (Yugoslavia, Iran and India), became increasingly sceptical of the possibility of establishing a unified state of Palestine in which Jews and Arabs could live peacefully together. Both groups, therefore, majority and minority alike, turned towards a solution providing for some degree of division between the two peoples. The difference between them consisted mainly in the nature and extent of the links between the two parts which they proposed.

The majority report in effect accepted the case for a Jewish state. It concluded that immigration had already taken place on such a scale that the Jewish population was too great to be easily assimilated in an Arab-dominated state. There were substantial and clearly defined areas in which the Jews were in a majority. Socially, politically and even economically the two populations had remained largely separate. They therefore recommended the establishment of a Jewish territory that would include eastern Galilee, the central plain from south of Acre to just north of of Isdud, and the Negev desert. The Arabs would get western Galilee, central Palestine and the coastal areas to north and south. Jewish immigration would continue at the rate of 75,000 a year for the first two years and 60,000 after that. The Jerusalem – Bethlehem area would be an international zone under UN trusteeship. An economic union would be established between the two territories, and a ten-year Arab–Jewish treaty drawn up. There would be a two-year probationary period during which the states would come into existence under British supervision.

The minority report, which was closer to Arab views, provided for a single state with its capital in Jerusalem, within which there would be Jewish and Arab zones, linked in a federal structure. For a period not exceeding three years the state would be under the administration of an authority designated by the UN. During that time Jewish immigration would continue according to the absorptive capacity of the Jewish state, which would be determined by an international body. After that immigration policy would be for the new state to decide. The federal government would have responsibility for defence, foreign relations, immigration, federal taxation, currency and communications. The Arab and Jewish governments would control education, police, housing, health, land rights and agriculture. There would be two chambers of parliament at the federal level, and a federal court. An international body would supervise and protect the holy places.

As had been requested, these reports were completed by 31 August, to be ready for the regular Assembly session beginning in mid September.

THE ASSEMBLY RECOMMENDS PARTITION

While the Special Committee was in Palestine, the British had given little indication of their own views. They were thought by some to be stalling, in the hope of maintaining the mandate for a number of years (and it is true that over the previous year or so a considerable amount of military equipment had been moved to Palestine from the Canal Zone, showing that the British War Office at least had hoped for a prolonged British stay in Palestine). Whatever its earlier intention, however, by September 1947 the British Government had decided that it had had enough of its costly and intensely unpopular burden in Palestine.

As soon as the General Assembly began to consider the Palestine issue, in late September, the British Colonial Secretary, Arthur Creech Jones, announced that it was the intention of the British Government to withdraw from Palestine. His government, he said, 'endorses without reservation the view that the mandate should now be terminated'. Any proposal made by the UN must take account of this intention. The British Government 'would be in the highest degree reluctant to oppose the Assembly's wishes in regard to the future of Palestine': it would thus give effect to any plan which had the agreement of Jews and Arabs. But if the plan was not so acceptable then some other authority might have to take the responsibility for implementing it. In any case, the British Government must plan for an early withdrawal of British forces and an end to British administration.

On 23 September the Assembly decided, against the wishes of the Arabs, to establish an *ad hoc* committee to consider the Palestine problem in the light of the Special Committee's report. Like many Assembly committees, this would be a committee of the whole, representing every member. Within the *ad hoc* committee the Arabs were naturally anxious to prevent endorsement by the UN of the proposals of the majority report for partition. Sensing the bandwagon in favour of partition, they proposed that an advisory opinion of the International Court of Justice on various legal points concerning the mandate should be obtained before any definite decision was made. This at least would cause some delay. Indeed, from their point of view the best hope was that the UN would fail to make any decision at all. The British, who had never endorsed partition, might then decide to give rapid independence to a unitary state. The representatives of the Arab Higher Committee announced that the Arabs of

Palestine would oppose partition, or any policy providing a special position for the Jews in Palestine, by every means at their disposal.

But the majority were determined to go ahead and reach a decision. This was not merely because a request for an Assembly recommendation had been made by the mandatory power. It was because there now opened the opportunity, in the eyes of many, to solve not only the problem of Palestine itself, but the wider problem of the Jews as well, the homeless people whose age-old wrongs, it was felt, could now finally be rectified. Even on practical grounds partition seemed the most sensible step, given the intense hostility between the two communities and the unlikelihood of their ever settling down in peace within the same state. In October the Soviet Union announced that it supported partition (at this time the Russians apparently hoped that a Jewish state, run largely by Russian Jews, many of leftist views, would be a progressive force in the Middle East, and subject to Soviet influence). The United States, as was expected, endorsed the majority report. Soon a large proportion of the existing international community, including its two chief powers, were clearly committed to the idea of partition. For this reason it was the Jews who at this time demanded a strong UN role in determining the country's future, and the Arabs who took the opposite view.

Most members of the UN accepted that the matter should be resolved by a vote within the organisation. This was partly because many of them favoured a particular solution, partition, which was only likely to come about through a UN decision, and partly because at this period there was a general belief that the UN could 'settle' difficult questions by passing resolutions on the subject. Just as the UN could settle the future of the Italian colonies or of Indonesia, so it could 'settle' Palestine. This would be done by the Assembly's (not the Security Council's) passing an edict on the matter. One effect of this god-like approach of the Assembly was that there was never any serious attempt at conciliation, negotiation or peace-making.

If ever there was a moment in the entire history of the Palestine issue when a genuine opportunity for conciliation existed, it was now. The obvious course for the organisation at this time was to promote further negotiation between the parties themselves (that is, between the Higher Arab Committee and the Jewish Agency) under UN auspicies, so as to find some middle course between the majority and minority reports. A UN mediator (as over Kashmir) or a UN commission (as over Indonesia) might have been appointed to achieve this. The exact form of a federal relationship, the exact type of autonomy to be enjoyed by the two proposed states, the nature and extent of the links, economic and political, between them, the way in which immigration was to be controlled, the territorial boundaries between the two zones, all these might have been discussed. It is such a course as an impartial majority within the organisation might have been expected to promote. But on this issue no impartial majority existed. Most of the membership was fully committed to one viewpoint or the other.

Only El Salvador proposed a serious attempt to promote negotiation and she was almost wholly disregarded. Far more influential was the proposal of the United States to set up a sub-committee to elaborate in greater detail the proposals of the majority report. This was followed by a demand for a corresponding sub-committee to do the same thing for the minority report. As a result two such sub-committees were set up to reconsider and refine the proposals of the majority and minority reports. Each would consist of members favouring those reports. In other words, instead of an attempt at compromise there were to be two further sets of proposals, one pro-Jewish and the other pro-Arab. It is true that there was also to be a 'conciliation group', consisting of the chairman, vice-chairman and rapporteur of the *ad hoc* committee, which would try to bring the two parties together. But in practice this was largely inactive. It had no power to make compromise proposals of its own. And it never even set in motion negotiations between the parties: its chairman briefly reported later that the efforts of the group 'had not been fruitful'. Most of the activity of the organisation was devoted to drumming up support for one or other of the two rival solutions proposed. Thus, instead of seeking a middle way, the membership was eventually given a straight choice between the Jewish and Arab cases. The chosen solution was then to be imposed on the losing side, regardless of its own views.

The 'minority' sub-committee, consisting mainly of Arab

states under the chairmanship of Zafrullah Khan of Pakistan, argued that, under the terms of the mandate, the Assembly had no right to split the territory in two against the wishes of the majority of its population. It called for a judgement of the International Court on the legality of such a course, in the light of the Covenant of the League and the mandate agreement, and on whether the UN was competent to enforce a solution which was adopted without the consent of the people of Palestine. It also recommended the establishment of a provisional government of Palestine, which should take over authority from the mandatory power. This would prepare elections for a constituent assembly, which would then establish a constitution for a unitary state. There would be guarantees for the rights of minorities, and wide powers for local authorities in the field of education, health and other social services. Hebrew would be the second official language of the state. But there would be no federal system, nor a separate Jewish zone as suggested by the earlier minority report. Thus, though possibly intended as a bargaining position, the proposal represented a partisan statement of the view of one side rather than an attempt at compromise. In any case, perhaps because it was known from the start that such a plan would not receive majority support, it never received any significant attention in the Assembly.

The other sub-committee, consisting entirely of powers which were sympathetic to Jewish aspirations in Palestine, set out proposals for implementing the majority report of the Special Committee. Its proposals were more favourable in many ways to Jewish aspirations than the original. They provided for a timetable that would bring about the establishment of a Jewish state within nine months. British forces would be withdrawn by 1 May 1948 and the new Arab and Jewish state would be set up by 1 July. A new UN Palestine Commission, of three to five members, would be set up to supervise the implementation of the plan almost immediately. This would be composed of Uruguay, Guatemala, Poland, Norway and Iceland (a composition extremely favourable to the Jews and later somewhat modified). Against this, Jaffa, which had a largely Arab population, would be established as an Arab enclave within the Jewish state. After British views on the plan had been taken into account, the timetable was slightly extended to allow for the ending of the mandate and evacuation of British forces by 1 August. The proposed Arab and Jewish states and a special international regime for Jerusalem would then come into existence on 1 October. But provisional councils of government, each controlling its own militia forces, would take over power on 1 April. These would arrange for elections to take place within their own states within two months of British withdrawal.

The British Government gave notice that it could not undertake to be responsible for implementing either of the two rival plans. Since they both represented partisan solutions, likely to be acceptable to one side but not to the other, they could not be put into effect without violence and bloodshed and, though Britain would not necessarily seek to oppose either of them, it could not take on the burden of putting them into effect.

This warning did not deter the *ad hoc* committee from proceeding to decide on an imposed solution. The 'majority' proposals were revised marginally. The Jewish Agency offered to transfer a small part of the Beersheba area and the Negev desert to Arab control. In the last few days before the committee's reports were to be voted on, a few other adjustments were hurriedly made. The membership of the proposed commission for Palestine was changed slightly. A statute for the international zone in Jerusalem–Bethlehem was suggested. The proposed boundaries were altered to give the Arab cities of Jaffa and Beersheba to the Arabs. On Soviet initiative the Security Council was asked to treat any breach of the partition arrangements as a threat to the peace, which it would meet with its enforcement powers if necessary: this might act to protect the embryonic Jewish state from attack from its neighbours.

Apart from these minor changes, there was no attempt to reconcile the two plans. The aim continued to be to put the two rival alternatives to the Assembly and see which got more votes. On 24 November the main Arab proposal for a unitary Palestine was defeated in the *ad hoc* committee by 12 to 29, though the proposal to ask for an opinion of the International Court on whether the UN had the right to enforce a settlement against the wishes of the people of Palestine was lost by only one vote. On the following day the partition plan was passed by 25 votes to 13, with 17 abstentions. This was not, however, a two-thirds majority; and, since it was accepted that the matter was an 'important one' for which such a majority was necessary, there remained doubt about the outcome in the Assembly itself.

The Assembly met to discuss the question only two days later, on 26 November. Intense lobbying by the US Government, as well as by the highly energetic and successful Jewish lobby, had meanwhile been going on. Haiti, which had spoken strongly against partition during the committee debate, was induced to vote in favour of it in the Assembly. The Philippines delegate, General Romulo, who had previously spoken against partition, disappeared on a long voyage before the vote; and the Philippines then voted for the partition plan. Paraguay and Liberia at the last moment were induced to vote 'yes'. Belgium, the Netherlands and New Zealand, which had been intending to abstain, suddenly decided to vote in favour. Just before the vote was to be taken, France requested a twenty-four hour postponement for one day, nominally to allow a last minute attempt at reconciliation, but in fact, it was generally believed, to show her own Muslim peoples and associates that she had done her best to secure a compromise. But, after this brief delay, France too came down for partition.

It was anyway far too late for conciliation. Everybody was now awaiting the final decisive vote. The Jews in particular, sensing victory, had no reason to compromise. Thus, when Iran proposed that a decision should be postponed for a further six weeks to allow further negotiations, the proposal was easily rejected. A reversion by the Arabs to the idea of a federal state, with self-governing Jewish and Arab cantons, was equally turned down.

The final vote was taken on 29 November. The proposal for partition was passed by 33 votes to 13, with 10 abstentions. So the necessary two-thirds majority had been obtained. The UN Assembly, overruling the wishes of the majority of the people most concerned, had reached its decision on the future of Palestine.

The British continued to adopt a highly detached position. They continued to insist that they could not accept responsibility for implementing any plan that was totally unacceptable to one side or the other. And they demonstrated their impartiality by abstaining in the votes on the two rival proposals.

The final decision would have created, of course, a Jewish state far smaller than Israel was to become less than a year later. But it was none the less greeted in Jewish Palestine (and Jewish New York) with jubilation; in the Arab countries with despair; and in Palestine with a renewal of inter-communal fighting. Both Arab and Jewish communities in Palestine started intensive recruiting campaigns.

THE DEMAND FOR ENFORCEMENT POWERS

Under the Assembly's resolution the British were to hand over the administration gradually to the UN Commission for Palestine. This would in turn transfer authority to the proposed Jewish and Arab provisional councils of government. The Commission, though subject to the Assembly, was to report to the Security Council, which would take the necessary measures, including enforcement action if necessary. At the same time the Trusteeship Council was given certain responsibilities in relation to Jerusalem. It in turn established a sub-committee to prepare for the internationalisation of the city.

Responsibility for Palestine within the organisation was thus highly dispersed, and was to remain so until the mandate came to an end. Moreover, the constitutional position was obscure. The Assembly's resolution could only be a recommendation: for it to be mandatory it would have to be endorsed by a 'decision' of the Security Council. And for this the Council would first have to find a threat to international peace.

In January 1948 the new Commission for Palestine met for the first time. It consisted of representatives of Bolivia, Czechoslovakia, Denmark, Panama and the Philippines. This composition, though slightly amended from the original proposal, was still markedly pro-Jewish, since the first four were all distinctly favourable to the Jewish cause. The Czech member, Lisicky, was elected chairman, and Ralph Bunche, head of the Trusteeship Division within the UN Secretariat, was given the leadership of its staff.

The Commission had twenty meetings in January and issued its first report to the Security Council at the end of that month. Representatives of the British Government and the Jewish Agency appeared before it, but it was boycotted by the Arab Higher Committee, which refused to recognise the partition decision.

One subject about which the Commission was concerned was the question of immigration into Palestine. The Assembly's partition resolution had called upon the mandatory power to ensure that, as early as possible and at any rate not later than 1 February, it would make over to the Jewish state a port and hinterland 'suitable to ensure substantial immigration'. Britain had not undertaken this by 1 February, arguing that to allow the uncontrolled arrival of a substantial number of Jews, probably armed, at a time of widespread civil conflict could only make the existing disturbed situation even worse. Despite pressure from the Commission she did not alter this decision. The Assembly's resolution, she argued, was only a recommendation, which could not bind the mandatory power, and she was therefore not prepared to make over a port for this purpose.

The Commission also pressed to be allowed to take a share in the administration of Palestine, as the resolution likewise demanded. This too the British Government was not prepared to allow, on practical grounds, 'until a short period before the termination of the mandate'. A situation of divided authority would indeed scarcely have been workable. It would have made it almost impossible for effective decisions to be reached in a critical emergency situation. Eventually the British Government announced that it would allow the Commission to enter Palestine on 1 May, before finally withdrawing, on the termination of the mandate, on 15 May.

In any case, the Commission could have exercised no effective authority without some forces to maintain order. This was increasingly clearly recognised by the Commission itself. It therefore decided to turn to the Security Council for assistance.

The security situation in Palestine was by this time rapidly worsening. Besides regular attacks on the British forces there, there were continual inter-communal incidents. Local Palestinian Arab groups organised attacks on Jewish settlements

and convoys, occasionally assisted by Arab irregulars who
infiltrated from neighbouring countries. Jewish groups became increasingly better organised and better armed. Two
Jewish terrorist organisations, the Lechi and the Irgun (Stern
gang), undertook bombing and other attacks against British
and Arab targets alike, while the Haganah, the more official
Jewish armed force, now began to procure arms on a wide
scale abroad, trained and recruited a substantial force and
undertook attacks on mainly Arab targets.

The UN Palestine Commission became increasingly concerned about the worsening situation. In the middle of
February it therefore addressed a special report to the
Security Council. It recognised that it was only the security
forces of the mandatory power which at that time prevented
the situation from deteriorating into 'open warfare on an
organized basis'. It therefore proposed that these should be
replaced by a new international force which could 'assist
law-abiding elements in both the Arab and Jewish communities, organised under the general direction of the
Commission', in maintaining order and security in Palestine.
The Commission therefore called on the Council to consider
making available 'military forces in adequate strength to
ensure that the Assembly's decision on Palestine could be
carried out'.[2]

The Security Council met on 24 February to consider this
proposal. The chairman of the Commission, appearing before it, declared that the only way of implementing the
Assembly's plan for Palestine would be through the creation
of an effective non-Palestinian military force, which could
maintain law and order during the transition. Creech Jones,
the British Colonial Secretary, said that, while Britain deplored the present situation, she had always warned that the
adoption of a plan that was acceptable to one side only was
almost certain to lead to widespread violence and so prove
almost impossible to implement. Britain must persist in her
own decision to withdraw, since British public opinion would
no longer tolerate the continued loss of life involved in
enforcing a policy which Britain herself had not chosen. If the
plan was to be enforced, therefore, it could not be by British
forces. The US representative pointed out that the Security
Council could use force under the resolution only if it found

that there was a threat to international peace and security, not simply to enforce the partition plan. At present there was not sufficient evidence to suggest this. He therefore proposed that the Council should set up a committee of the five permanent members, to consider whether the situation in Palestine represented such a threat to the peace and report back to the Council.

There was prolonged discussion of this proposal. Many detailed amendments were suggested. The Soviet Union, while welcoming consultation among the permanent members, felt that this could take place directly, without setting up a special committee for the purpose. Colombia and Belgium proposed amendments which would have avoided any specific endorsement by the Council of the partition plan, and would have made possible a further attempt at conciliation among the parties. Eventually the United States herself amended her proposal, so that it did not specifically commit the Council to accepting responsibility for enforcing the partition plan. The final resolution, endorsed by the Council on 5 March with only three abstentions, thus called on the permanent members to consult and to make recommendations 'regarding the guidance and instructions which the Council might usefully give to the Palestine Commission with a view to implementing the resolution of the General Assembly'. In other words, the Council made no commitment even to implement the partition plan, let alone to undertake enforcement measures for this purpose.

Two weeks later, on 19 March, the permanent members issued their report. This had been endorsed by the United States, France and China, with only small reservations from the Soviet Union. Britain, at her own wish, had not participated in the consultations (presumably to demonstrate that she would take no responsibility for enforcement), but she provided factual information. The report was equivocal. It stated that consultation with the parties showed that the partition plan could not be implemented peacefully under present conditions (a statement which the Soviet Union and the Jewish Agency strongly contested). It recommended that the Council should declare that it was none the less 'determined not to permit the existence of a threat to international peace in Palestine'. It would 'act by all means available to it to bring about the immediate cessation of violence and the restoration of peace and order in Palestine'. But it gave no indication at all of how it would secure these admirable ends. And it manifestly refused to make any commitment to the use of force to implement the partition plan, as the Commission had demanded.

So the position was that the Assembly had adopted a plan for Palestine that was totally unacceptable to a majority of its inhabitants. Britain had refused to enforce the implementation of the plan. So now had the Security Council. Yet the level of violence in the territory became worse day by day.

At this point there occurred a sudden, totally unexpected *volte-face* in US policy. While the report of the permanent members was being discussed, the US delegate suddenly proposed the abandonment of the whole partition plan, at least for the moment. This abrupt change of mind was no doubt caused by the realisation that an attempt to impose a solution which, though it might be acceptable to a majority in the UN, was totally unacceptable to a majority of the people mainly concerned could well lead to prolonged and bitter violence. It could even be the cause of an immediate attack on the Jewish state from its Arab neighbours, and so to the destruction of the Jewish community in Palestine. Alternatively, the Jewish state would be established only by force; and this could cause widespread resentment among Arab states, expecially against the United States, with possible damage to US commercial and strategic interests. The US delegate, Warren Austin, thus called now instead for a UN trusteeship over Palestine, to be exercised by the Trusteeship Council. This might allow further negotiations in which the parties could reach agreement on the future of Palestine. President Truman, in a statement justifying this change of policy, declared that it was not a substitute for partition but an effort to fill the vacuum that would shortly be caused by the termination of the mandate.

If proposed the previous autumn this idea might have had something to be said for it (though the problem of enforcement would still have arisen). At this late stage, when independence for the two proposed states was already imminent, it was a somewhat extraordinary proposition. Whatever chance there might have been of successful negotiation between the parties before the UN had committed itself to any particular solution, they were non-existent at this stage, when the Jewish demand for a national state had already been officially endorsed by the UN Assembly and was now on the point of realisation. It was inconceivable that Jewish representatives would now have been prepared to renounce that aim in order to seek an agreement with the Arabs for some lesser form of autonomy. Nor did the new US trusteeship plan offer any solution to the essential problem which had caused the Security Council to meet: what provisions should be made for maintaining law and order in Palestine before independence was granted? There had been no apparent consultation with the British, the power whose co-operation would be most essential in implementing the move, still less with the two Palestinian communities concerned, before the plan was announced. US policy, from having sought to promote the partition solution with almost indecent speed the previous year, now, at the last moment, when that plan was almost realised, suddenly reversed itself and sought to postpone independence indefinitely.

The new United States proposal was none the less supported by China, and, with modifications, by France. It was strongly attacked by the Soviet Union (in whose eyes UN trusteeship meant, effectively, United States trusteeship) as a violation of the Assembly resolution, designed to promote United States strategic and political interests. And it was, not surprisingly, angrily denounced by the Jewish Agency as a 'shocking reversal of United States policy'.

The United States proposed two resolutions in the Security Council. One called for a truce in Palestine, and invited the Jewish Agency and the Arab Higher Committee to confer with the Council on this question. The other called for another special session of the Assembly, to reconsider the whole Palestinian situation, including the new United States trusteeship proposal. If there was to be a change of plan it was logical to recall the Assembly which had adopted the earlier partition proposal. And this would, moreover, remove the possibility of a Soviet veto.

The two resolutions were both passed, by large majorities, on 30 March, with only the Soviet Union and Britain abstaining. In Palestine the truce call was broadcast by the

British High Commission. The president of the Security Council called a meeting with representatives of the Jewish Agency and the Arab Higher Committee in New York to discuss how to restore peace in Palestine. But these talks broke down within a day. Neither side would modify its position on the merits of partition, nor discuss peace independently of politics. Meanwhile the security situation in Palestine deteriorated further, with both sides jockeying for positions of power by the time the mandate ended on 15 May.

On 17 April the Security Council met again and reaffirmed its call for a truce, calling on the Jewish Agency to suspend its violence and sabotage; on the Arabs to cease bringing armed bands and fighting personnel into Palestine; and on both parties to stop the import of weapons and raw materials, to help Britain maintain law and order, and to suspend all political activity which might prejudice the rights of either community until the Special Assembly had taken a decision.

THE SECOND SPECIAL ASSEMBLY ON PALESTINE

The Special Assembly met on 16 April. By this time, with the British to withdraw in less than a month, the stage was being set for all-out war in the area. Between January and April inter-communal fighting had steadily intensified. The Jewish Agency and the Jewish National Council had already, in January, agreed on the formation of a provisional government which would take power in the proposed Jewish state as soon as the mandate was ended. Soon afterwards it was announced that registration had been completed for the recruitment of 15,000 Jewish men and women for full-time military service. Arms were being bought from abroad. On the Arab side, bands of guerrillas had increasingly infiltrated from neighbouring countries. As the end of the mandate approached, neighbouring Arab states threatened military intervention if partition went ahead. In April, Arab governments, under the leadership of King Abdullah of Transjordan, announced plans for military action in Palestine, to 'maintain the Arab character of Palestine', when the mandate expired. The Arab League announced that it would accept the idea of trusteeship in Palestine for a few months, but only as a prelude to independence for a united Palestine.

In the Special Assembly, the United States once more presented its proposals for a period of UN trusteeship. This would be for an indefinite time, but would end as soon as Arabs and Jews agreed on the future government of their country. The UN Trusteeship Council would appoint a governor-general, responsible to the Council, to head a government that would eventually include a cabinet and a democratically elected legislature. Meanwhile the governor-general would legislate by decree. The government which he finally established would take over responsibility for maintaining law and order through locally recruited police and a volunteer UN force: and he could if necessary call on certain member states to assist him in maintaining law and order. The trusteeship agreement would include provisions governing immigration, the sale of land, and the protection of the holy places. The United States would if necessary provide police forces to help implement the plan.

Most governments accepted that, with the mandate due to end in a month, it was now far too late for any such plan. The proposal was thus not warmly received in the Assembly. The representative of the Jewish Agency denied that it had yet been proved that partition could not be implemented peacefully: the Security Council had merely capitulated before Arab threats of violence. The representative of the Arab Higher Committee said that the Arabs of Palestine would accept a temporary arrangement for Palestine of the type proposed, on the clear understanding that this would lead to a united independent Palestine: otherwise they would continue to defend their land, by force, if necessary, and seek to establish an independent Palestinian government in accordance with the mandate and the Covenant of the League. The British representative pointed out that his government had always warned of the difficulties in implementing partition. It would, as before, co-operate in any new policy which the Assembly decided upon, but it could not share its authority so long as British responsibility remained, nor could it rescind its decision to withdraw. The Soviet Union, Australia, New Zealand and a number of Latin American countries declared that the UN was already committed to the partition plan, which was the fairest solution of the Palestine problem and should not now be abandoned. No more force would be needed to implement partition than would be needed to implement the trusteeship proposal now being put forward by the United States.

The Assembly was more willing to take emergency action to save Jerusalem and the holy places. France, following a long national tradition, with Sweden, expressed special concern for the protection of these places. A resolution was passed calling on the Trusteeship Council to take the necessary action to protect Jerusalem by taking it under international trusteeship. On 27 April the Trusteeship Council accordingly met to consider how this should be achieved. France proposed that an international police force of 1000 volunteers should be established and sent to Jerusalem to protect the holy places. Britain pointed out that, given the strategic importance of Jerusalem and the size of the local Jewish and Arab forces, a force of this size would be far too small to have any effect.

The president of the Trusteeship Council secured the agreement of the Jewish Agency and the Higher Arab Committee to recommend to their communities a truce in Old Jerusalem and an agreement to respect the holy places. Subsequently Britain asked for an extension of this truce to the whole Jerusalem area and proposed the appointment of a neutral municipal commissioner for Jerusalem, who should be chosen in agreement with both Jews and Arabs to supervise the truce. This too was agreed in principle both by the Council and by the representatives of the Jewish Agency and the Arab Higher Committee in New York. Eventually Harold Evans, a prominent United States Quaker, was appointed with the agreement of the two communities to fill the post. As a result of these moves the ceasefire in the Jerusalem area was in practice fairly well observed. Though fighting in other parts of Palestine became increasingly intense, and a Jewish force captured Jaffa on 28 April, the ceasefire in Jerusalem was maintained reasonably effectively until the end of the mandate. At least in this limited area the UN could point to some achievement.

The Security Council was meanwhile becoming concerned at the failure of its earlier general ceasefire call. On 23 April it met again and set up a Truce Commission for Palestine, consisting of the United States, French, and Belgian consuls, under the chairmanship of the first.[3] This was to try to bring about a ceasefire between the parties and act as an umpire in case of dispute. Efforts to achieve a political settlement of the affair were now almost abandoned. Activity from now on was concentrated on at least mitigating the worse excesses of the fighting that resulted.

The Special Assembly none the less continued to meet during the final three weeks of the mandate. The discussion was desultory, confused and entirely without effect. The Assembly made no decision either to reaffirm, to suspend or to rescind its partition plan. Nor did it adopt the trusteeship proposal suggested by the United States. It appointed a sub-committee to consider (only ten days before the mandate was to end) a 'future regime for Palestine'. But a week later it realised the futility of this exercise and concentrated on more immediate measures. It began to be accepted, as in the Council, that little could now be done to influence the political future of Palestine. Indeed, it seemed to be widely accepted that this could now be resolved only through military conflict between the parties. Discussion therefore became concentrated on steps to mitigate the scale of this conflict.

Much of the debate was focussed on an elaborate and totally impractical scheme, supported by both France and the United States, to place Jerusalem under UN trusteeship and administration. A UN commissioner was to be appointed (in addition to the Municipal Commissioner and the Truce Commission already set up there) who would be empowered to take over the government of Jerusalem, with full powers of 'administration, legislation and jurisdiction', to secure the protection of the holy places and to maintain law and order. Little was said about the physical means by which these admirable aims were to be achieved. The commissioner should somehow set up a police force of undisclosed composition, and could organise volunteer forces from among the inhabitants of Jerusalem, to provide for local defence and to 'assist in the maintenance of law and order': a somewhat forlorn proposal when most of those inhabitants were already engaged in fighting one another. During the final days before 15 May there was a wild rush to get this hairbrained scheme agreed before the mandate came to an end (after which the

UN would have no legal powers to pass such a plan). The final Assembly meeting took place only an hour before the deadline. According to most people's watches, the final vote in fact came a few minutes after the mandate had ended, and therefore after the Assembly's authority was exhausted. This, however, was not of fatal consequence, since, although the proposal received a small majority (20–15, with 19 abstentions), the president announced that, since the question was an important one and had not received a two-thirds majority, the resolution was lost.

On the same day, 15 May, the Special Assembly did agree to a proposal to appoint a UN mediator for Palestine, who was to arrange for the operation of essential common services, secure the protection of the holy places, and promote a 'peaceful adjustment of the future situation' in Palestine – still a somewhat tall order for even the most skilful mediator.

By this time widespread fighting had broken out all over Palestine. Already at 10 a.m. on the day before, 14 May, the independence of the state of Israel had been declared and was immediately recognised by the Soviet Union and the United States. On 15 May, Arab armies from neighbouring states entered the new state from the south, east and north. Arab governments announced their intention of 'maintaining law and order' or 'preserving the Arab character of Palestine'. One thing was certain: whatever chance the UN had ever had of determining the political future of Palestine had now gone for ever.

CONCLUSIONS

The failure of the UN to exercise any worthwhile influence on the ultimate destiny of Palestine is a supreme example of its characteristic failing at this time: its determination to resolve problems by counting heads and voting victories, rather than by any serious effort at conciliation and compromise between the parties mainly concerned. Just as on cold-war issues a majority of members, led by the United States, felt that the main role of the UN was to pass majority judgements on the merits of such issues (so demonstrating overwhelming support for Western positions), so on this issue a majority, again led by the United States, felt that the future of this territory, for which international responsibility was generally recognised, should be simply determined according to the majority views of the member states, however remote their own concern or knowledge of the area (and so, in this case too, to endorse and support the solution supported by the United States). Ironically enough, this was precisely the method which was later to be so often denounced and decried by Israel after that state came into being. Certainly the record of the UN's actions in this case hardly provided a high recommendation for that procedure as a means for securing peaceful settlement.

Because it was from the start intent on that procedure, the UN never made any serious attempt to explore the possibilities of a compromise middle course between those favoured by the two main interested parties. Nor did it at any point even seriously promote negotiations between those parties. From the beginning it was intent on discovering some 'ideal' solution (which turned out to be close to the one favoured by the Jewish side), which it then determined to impose on both parties.

Even the procedures employed by the UN worked in this direction. They all the time implied a *choice* between two rival solutions, rather than any attempt to discuss or attempt a compromise between them. The appointment of the Special Committee on Palestine, most of whose members were firmly committed to one side or the other, the decision of this to produce majority and minority reports each favouring a different side, rather than to seek generally agreed recommendations, the decision of the subsequent Special Assembly to eatablish separate sub-committees to refine the two rival viewpoints rather than to reconcile them, to promote negotiations or to discuss meeting-points – all had the effect of compelling the Assembly as a whole to reach a simple choice between two courses, rather than to seek to find an acceptable middle way. The effect was that the losers, the Arabs, inevitably had the sense of having a solution imposed on them against their will, rather than of having been given a real chance of influencing the outcome. A compromise would admittedly have been difficult, if not impossible, to achieve, given the attitude of both parties at the time. But at the very least the attempt should have been made; and it should have been the UN's chief role to make that attempt.

When the issue first came to the UN in the spring of 1947, the majority of members probably had little idea what solution might be possible in Palestine. For a time there were probably a number who felt that the establishment of a single binational independent state in which the two communities could live peacefully together was the optimum outcome. But to the Jewish Agency, and to those states which strongly supported the Jewish cause, including the United States and the Soviet Union, the only acceptable settlement was one which would produce a Jewish state in control of its own immigration policy: in other words, partition. This solution also appealed to many other governments, especially in Europe and Latin America, partly because of the difficulty of creating a viable state including both the two warring peoples, but above all because it could help to atone for the unimaginable wrong done to the Jews over the previous decade in Germany, and, less dramatically, over the previous millennium in Europe as a whole. To the Arabs, this solution, however convenient to the consciences of Europe and the Western world, represented the alienation of a primarily Arab land to suit the interests of a Western people who for a thousand years had had little contact with the region, and of their previous oppressors in Europe. The only logical aim for Palestine, in their eyes, was the same as for any other non-self-governing territory: independence for the entire area under majority rule. Thus the only point for discussion was the date of independence, the type of government to be established, and perhaps the arrangements to be made for the protection of minority rights.

In all its discussions in the year between April 1947 and early May 1948, the UN never seriously addressed itself to the ways in which these two alternative views could be reconciled. There was no deep-going discussion of the type of federal stature that might have combined effective autonomy for the Jewish population with some common institutions at the centre; or of an immigration policy that could have provided a continuing hope for Jews abroad without a continuing fear among the Arab population in Palestine. Such a plan would have been accepted by either side only if each had been convinced that it could not secure its optimum aim: partition or a unitary state, respectively. But at least a peace-making organisation might have been expected to explore the possibilities. The result could scarcely have been greater conflict and bloodshed than has been witnessed in the area over the subsequent thirty years.

Instead a decision was made to impose upon the one community a course favoured by the other. The decision was reached by governments whose own knowledge of the area and its problems was in many cases minimal. And, though the final vote in favour of partition was fairly decisive, it was obtained only by intensive lobbying and arm-twisting. Moreover, it was put through against the outright opposition of many of the countries most closely concerned (those of the Middle East), as well as of the majority in the territory itself.

The error of devising an imposed solution was compounded by the failure to create the means of imposing it. Even if a decision in favour of partition was ultimately inevitable, this should have immediately entailed consideration of how it was to be put into effect. Precisely because it was a solution totally rejected by one of the two communities, in the final resort it could be implemented only by force. Since Britain from the start made clear her reluctance to continue to bear the opprobrium and military costs of administering the area, and her refusal to implement a policy unacceptable to one of the parties, it should have been clear from the beginning that some alternative security force would be needed. The Assembly did in its initial resolution demand that the Security Council should be called on if there were a 'threat to international peace and security'. But it failed at that time to consult the Security Council on its views on the matter; and in any case never seriously considered the *internal* security problem involved. When the Security Council did consider the matter in March of the following year, it was unwilling to offer the force requested. By this time, in any case, with the parties jockeying for position, it was probably already too late to interpose any effective security force. Yet without such a force the whole concept of creating a transitional authority for the area under the Palestine Commission, as the Assembly had demanded, was a wholly unrealistic one. Still more so was the belated United States idea of a UN trusteeship for the area, to be imposed against the will of both parties, and again without any clearly defined security arrangements.

Another oddity of the UN's handling of the matter was the extraordinary dispersal of authority within the organisation. The Assembly, the Security Council and the Trusteeship Council and various committees of each were all involved in different aspects at different times. There was never any effective consulation between them. The Security Council and the Assembly made different arrangements for a truce within two or three weeks of each other (and the Security Council later added a mediator over and above). The Security Council was unwilling to implement the solution favoured by the Assembly. The Assembly then turned down the solution favoured by some in the Security Council and recalled the Trusteeship Council into action. This extraordinary division of responsibility certainly did not help the UN in making an effective response.

Many would no doubt lay part of the blame for the UN's ineffectiveness at the door of Britain, which adopted throughout a wholly ambivalent attitude to the UN's role. On the one hand she asked the UN for its considered advice on the matter. On the other, when the advice was given she refused to implement it. She gave no clear idea of her own favoured course; yet gave no co-operation in implementing that favoured by the UN. But this was not perhaps such a total contradiction as it appeared. Since Palestine was a mandated territory, there was some point in seeking an international view on its future. But, since she had made clear from the start that she would not implement a solution totally unacceptable to one of the communities, since the Assembly's resolution was, anyway, only a recommendation, and since Britain had far greater knowledge of Palestine than any other UN member and the main responsibility there, she was entitled to make her own judgement of the solution that was finally offered. In effect she recognised, six months before the United States and others were to recognise, that the partition plan could not be put into effect by peaceful means, and therefore refused to be responsible for implementing it. If she is to be blamed, it is rather for failing to reach any clear view of her own as to what the final settlement in Palestine should be and for her unconstructive attitude to most subsequent UN discussion of the matter. The effect of this attitude of non-co-operation was that, in the eyes of the Jews, the partition plan, which had received international endorsement but was not to be fulfilled by the mandatory power, might need to be fulfilled by force; while in the eyes of the Arabs it might have to be prevented by force. Both the UN and Britain must thus share responsibility for creating a situation in which the parties themselves finally came to the conclusion that the future of the territory could only be resolved by force of arms.

The entire episode was therefore one of the least glorious in the UN's history. And it was one which was to be the prelude to successive rounds of conflict in the area in the years to come. The UN cannot take all the blame for the violence which was to follow. But it must be blamed for not making more intensive efforts to seek the kind of mutually acceptable solution which could alone (if anything could) have prevented conflict occurring in the first place; and for not providing the security arrangements which alone were likely to stop it erupting into open warfare when agreement proved impossible.

11 Round One in the Middle East: the Arab–Israeli War of 1948

For weeks before the British mandate in Palestine came to an end, sporadic fighting had occurred. At the beginning of May the Palestine Truce Commission had informed the Security Council that the security situation was worsening daily. During the next fortnight fighting by organised units became more frequent. Regular forces from Syria and Lebanon entered Palestine to assist the local Arabs. And on 15–16 May, as the mandate came to an end, the governments of Egypt and Transjordan informed the UN that their forces were entering Palestine to 'maintain security and order' and to 'protect the unarmed Arab population': in effect to make war on the newly declared state.

Until the very day before the mandate came to an end, the Special Assembly had still been devoting itself to securing a *long-term* settlement of the Palestine problem. With a questionable sense of priorities it had devoted itself above all else to the question of internationalising Jerusalem. Only just before the deadline, as large-scale fighting increased, did it turn its attention to the more immediate, but far more urgent, object of securing a truce (a question on which the Security Council had appeared equally indifferent).

It entrusted this task primarily to the Truce Commission, which had been first set up on 23 April. The job of securing a political settlement, under the terms of its resolution of 14 May, it placed in the hands of the mediator it had then appointed. In the original resolution, no individual was named for this task. But within a few days, a committee of permanent members, to whom the task of choosing the mediator had been delegated, announced the appointment of

Count Bernadotte, president of the Swedish Red Cross.

With that the Assembly dispersed. For three days the Security Council remained totally inactive, while the fighting intensified. Various attempts by the Secretary-General to stimulate it to action had no effect. Lie (who was a strong supporter of the new state) regarded the attack by the Arab armies on Israel as the most serious act of aggression the organisation had yet had to confront. He strongly urged on the US and British governments the need for a prompt and firm UN response. And he addressed a personal letter to all the permanent members, demanding that the UN should act quickly.

Despite this it was only on 18–19 May that the Security Council finally met to consider the fighting. The United States then proposed a resolution, under Chapter VII of the Charter, ordering a ceasefire within thirty-six hours – a demand which would have been mandatory. This was not accepted. The Council agreed only to her proposal that it should send a questionnaire to the Arab governments, the Arab Higher Committee and the 'Jewish authorities in Palestine' asking how far their forces were involved in the fighting, the areas they controlled, and so on. Nothing else was to be done till the answers to this were received.

This was an extraordinarily long-winded procedure, and the replies inevitably took several days to come in. When they did arrive, they contained more propaganda than fact. Each party tried to show that it controlled large areas of Palestine, and was attempting to hold them against violent incursions by the enemy. The information made no significant difference to the action the Council took. But at least intense discussion now began about the terms of a ceasefire. The Council eventually adopted a British amendment to the resolution first proposed by the United States. This avoided invoking Chapter VII, but 'called on' the authorities concerned to implement a ceasefire within thirty-six hours.

This was in effect rejected by the Arabs, who demanded various conditions for accepting it. The Soviet Union then proposed another resolution, again invoking Chapter VII and 'ordering' a ceasefire. But this did not secure sufficient votes to carry. Meanwhile the fighting continued as intensely as ever, with Israel getting rather the better of it. Eventually, on

29 May, the Council adopted a stronger resolution, proposed by Britain, calling for a four-week ceasefire. The mediator and the Truce Commission were to supervise its implementation with the aid of a team of observers. During the period of the truce no new war material or fighting personnel were to be introduced into the area. If either party rejected the resolution or violated it, the Council would consider bringing the sanctions of Chapter VII into play.

By this time it had become clear that neither side could be sure of securing its aims by force. The Arab armies had not succeeded in crushing the new state, which had indeed slightly extended its original borders. But it was also probable that, if new and stronger Arab forces were now brought to the front, the Jewish state would have great difficulty in ensuring its survival. Both sides therefore had different reasons for accepting the ceasefire, and within a few days each did so. Acceptance by the Arab governments was said to be on the understanding that this was a means towards achieving a 'just solution' of the Palestinian problem; a solution that would ensure the political unity of Palestine and respect for the will of the majority there. However, the president of the Council said that the Council interpreted all replies as an unconditional acceptance of the resolution. For the first time the UN had functioned exactly as intended: in a conflict situation it had called for a ceasefire, which had been accepted.

The mediator proceeded to organise a team of observers, consisting of American, Belgian, French and Swedish officers, to supervise the truce, with headquarters in Haifa. The Soviet Union challenged these appointments. She proposed that the nationality of the observers should not be left to the choice of the mediator, but that they should be drawn from all member-states of the Council (in other words, should include observers from the Soviet Union). This proposal was, however, defeated in the Council. In practice the observers were entirely from Western countries. The mediator proceeded to try to negotiate with the parties the arrangements for the implementation of the ceasefire. Eventually he had to dictate himself the terms of the truce; and he named 11 June as the day it should come into effect. On that day fighting ceased.

During the truce period there were attempts at securing a more long-term settlement. The UN mediator put forward a plan for a federal state, including the whole of the original mandate area. This would consist of two parts, one Jewish and one Arab, with common policies for development and co-ordinated foreign and defence policies. The borders of the two zones would be negotiated with the help of the mediator. These proposals were rapidly rejected by both Arabs and Jews. They were regarded as particularly unacceptable in Israel. Both sides began to hope they could get better terms by resuming the fighting. And in spite of the efforts of the mediator and the Council, attempts to extend the ceasefire after a month had elapsed proved unsuccessful.

The Arabs believed that their position had been weakened by the ceasefire, which had enabled the Jewish forces to rearm and redeploy in relative security. They thus wished to try once more to secure their ends in Palestine by force of arms. On 12 July, shortly after the ceasefire ended, fighting broke out again. The Israelis, who had undertaken feverish military preparations in the intervals, immediately captured Nazareth, Lydd and Ramleh, and other strategic areas. The Arab governments once again vowed the total destruction of Israel.

Again the Security Council met to try and restore peace. The Soviet Union and the United States joined this time in demanding strong action to stop the fighting, and to ensure the continued survival of the young state of Israel. Reservations to the use of Chapter VII were now everywhere abandoned. On 15 July a new resolution was passed stating unequivocally that the situation in Palestine constituted a 'threat to the peace' within the meaning of Article 39 of the Charter, 'ordering' a ceasefire, and declaring that any failure to comply with this call would demonstrate the existence of a 'breach of the peace', which might require action under Chapter VII.

The more peremptory tone of this resolution secured an even more prompt response than before. Israel, having already achieved substantial territorial gains, announced her acceptance the following day. The Arabs accepted a ceasefire for Jerusalem on 17 July; and on the next day, with evident reluctance, they announced that because of the threat of sanctions they too would accept the general ceasefire.

This time the truce was even less effectively observed than before. There was sporadic fighting everywhere. By the middle of August there were open hostilities, especially in the Latrun sector (where Arab guerrillas destroyed the water supply) and in Jerusalem. Much of the activity was now by 'irregulars', by snipers, night raids and bomb attacks, rather than by the regular armed forces on either side. The Israeli Government gave notice that, unless the truce was better observed, they might abrogate the agreement. On 18 August the mediator himself asked the Council to meet to consider the serious situation that had arisen because of constant violations of the ceasefire. On 19 August the Council met again. It now passed a new US resolution declaring that each party had the obligation to ensure respect for the ceasefire by all individuals and groups in its own territory, whether regular or irregular, and that neither side should be allowed to gain any military or political advantage through violation of the truce. Again for a period there was some improvement; but sporadic raids and outbreaks of violence continued to take place.

On 17 September, Count Bernadotte, the mediator, while travelling in a part of Jerusalem under Jewish control, was shot and killed, together with Colonel Serot, a senior French officer of the UN observer force.[1] A number of Jewish extremist organisations and individuals had been intensely critical of the role of the UN mediator, especially of the proposals he had made three months earlier for a bizonal Palestine; and it seems probable that the assassin came from one of these groups. The Israeli authorities instituted an immediate investigation. But, though the leader of one organisation suspected of responsibility was arrested, he was later released. The assassin was never found and no charge was ever brought.

The event shocked the world. In the UN itself it aroused a new awareness of the explosive nature of the situation in Palestine and a determination that the organisation should continue to try to seek a long-term settlement. Ralph Bunche, previously head of the UN team working with Bernadotte, was appointed 'acting' mediator, and in practice, though retaining that title, assumed all of his functions. General Lindstrom, the Swedish officer who had been chief-of-staff of the Truce Supervisory Organisation (UNTSO), now established, resigned at the same time and was succeeded by

General Riley of the US Marines: thus once again the mediator and the chief military officer on the spot were of the same nationality.

The new mediator, however, had no better success than his predecessor in securing a more general observance of the truce: still less in making progress towards a peace settlement. At the end of September he complained to the Security Council of the difficulties being placed by both parties in the way of the UNTSO. On 19 October, as a result, the Security Council passed another resolution calling on both sides for better observance of the truce.

But in the middle of October there was a new and much more serious outbreak of fighting. One of the complexities of the previous situation, and the cause of many armed incidents, was that part of the Egyptian army had penetrated into southern Palestine, leaving in their rear Jewish settlements which thus became virtually cut off from the rest of Israel. Attempts to supply these settlements from Israel, and corresponding efforts to prevent this by Egypt, led to a series of clashes. Finally the Israeli authorities determined on a military action designed not only to relieve the settlements but also to occupy much of the Negev to the south, and so to secure access for Israel to the Gulf of Aqaba.

Bunche made an immediate appeal for a ceasefire. This was accepted by Egypt. Israel, however, which now had the initiative, demanded negotiations with Egypt (direct negotiations became then, as for the next twenty-five years, one of the principal objects of Israeli policy). On 19 October the Security Council passed a resolution calling for an immediate ceasefire, after which there should be negotiations. These would be 'on the basis of' a withdrawal of forces to the positions occupied before the recent fighting, acceptance of the proposals of the UNTSO concerning the supply of Jewish settlements, and an agreement to negotiate on certain specific questions affecting the Negev so as to prevent the recurrence of similar attacks in the future. This was a highly ambiguous formula, interpreted by some (the Arabs) to mean that the three conditions should *precede* negotiation, and by others (the Israelis) that the negotiations were to *cover* such questions.

22 October was subsequently given as the date for the ceasefire to become operative. On 26 October, however, the

Council was called together again. Although there had been agreement on the question of convoys to the settlements, there had been no withdrawal of forces, nor any effective ceasefire. The Israeli representative stated categorically that in Israel's view the main aim of the previous resolution had been to ensure that outbreaks of fighting in the area were not renewed, and a simple return to the *status quo ante* could not secure this. The acting mediator reported on 28 October that Israel had made a similar communication to him. He suggested that the time had come when the Council should assert itself and make clear that resort to force would not be tolerated.

Britain and China proposed that the Council should set up a committee to consider the use of sanctions under Chapter VII of the Charter, as the previous resolution had threatened, to ensure compliance with the Council's resolutions and with the orders of the acting mediator. The Council took several days to consider the exact form that such a resolution should take. Eventually, on 4 November, it simply called on the parties to withdraw any forces which had advanced beyond the positions of 14 October, and to establish, through direct negotiations or through intermediaries, permanent truce lines and demilitarised zones, failing which these were to be established by the acting mediator. It also, however, set up a committee to study the use of sanctions in the case of non-compliance, as Britain and China had proposed.

This now made clear that a withdrawal was to precede the negotiations. That interpretation was, however, contested by Israel. In any case, the resolution failed to have much effect. Israeli forces did not withdraw and the situation on the ground remained disturbed.

Bunche now began to become convinced that only an overall settlement of all outstanding issues would succeed in restoring peace. This might involve a substantial withdrawal of forces and the creation of broad demilitarised zones. On 9 November he reported this at two private meetings of the Council (one of the rare occasions till recently that private meetings of the Council have taken place). The Soviet Union, still Israel's strongest supporter, demanded that such negotiations should be direct, and not merely through the acting mediator (the opposite of the position she was to adopt twenty years later), and that they should be aimed at a final peace rather than an armistice only.

Most other members were less ambitious in what they thought could be achieved. On 16 November, therefore, the Council adopted a resolution proposed by Canada, Belgium and France which decided that, to facilitate the transition to permanent peace, an armistice should be established in all sectors in Palestine. It called on the parties to agree, either through direct negotiations or through the acting mediator, the delineation of the armistice lines and the withdrawal and reduction of their forces so as to ensure the maintenance of the armistice. Though it was said in the preamble to the resolution that it was 'without prejudice to the implementation' of the 4 November resolution calling for withdrawal, in effect it clearly replaced it. It thus let Israel completely off the hook so far as withdrawal from the area of the Negev she had occupied was concerned.

During December, indeed, Israeli forces advanced further, and now succeeded in cutting off an Egyptian division altogether at Al Saluja. The acting mediator reported to the Council that he was still unable to supervise the truce in the Negev, because the Israelis refused to allow observers access to the area. He expressed the view that the 'intransigent attitude assumed by the Israeli authorities in the situation at Al Saluja is a major factor in preventing progress towards implementation of the resolution of the Security Council of November 16'. Accordingly on 29 December the Council passed yet another resolution, calling for implementation of the call of 4 November (that is, for a withdrawal to the positions occupied before 14 October) without further delay, and instructing the committee on sanctions set up earlier to consider whether both resolutions had been complied with.

The Council thus showed considerable ambivalence during this period: it never quite made up its mind whether or not Israeli withdrawal should precede negotiations (an ambivalence repeated, more deliberately, nearly twenty years later after the Six Days War). Meanwhile the Assembly had now got into the act once more (thus continuing the long history of divided responsibility on this question). At least the Assembly was able to raise its eyes towards the more long-term issues. On 11 December, amid much other ineffectual discussion of 'the Palestine question' (as it was still formally called), it set up a conciliation commission, to try to bring about not merely an armistice, but a final settlement of the issues between Arabs and Jews in the Middle East.

THE ARMISTICE NEGOTIATIONS

The new commission, however, was for long unable to play any effective role. Thus it was the acting mediator who continued to hold the centre of the stage. On 6 January, Bunche was able to report that the governments of Egypt and Israel had both accepted his proposal for a ceasefire and for direct negotiations, under UN chairmanship, as well as for implementation of both the November resolutions. By its specific reference to the 4 November resolution, this seemed to imply that the negotiations would lead to a withdrawal of Israeli forces from the Negev and a return to the pre-14 October lines, as the Council had demanded. It seemed therefore to be a kind of deal: a promise to withdraw in return for direct negotiations on a final settlement.

In fact, however, Israel had no intension of making any such withdrawal. In her eyes the negotiations would simply be to establish an armistice, and to secure a ceasefire on the present lines. By the Negev operation in November, Israel had created facts which she had no intention of uncreating. Moreover, in the negotiations Egypt did not seriously contest this point. In practice the negotiations were merely for an armistice on the existing ceasefire lines, and the question of an Israeli withdrawal was not even seriously pursued.

Negotiations opened in Rhodes on 12 January. Though the agreement had spoken of direct talks, in practice they were only semi-direct: Bunche, as mediator, had to shuttle from one lot of hotel rooms to another to resolve the issues between the two sides (a precedent which became famous, so that twenty years afterwards 'Rhodes-type talks' was the phrase used to describe semi-direct, proximity discussions of this kind). As a result of Bunche's diplomatic skills, and because both sides in fact genuinely desired disengagement, the talks fairly rapidly came to a conclusion. Six weeks later, on 24 February, an armistice agreement was signed.[2] This became the basis for the settlement between the parties for the next seven years.

The parties agreed to obey the Security Council's injunctions for a cessation of military force against each other and it was accepted that the armistice was a step towards 'lasting peace in Palestine'. The Egyptian military forces trapped in the Al Faluja area were to be withdrawn, but Israel was to retain the Negev. A demilitarised zone was to be established around Auja. A mixed armistice commission – consisting of members of the two sides under the head of the UNTSO or one of its senior officers – based in the zone, was to be established to supervise the execution of the agreement. The arrangement was not to prejudice final claims by either side, and no military or political advantage was to be gained under the terms of the armistice.

The evacuation of the trapped Egyptian force was completed by 1 March. Armistice negotiations between Israel and Lebanon began on the same day, and between them too an agreement was signed on 22 March. Agreements with Jordan and Syria followed on 3 April and 20 July. The agreement with Jordan provided for a special committee, with representatives from Israel and Jordan, to safeguard the holy places and (since the fighting had left Jerusalem divided between the two countries) to ensure free movement between the two halves of the city: a provision Jordan later refused to implement. It also provided for the replacement of Iraqi forces in Jordan by Jordanian forces.

Thus some kind of peace in the area seemed to have been restored. As the acting mediator reported, the imposed 'truce' demanded by the Security Council on 15 July had been replaced by general 'armistice', as the Council had requested on 16 November.

On 11 August 1949, the Security Council met to consider the situation in the light of these agreements and the acting mediator's report. One of the main questions to be decided was whether the restrictions on the immigration of men of military age and on the import of military arms, which had been laid down in the original truce arrangement, should now be maintained. Eventually the Council decided to reaffirm the ceasefire 'order' of 15 July, made under the mandatory provisions of Article 40 of the Charter. At the same time it relieved the acting mediator of his duties 'under Security Council resolutions'[3] and confirmed the role of the Mixed Armistice Commission. And it asked the chairman of the UNTSO to make regular reports on the observance of the ceasefire, both to the Council and to the Palestine Conciliation Commission.

THE SEARCH FOR A FINAL SETTLEMENT

So the task of seeking a more permanent settlement was handed over to the Conciliation Commission. This consisted of the United States, France and Turkey. It had set up its headquarters at Government House in Jerusalem, in a zone neutralised by the agreement between Israel and Jordan. It started work on 24 January 1949, while the armistice discussions were still proceeding. Its main objective, to institute direct negotiations between the parties for a permanent peace, had to await the end of those negotiations. But it held discussions with each of the governments of the area during the next month or two. And on 21 March it organised a conference of Arab states at Beirut to hear their views.

Finally, on 27 April, the Commission arranged a meeting between the Arab states and Israel at Lausanne. But Israel's representatives were willing to meet the Arab states only separately, while the Arab states insisted on negotiating as a bloc. The main aim of bringing the two sides together was thus frustrated. But a number of questions were discussed through the mediation of the Commission.

One of the main questions the Commission had been mandated by the Assembly to pursue was the problem of the refugees, mainly Arabs, evicted from their homes during the fighting in the previous year. The General Assembly resolution of 11 December 1948 had resolved that refugees wishing to return to their homes and live at peace with their neighbours should be permitted to do so; 'and that compensation should be paid for the property of those choosing not to return'. The Commission when it was established was asked to 'facilitate the repatriation, resettlement and economic and social rehabilitation of the refugees and the payment of compensation'.[4] The principle that the refugees had a definite right to return to their homes, which this resolution implied, was not accepted by Israel, but in May 1949, at Lausanne, the Commission secured the agreement of Israel and the Arab governments to a protocol declaring that the boundaries for the Arab and Jewish states contained in the General Assembly resolution of 29 November 1947 should be taken as a basis for discussion on the refugee question. Though confused and imprecise (no doubt intentionally), this seemed to suggest that Arabs from the areas defined as Arab in 1947 but now under Israeli rule would qualify as Arab refugees for the purposes of the resolution.

But there was little further progress. The Arab states demanded a settlement on the question of the refugees as a precondition of even discussing other matters. Israel, on the other hand, demanded that the matter should be discussed only in the context of general negotiations for a final settlement. The only point on which there was any agreement was a scheme for the return of refugees separated from their families by the war; and a few thousand refugees were subsequently returned on the basis of this understanding. Israel eventually agreed in principle to accept 100,000 refugees, but this was to include 25,000 who had already returned, as well as any who were repatriated under the separated-families scheme. Against this the Arabs demanded an unconditional commitment by Israel that she would receive back all the refugees from areas then occupied by Israel (though they might have been prepared to negotiate about the timing). The United States urged Israel, it was reported, to accept about 300,000 refugees (as well as to return a part of the Negev), but this was rejected by Israel.

On a territorial settlement too there was an impasse. The Conciliation Commission sent out to all the states concerned a questionnaire on this and other matters in dispute. The Arab states called for the return of the Negev, Galilee and the Latrun salient, as well as the internationalisation of Jerusalem and Jaffa: the total effect would have been to reduce Israel to a third of the area allocated to her under the original UN partition plan. Israel wanted to retain the frontiers established in the armistice agreements, and was firmly opposed to any idea of internationalising Jerusalem. She demanded that the whole question should be discussed again in the forthcoming session of the Assembly (at this time a body still relatively favourable towards Israel). The differences revealed by these answers, both on frontiers and on the refugees, was so great that the Conciliation Commission decided to abandon the Lausanne meetings and issued a warning that, unless the parties showed themselves more conciliatory, it could not organise successful negotiations, as the Assembly had asked. The 1949 Assembly none the less asked the Commission to continue its work. It also discussed yet another plan for the internationalisation of Jerusalem which the Commission had produced. The city would be demilitarised and neutralised. There would be a Jewish zone and an Arab zone with their own local authorities, but with a general council drawn from representatives of the two zones. The plan was, however, rejected by both Israel and Jordan, which declared that they would refuse to implement it (though both agreed to secure the protection of the holy places). The idea of internationalising Jerusalem continued to be discussed for the next two or three assemblies. The 1949 Assembly reaffirmed the aim of internationalising Jerusalem and the surrounding area, and designated the Trusteeship Council as the administering authority. It requested the Trusteeship Council, as it had a year and a half previously, to undertake the preparation of a 'statute' for Jerusalem. The Trusteeship Council proceeded once more to prepare such a statute; but this remained as much of a dead letter as all previous plans proposed for that troubled city. The only visible outcome was that the Commission appointed a UN representative in Jerusalem, who acted for many years as a source of information and advice for the UN on developments in the area.

The Conciliation Commission then tried once more to bring about negotiations for a final settlement. But it had no more success than before. Many of the differences continued to be about procedure. Israel still insisted on direct negotiations with each Arab state separately, while the Arab states were determined to negotiate as a bloc, with the Commission acting as mediator. The Arabs wanted negotiations about the refugee question to be completed before going on to discuss other points, while Israel wanted it considered as one aspect of the general peace settlement. Eventually, on 29 March 1950, the Commission proposed as a compromise the establishment of joint committees meeting under the chairmanship of a representative of the Commission. Each meeting would be attended by those countries concerned with the subject under discussion. The Arab League accepted these proposals (which were somewhat nearer to the Arab point of view), but its secretary-general subsequently said that this was conditional on Israel accepting earlier UN decisions on partition and the internationalisation of Jerusalem. Israel, on the other hand, at first rejected the Commission's proposals, but subsequently changed her mind. On 15 May the Commission interpreted these conflicting answers as opening the way to a conference on the lines it had suggested. On 13 June, however, the Egyptian Government withdrew its delegate to the Commission; and soon afterwards Egypt, Syria and Lebanon all rejected the proposals for joint committees, declaring that they would no longer negotiate with Israel under the auspices of the Commission.

This was believed to be a response to an unexpected initiative at this time by the Western powers. It had now become apparent that the Commission's efforts to secure a final settlement were having little success. The frontiers were still disturbed, Israeli shipping was unable to pass through the Suez Canal, and public Arab hostility to Israel was becoming if anything more intense rather than less. Since it was clear that neither the UNTSO nor any other UN body was likely to be able to preserve the peace of the area in the case of a major outbreak of fighting, the three major Western powers, the United States, Britain and France, decided that some further action, outside the auspices of the UN, was needed to deter further violence and to demonstrate Western concern for the area. On 25 May 1950, they issued a statement which became known as the Tripartite Declaration. In this they declared that they would take joint action to prevent any alteration of the armistice borders by force. They would themselves seek to avoid an arms race in the area, which would add to existing instability, though they would not cut off all arms supplies – for example, where needed for local security needs, or for the 'defence of the area as a whole' (that is, against communism). The announcement was greeted with mixed feelings by both sides in the area. Ben Gurion declared that he did not regard it as binding on Israel, though he welcomed it to the extent that it was designed to increase security and peace. The Arabs denounced it in so far as it seemed to assure to Israel the retention of at least the territory she held at that time. The main defect of the declaration was that the Western powers at no time made clear how they intended to fulfil it, nor did they have adequate forces themselves in the area to do so. Only after 1955, when British policy turned sharply against Egypt, did Britain seek to persuade the United States that the declaration required teeth, to which the United States replied that she preferred acting through the UN: a preference which she was to put into effect in the following year.

The effect was the Arab states lost faith in the Conciliation Commission, since they felt it could not now bring about any revision of Israel's frontiers – guaranteed in this way – in their favour. Further efforts by the Commission in July in Jerusalem to overcome the procedural differences had no success. Increasingly the UN was concerned more with day-to-day violence on the frontier than with any serious hope of securing a long-term settlement. Jordan protested that 500 Arabs had been deprived of their belongings and expelled across the border when Israel occupied the Hebron area (regarded as a traditional holy place by Jews). UN observers reported in June 1950 that there had been a serious deterioration of the situation on Israel's southern borders. Israel was no longer willing to allow Arab farmers, with land partly on her side of the frontier, to harvest their crops there. In September, Egypt charged in the Security Council that 5000 Arabs had been expelled from their homes in Jerusalem, Haifa, Acre and other cities, to make room for Jewish families. General Riley, the chief-of-staff of the UNTSO, confirmed that their investigations showed that, in the Negev area, Arab bedouin had been systematically expelled from their homes and sent across the borders, though Israel claimed that these had only recently returned to the area, in violation of the armistice agreement. Eventually, in November, the United States, Britain and France brought forward a resolution in the Security Council calling on Israel, Egypt and Jordan to abide by the armistice agreements and to use the existing UN machinery in the area to resolve all their disputes. This was passed without contrary votes.

Meanwhile Egypt was preventing the passage of Israeli

ships or goods through the Suez Canal. Egypt justified this on the grounds that she was still in a state of war with Israel (since, though there was an armistice, there was still no final peace treaty). Israel protested strongly about this, in the first place to the UNTSO. The chief-of-staff of the UNTSO, General Riley, reached the conclusion that, though Egypt's action was clearly a 'hostile act', it did not constitute a violation of the armistice agreements, which had contained no specific obligation in this respect. Israel accordingly took the question up in the Security Council. In September 1951 the Council passed a resolution expressly calling on Egypt to cease interference with shipping passing through the Suez Canal. This, however, had no effect on Egypt's actions. And, when another attempt was made in 1954 to repeat the call to her, the resolution was vetoed by the Soviet Union, which by now had come out openly on the side of the Arab states.

In August 1951, the Conciliation Commission made one last despairing effort to reach a settlement. It invited the parties to attend a conference in Paris the following month. The Arab states accepted, so long as Arabs and Israelis were not required to sit at the same table. Israel accepted, so long as the aim of the conference was a final settlement of all outstanding problems. With these questions unresolved, the conference began in Paris on 13 September. The US chairman of the Commission defined the aims of the Conference as to discuss a settlement of the rights of refugees, including repatriation and compensation, to discuss the rights and obligations of the states represented, including the delimitation of frontiers, and finally to secure an agreement to abstain from all hostile acts and to promote peace in the area. The Commission subsequently submitted written proposals to implement this plan, including commitments to live in peace, to accept the return of a specific number of refugees, to pay compensation, to create a free port at Haifa, to create joint arrangements for economic development and so on. But again the discussions got bogged down on the question of priorities. Israel refused to negotiate unless the Arabs accepted a commitment to peace, so ruling out the blockade and interference with shipping, as a preliminary. The Arabs were willing to reaffirm the armistice agreements, but not to acknowledge Israel by entering into a non-aggression pact. They held that a settle-

ment of the refugee question should be the first consideration.
So once again no progress was made. Although the Assembly
once more renewed the Commission's mandate, it was becoming clear that the attitude of the parties was not such as would
allow it to promote any successful negotiations.

The Conciliation Commission remained formally in existence for a number of years longer. But it became increasingly
inactive, and its reports to the Assembly could only record the
continued unwillingness of the parties to implement earlier
Assembly resolutions – still less to come anywhere near an
understanding with each other on the basic points which
divided them.

CONCLUSIONS

The Arab–Israeli war of 1948 was the first major international
conflict the UN had to confront (the episodes in Indonesia,
Greece and elsewhere were too small in scale to merit such a
description). It was thus a challenging test of the UN's capacity
to fulfil its most important functions.

In some respects the UN came out of the test well. It was
slow in its initial response after the Arab governments
announced they were launching their attack on the new state,
on 14 May 1948. But, once the Security Council finally came to
grips with the affair, it immediately secured results. It passed
two resolutions demanding a ceasefire, one of them accompanied by the threat of Chapter VII enforcement. Both were
accepted by all parties within a few days. The UN also
established machinery, in the shape of the UNTSO, for
supervising the ceasefire: machinery that was to remain in
existence for the next thirty years.

More than this, the Security Council and the Assembly in
this case, unlike many others, never lost from sight that their
ultimate aim must be to seek a more lasting settlement. They
thus appointed first a mediator and then a conciliation
commisson, to bring this about. Though the attempt to
establish a final peace ultimately failed in the face of the
intense mutual suspicion between the parties, negotiations for
armistice agreements were successfully put in hand, and were
brought to a successful conclusion. These agreements pro-

vided the basis, insubstantial though they proved, of the settlement between the countries for the succeeding period. Their conclusion represented indeed a triumph for UN diplomacy. It is true that, if it had not been for the trapped Egyptian division, it is by no means sure that Egypt, for one, would have accepted the terms. But the willingness of the Arabs to sign an armistice, on somewhat unfavourable terms (given the Israeli occupation of the Negev), represented in practice a willingness to accept the continued existence of the state of Israel. Certainly the respite which Israel gained in this way gave her the chance to lay the foundations of a state which would never again be so vulnerable to attack from her neighbours as it had been in the first months after its foundation.

But the task of securing a long-term settlement, to make the acceptance of the new state explicit, proved beyond the powers of the UN. In some ways it should have been easier then than at any other time in the next twenty-five years. The Arab governments which ruled in Egypt, Jordan, Syria and Lebanon were probably more moderate in view than most which succeeded them (indeed, Jordan had almost reached such a settlement by private means when her ruler was assassinated). In return for some concessions – a willingness to deal with them as a bloc rather than individually, a readiness to accept in principle the right of the refugees to return (perhaps only over a twenty-year period), together with a willingness to pay generous compensation for those not returning, it is just possible that, at a not unreasonable price, Israel could have secured the recognition and the right to live in peace that she has been seeking ever since. Just possible. But not much more. For against all this was the fact that many in the Arab world still had not adjusted psychologically to the idea of the new state of Westernised settlers of alien culture, whose roots were far away from the region, becoming established in territory formerly occupied by Arabs. The acknowledgement of that state's legitimate existence, which any final settlement would have involved, was perhaps even more difficult in these early days than it was to become later.

The issue thus revealed the difficulty which has consistently faced the UN in confronting such conflicts: it was easier to deal with the *symptoms* of violence than with the disease itself, the long-term causes of conflict. On the former, both parties, for quite different reasons, could be persuaded eventually to accept a truce. On the latter, the difference between their positions and attitudes was so wide that all the UN's efforts at peace-making proved unavailing. Israel would never accept the idea of a united Palestine; she was unwilling to make any territorial concessions; she would not commit herself to receiving more than 100,000 Arab refugees on her soil; and she would discuss even this only in the context of an overall settlement, and with individual governments only. The Arabs would not accept the existence of the new state; they demanded that it should relinquish part of the territory it had occupied; they wanted a total commitment on the refugee issue as a precondition for discussing other matters; and they would deal with Israel only as a bloc, and even then only indirectly. These differences could not be bridged.

Though, therefore, on this occasion the UN did seek to bring about negotiations between the parties, and did tackle the long-term as well as the short-term issues, it still could not succeed in resolving the differences: it could bring the horses to the water – or near it – but could not make them drink. And its failure was to create its most persistent source of conflict over the next thirty years.

12 Trouble Spots in Europe

THE CORFU CHANNEL

Increasingly the cold war, now gathering in intensity, dictated the tone of debate in the UN on many issues, wherever they arose. But the real cockpit of the cold war was inevitably the area where the two great ideological blocs immediately adjoined each other: that is, in Europe. Many of the basic issues in that region – the future of Germany, the type of government to be established in Poland, the peace treaties with the East European states, and so on – never came up in the UN at all. This was partly because it had always been accepted that matters resulting directly from the war were to be discussed among the victorious powers and not within the organisation; and it was partly because there was, anyway, little hope of resolving them within the propaganda-laden, declamatory environment of the UN at this time. But there were a number of peripheral questions, resulting directly or indirectly from the cold war, which were discussed in the organisation during its early years.

The first of these concerned an incident in the Corfu Channel off the coast of Albania. On 22 October 1946 two British destroyers passing through the channel struck mines and were severely damaged. Forty-four British soldiers were killed and forty-two injured, and one of the ships became a total loss. Albania was not then a member of the UN. Britain therefore first approached her direct, asking for an apology and for compensation for the loss of lives and property. The Albanian Government, however, refused to accept any responsibility. Britain therefore, in January 1947, approached the Security Council on the matter.

There was provision in the Charter for the discussion of disputes with non-members. Albania was invited, under these arrangements, to take part in the discussion without a vote.

The discussion was conducted, as the Charter permitted (indeed, encouraged) in the form of a 'dispute', in which each party presented its case and the Council then reached a judgement.

On 18 February the British representative presented the British compliant against Albania, alleging that the mining of these waters, which were a commonly used maritime channel, without warning to other shipping, violated the rules of the Hague Convention of 1907 and was a 'crime against humanity'. The channel had been swept for mines only a few months previously by the British Navy, so that those which struck the ships had clearly been newly laid. The Albanian Government should be censured and should pay compensation for the losses. The Albanian Government claimed that it had not been responsible for laying the mines, did not know who had laid them, and was not responsible for the safety of navigation of ships which sailed in its territorial waters.

The Council decided to set up a small sub-committee, consisting of Australia, Colombia and Poland, to examine the evidence. This found that after the incident a minefield had been found in the area and swept by British naval vessels, though according to the Polish representative this did not prove that the mines which damaged the British vessels were part of the same field. On 25 March, on the basis of this report, the British representative put forward a resolution stating that an unnotified minefield had been laid in the channel with the knowledge of the Albanian Government. This received seven favourable votes from other members, but was vetoed by the Soviet Union and so was not carried (as a 'party to the dispute', Britain did not herself vote – one of the rare occasions when this provision was applied). Britain thereupon asked that the Council should recommend the two parties to take the dispute to the International Court of Justice. A resolution to this effect was carried, and this time the Soviet Union, with Poland, merely abstained.

In the following month Britain filed an application against Albania with the Court. There was some dispute about jurisdiction. Albania agreed to appear before the Court, though not a party to it; but she complained that Britain had not, as she should have done, reached an understanding about the conditions under which the dispute was to be submitted. This objection was rejected by the Court on the grounds that Albania had voluntarily accepted the Court's jurisdiction, so the application did not need to be jointly made. But Britain then voluntarily agreed with Albania on the terms of a joint submission to the Court. The Court was accordingly asked by the two countries to decide, first, whether Albania was responsible under international law for the damage and loss of life resulting from the explosions; and, secondly, whether Britain had violated Albania's sovereignty by entering her waters in the first place, and by subsequently unilaterally clearing the mines from them.

The Court took over a year to consider the matter, during which time it visited the area and listened to expert naval advice, especially on how far the damage to the ships was compatible with the particular mines subsequently found. In April 1949 it delivered its judgement. It found, by 11 votes to 5, that the minefield swept by the British Navy after the incident had been recently laid. Although it could not be proved who had laid the minefield, the fact that Albania, on her own account, had kept a vigilant watch on the strait (which could be easily observed from the Albanian coast) indicated it could scarcely have been laid without her knowledge. This created an obligation on her to notify foreign shipping of the mines, an obligation which she had not observed. The Court therefore found that Albania was responsible under international law for the explosions and loss of life.[1] On the second question the Court decided that, since this was a strait used for international navigation between two parts of the high seas, Britain was under international law free to send warships through even without authorisation, since their passage appeared to have been innocent. But the Court also found that, in sweeping the mines in the following month, Britain had violated Albanian sovereignty and her defence based on the right of self-help or self-protection provided no justification for this action.

The Court had been asked whether there was any duty to pay compensation. It decided that this must involve deciding the amount of compensation, which would require further hearings. Albania claimed that the Court was to decide only *whether* compensation was due, and not how much. But the Court declared that, if it omitted to decide this, an important part of the dispute would remain unsettled. It therefore continued to hear the British claim. And eventually it awarded compensation of £843,947 for damage to the ships and compensation for the loss of life.

Albania refused to accept this judgement or to pay the sums due. Britain attempted to pursue the matter through bilateral channels (though she had no diplomatic relations), but without success. Subsequently, when the International Court heard the dispute concerning the so-called 'Albanian gold', gold taken from Albania by Italy in 1939 and subsequently held in London after Italy's defeat, Britain maintained that a part should be awarded to her in settlement of her Corfu Channel claim. This was turned down by the Court. Albania remained unwilling to pay; and so Britain never got her compensation.

The case was a fairly minor one but it received much publicity at the time. The main thing it proved was that recourse to international arbitration was not a sure way of resolving international disputes. There was no attempt to get the Security Council to consider enforcing the Court's judgement, as the Charter provided for in Article 94 – presumably because the Soviet Union was bound to veto such a proposal. So the first major attempt by the Council to resolve a dispute through international adjudication was a dismal failure. Albania has still not paid the sums awarded.

TRIESTE

The next cold-war issue concerned Trieste. Trieste had come under Italian rule at the end of the First World War, as part of her acquisitions on the Dalmatian coast. At the end of the Second World War the southern part of this area was occupied by Yugoslavia and became known as 'Zone B'. The northern part, including the port, was occupied by Anglo-American forces and became 'Zone A'. Each was, for the moment, administered by the military command of the controlling side, pending a final peace settlement.

In December 1946 the Council of Foreign Ministers (the United States, the Soviet Union, Britain and France) agreed on the terms of a peace treaty with Italy, which included a settlement concerning Trieste. Trieste was in effect to be internationalised. A free territory of Trieste was to be created, which would be the direct responsibility of the UN Security Council and controlled by a governor under its authority. A permanent statute for the territory, a provisional regime to be applied meanwhile, and an instrument governing the operation of the proposed free port of Trieste were also agreed.

This peace treaty governing Italy was due to be signed by 15 January 1947. The foreign ministers therefore asked that the Security Council should approve the proposals for Trieste before that date. When the Council met, the Australian representative expressed considerable doubts about the idea of Security Council supervision of the territory, stating that the obligations proposed for the Council exceeded anything provided for in the Charter. This was contested by the permanent members. And eventually the Council, on 10 January, passed a resolution approving the three documents submitted by the Council of Foreign Ministers on the future of the territory.

But this left to be decided a matter of crucial importance, the appointment of a governor. Since it was believed that the governor would acquire substantial authority in an area whose political and strategic importance was great, this was a decision of considerable significance. In June 1947 Britain asked for the matter to be put on the Security Council's agenda. This was resisted by the Soviet Union, on the grounds that the decision could only be made by the four powers themselves. The item was none the less inscribed, and the Council agreed, for once, to go into private session to consider the matter. No decision was reached, but the Council did set up a sub-committee, consisting of Australia, Colombia and Poland, to consider possible candidates. This presented a report suggesting certain names, which were in turn submitted to the permanent members meeting informally. The permanent members were unable to agree, and Italy and Yugoslavia, the powers most directly concerned, were then asked to try to reach an understanding between them. They too reported failure, though they came up with certain new names. Again, neither the Council, nor the permanent members meeting alone, were able to reach agreement, and the matter was dropped for the moment.

The Western governments began soon after this to have considerable doubts about the feasibility of the proposal to internationalise Trieste. In March–April 1948 they introduced measures bringing about a considerable degree of monetary, economic and commercial integration of Zone A with Italy. The Yugoslav Government accused the Allied Military Command of violating the Italian Peace Treaty, and moving towards a merger between the zone and Italy. It also accused the Anglo-American authorities of encouraging pro-Italian irredentist groups in their zone, and blocking trade between it and Yugoslavia. The United States and Britain declared that the measures they had taken did not violate the Italian Peace Treaty, and were in any case provisional, pending the setting up of the free territory. They countercharged that the Yugoslav Government had not submitted reports to the UN on its administration of its own zone. Britain also accused Yugoslavia of violating essential human rights within its own area. And of course each side accused the other of blocking the appointment of a governor.

By this time the Western governments were being pressed hard by Italy for a reassertion of Italian rights in the area. In March 1948 (before a vital election in Italy) they called for a revision of the Italian Peace Treaty to allow this, though the United States said she would continue to apply the Italian Peace Treaty if no amendments were made. Yugoslavia and the Ukraine then proposed resolutions in the Security Council declaring the agreements on monetary and economic co-operation to be incompatible with the status of the free territory of Trieste, and declaring it was urgently necessary to appoint a governor. But these were defeated.

The question of the appointment of a governor was raised again by the Soviet Union in February 1949. This time she specifically named a candidate, a Swiss national, Colonel Fluckinger, previously Swiss minister in Moscow, who had originally been nominated for the post by Britain. This put the Western powers on the spot, and compelled them to state openly that they no longer regarded the provisions of the Italian Peace Treaty as workable. Yugoslavia, they said, had largely incorporated her own zone into Yugoslavia, and there had been for long no agreement on the appointment of a governor. There was therefore no advantage in the Council's even discussing the question at this stage. And the Soviet proposal was once more defeated through the abstentions of the Western powers. Again on a cold-war issue the West's majority could be used to secure its will, this time without recording a vote at all.

The matter was not discussed again for four years. In October 1953 the United States and Britain announced that they intended to wind up the Allied military government in Zone A, and to hand over the administration to the Italian Government. The Soviet Union immediately raised the question in the Security Council again. She again proposed the appointment of Colonel Fluckinger as governor, and the implementation of the provisions of the Italian Peace Treaty for a free territory of Trieste. The threat of unilateral action by the United States and Britain also brought some response from Yugoslavia (no longer an Eastern-bloc power). It began to be clear to her that the alternative was no longer between the free-territory idea and partition, but between a partition unilaterally affected and one whose terms had been agreed with her. She now agreed, therefore, to take part in intensive diplomatic discussions on the matter.

On 12 March 1954 the Yugoslav ambassador in Washington indicated that, provided there were some adjustment of the border between the two zones, Yugoslavia might accept the sharing of the territory between the two countries. In September of that year, Robert Murphy, the State Department trouble-shooter, paid visits to Yugoslavia and Italy, and early in the following month there were further discussions in London between the United States, Britain, Italy and Yugoslavia. These resulted in the signature of a memorandum of understanding on the future of the territory. Under this the whole idea of a free territory of Trieste under a neutral governor, as laid down in the Italian Peace Treaty, was abandoned. Military forces were to be withdrawn from the two zones, which would be placed under the civilian administration of Italy and Yugoslavia. There would be marginal boundary changes. Italy undertook to maintain the port of Trieste as a free port, and a mixed Yugoslav–Italian commission was to be set up to protect the rights of Yugoslav and Italian ethnic groups in the two areas.

On 5 October the text of this memorandum was transmitted

to the Security Council by the United States, Britain, Italy and Yugoslavia. A few days later, on 12 October, the Soviet Union informed the president of the Council that she had noted the terms of the agreement and, since it would restore normal relations between Italy and Yugoslavia, had 'taken cognisance of it'.

On 17 January 1955, the four governments informed the Security Council that the arrangements provided for in the Memorandum had been carried out. A preliminary demarcation of the boundary between the two zones had been made, including the adjustments already agreed. A boundary commission would demarcate the boundary more accurately and on a permanent basis. The US–UK military government in Zone A had been brought to an end and administration handed over to Italy. On the Yugoslav side the military government of Zone B had also been replaced by a normal civilian administration.

There was no discussion in the Security Council of this report. Trieste was one of the many East–West issues which were resolved outside the ambit of the UN: in discussion among the powers most directly concerned. The Council merely took note of the information it had received, and congratulated itself that this was at least one dispute which it would not need to discuss again.

CZECHOSLOVAKIA

The pro-communist 'coup' in Czechoslovakia in February 1948 was also briefly raised at the UN. The word scarcely describes what really happened. Since 1945 the communists had shared in the government of Czechoslovakia and had occupied, among others, the post of Minister of the Interior. In the most recent elections they had also become the largest single party in the Czech assembly. In February 1948 the communist Minister of the Interior began dismissing pro-Western security officials and promoting instead those favourable to the communists and to the Soviet Union. Non-communist members of the Government strongly protested at this action; and, when their protests were ignored, resigned. President Benes then reformed the government, which was now almost totally dominated by the communists. Jan Masaryk remained as Foreign Minister, and publicly defended the newly formed government. But a week or two later he mysteriously fell to his death, probably through suicide.

The permanent representative of Czechoslovakia at the UN under the previous government, Jan Papanek, wrote to the UN Secretary-General calling for an investigation into the events, on the grounds that there was strong evidence of foreign involvement (principally the fact that the Soviet Deputy Foreign Minister, Zorin, formerly Soviet ambassador to Czechoslovakia, had been in Prague at the time of the developments). Since Papanek was no longer recognised as the representative of the new government, however, he was not recognised as competent to raise the question at the UN. Shortly afterwards the representative of Chile, though not then a member of the Council, asked the Security Council to investigate the matter and circulated Papanek's letter to all members. After considerable discussion, the Security Council agreed to consider the matter and invited Papanek himself to appear. Papanek spoke eloquently about the attempt of the Benes government over the previous three years to retain its independence, about the attempts of the Soviet Union to extend her influence over it and repeated the accusations of foreign involvement in the February events.

It was then proposed by pro-Western powers that a sub-committee be set up to examine the question. There was a prolonged discussion, lasting for three meetings of the Council, on whether or not this proposal was a procedural or a substantive decision. If it had been procedural, it would not have been subject to veto. The Soviet Union was able to quote the formula agreed during the San Francisco Conference (p. 46 above), under which the decision whether or not a question was procedural was itself subject to veto. The president of the Council ruled accordingly. The Western permanent members could, if they had so wished, have prevented this formula from being applied by opposing the president's ruling. But in fact they submitted: the words of the understanding were so clear that they could scarcely have done otherwise without a blatant breach of faith. Since the action to establish a committee, the only one which was in effect open to the Council, was excluded, it decided to allow the entire matter to drop.

BERLIN

In June 1948, the three Western occupying powers in Germany, the United States, Britain and France, had undertaken a currency reform in their zones and in West Berlin. This was taken by the Soviet Union as an indication that the three powers were seeking to build up a wholly separate economic, and possibly political, system in the west of the country and to abandon the occupation statute. She immediately forbade the circulation of the new currency in East Berlin. And she proceeded to institute a tight blockade of West Berlin, preventing any contact by land from West Germany and so preventing the city from receiving the supplies of food and other goods on which it depended. The Western powers in turn retaliated by instituting an airlift to maintain these supplies.

Intensive negotiations in Moscow, London and elsewhere terminated in an apparent agreement on 30 August. An agreed directive was sent to the commanders-in-chief of the four powers in Germany. This provided for ending the blockade and the re-establishment of a joint currency for Berlin, but under four-power control. However, disagreements immediately broke out over the implementation of this agreement, and the blockade continued.

On 29 September 1948, the Western powers wrote to the UN Secretary-General drawing attention to the serious situation resulting from the blockade. This was a violation of the Allied rights of occupation, and was designed to secure by force what the Soviet Union had been unable to obtain by peaceful means. They asked that the Council should consider the threat to the peace which resulted. The Soviet delegate protested that it had been generally agreed that questions arising immediately out of the war, especially those concerning Germany, were matters for the Allies and not for the UN. He quoted Article 107 of the Charter, under which nothing in the Charter 'shall invalidate or preclude action in relation to any ex-enemy state, taken or authorised as a result of the war, by the governments having responsibility for such action' (it is doubtful how far this supported the Soviet Union's position, since the Soviet blockade of Berlin could scarcely be said to result from the war). He stated that four-power agreements governing Berlin provided procedures for settling any disputes which occurred there. In any case, the 'restrictions' on transport and communications did not represent any threat to the peace. They had been made necessary because East Berlin and the Soviet Zone of Occupation had been 'threatened' by the Western currency reform and the flow of currency coming from the West.

The Council decided, against the votes of the Soviet Union and the Ukraine, to consider the matter. The Soviet Union and the Ukraine thereupon announced that they would take no part in the discussion. The Western powers then expounded their charge that the Soviet measures represented an illegal violation of their occupation rights in Berlin.

At this point a new type of UN initiative occurred: the non-permanent members took it on themselves to seek to adopt a mediating role between the two blocs (a precedent that was to be repeated in later years). The president, on their behalf, requested further factual information on the background to the dispute. Such information was provided by Western delegates. But the Soviet Union reaffirmed that she was not prepared to discuss the matter in the Council at all (though she continued to attend its meetings).

On 22 October the six non-permanent members introduced a resolution which was intended as a compromise. It called for the removal of the Soviet restrictions, but also for an immediate meeting of the four military governors to arrange for a unified currency throughout Berlin, based on the Soviet Zone mark. This was a reasonable proposal which, since it was the currency question which had sparked off the blockade, might well have been acceptable to the Soviet Union. But she was in a highly suspicious mood, and, moreover, believed that she had might on her side. She resisted the proposal that she should raise the blockade before the introduction of the joint currency, and accordingly vetoed the resolution when it was put to the vote.

In the following month, while the Security Council was meeting in Paris, the president of the Council made another move. He tried to secure agreement from the four powers for the establishment of a technical committee to discuss the means of creating a joint currency. Meanwhile the presidents of the Security Council and the General Assembly joined in an appeal to the powers to settle the Berlin dispute peacefully among themselves. The Technical Committee was duly set up as proposed. It was at first asked to report in ten days. Its life was twice extended. But this still did not succeed in securing agreement. Eventually, in mid-February, it had to report that it had been unable to resolve the differences. At the beginning of March the Western powers imposed certain counter-measures against trade between East and West Berlin.

By now it was clear that all formal UN moves had failed. It was time for informal measures. The Secretary-General brought together the chief delegates of the United States and the Soviet Union at the UN in private discussions under his chairmanship. The representatives of Britain and France later joined these talks. For once the great powers were able to meet at the UN without the glare of publicity and propaganda. By this time the failure of the Soviet blockade, as a result of the Western airlift, had become apparent. Some softening of the Soviet position emerged. At any rate, on 4 May it was announced by the Secretary-General's representative that agreement had finally been reached on all major questions affecting Berlin. The agreement provided that both the Soviet and the Western restrictions were to be removed on 12 May. Nine days later, on 23 May, all questions concerning Berlin, including the currency question, were to be considered at a meeting of the Council of Foreign Ministers in Paris, in the context of the German question as a whole.

This was a considerable coup for UN diplomacy. There was no final settlement of the Berlin question, or even of the currency problem. But at least the blockade was brought to an end. The Berlin dispute was undoubtedly the most serious East–West issue which had so far come up at the UN. It was widely believed at the time that, if unresolved, the blockade could culminate in world war. It was for this reason that the Assembly had so urgently pleaded with the four powers for a negotiated settlement. No doubt it is true that, even if the Secretary-General had not instituted the final round of discussions, they might still have taken place in some other forum. But the fact that it was the UN which in this case laid on the successful negotiations did much to enhance its faltering prestige. At last, it was felt, the new organisation was doing exactly what it had been set up to do: settling disputes between the major powers and averting the danger of war.

Another conclusion, less obvious, but perhaps more important to the organisation, was less widely drawn: that on such issues private negotiation is often more successful than public confrontation.

HUMAN RIGHTS IN EASTERN EUROPE

Another East–West issue at this time concerned human rights in Eastern Europe.

We saw earlier (p. 32) the disputes which had occurred during the drafting of the Charter on the powers which the organisation was to enjoy on human rights questions. Eventually it had been laid down that one of the purposes of the organisation was to 'promote and encourage respect for human rights and for fundamental freedoms'; and in Chapter x the Economic and Social Council (ECOSOC) had been empowered to 'make recommendations for the purpose of promoting respect for, and observance of, human rights and fundamental freedoms for all'. The Security Council, being concerned with threats to the peace, breaches of the peace and acts of aggression, was not, in the original conception, given powers in this field at all. Thus discussion of such matters at first took place in the Assembly alone.

The first move on this question was sparked off by the arrest of Cardinal Mindszenty, Primate of Hungary, by the Hungarian Government in December 1948 and his subsequent trial by a 'people's court'. On 16 March 1949 the Bolivian Government asked that the General Assembly, unusually in session in the spring, should consider the question; and a few days later Australia formally tabled an item 'observance of fundamental freedoms and human rights in Bulgaria and Hungary, including the question of religious and civil rights, in special relation to recent trials of Church leaders'. The Assembly referred the matter to its *ad hoc* political committee. Hungary and Bulgaria were not members of the UN at this time and, when invited, refused to take part in the discussions; instead they denounced them as an illegal interference in their internal affairs.

During the discussions Western and Latin American delegates declared that in each country the Communist Party, though receiving only a small number of votes in the elections held immediately after the war, had gradually extended its hold on power, had reduced political and other freedoms, and had in some cases executed opposing political leaders. They had recently proceeded to persecute Church leaders as the principal remaining threat to their own power. Cardinal Mindszenty, after he had forbidden the members of religious orders to teach in the confessional schools which had been taken under national control, had been subjected to a campaign of vituperation and threats, and finally been arrested and tried, as had Church leaders and priests in Bulgaria. All of this represented a clear violation of fundamental human rights. The Assembly in Articles 10, 14, 55 and 56 of the Charter had a general jurisdiction over such questions, which overrode the reservation of domestic matters in Article 2(7). Moreover, in this particular case the two governments had undertaken in their peace treaties to safeguard civil and religious rights and this had created clear international obligations.

Representatives of the communist countries claimed that in both states religious freedoms were assured in law and in practice. The Church in each case occupied a privileged position and enjoyed financial assistance from the state. In Hungary religious teaching was compulsory and there was no propaganda against religious beliefs. In Bulgaria the new constitution assured freedom of worship, and here too the Church received financial assistance from the state and special facilities for propagating its religious views. Cardinal Mindszenty had been arrested not for his religious ideas, but because he had been conspiring to overthrow the state by force, to establish a 'monarcho-fascist system' in Hungary. By his own confession he had transmitted confidential political information to the United States. Similarly, the fifteen Bulgarian pastors recently put on trial had been trying to overthrow the Government by force and engaging in espionage for the US Government. In any case, all these matters were beyond the competence of the Assembly. So far as the peace treaties were concerned, a special procedure had been set up for considering any alleged violations, and these should be put in motion if there was any doubt about their implementation.

A number of resolutions were put forward, calling for the setting up of a special committee to examine the situation on the spot in the two nations, or proposing that they should be refused admission to the United Nations. Even among the Western delegates there were doubts about the usefulness of setting up a special committee. The two governments were not likely to provide facilities for this. Not surprisingly South Africa, whose internal affairs were already attracting comment in the Assembly, voiced especially strongly the view that the Assembly had no competence in the matter. These views prevailed and the proposal to set up a special committee was rejected by a substantial majority. But a resolution was adopted expressing 'deep concern at the grave accusations made against the governments of Bulgaria and Hungary regarding the suppression of human rights and fundamental freedoms' in these countries, noting 'with satisfaction' the steps being taken by signatories to the treaties with them to ensure that human rights were protected – the United States and Britain had already tried to invoke the treaties – and drawing the attention of the two governments to their obligations under the treaties.

However, the measures taken by Western powers under the peace treaties did not get anywhere. All that happened was that the two governments (and Romania, when similar steps were taken there) refused to appoint representatives to the committees which were supposed to examine alleged violations. This refusal, apparently in defiance of the treaties, provided a new justification for raising the matter at the UN. Thus in August the matter was raised again. Romania was now added to the list of countries involved. Again she was invited to send representatives to the debate, but she too refused. During the discussion the US delegate recounted further developments in the three countries, declaring that they had now fallen totally under the control of their communist parties and recounting the steps taken by those parties to suppress fundamental freedoms. The Christian churches had been persecuted and minority parties suppressed. He therefore proposed that an application be made to the International Court of Justice, asking whether it confirmed that a dispute existed concerning the application of the peace treaties, and whether this obligated the three governments to appoint representatives to the commissions established in the treaties. It also asked whether the Secretary-General could appoint a third member to such a committee. The communist states again denied that any violation of human rights had occurred in the three countries or that any 'dispute' concerning the application of the treaties existed. None the less, the US resolution was adopted by a large majority.

Meanwhile a similar charge of violation of human rights had been brought against the Soviet Union too. Here a different procedure was required, since there were of course in this case no peace-treaty obligations. The particular action of the Soviet Union which provoked attack was her policy at this time of refusing permission for Soviet citizens who had married citizens of other countries to leave the Soviet Union. There were, for example, 350 wives and sixty-five husbands of US citizens alone who wished to leave to join their spouses but had not been permitted to do so. And in February 1947 the supreme Presidium of the Soviet Union passed a decree forbidding Soviet citizens to marry foreigners at all: an even more serious violation of human rights.

At the 1948 General Assembly, the issue was raised by Chile (the Russian daughter-in-law of the former Chilean ambassador in Moscow was one of those refused permission to leave with her Chilean husband) and Australia. Western speakers declared that the Soviet measures were a violation of the Charter and of the Universal Declaration of Human Rights. The Assembly was competent to consider the question because the measures could damage friendly relations between states. It therefore supported a Chilean resolution calling for the restrictions to be withdrawn. Australia demanded that the International Court of Justice should be asked to advise whether, in the case of the wives of members of diplomatic families, a breach of international law or practice was involved. The Soviet and other communist delegates maintained that the issuing of exit visas and marriage legislation were purely domestic questions which were outside the competence of the UN. The Soviet Union had voted against the provision of the Universal Declaration of Human Rights relating to freedom to emigrate, and had always made clear its views on the point. Diplomatic immunity was not affected since this did not extend to all members of a diplomat's family; nor could anybody claim diplomatic immunity in his own country.

The Australian proposal was defeated, but the Chilean resolution, slightly amended, was carried by the Assembly by 79 votes to 6. This 'declared' that measures preventing wives of foreign nationals from leaving their own country to join their husbands were 'not in conformity with' the Charter and that, if the wives were persons belonging to foreign diplomatic missions, such measures were contrary to diplomatic practice and likely to impair friendly relations between states. The resolution therefore called on the Soviet Union to withdraw the measures. There was not, however, any immediately discernible effect and this was the last that was heard at the UN of the matter of the Soviet wives.

In March 1950 the International Court of Justice delivered its advisory opinion on the questions involving Hungary, Bulgaria and Romania. By a substantial majority it found that it had competence in relation to the question it was asked (though not on the merits of the human-rights issues themselves). It concluded that disputes did exist on the interpretation of the treaties, that these had not been resolved directly between the parties, that they were thus suitable questions for the commissions established in the treaties to decide, and that the parties were under an obligation to appoint representatives to these commissions. The three communist states still declined to appoint their own representatives. Subsequently, therefore, the Court went on to consider the third question: whether the UN Secretary-General might himself appoint the third member provided for in each commission, which might then operate on this basis. Here the Court found that this would not be lawful, since such a step was not provided for in the treaties: the refusal of the other parties to appoint representatives could not alter the position in this respect.

This result was not a total victory for either side. It put the communist countries in the wrong over their refusal to appoint their own representatives, but did not justify the West in seeking to establish commissions by other means. The 1950

Assembly considered the position again in the light of this judgement. The communist delegates continued to maintain that human rights were adequately protected in the three countries and that no dispute existed between the parties, since the Soviet Union had not joined with the other signatories in making a complaint. The Western powers repeated their charges against the three governments and declared that the refusal to appoint representatives showed that they knew that breaches of the treaties had occurred. Eventually a resolution was passed by an overwhelming majority condemning the refusal of the three governments to appoint representatives to the treaty commissions, and inviting all members to submit to the Secretary-General any further evidence which they received on the question. So the matter was allowed to drop.

FREE ELECTIONS IN GERMANY

A final Western attempt to win support in the UN on a cold-war issue concerned elections in Germany. For several years the United States, Britain and France had been calling in their discussions with the Soviet Union for free elections throughout Germany as a means towards the reunification of that country. Pressure for reunification was of course strongest in West Germany itself, and it was the West German Government, Dr Adenauer in particular, that demanded that the Western powers should raise the issue in the UN.

At the 1951 General Assembly the United States, Britain and France therefore proposed the setting up of a UN commission to examine whether conditions existed for the holding of free elections throughout Germany. The communist states opposed any discussion of the question as an intervention in domestic affairs. And they pointed out that matters arising from the war were the responsibility of the victorious powers and not of the UN. The item was none the less accepted and it was decided to invite representatives of the West and East German governments, and of the two sectors of Berlin, to take part in the discussions. Dr von Brentano, on behalf of West Germany, declared that the rebuilding of a united Germany was an imperative necessity and that free elections would be a decisive step towards this. The Federal Government in West Germany, with the support of its parliament, had called for the setting up of a UN Commission to investigate how these could be held. The representatives of the German Democratic Republic and East Berlin said that any examination of the conditions for elections was the responsibility of the German people themselves, and should be done by a joint commission composed of representatives of the governments in the two halves of the country (a proposal the West German representative had rejected on the grounds that the East German Government was not representative of the East German people). An investigation by the UN would represent interference in the internal affairs of Germany and would be contrary to the principles of the Charter.

On 20 December the Assembly none the less decided to set up a commission to investigate conditions in both halves of Germany, to consider the constitutional provisions in force there, the freedom of political parties, and the organisation of judiciary and police, and to report to the Secretary-General whether conditions for genuinely free and secret elections existed. The communist states denounced this as a gross interference in domestic matters, and Poland refused to take part in the proposed commission, as she had been invited to do. The Western powers, on the other hand, maintained that Germany was still under military occupation, and so had no real sovereignty to violate: the proposal was designed, on the contrary, to promote the restoration of German sovereignty. A less political Swedish resolution, which recognised that the commission would certainly not be allowed to travel throughout Germany and therefore merely declared the desirability of holding elections and called on the four powers to establish the necessary conditions for them, lapsed.

As was widely predicted, the Commission was not given permission to travel in East Germany or East Berlin. It had to report on 30 April of the following year that, while it had travelled freely in West Germany and West Berlin, and had had satisfactory discussions with the authorities there, it had been unable to undertake any investigation in the East. Meanwhile, in diplomatic correspondence with the Western powers, the Soviet Union had held that the only commission acceptable to it would be one composed of representatives of the four occupying powers. Thus the UN Commission did not feel it could pursue its task any further, though it would remain at the disposal of the UN in case conditions became more favourable. So the whole venture was clearly hopeless. The report was not taken up at the next meeting of the General Assembly, and the whole matter lapsed.

It was of course only too clear, even before the Commission was established, that it would not be permitted to travel in East Germany and East Berlin. If a constructive effort to bring about elections was wanted, the Swedish proposal for discussions among the great powers would have been more to the point, though its chance of success was slender. The whole episode must therefore really be regarded primarily as a propaganda exercise, designed to expose to the world the reluctance of the East German Government to submit itself to free elections, and so to demonstrate its unrepresentative character. The move's practical purpose was almost nil. No doubt the Western powers were being pushed hard by Dr Adenauer, and went through the motions of proposing a commission, however small the hope of a favourable outcome, to please him and his government.

This was only one of a number of propaganda items raised by the West at this time of its domination. That they were largely propaganda does not necessarily condemn them – since, some held, the public exposure of abuses was precisely one of the purposes the UN should serve. But it was a purpose unlikely to produce results. And it was one which the West would be able to pursue only at a time when it held a majority. Within a few years it was to find itself on the receiving end as a different majority made use of the organisation, equally ineffectively, for the same purpose.

13 The Korean War

The Korean question had been intensively discussed at the UN for four years before, in 1950, it was faced there with the greatest challenge of its history.

During the Second World War it had been agreed among the Allies that, after the defeat of Japan, Korea would be restored to independence. At the Yalta Conference there had been a brief discussion of the possibility of some sort of international trusteeship for the country, but this was not pursued. It was, however, agreed there that the Soviet Union should join the war against Japan at a time of her choosing. The obvious place for the Russians to attack was Korea, so this raised the possibility of a Soviet occupation of the country. In May 1945, when Harry Hopkins went to Moscow on behalf of President Truman, Stalin again raised the possibility of some sort of international trusteeship for Korea. But nothing was agreed.

On 8 August the Soviet Union entered the war against Japan, and four days later sent her troops into northern Korea. Within the next few days it was proposed by the United States, and accepted by the Soviet Union, that the Japanese surrender should be accepted by Soviet forces in northern Korea and by the United States in the south. The division between the areas occupied by the two allies should be the 38th parallel. This was a proposal of the US joint chiefs-of-staff. It was a fateful decision, since it effectively determined the political future of Korea for the coming decades. A month later, on 8 September, US forces landed in Korea. By that time Soviet forces could, if they had so wished, have occupied the entire country. But the agreement was observed. Soviet forces occupied the area north of the 38th parallel, and US forces the part to the south.

This had originally been regarded, at least in Western

229

quarters, as a purely temporary arrangement. The Allies were committed to restoring independence to Korea and to establishing there a unitary state. But this immediately raised the question, to what government should power be handed over?

In December 1945 the Council of Foreign Ministers, meeting in Moscow, agreed in principle to establish a 'provisional Korean democratic government' for a united Korea. A joint commission was to be established, consisting of representatives of the US and Soviet commands, to prepare proposals in consultation with democratic parties and organisations in Korea. Meanwhile there would be a four-power trusteeship for the country, to be held by the United States, the Soviet Union, Britain and France.

The proposal for trusteeship, implying a kind of colonial tutelage, was strongly resisted by many Korean politicians in the South; and the United States subsequently declared that this proposal need not be implemented if a viable and representative Korean government could be established. This view was contested by the Soviet Union, which continued to attach importance to the trusteeship idea. For nearly two years inconclusive negotiations proceeded between the US and Soviet occupation authorities in the two zones about the future government of the country. A joint commission was set up to assist in this process but was frustrated by a total conflict of views. There was prolonged disagreement about which groups and organisations within Korea were 'democratic' and should be consulted about the constitutional system to be established. The Soviet Union held that any groups opposed to the Moscow Agreement and the trusteeship proposal had no right to be given a voice. The United States in reply proposed that elections should be held separately in the two zones; representatives from each zone would then come together in numbers proportionate to population (the population of the South was twice that of the North) to establish a provisional government for a united Korea. But the Soviet Union wanted the provisional assembly to be *appointed*, with equal numbers from North and South, and with representatives only of those parties which fully supported the Moscow Agreement. The United States then suggested that the various proposals should be considered by a joint meeting of the four signatories of the Moscow Agreement. This in turn was rejected by the Soviet Union.

Finally the Soviet Union proposed that all US and Soviet forces should be withdrawn by 1 January 1948, handing over to local authorities in each zone, and so in effect perpetuating the division of the country. The United States was not unwilling to withdraw its forces, under reasonable safeguards, since the joint chiefs-of-staff regarded the commitment in South Korea as both a military and a political liability.[1] But it was not yet willing to renounce all hope of eventual reunification.

In the late summer of 1947 the United States decided to bring the question before the UN. On 17 September, Secretary of State Marshall declared to the Assembly that it now seemed evident that

further attempts to solve the Korean problem by means of bilateral negotiations will only serve to delay the establishment of an independent united Korea.... Although we shall be prepared to submit suggestions as to how the early attainment of Korean independence might be effected, we believe that this is a matter which now requires the impartial judgement of the other members. We do not wish to have the inability of two powers to reach agreement delay any further the urgent and rightful claims of the Korean people to independence.

In the eyes of the United States, the advantage of this initiative was that she might now be able to mobilise world opinion on her side on the issue. In the eyes of the Soviet Union this was precisely its defect. Gromyko declared that, as a matter resulting directly from the war, the question was not one for the UN; the great powers had already laid down the lines of a solution in the Moscow Agreement and there was therefore nothing now for the UN to do.

The item was none the less inscribed. In the Assembly's First Committee the US proposed that the occupying powers should hold elections in their own zones, under UN supervision, by 31 March 1948, so as to establish, in due proportions, a single national assembly and a national government. This united assembly would establish its own security forces, after which foreign forces would be withdrawn. A UN commission would supervise the whole affair and report back to the Assembly. The Soviet Union proposed simply the withdrawal of all foreign forces by the beginning of 1948, after which the people of Korea would be left to establish a Korean national government (a sure prescription for permanent division).

The Assembly accepted the US proposals with only minor modifications. The Soviet Union had proposed that representatives from both North and South should take part in the UN discussions themselves. The United States therefore modified her proposals so that the UN commission might arrange for the participation of Korean representatives, so long as these were genuinely elected and not 'mere appointees of the military authorities in Korea'. The resolution finally adopted established a temporary commission on Korea, to observe elections throughout Korea and subsequently to assist the elected representatives to establish a united and independent Korea under a national government. Elections would be held not later than 31 March 1948, and the Commission should have the right to travel freely throughout Korea to observe them and consult with the Korean people. Armed forces should be withdrawn 'as early as practicable and if possible within 90 days of the establishment of a Korean government'.

The decision of the Assembly itself to lay down the political future of Korea was an ambitious one, paralleled only by the decision on Palestine reached at the same Assembly. But it was not untypical of its mood at this time. Under a narrow interpretation of the Charter, it could have been held to be a violation of Article 2(7), prohibiting interference in matters within the jurisdiction of any state. Since, however, Korea at this time consisted in effect of two states, it could be held that the matter was not purely domestic and that the UN was in practice seeking to resolve a dispute between them. In any case, the area, as one taken from one of the defeated powers in the Second World War, could be held to be, like the Italian African colonies, now an international responsibility.

The procedure adopted was, however, unneccessarily precipitate and uncompromising. It may be compared with that adopted over Palestine at about the same time. In neither case did the Assembly have authoritative powers to decide on a solution: all it could do was to pass recommendations on the procedure to be adopted. Over Palestine the Assembly at least decided to undertake an investigation of the situation, before later considering what long-term solution to recommend. It invited representatives of the main parties concerned to appear at the Assembly itself, and then proceeded to consult them through the special committee it established. And the country which brought the problem to the Assembly, Britain, made no attempt to dictate or even recommend the position it should take. In contrast over Korea, the Assembly decided to make no initial investigation of the situation. It made no attempt to listen to representatives of the Korean people. And the country which raised the issue, the United States, itself proposed and effectively determined the procedure to be followed.

That procedure certainly received the overwhelming endorsement of UN members. It was no doubt acceptable also to many Koreans, at least in the South. But it could be passed by the Assembly only at the cost of provoking the unqualified hostility of the Soviet Union and the North Korean authorities. What it therefore could not do was materially to promote the unification of Korea; for, if attainable at all, this would only be achieved with the goodwill and consent of the Soviet Union and the authorities at that time controlling the North. Here, if ever, was an occasion where the UN object should surely have been to promote negotiation; if necessary, under its auspices, even within its portals. Once again UN members preferred a voting victory, and the endorsement of an ideal solution, to the institution of political procedures which alone might resolve the dispute.

The Soviet Union from the start announced its opposition to the course determined by the Assembly. The Ukraine refused to serve on the Temporary Commission. The other members met at Seoul on 12 January 1948. The Commission made no attempt itself to organise or conduct elections. It confined itself to observing and reporting elections undertaken by the authorities in the two territories. In the South it was able to establish contact with the US military government and the local Korean authorities, though it could have little direct control over the registration of voters, parties, and electoral procedure. In the North it was unable even to obtain entry, let alone to influence elections. Some members of the Commission, and some of the political groups in the South, concluded that in these circumstances the entire mission of the Commission should be abandoned. Elections in the South alone could not establish a Korean national government, nor re-establish the unity of the country. On the contrary, they might perpetuate its division. Even in the South alone it was doubted by the majority of the Commission, after consultation with opposition Korean groups, whether conditions obtained under which free elections could be held. Despite this, a small majority held that it should still supervise elections in the South alone: at least this could produce Korean representatives who could be consulted by the General Assembly in the future. This view was opposed by Australia, Canada and India, who felt that the result would be to harden the division of Korea. Because of this conflict of views the Commission decided to consult the Interim Committee of the Assembly.

The Interim Committee, established to represent the Assembly, with the same membership, when it was not in session, heard the conflicting views of the Commission. It decided on 26 February to adopt the view, strongly supported by the United States and the majority, that the Commission should implement the programme previously laid down 'in such parts of Korea as are accessible to the Commission'. This could be a 'stage in the formation of a Korean government'. The new Korean assembly would be free subsequently to negotiate with other groups about the form of a Korean national government and who should participate in it.

In effect this was a commitment not only to elections but also to the establishment of a separate authority in the South. It was thus felt by many to make more difficult in the long run the establishment of a united Korea. Indeed, it was clear that both super-powers, supported by their Korean partners, were pursuing policies which, however much the aim of unification was declared, were only likely to lead to permanent division. Failure to regain the other half was felt better than to risk a united country controlled by the enemy. The decision also meant adopting a course that was wholly opposed by one of the great powers concerned, with little attempt to take her concerns into account. It was therefore another expression of the politics of confrontation and cold war, rather than of consultation and consent among the great powers, so common at this stage of the UN's history. The decision to go ahead was, largely on these grounds, opposed by Canada and Australia and eleven other members of the Interim Committee; while three Latin American, five Middle Eastern and three Scandinavian countries abstained. It was none the less carried.

Two days after the decision, the Temporary Commission, announced that it would observe elections not later than 10 May 1948. General Hodge, the US military commander in South Korea, subsequently announced that elections would be held on 9 May. The Commission agreed to observe these elections, provided it was satisfied that the elections would be held 'in a free atmosphere, wherein the democratic rights of freedom of speech, press and assembly would be recognized and accepted'. Out of the eight members of the Commission two (Australia and Canada) opposed the decision to observe elections in the South alone even after the Interim Committee's decision, and two more (France and Syria) abstained: these countries were not convinced that the Interim Committee's decision (as opposed to an Assembly resolution) was binding on the Commission, nor satisfied that it was wise to proceed to an election in conditions prevailing in the South at this time.

The Commission laid down certain elementary conditions, which it held should be observed. For the most part these were accepted by the US military command. During the elections the Commission interviewed US officials and Korean election officers and candidates, and travelled throughout the country. There were, however, only thirty non-Korean personnel engaged in observing the election in an area of about 40,000 square miles with a population of 20 million (this may be compared with the thousand neutral observers used in the Saar plebiscite, among a far smaller population, in 1935).

When the election took place, 72 per cent of the qualified voters were said to have taken part. The result was a victory for the right-wing parties, especially Syngman Rhee's National Association for the Rapid Realisation of Korean Independence, and the Korean Democratic Party. The UN Commission accepted the elections as a valid expression of the free will of the electorate in those parts of Korea which were accessible to the Commission. But it carefully avoided recognising the resulting assembly as a national assembly, capable under the UN resolution of setting up a national government for an independent Korea. The new South Korean leaders had other views. They showed little inclination for consultation with the Commission, which in any case had no power at its disposal. Apart from addressing a message to the people of North Korea inviting them to hold an election to find representatives for the new Assembly, they also took no steps to approach the North Korean authorities on unification. Syngman Rhee was elected chairman of the new assembly, and proceeded to form a national government. On 12 July, within two months of the election, a constitution for the Republic of Korea was adopted, in theory covering the whole 'Korean peninsula and its accessory islands'. Three days later Syngman Rhee was elected President of the Republic.

Early in August this South Korean government was officially established. It proceeded, with the consent of the US military authorities, to take over responsibility for the government of the South. On 12 August the United States, in a public statement, declared that the administration was 'entitled to be regarded as the government of Korea'.[2]

All of this was paralleled by similar developments in the North, where elections for a 'supreme people's assembly' were held on 25 August. This included the 'election' of delegates said to represent the South. On 7 September a government was set up under the leadership of Kim Il Sung. Like its counterpart in the South, this too claimed to be the government of all Korea. It was quickly recognised by the Soviet Union and other communist states. Soon afterwards, on 19 September, the Soviet Union announced that all Soviet forces would be withdrawn from Korea by the end of December.

The Temporary Commission reported to the Assembly the transfer of the functions of government to the new regime in the South. It considered that the new republic might be expected to perform adequately the normal functions of a government and to provide a basis from which unification might be achieved, especially through economic contacts. The Commission strongly urged that peaceful negotiations should take place between North and South before the evacuation of foreign forces. Otherwise, it shrewdly forecast, Korea might be abandoned 'to the arbitrary rule of rival political regimes whose military forces might find themselves driven to internecine warfare'. But by this time the evacuation of US forces had already begun (it started on 15 September). Soviet evacuation began shortly afterwards. Nor was the slightest inclination to negotiate manifest among the rival leaders in the two halves of Korea, who passionately distrusted each other.

The Assembly thus took little heed of the warnings of the Commission. On the proposal of the United States it passed a resolution recognising the new South Korean government as a 'lawful government', based on elections which were 'a valid expression of the free will of the electorate'. It recommended that the occupying powers should withdraw their forces 'as early as practicable', and established the Commission on a permanent basis to help bring about reunification. This left ambiguous whether the South Korean Government was being recognised as the government of the South alone, or as a national government whose authority was eventually to extend to the North. A US Government spokesmen said its authority under the resolution was recognised only in the areas it controlled. But the new government itself claimed to be the government of all Korea. In the same resolution members of the UN were requested to enter into diplomatic relations with the new government. Though its application for UN membership was inevitably vetoed by the Soviet Union, it was within a year accepted (under the title 'Republic of Korea') as a member of the FAO, the World Health Organisation (WHO) and the Economic Commission for Asia and the Far East (ECAFE). Applications from the 'People's Republic of Korea' to these bodies were turned down.

The new permanent commission made a few hesitant steps to promote unification. But it had little influence with either North or South. It decided not to communicate with the government in North Korea, whose authority it rejected. It made some approaches to individuals in the North but, not surprisingly, received no reply from them. Its efforts to make the South Korean Government more representative of the population there were turned down out of hand by Rhee, who considered that the Commission's mandate extended only to promoting democratic elections in the North. And its attempts to promote economic and other contacts between the two zones had no effect. On the contrary, on 1 April 1949 Syngman Rhee banned all trade with the North, on the ground of the illegality of the northern regime and the alleged danger that trade would be used 'for subversive purposes', whatever that might mean.

The Commission could therefore only report on the increasing friction between the two halves of the country and 'much military posturing on both sides of the parallel'. The withdrawal of foreign forces and occasional raids over the border from the North had, it recognised, produced a considerable sense of insecurity, especially in the southern half of the country. As a result, at the 1949 Assembly a resolution was put forward, proposed by the United States and other countries, authorising the Commission 'to observe and report any developments which might lead to, or otherwise involve, military conflict in Korea'. As the US delegate observed, with prophetic accuracy, 'this would enable the UN, should a conflict occur, to obtain all the necessary information concerning the conflict, its causes and those responsible for it from a duly constituted body'. Thus the Commission established a series of posts, with trained observers, along the borders between North and South. These were to have only a few months to wait to perform their functions.

If the UN's overriding aim at this time was to secure the unification of Korea, it can scarcely to be said to have followed the course most likely to achieve it. Given the political and military realities, reunification could only be achieved, if at all, by negotiations. These must involve the two super-powers and their Korean partners, who were wholly dependent on them. The UN at no time made any attempt to organise or promote these. It would have no communication at all with the North Korean regime. It made no real contact with the Soviet Government. It called for no discussions among the super-powers. The Soviet and North Korean leaders more than once proposed a conference of political leaders in the two halves to discuss their common problems, but these were always turned down by the South. It is uncertain that such talks, even if held, could have succeeded. It is unlikely that elections for a single government throughout Korea would have been accepted by the North, except on terms that would have denied any real freedom of choice. But certainly the course favoured by the UN, promoting elections and the formation of a government in the South alone, without any serious discussions of joint institutions for contact, could only serve to harden the division between the two territories. The two governments which were established inevitably regarded each other as rivals rather than as potential political partners. Relations between them rapidly worsened. And both were at times prepared to hint at military action as the only means of re-establishing the unity of the country.

There was, however, one major difference between them in this respect. Though the Soviet Union finally withdrew its forces somewhat earlier than the United States (by December 1948 instead of June 1949), it did so only after it had fully trained and armed powerful and effective North Korean forces. It supplied these with modern equipment, including heavy artillery, tanks and aircraft. The United States, on the other hand, though it allowed the formation of substantial ground forces in the South, with over 100,000 men, specifically designed that force for defence only (perhaps already fearing its possible intentions towards the North). She provided no tanks, no aircraft and no heavy artillery. The leaders on both sides were fully aware of this difference in armed strength. Though the public statements of Syngman Rhee were therefore sometimes even more bellicose than those of Kim Il Sung and his colleagues, specifically asserting the right of his government to use force if necessary to unify the country, they were taken seriously almost nowhere. The statements of Northern leaders, though perhaps outwardly more restrained, were in reality more dangerous. For they were capable of being put into effect.

WAR BREAKS OUT

During the early part of 1950 there were a series of small-scale incidents on the border between North and South. Statements on either side became increasingly warlike. In June, John Foster Dulles, foreign-policy adviser to the Truman administration, paid a visit to South Korea and gave assurances of US support, both moral and material. He visited South Korean forces on the border and declared that 'any despotism which wages aggressive war dooms itself to unalterable disaster'.

At 1.30 p.m. on 25 June 1950, the South Korean Foreign

Minister informed the UN Commission of a large-scale attack by North Korean forces across the border. A few hours later similar reports were sent by the Commission's observers on the border. The Commission immediately reported to the Secretary-General 'a serious situation developing, which is assuming the character of full-scale war and may endanger the maintenance of international peace and security'. It suggested that the Secretary-General might wish to call together the Security Council. In a broadcast in South Korea, the Commission's chairman appealed for an end to hostilities and offered the Commission's good offices in arranging a ceasefire.

At 3 a.m. on 25 June (New York time), the US representative at the UN, Ernest Gross, called for a meeting of the Security Council to consider 'a breach of the peace or act of aggression' in Korea. At 3 p.m. the Council met. The Soviet Union was at this time absent from the Council, having walked out in January over the issue of Chinese representation (p. 314). This of course ruled out from the start the danger of a Soviet veto, and made it possible to contemplate resolutions in terms which would have been unthinkable if the Soviet Union had been present.

Addressing the Council, the Secretary-General declared that the situation represented a serious threat to international peace, and it was 'the clear duty of the Security Council to take the steps necessary to re-establish peace'. The US representative put forward a draft resolution declaring that a breach of the peace had been committed and calling on North Korea to cease hostilities and withdraw its armed forces. With small amendments this was accepted. The resolution noted with grave concern the 'armed attack upon the Republic of Korea by forces from North Korea', called for an immediate end to hostilities and the withdrawal of North Korean forces to the 38th parallel, and asked all members to render every assistance to the UN in the execution of the resolution and to refrain from giving assistance to North Korea. In its unequivocal attribution of responsibility to the North, this resolution differed from nearly all UN ceasefire calls before and since (which almost always call impartially for a ceasefire and withdrawal); but this could perhaps here be justified in view of the circumstantial reports of the UN Commission which were before the Council. At any rate, an alternative resolution, put forward by Yugoslavia, which called for a ceasefire without any finding of guilt and invited the North Korean Government to state its case before the Council, received no support (Norway, India and Egypt abstained on this proposal).

On the same day, 25 June, President Truman, after consulting with defence and State Department advisers, sent naval and air forces to South Korea to protect the evacuation of US civilians there. He decided to supply arms to South Korea, and moved the Seventh Fleet from the Philippines to the Taiwan Straits. On the following day he went further. He sent naval and air units to give active support to South Korea; and he announced that the Seventh Fleet would be used to neutralise Taiwan (in effect to defend it against a possible invasion by communist forces then being massed on the mainland coast). Announcing these measures on the following day, Truman justified them on the basis of the Security Council resolution. This required a somewhat ingenious interpretation of the resolution, which had not asked for the despatch of armed assistance to South Korea but had called on all members to give every assistance in the execution of the resolution – that is, it seemed, to assist in bringing about a ceasefire. US action to help defend a state under attack did not necessarily require justification in terms of a UN resolution. But her decision to interpose the Seventh Fleet between mainland China and Taiwan was much more questionable, since this in effect represented a direct intervention in a civil conflict not yet completed. And it was this feature of US action which aroused most criticism among UN members, and above all from mainland China.

On 26 June, the UN Commission in Korea reported that there were no signs that the North Koreans were heeding the Security Council resolution; and on the following day it reported that they seemed to be carrying out a 'well planned, concerted and full-scale invasion of South Korea'. The same day, 27 June, the Security Council met again. The US representative now presented a stronger resolution, calling specifically on members to 'furnish such assistance to the Republic of Korea as may be necessary to repel the armed attack and to restore international peace and security in the (area'. The resolution was not, however, explicitly based on Chapter VII of the Charter (dealing with breaches of the peace and acts of aggression), and did not 'decide' what action should be taken by members – a decision which would have had mandatory force. It represented in effect only a recommendation to members. The Yugoslav representative, Alex Bebler, proposed that the Council should use a procedure of mediation and again asked that North Korean representatives should be invited to take part in Council discussions. Once more this proposal received no support. And the US resolution was then passed by a large majority, with only one vote against (Yugoslavia).

The passage of this resolution was a major event in UN history. It was the first time that the UN had taken action calling on its members to come to the defence of a member-state under attack. It was thus a classic example of the principle of collective security being put into effect. Ironically, the action taken, a *recommendation* to all members to assist an attacked nation, fulfilled far more closely the League concept of peace-keeping, joint action to defend the peace by individual decision, than that of the UN, a collective decision by the Council which would be binding on all members. Even in this limited form, the Council was able to take action only because of the chance that the Soviet Union was absent.

For this latter reason the decision was denounced by the Soviet Union as illegal. She claimed that the necessary 'concurrence' of the permanent members had not been obtained. This view could in fact scarcely be seriously sustained. It had already been accepted by all the permanent members, including the Soviet Union, that an abstention by a permanent member did not constitute a veto. The Soviet Union, however, held that the *absence* of such a member was different and could prevent any action from being taken. This would have meant that all Security Council decisions since January were illegal (which the Soviet Union had not previously maintained); and that any permanent member could at any moment prevent the Security Council from reaching a decision by the simple procedure of staying away from its meetings, a conclusion that no reading of the Charter could plausibly sustain.

On 27 June the Secretary-General cabled all members,

asking what assistance they proposed to give to South Korea in accordance with the terms of the Security Council resolution. Most of the replies were vague or evasive. Nearly all governments approved the general principle of resisting aggression and support for the UN, but were carefully uninformative about what particular action they proposed to take to implement it. Only a very few undertook to send military assistance. The scale of US action was, however, stepped up. On 29 June naval and air strikes against targets in North Korea were authorised. A naval blockade of the North Korean coast was instituted. And on 30 June it was decided, on General MacArthur's recommendation, to send two divisions from Japan to help in the defence of the South. By this time the South Korean forces were in full retreat.

A few other countries made contributions, though on a far smaller scale. Within two weeks of the passage of the resolution, naval and air units from the United Kingdom, Australia and New Zealand were actively engaged, and units from the Netherlands and Canada were on the way. By the middle of September fourteen members, Western or pro-Western, had sent ground forces. By the end of the year this had become fifteen; and early in 1951 the total of contributing states became, as it remained, sixteen.[3] But two-thirds of the UN force consisted of US forces, even if the South Korean forces were included. At the end of 1951 the land forces were 50 per cent US and 40 per cent South Korean, the air forces 93 per cent US and 6 per cent South Korean, the naval forces 86 per cent US and 7 per cent South Korean. Thirty Governments offered assistance of other kinds, including civilian relief, Red Cross units, field hospitals, blood, rice, blankets and medicines.

The problem arose of how the UN was to organise the command of this motley force. The Secretary-General proposed that the United States should have the main responsibility for directing it, with the assistance of a co-ordination committee. But this was not accepted by the United States. Eventually, on 7 July, the Security Council passed a resolution, originally put forward by Britain and France, asking members providing military forces and assistance to make them available to 'a unified command' under the UN. The force was authorised to use the UN flag. The United States was to designate the commander of the force and to provide regular reports to the Security Council on the conduct of the operation. Apart from this obligation to report, the United States was given unlimited authority to direct the operations. On 8 July, President Truman announced that General MacArthur had been appointed by the US Government as commander of the UN forces. On 15 July, South Korean forces were also placed under General MacArthur's command.

This was a somewhat extraordinary arrangement. General MacArthur was now under the authority both of the Security Council and of the US Government. He remained US Commander-in-Chief, Far East, and Supreme Commander Allied Forces in Japan. He reported regularly to the US President and chiefs-of-staff and received orders from them. Reports to the UN were sent in the first place to Washington and were amended and edited by the US Government before being presented by them to the Security Council. There was no suggestion, as with subsequent peace-keeping forces, that the UN commander should report direct to the Security Council or the Secretary-General. It was as if in effect the United States had been given control of the UN, or at least of an important aspect of its activity.[4]

On 31 July the United States introduced a new resolution in the Security Council. This would condemn the North Korean authorities for their defiance of the UN and called on all states to try to bring an end to this defiance, and to refrain from giving any assistance or encouragement to the North Korean authorities. The next day, however, the Soviet Union decided to return to the Council. By mischance it was her turn to be president. This may indeed have been the fact that caused her to return. For the following month, during thirteen meetings devoted to the question of Korea and related matters, Gromyko, the Soviet representative, used every possible device his position made available to frustrate and disrupt offective discussion of the issue. He proposed an agenda of his own, voted against all attempts to change it, refused to implement procedural decisions of the Council (for example, to seat a representative of South Korea), and so on. By these means he made it impossible to vote on the proposed US resolution for more than a month. Only after the British delegate (Sir Gladwyn Jebb) took over the presidency in September did the resolution finally come to a vote. Though it then obtained an overwhelming majority in its support (9–1, with 1 abstention), it failed, to no one's surprise, because of a Soviet veto. Similarly, a number of Soviet resolutions condemning UN action in Korea, calling for representation of North Korea or the Korean people, and demanding the transfer of the China seat to the Chinese People's Republic were overwhelmingly defeated.

Throughout this critical period, therefore, there were no effective decisions taken by the Council. Meanwhile, the position on the ground had radically altered. For nearly a month after the invasion, the North Koreans advanced rapidly and approached near to the southern coast of Korea. Only towards the end of July did General MacArthur report that the advance had been held and a defensive line established along the Naktong River, and towards the east near Taegu. For some weeks the situation remained roughly stable, with even a small UN advance. On 15 September, a skilful amphibious operation was undertaken by UN forces at Inchon behind the North Korean lines. This took the North Koreans completely by surprise. Their front line collapsed and their forces rapidly retreated. By the end of September UN forces were approaching the 38th parallel.

Now a new problem arose. Should the UN forces halt there, where the war had begun, or advance beyond to secure the total defeat of North Korea and the reunification of the country? When UN forces were first sent to Korea, it was almost everywhere assumed that the purpose of its intervention was to help South Korea defend its territory, to drive the North Koreans back to their own borders, but not to occupy any part of the North. Dean Acheson, US Secretary of State, had made a speech within a few days of the invasion in which he declared that US action in Korea in support of the Security Council resolution 'was solely for the purpose of restoring the Republic of Korea to its status prior to the invasion from the north and of re-establishing the peace broken by that invasion'.[5] The terms of the two main resolutions passed by the Council in June supported this interpretation of UN aims: they spoke of assistance by members of the UN to South Korea to help her 'repel the armed attack from the north' and 'restore international peace and security in the area'. There was at this time no hint that UN forces might seek to enter North Korean territory.

As UN forces rapidly approached the 38th parallel, however, opinion in some quarters began to change. The US military, in particular, feeling that they had the enemy on the run, believed that it would be folly to leave the job half done, and to restore the very situation which had previously led to war. This was not perhaps a very strong argument. It was not really very likely that the North Koreans, once badly mauled in such an operation, and having learnt that such an attack would provoke worldwide retaliation, would seek to repeat the operation, especially if significant UN forces remained in South Korea. There was, however, another argument. This was that the UN had been engaged for four years in seeking to bring about the peaceful unification of Korea under a freely elected government. It had been frustrated in this task by the obstruction of the authorities in North Korea. Now surely, when its forces, it seemed, were easily able to subdue that country, was the ideal opportunity to bring this task to fruition and so resolve the whole Korean problem for good.

Against this it could be held that UN military action for such a purpose could not possibly be justified by the UN Charter. By it a defensive war, to preserve a nation under attack, would be converted into a war of conquest. Besides this question of principle – of what the UN was justified in doing, in accordance with its own Charter and the terms of its resolutions – there was an additional question, that of expediency. Even if the UN were justified in crossing the frontier, would it be wise to do so? Might it not enormously exacerbate an already sufficiently dangerous situation? Might it not risk provoking intervention by the Soviet Union or China or both? Could a UN force, even though militarily successful in the South, occupy and hold down a population of 10 million or so in the North, who might not support UN intervention so readily as some optimists seemed to assume? All of these were powerful arguments against crossing the border, and were strongly voiced by some UN members.

Finally, there was still another related question: who was to reach the decision? Could the UN commander, in effect the US Government, unilaterally decide whether the frontier should be crossed? Or would it require a further UN decision? The US Government itself was not at one on this point. At one stage Truman suggested that a new UN decision would be required. Later both the State Department and the US military authorities, notably General MacArthur, asserted that the UN Command could take the decision, on the authority of the earlier resolution; the need to 'restore international peace and security in the area' could be used to justify such action. At the same time the US Government dismissed as unrealistic the fears, urgently presented to it by both India and Britain, that there was a strong risk of Chinese intervention if the parallel was crossed.

Uncertainty on all these points persisted when the General Assembly met for its normal session on 19 September. Dean Acheson, in addressing the Assembly, while not specifically arguing in favour of crossing the parallel, stressed that the opportunity was now presented to the UN of establishing a unified and independent Korea. The two resolutions that were presented by West and East on the Korean question similarly made no explicit reference to the parallel, though the implication of each was clear. One, which was essentially a US draft though presented by a number of Western countries, demanded that all appropriate steps be taken to ensure conditions of stability throughout Korea; that everything necessary be done, including the holding of elections under the auspices of the UN, for the establishment of a unified, independent and democratic government in the sovereign state of Korea; and that all necessary steps be taken to ensure the economic rehabilitation of Korea. By calling for the establishment of stability 'throughout Korea', and the setting up of a government for the whole country, this really gave, and was intended to give, explicit authority for a crossing of the parallel. The resolution sponsored by the Soviet Union and other communist countries also demanded the holding of all-Korean elections under UN auspices, together with a programme of economic and technical aid to Korea. But this asked for an immediate withdrawal of foreign troops from Korea and demanded that the elections should be organised by a commission drawn equally from the assemblies of North and South Korea. This therefore opposed any crossing of the frontier and demanded that the UN force should be withdrawn so that the country's future could be settled bilaterally between the two local governments.

If there had been any doubt about the intention behind the Western draft it was immediately dispelled by Acheson's speech to the Assembly in support of it. In this he set out with cogency the arguments in favour of crossing the parallel.

> Today the forces of the UN stand on the threshold of victory.... The aggressors' forces should not be permitted to have refuge behind an imaginary line, because that would recreate a threat to the peace of Korea and of the world.... The artificial barrier which has divided North and South Korea has no basis for existence either in law or in reason. Neither the UN, its Commission on Korea, nor the Republic of Korea recognized such a line. Now the North Koreans, by armed attack on the Republic of Korea, have denied the reality of any such line. Whatever ephemeral separation of Korea there was for purposes relating to the surrender of Japan was so volatile that nobody recognizes it. Let us not, at this critical hour and in this event, erect such a boundary. Rather let us set up standards and means ... by which all Koreans hereafter can live in peace among themselves and with their neighbours.

These arguments found widespread support. Only India and a few other Asian and Latin American countries raised some doubts about the wisdom of carrying the war to the enemy's territory. Yugoslavia thought 'the aims of the Security Council had been to prevent the alteration by force of a given situation, not to use armed force to change the *de facto* situation existing at the beginning of hostilities'. The Soviet Union and her allies of course expressed total opposition. But the majority were for pushing ahead. The Western resolution was passed by an overwhelming majority (45–5, with 7 abstentions). So the UN force was given the go-ahead.

This resolution, quite apart from the major issue of principle – was the UN justified in taking military action not merely to reverse aggression, but to conquer the territory from which it came? – raised an important constitutional issue. Under the Charter all enforcement powers rested with the Security Council. The Assembly merely had the power to pass resolutions recommending action by member-states: and even then only when the Security Council was not itself dealing with a particular question. In this case a major decision, directly concerning the UN's security role and the use of UN forces, had deliberately been taken within the Assembly, primarily because, with the return of the Soviet Union, any such proposal in the Council would inevitably have been vetoed. It could just be argued that Article 11 of the Charter, under which the Assembly had the right to discuss any questions relating to 'the maintenance of international peace and security' brought before it and to 'make recommendations to the states concerned or to the Security Council', gave some basis for Assembly action. But this was certainly not an interpretation that would have been generally accepted when the UN was founded. The debate was essentially the culmination of the gradual switch from the Council to the Assembly which Western countries had been steadily instituting over the past four years.

The resolution was passed on 7 October. Already before this, on 1 October, South Korean forces (which need not, it was felt, be bound by a UN decision in a matter directly affecting their own country) had crossed the parallel into North Korea.

As soon as the Assembly resolution had been passed, General MacArthur called on the North Koreans to lay down their arms. Failing this he would 'at once proceed to take such military action as may be necessary to enforce the decrees of the United Nations'. Receiving no reply, UN forces crossed the border.

China too made a distinction between South Korean and other UN forces. Since the beginning of the war China had made a number of communications to the UN. At first she had been far more concerned about US action in ordering its naval forces to defend Taiwan than with the intervention by the UN in Korea. For some months, in any case, things had gone badly for the UN, and no serious threat was presented to China. On 6 July Chou En-lai had sent a telegram to the Secretary-General protesting against US intervention and aggression in Korea. On 20 August, when UN forces were beginning to be more successful, he warned that the Chinese people 'cannot but be most concerned about the solution of the Korean question' and called for the withdrawal of all foreign troops

from Korea. He demanded too the right of China to participate in UN discussions, especially those which concerned the
'illegal US occupation' of Taiwan. On 29 September the
Security Council decided to accept the request for Chinese
representation in discussions of that question.[6]

By this time the possibility of UN forces' crossing the parallel
was being discussed. If they eventually arrived at the
northern part of North Korea, these would have come to the
Chinese border, and so appeared as a serious potential threat
to China. It was known that large Chinese forces had already
been moved from south China to Manchuria. On 30 September, in a speech to the People's Political Consultative
Conference, Chou En-lai declared that the Chinese Government 'would not stand aside' if North Korea was invaded.
Three days later he directly warned the Indian ambassador in
Peking that, if any UN forces, other than South Korean,
crossed the border, China would feel obliged to intervene.
These warnings were transmitted to the US and other
governments, and were known before the Assembly vote.
After the Assembly had voted, an official Chinese Government statement declared that 'the US invasion' of Korea
menaced Chinese security, and China could not 'stand idly
by. . . . The Chinese people loved peace but, in order to
defend peace, they never will be afraid to oppose aggressive
war.' As the UN forces crossed the border, Chinese forces
massed on the Yalu River dividing Manchuria from North
Korea.

As Chinese warnings became more insistent, more UN
members, including some close to the US, became concerned
about the dangers of Chinese involvement. Britain, in particular, warned repeatedly that this was likely if UN forces
approached close to the Yalu, not only because Chinese
security would be directly threatened, but also because
Chinese industry in Manchuria depended on power supplied
from power stations in North Korea. Perhaps as a result,
General MacArthur had been given instructions, even before
the frontier was crossed, that only Korean forces should be
used in the areas adjoining the Soviet and Chinese borders.
On 24 October, however, despite these specific instructions,
General MacArthur told his field commanders that all earlier
restrictions were lifted, and he authorised them to enter any

part of North Korea. When challenged on this by his superiors in Washington, he argued the imperative needs of military necessity. He publicly discounted the danger of intervention by Chinese forces.

However, two days after he had issued these instructions, on 26 October, UN forces captured prisoners from Chinese units. On 6 November, MacArthur officially reported to the Security Council that UN forces 'were in hostile contact with Chinese Communist military units'. Three weeks later, MacArthur launched a last attempt at a 'general assault' on the communist forces in the North. But this was a total failure. Within two or three more weeks, the UN forces had once more been driven out of North Korea altogether by the combined Chinese and North Korean forces.

ATTEMPTS TO REACH A SETTLEMENT

This new situation brought two responses.

One was a decision to increase the military effort in Korea to meet the far more powerful forces now encountered there. The other was new consideration of means of securing a settlement, especially by bringing China into UN discussions of the conflict. Although the Security Council had already agreed in principle to receive a representative from the mainland, this had been only to discuss the question of Taiwan, and in any case was not to be taken up until after 15 November. On 8 November, not long after the first confirmed encounters with Chinese forces, Britain proposed that representatives of Peking should be invited to discuss the report just received from General MacArthur describing these encounters. This proposal was adopted by 8 votes to 2. Even then, however, a proposal for a general invitation to China to take part in discussions of the Korean issue was narrowly defeated.

One of the main reasons for seeking discussions with China was to assure her that the UN forces had no hostile intentions against Chinese territory. It was believed that, if China could be reassured on this point, she might be less inclined to become involved in a protracted military confrontation with the UN. The United States therefore proposed a resolution for this purpose. This, while calling on the Chinese to withdraw, declared that 'it is the policy of the UN to hold the Chinese frontier with Korea inviolate and fully to protect legitimate Chinese and Korean interests in the military zone'. The British Government delivered, through the British representative in Peking, a message to the same effect. The UN Commission on Korea also offered to try to mediate, but this idea was turned down by the US Government. To believe that China would have withdrawn her forces on the basis of such assurances, and perhaps allowed a resumption of the UN advance to the north, was an illusion at the best of times. But, after the Chinese had begun to win spectacular military victories, and, by the end of November, begun to pursue UN forces into the South, it became a still more unrealistic hope.

On 11 November, Chou En-lai refused the invitation to discuss the MacArthur report, because it would not permit discussion of the issue most pressing to China: 'the armed intervention in Korea and the aggression against China by the US government'. None the less, three days later it was announced that a Chinese delegation, headed by General Wu Shin-chuan, was leaving Peking to present the Chinese complaint against US 'aggression' in Taiwan, as previously invited. When the Council met on 16 November to discuss Korea, a Chinese statement was read out at the request of the Soviet representative. This denounced US action in Korea and demanded that, 'in order to achieve a peaceful settlement of the Korean question, it is essential, above all, to withdraw all foreign forces from Korea'. The Korean question could be solved only by the people of North and South Korea themselves. In reply the US delegate referred to a statement of President Truman's that the US Government had 'no intention to carry hostilities into China' and would do everything possible 'to prevent any extension of the hostilities in the Far East'. Further discussion was postponed until the Chinese delegation had arrived.

But there was still dispute about what China was being invited to discuss. When the Council met again on 27 November a compromise was reached. It was decided to consider together the items on 'complaint of armed invasion of Taiwan' and the 'complaint of aggression upon the Republic of Korea' (mutually opprobrious titles). This meant hat the Peking delegate would be able to participate in a general way on both items. When the meeting began, the US delegate denied the charge of aggression in Taiwan, and in turn accused China of aggression in Korea, calling on her to accept the UN's resolutions on Korea, including those calling on states to refrain from assistance to North Korea. General Wu, after protesting against the title accorded to the Korean item, denounced the United States for aggression in both Taiwan and Korea. He demanded that the Council should take steps to bring this to an end. The United States was seeking to encircle China, with bases in Japan, Taiwan and Korea. The Korean War had been fermented by her as a pretext for aggression against North Korea and Taiwan. On the other hand, the action of Chinese nationals acting as 'volunteers' in Korea represented no threat to the United States. The Soviet Union introduced a resolution on behalf of China calling on the Council 'to ensure the immediate cessation of aggression against China by the US'. This was defeated overwhelmingly (1–9, with 1 abstention). The US resolution calling for Chinese withdrawal but affirming no hostile UN intention against China received wide support (9–1, with 1 abstention) but was vetoed by the Soviet Union. India abstained on both resolutions.

At this time the Assembly had very recently passed the so-called 'Uniting for Peace' resolution, empowering it to consider questions that had been deadlocked by veto in the Council and to authorise the use of force if necessary (p. 94). Now for the first time this procedure was put into use. The resolution that had been vetoed in the Council was now brought, virtually unchanged, into the Assembly. Here it might be expected to have an easy passage, since there was no risk of veto. However, the mood of the Assembly, with the increasing success of Chinese military action, had now become restrained and apprehensive. There was widespread fear of the possibility of a major war between the United States and China, which might eventually also involve the Soviet Union. There was a desire for a more conciliatory approach.[7]

In the Assembly the US representative argued that the main aim of the UN in Korea should be to maintain the security of the UN forces, to bring about the withdrawal of those forces assisting North Korean aggression, the localisation of the conflict, a quick end to the fighting and renewed assurances that the UN had no intention that could threaten Korea's neighbours. But there were calls for further efforts at compromise and negotiation before any new resolution that might antagonise China was passed. India proposed, on behalf of thirty Asian and Arab states, that a group of three representatives should be established to explore the basis for a ceasefire in Korea. And she later introduced a second resolution, calling for an international conference at an early date to recommend the basis for a settlement in Korea. The United States insisted that a ceasefire must precede any political negotiation or conference. The Soviet Union, on the other hand, was against any ceasefire in isolation. These positions clearly reflected the current military situation, with the communist forces at present successful. The first Indian proposal was accepted overwhelmingly (51–5, with 1 abstention). The Group of Three so established was to consist of the president of the Assembly (Entezam of Iran), Sir Benegal Rau of India and Lester Pearson of Canada.

This group proceeded to consult the governments chiefly concerned about the basis on which they would accept a ceasefire. The United States wanted a demilitarised zone about twenty miles wide to be established in the area north of the 38th parallel, a cessation of reinforcements or replacement of armed forces in Korea, and a ceasefire supervised by a UN commission. But by this stage Chinese forces were advancing steadily beyond the 38th parallel. China was therefore scarcely likely seriously to consider a ceasefire north of the parallel. In any case, the Chinese Government refused to recognise the legitimacy of the Group of Three, since it had been established by an Assembly from which it was excluded. It therefore refused altogether to enter into discussions with that body. Informal discussions with the Chinese delegation organised by the Secretary-General were no more fruitful.

But at the same time Chou En-lai, the Chinese Prime Minister, made various statements indicating the type of settlement China might accept. On 22 December he declared that

as a basis for a peaceful settlement of the Korean problem all foreign troops must be withdrawn from Korea and

Korea's domestic affairs must be settled by the Korean people themselves. . . . US aggressive forces must be withdrawn from Taiwan and the representatives of the People's Republic must obtain a legitimate status in the UN.

Clearly these were China's maximum demands. At the peak of her military success, she was using the opportunity to demand satisfaction on a number of issues, not all related to Korea, on which she felt aggrieved.

Because it had been unable to meet a Chinese representative, the Group of Three had to report to the Assembly on 3 January that it was unable to make any recommendation on the basis of negotiations for a ceasefire. At about this time, however, (between 4 and 12 January) the prime ministers of the Commonwealth were meeting in London. This meeting issued a statement setting out certain principles which the prime ministers felt should be used as the basis for the settlement. On 12 January, Lester Pearson, the Canadian representative in the Group of Three, presented a set of 'five principles' closely reflecting these Commonwealth attitudes, which he proposed should be submitted to Peking. The principles were (a) a ceasefire, with safeguards against secret preparations for a new offensive; (b) the use of this to promote further discussions for the restoration of peace; (c) the withdrawal of all foreign forces, followed by arrangements for elections throughout Korea; (d) arrangements for the peaceful administration of Korea according to UN principles, till these arrangements were completed; (e) the setting up of a body including representatives of the United Kingdom, the United States, the Soviet Union and the People's Republic of China to find a settlement of all Far Eastern problems, including Taiwan and Chinese representation. The principles were approved in the First Committee of the Assembly (50–7, with 1 abstention) on 13 January and transmitted to Peking immediately afterwards.

The proposals went some way to meet Chinese demands. The last point gave a hope for discussion of the two extraneous matters which China had introduced. The second proposed the withdrawal of foreign forces, which she had consistently demanded. And a ceasefire on the existing lines would have removed the danger of even a temporary presence of US forces close to the Chinese borders. But the Chinese leaders perhaps overplayed their hand. If they had at least shown a willingness to discuss the principles, there is a chance that serious negotiations could have begun. But in their reply on 17 January they denied even the legitimacy of the proposals and the source from which they came, and presented a counter-plan of their own.

Like the UN proposal, this too called for a withdrawal of all foreign troops. It too demanded a conference including representatives of mainland China, the Soviet Union, the United States and Britain; this was to be held in China and would discuss not only Korea but also 'the withdrawal of US forces from Taiwan and the Taiwan straits' and other Far Eastern problems. The plan said nothing about elections in Korea or the role of the UN in deciding Korea's future, merely referring, like previous communist proposals, to 'the settlement of Korean domestic affairs by the Korean people themselves' (presumably on the basis of the current military balance). But there was no demand for the transfer of the China seat in the UN to Peking. And, though the plan differed in significant ways from the UN proposals, it was not so different that it might not have been possible to negotiate a compromise. It was indeed probably intended, in traditional Chinese style, as a bargaining position from which concessions might well be later made.

However, on the same day that the plan was received, the US Secretary of State, Dean Acheson, issued a statement describing the 'so-called counter-proposal' as nothing less than an outright rejection. 'There can no longer be any doubt', he declared, 'that the UN has explored every possibility of finding a peaceful settlement of the Korean question. Now we must face squarely and soberly the fact that the Chinese Communists have no intention of ceasing their defiance of the UN.' When the First Committee met on 18 January, Acheson, having again declared that the Chinese reply amounted to a rejection of UN terms, proceeded to ask for the condemnation of China as an aggressor and for the institution of some measure of sanctions to be used by UN members against both China and North Korea.

This precipitate and ill-judged response arose from two causes. On the one hand, the war in Korea itself was now going very badly indeed for the UN forces. Chinese and North Korean units had advanced halfway to the south coast of South Korea. US opinion was thus now less ready than ever to treat with the Chinese, or to accept any ceasefire on the existing unfavourable line. Secondly, policy towards China had become a major issue in US domestic politics. On 19 January the House of Representatives had adopted a resolution demanding that 'the UN should immediately act and declare the Chinese Communists aggressors in Korea'. Four days later a similar resolution was adopted in the Senate. The Truman administration was already under fierce attack for its alleged 'betrayal' of China in not giving sufficient help to the nationalists during the civil war. They could come under still fiercer attack for 'capitulation' if they could be accused of negotiating a Korean settlement favourable to communist China.

In the First Committee, however, there were divided views on how to proceed. Britain, France, Canada and Australia all urged caution and recommended that the Chinese reply should be studied carefully to discover if there was hope of a compromise. The Indian delegate announced that his government considered the reply in part a request for clarification and in part a counter-proposal which should be examined. His government's request for further elucidation had already received an encouraging answer: the Chinese Government had undertaken to seek to secure the withdrawal of the Chinese 'volunteers' from Korea if her own plan was accepted. This, however, was not a sufficient advance to satisfy the US delegate, who declared that previous UN resolutions relating to Korea were still valid: if negotiations were to be worthwhile, China must accept their implementation. And he continued to insist that China should be condemned as an aggressor.

Other member-states, led by Britain, however, continued to argue that the Chinese reply should be explored further. Some points it left in doubt required elucidation. Even if, strictly, China was guilty of aggression against UN forces, the British delegate argued, efforts should be made to persuade her to reform before resorting to condemnation. No long-term solution of the Korean question was likely to be achieved except with the agreement of the largest neighbouring country, China, so that everything was to be gained by making a further effort to achieve a settlement with her. At least the UN should not, by instituting sanctions, make the situation still more difficult. Members of the Arab–Asian group shared this attitude. They thought the Chinese reply held out some hope, and felt time should be left for further negotiation before the UN committed itself to a condemnation of China. India thus proposed a seven-power conference to seek steps towards a ceasefire in Korea and enable the Chinese attitude to be elucidated. The United States accepted one very marginal amendment of its proposal: 'the good offices committee' which it proposed for exploring the possibilities of a settlement should report its results before any steps towards sanctions were taken. But this did not modify the denunciation of the Peking government for aggression in Korea and so could scarcely prevent the final rupture of all meaningful negotiation likely to result.

The Indian compromise proposal was rejected in the Assembly by 27 to 18, with 4 abstentions. The US proposal was then passed on 1 February by 44 to 7, with 9 abstentions. The resolution found that the Chinese Government 'by giving direct aid and assistance to those who were already committing aggression in Korea and by engaging in hostilities against UN forces' had 'itself engaged in aggression in Korea' (the word 'condemn' was avoided). It called on China to withdraw her forces. And it set up with a good offices committee an additional measures committee, which was to consider possible sanctions against the aggressors.

The Good Offices Committee was constituted of the president of the Assembly and the permanent representatives of Sweden and Mexico. These attempted to make contact with the Peking Government through the Swedish legation in Peking. They failed to obtain any reply. The Chinese Government, to judge by its press and public statements, was now so enraged at the accusation of aggression (also, perhaps, so militarily successful) that it was no longer prepared to maintain any communication with the UN at all.

From about this time, however, the military position changed substantially. During the second half of February, UN forces began to halt the Chinese and then to move forward again. By mid March they had recaptured Seoul. Not long afterwards they again approached the 38th parallel. Again there was considerable discussion on whether or not it should be crossed. At least, the states providing forces were agreed, before any crossing took place a statement should be issued offering a ceasefire and once more extending an invitation to negotiations. On 20 March, General MacArthur was informed that such a statement would be made by President Truman. Four days later, however, on his own responsibility, General MacArthur issued a statement of his own, inviting the commander-in-chief of the enemy forces to confer with him about the military means of achieving the UN's political objectives. If this was refused, direct military action against the mainland of China might be taken. And he unnecessarily declared the questions of Taiwan and the Chinese seat in the UN to be 'extraneous matters'. The imperious tone of this statement scarcely represented an inducement to the Chinese to negotiate. Other members of the UN, including those contributing forces, protested at the intransigent character of the announcement. And President Truman finally decided not to go ahead with his own, more conciliatory message.

Shortly afterwards General MacArthur was found guilty of another serious misdemeanour. In March he wrote a letter to a US Congressman, Representative Martin, supporting the use of Chinese nationalist forces in Korea and advocating carrying the war to the Chinese mainland. Both of these positions were contrary to declared US policy. This was the culmination of a series of occasions on which MacArthur publicly expressed his disagreement with the instructions or policies of his superiors in Washington. The statement aroused widespread anxiety among many members of the UN, including some of those supplying forces to Korea. A resolution in the British House of Commons, expressing no confidence in General MacArthur's handling of his duties, received many signatures.

On 11 April President Truman announced his dismissal of the General. In the United States this aroused considerable public demonstrations in support of MacArthur. Among most members of the UN it was greeted with heartfelt relief.

In the middle of April, and again a month later, the Chinese launched major offensives, apparently seeking to drive the

UN forces well to the south again. Though they were unsuccessful, they precipitated further moves to introduce sanctions against China. The Additional Measures Committee, after postponing action so long as there seemed to be any chance of negotiations, decided on 3 May to begin a serious study of possible economic measures. The United States then proposed an embargo on the shipment of raw materials to all areas under the control of North Korea and communist China. This suggestion was approved by the Committee, with only marginal amendments, and on 18 May it was overwhelmingly endorsed by the Assembly as a whole.[8] The resolution recommended all states to embargo the supply of 'arms and implements of war, atomic energy materials, petroleum, transportation materials of strategic value, and items useful in the production of arms, ammunition and implements of war'. This represented the first attempt within the UN to decide on an agreed policy of sanctions against a state accused of aggression. Six months later, thirty-eight members and six non-members reported full compliance with the resolution.[9] The Additional Measures Committee continued to report on the observation of the resolution (supplied with information by the United States). But far more significant in its effect was the committee (COCOM) set up in Paris early in 1950 with the object of controlling among Western countries, strategic exports to the whole of the Eastern bloc: this maintained an embargo far stricter than that demanded by the UN.

THE PEACE NEGOTIATIONS

Even while military measures in Korea were being intensified and sanctions brought to bear, the nations leading the UN effort began to be ready to reconsider their war aims.

Although the enemy forces had been pushed back beyond the 38th parallel, it had become evident that it would be difficult, if not impossible, to push them back to the far north of Korea as had been assumed in October 1950. After the failure of two Chinese offensives in the spring of 1951, it began to look as if a situation of military stalemate might develop. Even US leaders now began to state publicly that the UN mission might be complete with the successful repulse of the attacking forces beyond the 38th parallel. Speaking to the Senate Committee on Foreign Relations on 1 June 1951, Dean Acheson, the US Secretary of State, declared,

> Our objective is to stop the attack, end the aggression, restore peace and provide against the renewal of aggression. These are the military purposes for which, as we understand it, the United Nations forces are fighting. . . . A united, free and democratic Korea . . . is still the purpose of the UN but I do not understand it to be a war aim. In other words, that is not sought to be achieved by fighting, but it is sought to be achieved by peaceful means, just as was being attempted before this aggression.

These were very different words from those which Acheson had uttered in the UN Assembly only nine months earlier. But he was not alone in his view. Trygve Lie, speaking in Canada on the same day, declared that he believed 'that the time has come for a new effort to end the fighting in Korea. The UN forces there . . . have repelled the aggression and thrown the aggressors back across the 38th parallel. If a ceasefire could be arranged along that parallel, then the main purpose of the Security Council resolutions . . . would be fulfilled.' Such statements seemed to reflect a considerable change from the war aims widely declared during the previous year. The real change, of course, consisted not in a new conception of desirable outcomes but in a wholly different military situation.

On 23 June, no doubt in response to these indications, during the course of a broadcast on the UN radio, Jacob Malik, the Soviet permanent representative at the UN, declared his belief that the conflict in Korea could be settled if the parties were ready to enter the path of peaceful settlement. 'The Soviet peoples believe that, as a first step, discussion should be started between the belligerents for a ceasefire and an armistice providing for the mutual withdrawal of forces from the 38th parallel.' Two days later, the Peking *People's Daily*, usually the mouthpiece of official Chinese Government policy, also spoke of the possibility of a peaceful settlement of the conflict, provided all foreign troops were withdrawn from Korea and the Korean people were allowed to settle their own future for themselves. On 27 June

Gromyko informed the US ambassador in Moscow that ceasefire negotiations could be purely military in scope, leaving the settlement of the political problems of Korea to the future.

These various statements reflected the general weariness with the war after a year of bitter fighting. Both sides had, at one time or another, sought to secure their political objectives by military force alone. Neither had achieved this. Each was now willing to settle for a draw (roughly speaking), and to defer the interrupted discussions about unification until a later date.

The United States decided to seek a military settlement on the existing fighting lines. This, however, raised the question, who had the authority to seek terms from the enemy? Would a decision be needed from UN political bodies for such an initiative? The Secretary-General consulted his legal counsel, Abraham Feller, on the point. On 29 June Feller submitted a memorandum expressing the view that the United States had the right to conclude a ceasefire agreement of a purely military kind without any new authorisation from the Security Council or the General Assembly. This would, of course, need to be reported to the Security Council, which had originally placed the united command in the hands of the United States. Only if political matters, relating to the future of Korea as a whole, were discussed would the UN's political bodies be required to take the necessary decisions.

Contacts between the US commander and the commander-in-chief of the communist forces accordingly took place, and the first meeting of liaison officers of the two sides was held at Kaesong on 8 July. At this time there is no doubt that many hoped that the fighting in Korea would quickly be brought to an end. Such hopes were very far from being realised. No substantial change in the military positions occupied by the two sides was to take place after this time, yet only a third of the war had so far been fought.

At first the Chinese wanted the agenda to include the withdrawal of all foreign troops from Korea. This was not accepted. On 26 July an agenda was agreed. It included arrangements for a ceasefire, the fixing of a demarcation line between the two sides, arrangements covering prisoners of war, and a vaguely worded item 'recommendations to the governments of countries concerned on both sides' – this might perhaps have allowed the Chinese to raise the question of withdrawal of foreign troops or other items.

There was argument at first over the line of demarcation, the Chinese and North Korean delegations insisting that this should be the 38th parallel (in accordance with Acheson's statement that the UN wanted only to restore the pre-war situation), and the US negotiator insisting that the line should be north of the parallel to create a defensible position. For a time the US team continued to demand that the line should pass well to the north of the fighting-line. However, by 27 November there was agreement that the line of demarcation should be the current 'line of contact', or fighting line, at the time the ceasefire came into effect, with a two-mile demilitarised zone on either side.

On the arrangements for a ceasefire, the US negotiators demanded, in addition to a withdrawal from the demilitarised zone, an assurance against reinforcements from either side and the construction of new airfields, with widespread inspection to ensure that this was carried out. It was eventually agreed that inspection teams should be posted at five points of entry on either side, supported by ten mobile teams to investigate suspected violations. There would be a limit of 35,000 on the rotation of troops in each month and no limitation on airfield construction. There was some disagreement about the composition of the supervising commission, but finally it was accepted that Sweden, Switzerland, Poland and Czechoslovakia should be its members. It was agreed too that within ninety days of the ceasefire there would be a conference to consider the withdrawal of foreign troops, the peaceful settlement of the Korean question and 'other matters related to peace in Korea' (this would therefore not include US activity in the Taiwan Straits or Chinese representation at the UN).

Agreement on all these points was reached by February 1952. But it was still to be well over a year before final agreement on an armistice would be reached. The vital point which held up an agreement concerned prisoners of war. At first this was simply a matter of discrepancies over the numbers of prisoners held on each side. But it quickly developed into a much wider argument on an important point of principle: should all prisoners of war be returned automatically, or only those who wished to be? The two communist states demanded that every prisoner must be returned to his country of origin and held that this was an obligation under the Geneva Convention on prisoners of war, passed only two years previously, in 1949. On the face of it, the Convention did support this position. It laid down in Article 128 that 'prisoners of war should be released and repatriated without delay after the cessation of hostilities'. The United States, however, held that this was counterbalanced by other provisions of the Convention relating to the need to show humanitarian concern for the welfare of prisoners: this meant that, if a prisoner expressed a strong aversion to or fear about returning to his country of origin, other arrangements must be made. The United States therefore demanded that repatriation should be in accordance with the prisoners' wishes and that the Red Cross should be empowered to interview the prisoners to find out their views.

For a time it seemed there was a chance that this principle of voluntary repatriation might be accepted by the communist states, so long as only a handful would exercise their option not to return. But, when it was announced that a survey showed that almost half (about 60,000 out of 130,000) of all the prisoners wished to do so, the two states promptly stiffened their resistance. The UN negotiators offered a screening of the prisoners by neutral third parties, or release of the prisoners in the demilitarised zone, after which they could exercise their own choice. But both proposals were turned down by the two communist powers. And at the beginning of October 1952 the negotiations were suspended for nearly six months.[10]

The General Assembly, which was meeting at this time, discussed ways of meeting the difficulty. The United States and the Soviet Union both proposed resolutions embodying their own position. The US resolution approved the conduct of the negotiators so far and called on the Peking government and the North Korean authorities to avoid further bloodshed by accepting the principle of non-forcible repatriation. The Soviet resolution provided for an 'immediate ceasefire' and the establishment of a commission to seek a political settlement and to give every assistance in the repatriation of all prisoners.

But many members were unwilling to go along with either of these familiar propositions. Eventually India put forward a compromise proposal: this suggested that force should not be used either to keep or to return prisoners, and the prisoners should be handed over to a neutral nations repatriation commission, which would arrange for their repatriation after both sides had had the opportunity to explain their own point of view. If, after ninety days, some had still not chosen to return home, their ultimate disposition would be decided by the political conference which was to be called after the ceasefire. This somewhat ambiguous proposal attracted considerable support, mainly, no doubt, because it looked like a reasonable middle way. But it left the prisoners' ultimate future quite uncertain. The United States succeeded in securing the passage of an amendment which provided that prisoners not choosing to return would not be detained indefinitely. The implication was that those choosing not to return would eventually be released, and for this reason the resolution was not acceptable to the communist states. It was none the less passed by an overwhelming majority (54–5, with 1 abstention).

The resolution had no immediate effect on the situation in Korea. The negotiations themselves were still in recess. There was no move to reopen them by either side. The communist rejection of the Indian resolution did not suggest that it could provide the means for resolving the dispute. For some months nothing happened. Then, on 28 March, the Chinese and North Korean negotiators informed that UN Command that they were prepared to proceed with the repatriation of seriously sick and wounded prisoners. Negotiations were resumed and in two weeks an agreement on this point was reached.

On 26 April full-scale armistice negotiations began again. It became clear that there was considerable anxiety on the communist side to reach an agreement quickly. They accepted the principle of a period of custody during which explanations should be made to the prisoners, as in the Indian proposal. Discussion centred on the nature of this temporary custody, the arrangements for explanations, and the body responsible for deciding the ultimate fate of the prisoners. On 8 June agreement was reached on the procedure to be used.

A neutral nations repatriation commission was to be created, to take custody of the prisoners and supervise the explanations. After ninety days the explanations would cease and the future of any prisoners not wishing to return home would be submitted to the political conference. If the conference reached no decision about this in 120 days, they would be released to civilian status. In effect, therefore, the communist powers had accepted that, unless the Western nations unaccountably gave way at the subsequent conference, some prisoners would not be forced to return home and within less than a year would be free to make their homes elsewhere.

Even so, there was a further hitch before the agreement came fully into effect. On 18 June President Syngman Rhee suddenly ordered the immediate release of several thousand of the prisoners. They quickly disappeared, and in this way escaped the procedure that had been laid down for them. This was of course a deliberate effort to sabotage the agreement. The communist powers broke off the negotiations. They demanded the immediate recapture of the prisoners and assurances that South Korea would regard itself as bound by the agreement. Since many of the prisoners immediately went underground, it was impossible for the UN Command to give any absolute assurance that all would be returned. But it did give an assurance that the governments it represented (meaning the United States) would, so far as they could, establish military safeguards to 'ensure that the armistice terms are observed' and would 'make every effort to obtain the cooperation of the government of the Republic of Korea'. Later, on 11 June, the US Government obtained from Rhee a signed agreement that he would not obstruct in any way the implementation of the agreement.

As a consequence, the Armistice Agreement was completed and signed on 27 July 1953. On the same day the sixteen nations with forces in Korea made a statement declaring that, if there were a renewed attack, 'we should again be united and prompt to resist'. In these circumstances, they threatened, it might not be possible to confine hostilities within the Korean peninsula. On 1 October the United States signed a military agreement committing itself to the defence of South Korea.

The final ceasefire line ran partly to the north of the 38th parallel and partly to the south. But there was more territory to the north under UN control than former southern territory conquered by the North. Thus it was possible to argue that UN forces had not suffered a defeat. They had in general achieved their original aim of repelling the invasion and restoring South Korean territorial integrity. The agreement prohibited the reinforcement of armed forces in both halves of Korea, so, it was believed, making a subsequent attack less likely. But it is doubtful if the observance of this provision was ever adequately verified. In practice both sides would no doubt have withdrawn forces from North Korea in any case after the conclusion of the war, so the obligation was not one which they were likely to have evaded.

The Armistice Agreement had provided that a peace conference should be called within three months after the Agreement was signed and became effective. This would bring about a peaceful settlement of the Korean question, discuss the withdrawal of all foreign forces, 'etc.'. The Chinese had succeeded in procuring the insertion of the word 'etc.', a word they probably intended to use to bring about discussion of the US presence in Taiwan and the Taiwan Straits, and possibly UN representation. The Agreement had not specified who would take part in the conference, when it should occur or where. The recommendation to hold the conference was made 'to the governments of the countries concerned on both sides'. The United States interpreted this to refer, on its own side, to the governments of the United Nations. The matter should therefore, in her view, be considered at the forthcoming Assembly session, which might also decide representation at the conference.

The General Assembly had already decided, at a special session in April 1953, that it should meet again as soon as an armistice was signed. After the signature of the Armistice, it was decided that the Assembly should be recalled, earlier than usual, on 17 August in a special session. The Assembly then had to discuss what kind of peace conference should be called and who should attend it. The United States supported by most of those having troops in Korea, proposed that the conference should be attended by those contributing forces, together with South Korea. Australia and New Zealand wanted the Soviet Union to be added to the list 'if the other side desired it'. Britain, Australia, New Zealand and Canada

wanted India to attend, as a leading Asian power which had
played a prominent part in mediating between the two sides
during the war. The Soviet Union proposed a list of fifteen
states, including three members of the Soviet bloc and five
Afro-Asian states, to be invited.

The proposal to invite the Soviet Union was accepted
without serious objection. But the proposal to invite India was
strongly resisted by the United States. This presumably
reflected the position of John Foster Dulles that all neutralism
was immoral. While an invitation to the Soviet Union might be
accepted as endorsing the view, long propounded by the
United States, that the Soviet Union had played an active role
in the Korean War, there was no good ground for inviting
India, which merely moralised on the touch-lines, she held,
but contributed nothing to the achievement of UN aims in
Korea. The proposal to include India received a small
majority in the First Committee (27–21, with 11 abstentions),
but, since this was short of a two-thirds majority, and was
regarded by many as an 'important' question, India requested
that her candidature should be withdrawn. The Assembly
therefore proposed that the conference should include,
besides North Korea and mainland China, the countries
having forces fighting under the UN flag, together with South
Korea and the Soviet Union.

China and North Korea were not, however, prepared to
accept this. They informed the Secretary-General that they
hoped the UN would reconsider the question at its forthcoming autumn session and would then agree to include India,
Indonesia, Pakistan and Burma. The General Committee of
the Assembly – the steering committee which considers proposed items – refused to accept the inclusion of this item on the
Assembly's agenda. It was held that the UN's position had
been laid down at the special session and that there was no
need to reconsider the matter merely because of the objection
of the two communist states. So it was not considered during
the Assembly session. Representativies of the UN and the
communist countries met again at Panmunjon between October and December but failed to resolve the matter.

Early in 1954 India sought to reconvene the Assembly
to reconsider the question. This was not accepted by other
UN members. But the whole question was discussed at the

Berlin Conference between the Soviet Union, the United States, Britain and France in January of that year. On 18 February it was agreed that a peace conference should take place in Geneva, beginning in April, partly to seek a settlement of the Korean question. The countries represented would include the United States, France, the Soviet Union, the Chinese People's Republic, North and South Korea and the nations whose forces fought in Korea.

By the time the conference began, on 26 April, however, world attention was focused far more closely on the problem of Indo China, also to be discussed There was by this time considerable scepticism about the possibility of reaching any overall solution of the Korean question. Here the most immediate issue, on which so much argument had taken place over the past two years, that of the prisoners of war, was now decided. Because of the delay in convening the conference, the maximum time-limit laid down in the Armistice Agreement, 210 days, had expired. The Neutral Nations Repatriation Commission had accordingly released those prisoners who still refused to return to their homelands, and they had gone, by way of India, to the destination of their choice. The general situation in Korea had thus to all extents and purposes returned to the position before the Korean War had ever begun.

This was reflected in the proposals made by the two sides at the conference when it finally took place, in Geneva in May 1954. These were virtually the same as each side had propounded between 1948 and 1950. The North Koreans called for general elections, conducted separately in the two halves, for an all-Korean assembly, which would then set up a united government. An all-Korean commission would be established with an equal number of representatives from each side, chosen from their legislatures, to organise the elections and make subsequent arrangements. It would draft the electoral law and take steps to bring about the economic development of the whole country. All foreign troops would be withdrawn within six months. The South Koreans demanded that the UN Commission for Korea should supervise elections in North Korea alone, to find representatives who would join the members of the South Korean assembly. Later, on 23 May, the South Korean Premier agreed that elections should take place throughout Korea, but this should be according to the electoral law already operating in the South. Representation in the all-Korean assembly would be in proportion to the population of the two areas. Chinese forces should withdraw from the North a month before the election took place. UN forces might begin to withdraw before the elections, but the withdrawal should not be completed until a new government had been established for a united country. The UN would then guarantee the integrity and independence of a united Korea.

There was little progress in reconciling these two positions during the Conference. On 6 June Molotov agreed, on behalf of the communist delegates, to elections throughout Korea, with representation in the assembly according to the numbers in each half. The election should be supervised by an appropriate international commission, whose composition was to be decided. An all-Korean commission would prepare the elections and seek to promote a rapprochment between the two halves. The powers most directly concerned in the maintenance of peace in the Far East would 'assume obligations to ensure Korea's peaceful development, which should facilitate settlement of the problem of unification'. These proposals represented a considerable advance on the earlier communist position and, if there had been more time and more goodwill, they might have been worth exploring further. But many of the most important questions had been left undecided in Molotov's proposals: the composition of the proposed commission, the electoral law it would apply, the countries which would be accepted as 'directly concerned in the maintenance of peace in the Far East', and so on. Both the US and British spokesmen, Bedell Smith and Eden, insisted that the UN should be given the role of supervising elections and would not consider the setting up of some other body (though this had been agreed in the case of Greece) for this purpose. To the Chinese, on the other hand, the UN still appeared a hostile body largely under enemy control.

There were no serious negotiations to reconcile these differences. After the final session on Korea on 13 June, both sides issued prepared statements largely reiterating their previous viewpoints. Chou En-lai proposed that there should be further discussions in restricted session, but this was not adopted. The truth was that both sides, after the years of bitter struggle, were more concerned to keep what they held than to risk the totally unpredictable outcome of all-Korean elections, which could have left the entire territory in the hands of their opponent. From the beginning of the war, and indeed for the five years before, each side had been more anxious to prevent the opposing party from winning a dominant control of the entire territory than with bringing about reunification of the country. In this situation, as in Germany, partition became the only possible outcome if the area was not to be reunified by force of arms. In Korea both sides in turn had failed to achieve this. So they were finally prepared to share the prize between them.

CONCLUSION

There was indeed a curious symmetry about the course of events in the Korean War. The initial North Korean objective, to overrun the South, was quickly defeated through the intervention of UN forces, and within three months they were driven back to their own country. The UN then in turn sought to convert what had been a defensive war into a war to reunite Korea, and so to conquer the North. This aim too was defeated within two or three months, this time through the intervention of Chinese forces. China in turn, when she reached and crossed the parallel, also transformed a struggle to defend North Korea and her own frontiers into a war to reunite Korea under a government of her own choice. This again was defeated within another three months. Thus by April 1951 the situation had been restored very close to what it had been at the beginning. After this, though fighting went on for another two and a quarter years, there was no significant change in the military position. So neither side attained its maximum objective, and both were finally forced to accept a compromise. But by that compromise each secured what had always been its most important aim: to prevent the control of a united Korea by its enemy.

In some ways the Korean episode can be regarded as the UN's finest hour. Here for the first and only time in its history the Security Council called on its members to go to the defence of a state under armed attack. Here, in consequence, the forces of a number of countries fought under the UN flag to defend the principle that aggression should not be allowed to succeed. Through these efforts a small state that would otherwise certainly have been defeated and annexed by its northern neighbour, was enabled to defend its borders and maintain its independence. This, in the eyes of many, was what above all else the UN was created to achieve.

There were no doubt many who hoped that this example set a pattern for the future, and that many times again the organisation might be able in the same way to come to the defence of a state under attack. This, however, was to ignore a number of special factors which had operated in this case. It was these alone which made possible prompt and effective UN control.

The first was the chance that the Soviet Union was not occupying her seat in the Security Council at the time the attack occurred. If she had been, it is beyond doubt that she would have vetoed almost all the Council's resolutions on the subject, especially that calling on members to come to the aid of South Korea. Though it might still have been possible for the Assembly to make a similar call, this would have provided the UN with a far more dubious moral authority, since it could easily have been held that such a call represented a violation of the provisions of the Charter. While Western forces would still no doubt have been sent to help South Korea, they would not have been able to claim the UN's authority.

A second qualification to the view that the UN action in Korea represented a glorious fulfilment of its responsibility to defend the peace was the fact that participation in that action was limited to a certain group of politically interested states. Only a quarter of the membership sent military assistance to South Korea. And the sixteen nations which did so were all Western countries, which had a common national interest in securing the defeat of communist aggression wherever it occurred. The episode was thus more an example of alliance strategy than of enforcement action by an international organisation; of collective defence rather than collective security. Because there existed at this time a pro-Western majority in the UN, such strategy could be provided with the legitimation of the UN flag. But the fact that a great majority of the UN membership, though pro-Western, were unwilling to send significant armed support to the country whose existence was threatened showed that the action could scarcely be said wholeheartedly to fulfil the ideals enshrined in Charter.

A third feature of UN action which deprived it of the name of genuine collective security was the dominance exercised from the beginning by the United States over the entire operation. This was demonstrated in the early stages by the fact that most of the Security Council initiatives and resolutions were all in origin US proposals. It was shown, more conspicuously, in the total control accorded to the US Government over the military operations, and subsequently over many UN command decisions. And it was witnessed equally conspicuously in its monopoly of the peace negotiations. This contrasted radically with the subsequent practice of the UN in organising peace-keeping forces from 1956 onwards. In these cases the super-powers were normally excluded from participation altogether. And no single power or even a group of powers was able to dominate policy in the way the United States was allowed to do in Korea. Since the orders to the UN forces in effect came from Washington rather than from New York, the operation in the eyes of many was not a UN operation in any normal sense but became instead a US action which happened to enjoy UN endorsement and support.

In so far as the majority of UN members were able to influence decisions at all, it was only indirectly. The fifteen other members having forces in Korea were engaged in regular consultations in Washington concerning the operation, though it is doubtful whether their voices carried any significant weight. Within the UN Assembly, neutral nations such as India were able sometimes to make proposals which had some influence on events. Assembly resolutions in the autumn of 1953, for example, were not always exactly to the taste of the United States. But none which succeeded diverged far from her policy on the most important points.

So far as the long-term discussions on Korea's future were concerned, there was always some ambivalence in US, and so in UN, aims. If reunification had really been the main objective, there were many ways in which their policy should have been modified. There should have been less haste in establishing a local administration in South Korea, and more readiness to consider the Soviet trusteeship idea. The latter perhaps was the only way in which the strategic interests of the great powers might have been satisfied without resort to partition. Mutual distrust, however, here as in so many other cases, was too great. Each super-power was more willing to see the territory divided than to risk the whole falling into the hands of its opponents. So, in the prewar talks, and later in the war itself, each eventually found the most comfortable position to be to tolerate the continued partition of the country.

But the most conspicuous feature of UN action, here as in so many other cases, was the failure to institute, or even to attempt to institute, any effective negotiations among the parties concerned. This was true of contacts between the authorities in North and South Korea; but it was even more true between the United States and the Soviet Union. As over Palestine, Kashmir and other areas, UN policy was essentially *declaratory*: it consisted in statements of ideal end-situations, rather than in any effective exploration of the means which might secure them. During the period before 1950, the North Korean authorities were largely boycotted by all UN bodies, including its 'Commission for Korea'. It seemed to be believed that, merely by stating the demand for all-Korean elections under UN auspices, such elections would magically be brought about. Once again the UN aimed too high. If it had been more willing simply to bring the parties into discussions, to seek to influence these discussions through periodic resolutions, or through a mediator or a good offices committee, it would have had a greater chance of securing success. The chances of achieving an agreed solution would still have been small; but they would without doubt have been better than they were in following the course which the UN in fact pursued.

The UN could justifiably hold that it had fought a successful war to defend a nation under attack. What it could not claim, after eight years of discussions, was that it had brought any nearer a resolution of the Korean problem.

14 Kashmir

HYDERABAD AND JUNAGADH

At the time of the independence of India and Pakistan in 1947 it was agreed that the former princely states, which had not been part of British India, should be free to choose their own future status. It was expected that they would join either India or Pakistan, though they were under no strict obligation to choose either. The choice was to be made by the ruler himself. This formula, though accepted by both India and Pakistan, led to a number of bitter disputes, one of which was to poison relations between India and Pakistan for more than twenty years.

The first dispute of this kind to come up at the UN concerned the state of Hyderabad. Here the ruler, the Nizam, was a Muslim, but most of his subjects were Hindus. The ruler in this case wished to remain, if possible, independent of both the two new states. In July 1947, a month before Independence Day, his government sent a delegation to Delhi to negotiate with the departing British authorities for the status of an independent dominion within the Commonwealth. The British discouraged this notion, but the matter was left undecided. After the transfer of power the ruler at first made no statement about accession to either state. Negotiations began with the new government of India about some form of association with it, but the Indian Government was unwilling to sign any treaty which might seem to acknowledge that Hyderabad already possessed some independent status.

The Nizam was willing to offer 'articles of association', covering arrangements for defence, foreign affairs and communications, but not a formal instrument of accession. This was unacceptable to India. She proposed instead a referendum (which, since the majority of the population was Hindu, would probably have led to a decision for accession to

275

India). Under pressure from militant Muslims the ruler rejected this and threatened instead accession to Pakistan. In November he none the less signed with India a 'standstill agreement', under which he agreed to work in close co-operation with India, while India gave assurances that she claimed no 'paramountcy' in Hyderabad (such as the British had possessed), nor the right to send troops into that country.

Soon afterwards the Nizam moved further towards Pakistan. He advanced a loan to that country (he was the richest ruler in India), and prohibited the export of precious metals to India. Intensive pro-Muslim and anti-Hindu activity began to be undertaken by a militant minority group, the Razakars. In March 1948 the Indian Government sent a note demanding, among other things, the withdrawal of the loan to Pakistan, the banning of the Razakars, and the cancellation of an agreement with United Press of the USA for a transmission station for foreign news. On 31 March Hyderabad rejected this and proposed that any points of difference concerning the standstill agreement should be put to arbitration. This was in turn rejected by India, which continued to demand the banning of the Razakars and other measures and began to institute an economic blockade of Hyderabad.

On 21 August Hyderabad turned to the UN. She formally appealed to the Security Council for assistance, complaining of India's action in threatening her with invasion and economic blockade so as to coerce her into the renunciation of her independence. She asked the Security Council for assistance and sent a delegation to put forward her complaint. India resisted all discussion, on the grounds that Hyderabad had no status to bring the question to the Council at all, since it was not an independent state.

The Council considered the matter during a number of meetings. Most of the discussion related to whether Hyderabad was able to initiate action in the Council at all, and to the credentials of the Hyderabad delegation. This debate was inconclusive, and the Security Council had still not decided what action it should take on the Hyderabad complaint when it was overtaken by events.

Early in September, India again formally demanded the banning of the Razakars and the control of 'communists', alleged to be gaining influence on the state's borders with

India. She demanded the right to send troops to Secunderabad to establish 'a sense of security' among the people of Hyderabad, and help to maintain the peace of India. On 13 September, before she had received any reply, India sent troops into Hyderabad. Within five days they had conquered the state and the Hyderabad troops had surrendered. The state was placed under a military government and the Razakar leaders were arrested. Hyderabad was then incorporated into the Indian union. On 23 September the Nizam withdrew Hyderabad's appeal to the Security Council. For a time Pakistan fought to keep the item on the agenda, claiming that the ruler had acted under duress in withdrawing it, and that the Indian invasion made Security Council discussion all the more necessary. Majority opinion in the Council, however, felt that since the complaint had been formally withdrawn, and since in any case there was now nothing that could be done, it would be best to let the matter drop.

Most of the other disputes about accession were not brought before the UN. One of them, however, should be mentioned, because of its implications for the major dispute of this kind which occupied the UN for many years. This concerned Junagadh in Western India. Here once more the majority of the population were Hindus but there was a Muslim ruler. In this case the ruler announced his decision to accede to Pakistan, though he had no common border with Pakistan (he apparently had some encouragement in this course from the Pakistani Government). Formally there was nothing illegal in such a decision, but India protested to Pakistan that it would be contrary to the wishes of the great majority of the people, as well as to the principle of geographical continuity, if such an accession took place. During October India occupied two regions of Junagadh which, she said, had themselves claimed independence from that state and accession to India. The ruler, in increasing economic and other difficulties, fled to Pakistan. And the government he left behind ultimately negotiated for accession to India. This was ratified by a plebiscite organised by the Indian Government.

The significance of the incident was that in this case India clearly regarded the wishes of the majority of the inhabitants as being the decisive factor, as she had too, in effect, over Hyderabad. Pakistan, on the other hand, even after the plebiscite, regarded the accession as illegal and said that the original choice of the ruler should be the decisive factor, as had been agreed by both states. In other words, on these two matters both countries adopted a position exactly opposite to that which they were to hold on the far more important dispute which broke out at about the same time over Kashmir.

KASHMIR

Kashmir was a far more important territory than either of these. Unlike Hyderabad and Junagadh, it was contiguous to both India and Pakistan. It had a population of over 4 million. It covered a large area, of crucial strategic importance, at the north of the sub-continent, commanding the approach to both India and Pakistan, and having borders with China, Tibet and Afghanistan. It covered a diversity of territories, including Ladakh, Baltistan and Gilgit in the north, Jammu to the south, and the beautiful and lush Vale of Kashmir itself. It contained various peoples of a number of races and languages. Of these about 80 per cent were Muslims; but the ruler was a Hindu.

As in Hyderabad, the ruler had made no decision about accession at the time of independence and he too apparently hoped to maintain his own state's independence if possible. Pakistan was not averse to continued independence, since immediate accession must almost certainly be to India, given the ruler's religion. The Maharajah had pursued, however, a highly autocratic and repressive policy. Muslim leaders had been put in prison during 1946 and there was already much simmering discontent among the Muslim population. After independence this restiveness among the Muslim people increased. There were some communal disturbances and in September 1947 there was a small-scale revolt in Poonch, not far from the Pakistani border.

This led, in the second half of October, to a large-scale incursion into Kashmir by the Pathan tribesmen of north-east Pakistan. This was, if not encouraged, by no means prevented by the Pakistani authorities. The Kashmiri forces were weak, and by 24 October it began to look as if the capital, Srinagar, might be overrun. On that day the Maharajah appealed to

India for help. V. P. Menon, the Indian Secretary of the Home Ministry, flew to Srinagar to discuss the request. On 26 October the ruler signed an instrument of accession agreeing to join the Indian union. This was in a sense a deal: the ruler exchanged accession, which he would have preferred to avoid, for a promise of military assistance from India, which, from that point, was defending what she regarded as her own territory.

The next day India sent a battalion of Sikh troops, who were able to secure the defence of Srinagar. Meanwhile Lord Mountbatten, the Governor-General, in accepting the offer of accession, announced that, consistently with his government's (the Indian Government's) policy, that 'in any case where the issue of accession has been the subject of dispute, the question . . . should be decided in accordance with the wishes of the people', it had informed the ruler that 'as soon as law and order had been restored . . . the question of the state's accession should be settled by a reference to the people'. This offer was repeated by Nehru in a broadcast on 2 November, in which he said that the question would later be settled by a referendum under international auspices.

Mountbatten soon afterwards visited Jinnah, the Governor-General of Pakistan. Jinnah denounced the accession as a fraud and the despatch of Indian troops as an act of aggression. But he agreed to use his influence to secure the withdrawal of the tribesmen if India withdrew her forces simultaneously. After this there could be a plebiscite organised by the two governors-general together. India agreed to the idea of a plebiscite, probably under UN auspices, but refused to withdraw her forces until all the tribesmen had withdrawn and order had been restored. This remained the essential point in dispute for many years.

During the autumn, India was able to clear the Vale area of invaders, but the Gilgit region in the north was taken over by tribesmen loyal to Pakistan. Further direct talks between the prime ministers of the two countries in December got nowhere. A temporary stalemate developed in the fighting, with the territory of Kashmir effectively partitioned between the two countries.

On 31 December, Nehru referred the dispute to the Security Council. On the following day, 1 January 1948, the Indian representative on the Council issued a memorandum of complaint against Pakistan. On 15 January, Ayyangai, the former Prime Minister of Kashmir, presented the Indian case in the Council. He laid stress on the agreement of both countries that accession was to be decided by the rulers. The ruler of Kashmir had legally acceded to India. This meant that India's forces were justified in being in Kashmir, while Pakistani forces there, whether regular or irregular, were guilty of aggression. The immediate step was for the raiders to withdraw. Once law and order had been restored it might be possible for India too to withdraw her forces. He therefore requested the Council to pass a resolution under Article 35 of the Charter,[1] calling on Pakistan to cease interfering in Kashmir and to prevent her nationals from doing so by denying them bases and supplies. This case was supported at the UN by Sheikh Abdullah, at this time a firm supporter of Indian rule in Kashmir.

For Pakistan Sir Zafrullah Khan, the Foreign Minister, denied that the question was one of interference from outside. He described the fighting as the effect of an internal revolt of the Muslim population against the oppresive and anti-Muslim policies of their Hindu ruler. He challenged the legality of the accession, which had been brought about by 'fraud and violence' and without any attempt to consult Pakistan. It violated the principle of self-determination; and he quoted the Junagadh case to show that India herself in other areas had supported the prior claim of the people's wishes in determining accession. He accused India of interfering in the affairs of Kashmir and of oppressing the local Muslim population, as she had oppressed Muslims in other parts of India. He proposed that the Council should set up a commission to arrange for a ceasefire, followed by the withdrawal of all outside troops, the establishment of an impartial Kashmiri administration (in Pakistan's eyes this excluded one led by Sheikh Abdullah) and, finally, a plebiscite to determine the wishes of the people.

The crucial questions concerned the order of withdrawal and the legality of the existing administration in Kashmir: questions which were to remain in dispute for the next twenty years. India insisted that the first step should be the withdrawal of the tribal forces and of any other Pakistani elements that might be assisting them. After this Indian forces might be reduced, though some would have to remain to maintain law and order. Later a plebiscite, under UN supervision but with the local administration remaining, could be held. Only if this went against union with India could the accession to India be reversed. Against this Pakistan wanted all foreign troops withdrawn simultaneously; the establishment of a new and 'impartial' administration; and a plebiscite which would be undertaken under 'international authority, control and responsibility'.

When the issue first came up, most members of the Council genuinely had no preconceptions and no firm political commitment to one side or the other. In the eyes of most members the first aim must be to bring about a ceasefire. On 17 January the Council passed a resolution calling on both sides to bring this about, to refrain from any action that might aggravate the situation and to keep the Council informed of any change in the situation. The British representative proposed discussions between the two parties at the UN under the chairmanship of the President of the Council. These took place in the next two or three days, and on 20 January the President was able to introduce a resolution which had been agreed between the two sides. This was to set up a UN Commission for India and Pakistan (UNCIP), to investigate the facts of the situation, to seek to smooth away difficulties between the two sides and to report to the Council.[2] The resolution said nothing for the moment on the tricky question of the timing of withdrawal.

In the following weeks there were intensive discussions. A majority were increasingly inclined to accept Pakistan's view that a call for a ceasefire would be ineffective unless accompanied by a commitment to a plebiscite to resolve the underlying problem. Since Indian military control might be used to influence the outcome, this plebiscite would have to be undertaken under some impartial interim administration to be set up by the UN. Meanwhile the armed forces in the area, including India's, would need at least to be reduced. A resolution to this effect was proposed by the Canadian president of the Council on 10 February. This was totally unacceptable to India, which demanded an adjournment to allow her delegation to return to Delhi for consultations. This was reluctantly agreed and there was no further discussion for a month.

When the Indian delegation returned, there were prolonged negotiations. The United States, Britain, Canada, Belgium, China and Colombia introduced a resolution which went a small way to meet Indian concerns. On 21 April this was passed with minor amendments. The resolution called for a withdrawal of the Pathan tribesmen first, followed by a progressive reduction of Indian forces to the minimum level necessary for the support of the civilian administration. This administration should itself be broadened to bring in all major political groups, while law and order would be placed in the hands of locally recruited personnel. A plebiscite administrator would be appointed by the UN Secretary-General and would operate as an officer of the Kashmiri Government, when appropriate conditions had been restored in organising a plebiscite. The plebiscite would be supervised by the UNCIP. This was passed overwhelmingly. India, however, announced that she refused to accept it and formally informed the Secretary-General that she would not be bound by it. Pakistan was also critical of certain features of the resolution, but undertook to accept it on the interpretation given to it by its sponsors.

The UNCIP had five members. The United States, Belgium and Colombia were nominated by the Secretary-General; Czechoslovakia and Argentina were nominated by India and Pakistan respectively. It first met in Geneva on 16 June and reached the sub-continent only on 7 July. From May of that year Pakistani regular forces had become engaged in the fighting on an increasing scale. The Pakistani Foreign Minister frankly informed the Commission when they saw him in the middle of July that three Pakistani battalions had been involved since May. This was said to be for self-defence and to prevent Indian forces from taking over the whole of Kashmir. The Indian Government, with same reason, regarded this as a confession of foreign aggression against what was now Indian territory. Nehru was insistent that Pakistan should be condemned and called on to withdraw.[3]

Pakistani forces had rapidly occupied much of the northwest of Kashmir, assuming control of Gilgit, Baltistan, and part of Ladakh. But they were pushed back by Indian forces from Kargil, the key communications centre controlling the route from Kashmir to Ladakh. In face of this intensive fighting the immediate task for the Commission clearly was to bring about a ceasefire.

On 13 August it produced a plan for peace. There would be a ceasefire, followed by the withdrawal of the tribesmen and the beginning of withdrawal by the regular Pakistan forces; followed in turn by a truce, under which the rest of the Pakistan forces and the 'bulk' of the Indian forces would be withdrawn. After this arrangements could be made for the plebiscite, with an administration of local authorities under the supervision of the Commission itself.

This was much more acceptable to India than any earlier proposals: it made a clear distinction between the rights of Indian and Pakistani forces in the area, and it did not presuppose the establishment of a new administration before the plebiscite. She therefore accepted the proposals, subject to certain assurances that sovereignty in Azad Kashmir (the part under Pakistani control) would not be accorded to the local authorities there. Pakistan on the other hand was, for the same reason, much less happy, demanding a return to the formula in the 21 April resolution. Thus her acceptance was hedged about by so many conditions that it was virtually a rejection. Subsequent negotiations brought about some qualifications. Pakistan received certain assurances concerning the powers of the plebiscite administrator and the right of political organisations to campaign, while India secured others to the effect that the administrator would not usurp the powers of the state government. Even this degree of agreement was a substantial achievement by the Commission.

This was the first UN resolution since mid-January which had been at least substantially accepted by both sides and it was accordingly to become the basis for many future proposals for the territory. Meanwhile the fighting continued. During the autumn Indian forces had pushed Pakistani troops from Poonch, and a Pakistani attempt to cut the Indian line of communication from west to east (a measure to be attempted again seventeen years later) failed. By this time something of a stalemate had been reached. The two armies both had British commanding officers, and even technically were still, during a transition period, under the same (British) supreme com-

mander, General Auchinlech. These were anxious to limit the
conflict between two Commonwealth countries. For these
various reasons, on 25 December a ceasefire was signed. This
took effect on 1 January 1949, and lasted reasonably well for
the next sixteen years. By this time Pakistan held much of the
north-east of the country and a narrow strip to the west of
Kashmir and Jammu. India held most of Kashmir and
Jammu, half of Poonch, as well as most of Ladakh in the
north-east. The Security Council on 5 January welcomed the
ceasefire and adopted the general scheme for a settlement
proposed by the UNCIP, including the appointment of a
plebiscite administrator. Admiral Chester Nimitz was nominated for that post by the Secretary-General.

Neither of the parties was entirely happy about the arrangements for the plebiscite. Pakistan was afraid that if it
took place under the existing government of Sheikh Abdullah
(who had now become Chief Minister) it would come up with
the answer that government wanted, and she therefore
demanded that a new and wholly neural administration
should be established during the interim. India, on the other
hand, would not accept any arrangement that seemed to
challenge the legality of the existing administration or the
accomplished fact of accession.

Meanwhile the Commission concentrated on the arrangements for the ceasefire and the demarcation of a ceasefire line.
Finally, under an agreement reached between the two sides at
Karachi in July 1949, a ceasefire line was agreed and the
sporadic fighting around it which had continued came to an
end. UN observers were placed along the line to police it and
remained there for over twenty years. Both sides also agreed
not to increase the size of their forces in the area.

Discussion now centred on the arrangements for withdrawal. Big differences emerged. The August resolution of
the UNCIP the previous year had said that the 'bulk' of the
Indian forces should be withdrawn before the plebiscite took
place, but there was no agreement on what this meant. India
in turn wanted assurances that the Azad Kashmir forces on
the Pakistani side of the line would be disbanded. She also
wanted to be able to send Indian forces to occupy the northern
territories which had been overrun by Pakistan's regular
forces. On 9 August the UNCIP proposed a conference on

these points, but because of disagreement about the agenda this never took place. The UNCIP then proposed arbitration by Admiral Nimitz on these issues. This was supported, on 31 August 1949, in a statement by President Truman and Prime Minister Attlee – an intervention that was bitterly resented by India, which began to feel that the Western powers were increasingly siding with Pakistan on the issue.

The matter was considered by the Security Council again in December. The basic differences, concerning the arrangements for withdrawal and for administration during the plebiscite, remained as wide as ever. These in turn reflected even more fundamental differences. India regarded herself as being in Kashmir by right, so that all arrangements which might be made for reducing her forces would be a voluntary concession, while Pakistan was an aggressor which must first of all 'vacate' her aggression by withdrawing. Pakistan, on the other hand, regarded the question as one of self-determination for the people of Kashmir, with India and Pakistan on an equal footing as interested outsiders. Any resolution, therefore, calling for a 'reform of' administration in Kashmir before the plebiscite took place was unacceptable to India; while any arrangement which left India effectively in control during that period was unacceptable to Pakistan.

UN ATTEMPTS AT MEDIATION

On 17 December the Council decided to appoint an 'informal mediator' to try to resolve these differences. The first mediator to be appointed was General McNaughton of Canada. He attempted first to tackle the question of withdrawal, or 'demilitarisation', as it came to be called (since total Indian withdrawal was no longer demanded). He tried first to tackle the question of the Azad Kashmiri forces, which had understandably concerned India (since Pakistani withdrawal would mean little if local forces loyal to her ramained). He proposed that these, as well as the local militia on the Indian side, should be reduced by disbanding, but not eliminated altogether. Some Indian regular forces would then remain in addition on the side they occupied, but no regular Pakistani forces on the other. In addition a UN 'representative' should be appointed (in addition to the plebiscite administrator) to supervise this process of demilitarisation. But even this was unacceptable to India, on the grounds that it 'legitimised' the concept of Azad Kashmir, which had been illegally established; the Azad Kashmiri forces should be totally disbanded and disarmed.

On 14 March 1950 the Security Council took up some of the McNaughten proposals. It decided to appoint Sir Owen Dixon, an Australian lawyer, as the 'UN representative' McNaughten had proposed. He would in practice replace the UNCIP in the area. His task was to bring about demilitarisation which would lead to a plebiscite, as the UN had already agreed. But he could make his own independent proposals if he wished.

Dixon spent more than a month in Kashmir, had long talks with Nehru and Liaquat Ali Khan, and organised a four-day meeting between himself and the two leaders. He became aware of the difficulty, even impossibility, of bringing about demilitarisation on an agreed basis, still more of organising a plebiscite for the disposal of the entire state, with its many disparate regions and the huge refugee problem that would be created, whichever side prevailed. He saw that the two sides did not much care about recovering the outlying areas. The real heart of the problem was in the Vale of Kashmir, claimed by Pakistan because of its Muslim majority, and by India because of the fact of accession and its strategic situation.

He began therefore, for the first time, to look for some totally different kind of solution. This was the only moment during the long history of the dispute that any proposals were made that had the slightest chance of securing a settlement. 'I have formed the opinion', he wrote, 'that if there is any chance of settling the dispute . . . it now lies in partition, and in some means of allocating the Valley, rather than in an overall plebiscite.' The way of achieving this should be left to the two parties themselves. But if they could not agree a neutral administration should be formed under UN supervision to undertake the plebiscite in the Valley if ever this proved possible. At the very least the conditions of the ceasefire should be improved and the UN observers kept in being on a permanent basis (which could in effect bring about a *de facto* partition).

This was by far the most realistic approach to the problem made at any time. The fact was that India had never really been concerned with what happened to Gilgit and Baltistan, nor Pakistan with Ladakh, or even Jammu. But, so long as the entire huge territory was all at stake, the incentive to obduracy was increased. The crucial question therefore concerned Kashmir itself, which should be considered in isolation. Even this could be partitioned on the basis of the plebiscite. And the report clearly hinted, in its final pages, that, provided the dangers of fighting could be reduced, even the continuation of the *status quo* might be supportable. Unfortunately the Council never seriously took up the opportunity the report offered for such a compromise. As always at this period, it looked for ideal solutions. The UN had been earlier committed to a plebiscite for the entire area; and Pakistan, with some help from her friends, would not now allow that commitment to lapse.

Instead of pursuing these proposals seriously, the UN became diverted by constitutional developments in Kashmir which it felt could prejudice its future. In October of 1950 the Indian-sponsored General Council of the All Jammu and Kashmir National Conference had recommended the convening of a constituent assembly to determine the future affiliation of the state. In December Pakistan called on the Security Council to demand that India should refrain from proceeding with this proposal, which might prejudice the holding of a free and impartial plebiscite. In March, after some delay, the Council did in fact pass a resolution which sought to negate the effect of any such conference, declaring that the holding of such a constituent assembly and any action it might take could not constitute a 'disposition of Kashmir' such as the Council had previously proposed by plebiscite. The constituent assembly none the less met and decided in favour of further integration with India.

Soon afterwards, in April, the Council appointed a successor to Sir Owen Dixon as UN representative in Kashmir. Dr Frank Graham, formerly a US Senator and a member of the UN Commission on Indonesia, was chosen. He too was to try and secure agreed proposals for bringing about the demilitarisation of Kashmir and report to the Council within three months. Where the parties disagreed, they were called on to accept arbitration by arbitrators appointed by the International Court of Justice (a proposal strongly rejected by India as an affront to her sovereignty).[4]

During the next two or three years Dr Graham undertook a number of missions to the sub-continent and presented five reports to the Council. During this time he made many alternative proposals concerning the exact timing of the demilitarisation process, the precise balance of forces which would remain after this was complete, the date when the plebiscite administrator would take up his duties, and so on. None of these resolved the differences between the two countries. While Dr Graham proposed that the forces on the Indian side should be three times larger than the local forces on the Pakistan side, India demanded forces five or six times larger. While Pakistan demanded a 'new and neutral' administration to take over in Kashmir, India continued to demand that the existing legally established administration should remain in full control, and that the plebiscite administrator should have responsibility only for the conduct of the plebiscite. Underlying these familiar difficulties was a wider problem (not unlike that preventing agreement over Korea between 1946 and 1950): because discussion was directed exclusively to the disposal of the entire territory in a single block, each party – above all India, which held the most valuable share – had every temptation to prefer the preservation of the *status quo* to the risk of losing the entire, immensely valuable territory at one fell swoop.

Attempts at direct negotiations during these years were no more successful. There were a number of talks between the leaders of the two countries, in London, Karachi and elsewhere, during the years between 1953 and 1956. But they produced no solution even to the initial problem of demilitarisation, let alone over the conduct of the plebiscite. The granting of US military assistance to Pakistan at the end of 1953, and her adherence to the South East Asia Treaty Organisation (SEATO) in the following year further embittered relations between the two countries and made India still more wary about demilitarisation in Kashmir. Conversely, the Soviet Union increasingly came out in support of India. So increasingly the conflict began to acquire cold-war overtones.

The negotiations did reach preliminary agreement, in

August 1953, on two small points: a date for appointing a plebiscite administrator; and the setting up of a committee to look at some of the differences on demilitarisation. But this only led to further difficulties concerning who should be appointed as plebiscite administrator: India was now unwilling to accept Admiral Nimitz, both because she increasingly distrusted any American, and because she wished if possible to remove the whole conflict from the hands of the UN. Because of these differences Nimitz shortly afterwards resigned. But this did not resolve the question. Again for a brief period in 1955, after direct talks between leaders of the two countries, Pakistan seemed willing to explore the possibility of partition, but after the Prime Minister of Pakistan had returned to his own country he was forced by public opinion there once more to reject any such idea.

During all this time Indian-occupied Kashmir was being progressively integrated into India, through the abolition of customs duties, the introduction of Indian taxes, and integration with the Northern Zonal Council of India. In 1953 Sheikh Abdullah had been dismissed as a result of a revolt within his own cabinet. He was later arrested and charged with corruption, 'disruptionism', and 'dangerous foreign contacts'. But there is little doubt that the real reason for his arrest was the fact that he was moving away from support for India, and was increasingly inclined to seek an independent future for Kashmir. His successor obediently followed the policy favoured by India – that is, increasing integration within the Indian union.

Because of these measures and the dangers of a *fait accompli*, Pakistan felt that that she had no choice but to return to the UN, where she had the weight of opinion of her side. In January 1957 the constituent assembly established in Kashmir had completed its work of drafting a constitution, and announced that this would come into force before the end of that month. Pakistan protested to the Security Council that this would lead to the further integration of the state into India and was incompatible with the previous UN decision for a plebiscite to decide the state's future status. She therefore demanded that the Council should call on India to allow no change in that status and to withdraw her forces from the state, allowing them to be replaced by a UN force (this was just after the first UN force, in the Middle East, had been created). Krishna Menon replied in a typically rhetorical speech, lasting for three meetings. He denied that there was any great significance in the constituent assembly's action. It was a 'sub-sovereign' body, without power to determine Kashmir's status, and its action was only declaratory. The basic factor in Kashmir's situation was the aggression committed by Pakistan nearly ten years ago, which the UN had still failed to reverse. Because of this failure, and in accordance with the ruler's legal decision on accession, the constituent assembly had been set up to enable the people of Kashmir to rule themselves democratically. The main task of the UN now was to bring an end to the Pakistan aggression and secure a withdrawal of her forces.

The Council first passed a preliminary resolution, reaffirming its earlier decisions on Kashmir and again declaring that the convening of the constituent assembly and any actions it might take would not constitute the final disposition of the state which its earlier resolutions had called for. On 14 February the Council passed a more positive resolution. This was the UN's last serious effort to resolve the problem. The Council now asked Gunnar Jarring, then its president and formerly Swedish ambassador in India, to seek to mediate on the conflict and to 'examine with the governments of India and Pakistan' ways of securing demilitarisation and any other steps necessary to resolve the dispute, bearing in mind the proposal for the use of a temporary UN force as well as the other statements made by the two sides. This resolution was violently rejected by India, above all because of its reference to a UN force. And the Soviet Union, having proposed amendments to eliminate any reference to demilitarisation or a UN force, proceeded to veto it. In consequence the United States, Britain and Australia introduced a simplified resolution, which merely asked Jarring to explore proposals likely to lead to a settlement and report back by 15 April. Even this was objected to by India, because it referred to earlier UN resolutions, some of which India had not accepted. But this time the Soviet Union did not veto, and Jarring set off for the sub-continent on 14 March.

He spent a month in the two countries. But the chances of effective mediation were now smaller than ever. There had been a significant change. The Indian Government no longer accepted even the principle of a plebiscite, or of demilitarisation for this purpose, on the grounds that circumstances had changed. In his report Jarring fastened on the resolution passed by the UNCIP on 13 August 1948, about the only UN resolutions which both parties had accepted. Since differences had arisen on its interpretation, Jarring proposed that those questions should be resolved by arbitration. Pakistan accepted this proposal, but India once again did not (since she claimed that to accept arbitration would put in question her rights in Kashmir and would give Pakistan a standing in a question that was not legally her affair).

The report was not debated in the Security Council till six months later, on 24 September. After more marathon speeches by Krishna Menon and his opponent Feroz Khan Noon, and more threats of a veto by the Soviet Union, an agreed resolution was eventually passed on 2 December. This asked Dr Graham, still the official UN mediator, to proceed once again to the sub-continent to see if he could resolve the differences still existing about the preconditions for de-militarisation, as well as on the other differences which had prevented a settlement; to meet Indian objections (and the threat of a Soviet veto) all mention of 'demilitarisation' was now removed.

Dr Graham spent about a month on the sub-continent in January and February 1958. On his return he made five recommendations: for a reaffirmation of earlier declaration by the parties relating to the creation of a peaceful atmos-phere; for a new declaration of respect for the ceasefire line; for a study of how administration should be carried out on the Pakistani side after withdrawal, including the possible use of a UN force on that side alone; for an attempt to reach agreement on the form of a plebiscite; and for a conference between the two prime ministers in the spring. Pakistan accepted all five recommendations in principle. India rejected all of them. She claimed that they ignored Pakistan's original aggression and her failure to abide by the earlier resolutions, and placed India and Pakistan on the same footing.

So yet another UN effort at conciliation failed. Over and over again, the UN had passed resolutions, most of which had been rejected by one party or both – usually by India. A whole

series of UN representatives had travelled to the sub-
continent and made proposals. Yet, after more than ten years,
virtually no progress towards a settlement had been made. No
undertakings made by the parties had carried matters any
further than the resolution agreed (partially) by both sides in
August 1948. This stalemate reflected the fact that India, the
country which occupied the lion's share of the territory, was
increasingly unwilling to contemplate any compromise which
might forfeit her control of it.

CONCLUSIONS

The UN was not again to be significantly involved in the affairs
of the territory until fighting once more broke out over it in
1965. Its handling of the matter during the first phase of the
dispute can scarcely be regarded as one of its triumphs.

Admittedly, it was a dispute of a particularly difficult kind
for an international organisation to influence. The legal rights
were unquestionably on India's side; and neither UN resolutions nor world opinion ever adequately acknowledged this
fact (again reflecting the UN's Western bias at this time).
Pakistan's case was based, against this, on considerations of
equity and principle: in particular, the 'right of self-
determination'. Thus each party could claim it had a principle
of a kind on its side. And neither was willing to compromise on
them. Moreover, the country in possession of the most
valuable and coveted part of the territory, India, was also the
more powerful. Pakistan never possessed military leverage
sufficient to make the threat of self-help a significant inducement to India to compromise. Neither the mediators nor the
purely declamatory action indulged in by the UN were in
these circumstances likely to achieve much. Finally, the sense
that the UN was committed, almost from the beginning, to a
particular type of solution, and to one that favoured Pakistan,
reduced its ability to mediate and made India increasingly
hostile to all attempts by the organisation to seek a solution.

Even without these difficulties, however, the UN did not
make the chances of a settlement easier by the methods it
adopted. There were two fundamental errors in its handling
of the conflict. First, it never seriously entertained the

possibility of compromise. It always presupposed, like Solomon in dealing with another conflict of possession, that both parties must want all or nothing. But, while Solomon had good reason for supposing that one party at least would not contemplate a compromise, the UN had no good reason for such a premise. There can be no doubt that the influence of its resolutions, its mediators and its 'representatives' on the spot would have been far greater if these had made some attempt to explore some kind of halfway solution which would have left part of the territory with one and given part to the other. Only Sir Owen Dixon recognised this realistically, seeing that the strategic, as well as the emotional, importance of Kashmir was such that India at least was never likely to implement any solution which would involve the danger of losing the entire territory. But his proposals were never seriously explored. If the UN had in a systematic way pursued a compromise of this kind, or even some fairly marginal adjustment of the existing ceasefire line – in other words, a solution which might give at least some satisfaction to both sides, rather than one which would represent total victory for one and total defeat for the other – it might have got somewhere near securing a settlement.

Secondly, as on so many other issues, the UN sought to lay down, by resolution, the required answer, rather than attempting simply, without preconditions, to institute the negotiations between the parties which alone were likely to produce a solution. Early on in the dispute the UN became committed to the notion of demilitarisation and an overall plebiscite as the required formula; and it was not willing at any later stage to modify this stand. It was not willing to do so because the majority sympathised with the Pakistani demand for self-determination (a demand which Indian words in the days immediately after accession made easier to justify); and because Pakistan could always quote earlier resolutions in support of the course of action she favoured.

A proposal for unconditional negotiation would of course have meant abandoning the decision to make 'self-determination' the basis of the settlement. But this was a principle that was scarely ever applied to other areas previously under colonial rule when they became independent. And it was one that was never, even in principle, to have been applied in the Indian sub-continent. It was Britain that decided, with the consent of India and Pakistan, that the destiny of the states should be determined by their rulers rather than by their peoples. And criticisms of the failure to apply the principle over Kashmir could as reasonably be raised against Britain as against India, which merely sought to stick to the rules concerning accession that both sides had accepted.

India therefore clung tenaciously to this legal justification of her stand and understandably felt aggrieved that few others sympathised with her. It is indeed strange that the legal rights and wrongs of the case were so little regarded in the UN. The real reason must be that the concept of 'self-determination' had acquired such a universal acclaim in this age that, once that magic formula was invoked by Pakistan, she managed to mobilise much of the world on her side. But India from an early stage had made up her mind not to concede the principle in this case (unless perhaps on terms highly favourable to herself, with Indian troops and a pro-Indian administration in attendance). So the dispute festered on, eventually to erupt years later when, Pakistan's patience finally exhausted, she attempted another last desperate bid to seize the territory, by methods essentially similar to those she first adopted in 1947–8.

15 Guatemala

In the summer of 1954 the Security Council was faced, for the first time, with an issue arising in the Western Hemisphere. On 19 June Guatemala asked for an urgent meeting of the Council, asking it to put a stop to an act of aggression against Guatemala.

Guatemala was at that time ruled by a government led by Arbenz Guzman. This was a radical but by no means communist government which had introduced a programme of drastic reform, nationalised a Western-owned railway and introduced other social and economic changes. In February 1953 it had expropriated a large part of the banana plantations of the United Fruit Company, a large US corporation; and its offer of compensation had been regarded by the United States as inadequate. During January 1954 President Arbenz accused the governments of Nicaragua and Honduras of plotting, with other Central American governments and the CIA, to train Guatemalan exiles for an invasion of the country: a charge resolutely denied by all concerned.

In May of that year the US Government announced that a shipload of arms had been landed in Guatemala which had been obtained from communist sources and shipped from Poland. The State Department described this as a 'development of extreme gravity'. President Eisenhower said that it would be a 'terrible thing if the communist dictatorship establishes an outpost on this continent'. The Guatemalan Government replied that it had been obliged to turn to communist sources because it had attempted and failed to get arms from the United States. And it again accused the United States of equipping and training Guatemalan exiles for an invasion from neighbouring countries. On 24 May the United States announced the conclusion of new military assistance pacts with Nicaragua and Honduras under which she was sending them arms. On 17 June the State Department

announced that it had requested the co-operation of other
maritime states in maintaining an embargo on all arms
shipments to Guatemala: it had therefore asked for the right
to search the ships of other countries on the high seas (a right
that was not, however, accepted even by some of her allies).

On 18 June forces based in Honduras launched an attack
against Guatemala. They quickly captured a number of
frontier posts and advanced about 15 kilometres into the
country. On 19 June aircraft flown from Honduras and
Nicaragua bombed and machine-gunned targets in
Guatemala City, San José and other towns. It was then that
Guatemala made its appeal to the UN.

The Security Council met to consider the Guatemalan
complaint on 20 June. The representative of Guatemala
stated that his country was being invaded by an expeditionary
force from the neighbouring states of Honduras and
Nicaragua: though the invaders claimed to be exiles engaged
in a revolution against their own government, they were in
fact mercenaries, organised and financed by foreign governments and led by the United States, and they could not have
operated at all without the connivance of the Honduran and
Nicaraguan governments. He asked the Council to call on the
governments of those two countries to halt the operations and
to apprehend those who were involved in organising and
directing them. In addition he asked that the Council should
establish an observation commission, to be sent to Guatemala
and its neighbours, to examine the situation on the spot, and
to verify whether the charges his government had made were
well founded.

This was a procedure not unlike that which the UN had
used in dealing with the somewhat similar charges raised by
the Greek Government against its neighbours. There was,
however, one big difference. Greece was a friend of the
governments which then dominated the UN, and her enemies
were their enemies. For Guatemala the opposite was the case.
The Guatemalan Government was distrusted, and indeed
reviled, by the United States and some other Western governments; and its enemies were therefore their friends. For
this reason the type of measures used in Greece, in almost
exactly parallel circumstances, were here by no means
favoured.

The representatives of Honduras and Nicaragua did not even attempt at this meeting to answer the factual accusations made against their countries, though they did subsequently address written communications denying the charges. They stated only that the accusations were matters for the Organisation of American States (OAS), an organisation designed explicitly, they held, to consider situations of this kind within Latin America. The matter should not therefore be discussed in the Security Council at all.

The representative of Brazil, a member of the Council, supported the proposal to refer the question to the OAS. With the Colombian representative, he introduced a draft resolution proposing that the Security Council should refer the matter to that organisation, asking merely that it should as soon as possible report to the Council on any action it took. They quoted Article 52 of the Charter, relating to regional arrangements, in support of this proposal. This article stated that the Security Council should 'encourage the development of pacific settlement of local disputes' through regional arrangements, if necessary by reference from the Council. This was the provision which, as we saw, when the UN was established the Latin American states (though not at that time the United States) had demanded in order to preserve the right of American states to deal with their own affairs. The reference to this article, however, ignored the point, firmly established when the Charter was adopted, that such arrangements were not to be used to usurp the authority of the Council itself, which should always remain available to be invoked in every case: a point on which originally the United States herself had insisted.

The representative of Guatemala protested that his government's appeal had been based on Articles 34, 35 and 39 of the Charter, which gave his country an unchallenged right to appeal to the Security Council. The Council should intervene directly on such questions and not through a regional organisation. The OAS might be appropriate for trying to resolve peaceful disputes among members, but was quite incapable of dealing with the situation where an invasion had already taken place. The French delegate then proposed an addition to the resolution of Brazil and Colombia by which the Security Council would at least, without prejudice to any measures taken by the OAS, call for the immediate termination of any action likely to cause further bloodshed and ask members to refrain from assisting such action. This was accepted, somewhat reluctantly, by the sponsors. But it was regarded by Guatemala as too weak to be effective.

The Soviet Union declared roundly that this was a clear case of aggression against a member-state by neighbouring states and it was therefore the duty of the Council itself to take action to end the aggression, not to refer it to some other body. But, apart from her, only the Lebanon and New Zealand half-heartedly defended the right of all members to have direct recourse to the UN. The United States, referring once more to Article 52 of the Charter, maintained that this was precisely the type of problem which should be dealt with in the first place by the OAS. She was obligingly supported in this by Britain and other Western states. Eventually ten members of the Council were willing to support the Latin American proposal to pass the matter to the OAS. The French request that the parties be asked to terminate armed action or assistance to that action was then passed by itself, without dissent.

The OAS took its time in considering the matter. Most of its members made no secret of their fear and detestation of the Arbenz government and were widely believed to be sympathetic with the invaders. It met only on 23 June. It then accepted a proposal by Nicaragua and Honduras (the states against which the complaint was raised) to send a fact-finding mission to Guatemala. That mission did not finally leave, however, for several days. By this time Guatamala was almost overrun. Meanwhile on 25 June, no longer prepared to wait, Guatemala, supported by the Soviet Union, again asked the Security Council to consider the matter.

The representatives of the United States, Brazil and Colombia now argued that the Council should not even discuss the question: it was, they said, already being dealt with by the OAS. They again emphasised the provisions in the Charter allowing local disputes to be considered by regional organisations, and maintained that it was essential for the UN to do nothing that could prejudice the use of such arrangements. On these grounds, they held, the item should not be placed on the agenda at all.

The Soviet Union said that the Council was under a duty to consider the complaint. It had the primary responsibility under the Charter for maintaining the peace. It had already, on these grounds, passed a resolution on the question. And it could not now be deprived of its responsibility on the grounds that the matter was being discussed elsewhere – least of all when the organisation in question had shown no concern or ability to defend the state being attacked.

Britain, France and China obediently supported the US view that there was no need for the Council even to place the question on the agenda. This did not mean, they maintained, that it was divesting itself of its responsibility (though they failed to explain what else it was doing). Only Denmark, New Zealand and the Lebanon supported the claim that the matter should at least be considered. When this request was put to the vote, there were thus only four votes in favour of discussing the item, five against – the three American states, Turkey and China – while Britain and France ingloriously abstained (knowing of course, that this meant there were not enough votes for inscription).

On 27 June, more than a week after the first complaint to the Council, the chairman of the Inter-American Peace Committee of the OAS informed the Secretary-General that that committee was establishing itself as a fact-finding body and intended to proceed to Guatemala, Honduras and Nicaragua. The Committee had been careful not to act too precipitously. It finally left by air on 29 June. By the time it arrived in Guatemala on the following day, the Guatemalan Government forces, without any aircraft or air defences, had been defeated and Arbenz had resigned. He was succeeded by a strongly anti-communist regime, imposed by the leaders of the invading forces. This proceeded to ban the Communist Party, to arrest 2000 alleged communists, and to reduce the numbers of those entitled to vote in elections.

On 8 July the Inter-American Peace Committee reported to the Council that the three governments concerned had now stated that the dispute between them was at an end and its services were therefore no longer required. The new Guatemalan Foreign Minister shortly afterwards informed the president of the Council that 'peace and order' had been restored in his country. The Guatemalan question could now therefore, he informed them, be removed from the Council's agenda. No members of the Council felt inclined to dispute this proposition. The invasion had succeeded; so the Council's work was done.

There has perhaps been no episode in the organisation's history to discreditable to its reputation as this. Instead of acting as an organisation to defeat aggression, it acted in a way carefully calculated to allow aggression to succeed. The fact was that the United States and the Latin American nations, weakly supported by a number of other Western states, did not wish that the UN should in this case take action to halt, or even to condemn, the invasion of a member-state. They used the ambiguous provisions of Article 52 to justify taking the affair out of the hands of the UN and shuffling off responsibility on to another organisation – an organisation that could be relied on to do nothing at all. For they knew that the political sympathies of the majority in that organisation were such as to make them quite unresponsive to the appeal Guatemala had raised, and wholly indifferent to, indeed enthusiastic about, the overthrowing of its government by invading forces.

The episode, besides reflecting once more the political bias of the Council at this time, revealed how vague and unsatisfactory was the wording of Article 52. In saying that the Council ought 'where appropriate' to refer a matter to a regional organisation, the article nowhere laid down, as it should have done, that if the appellant country itself (because of its distrust of the regional organisation or for any other reason) wished the Security Council itself to take action, it should be the duty of the Council to take the matter up. The same problem was to be raised in equally acute form ten years later in the case of the Dominican Republic.

It is of course arguable that it in practice made little difference whether the matter was referred to the OAS or discussed in the Council: the same majority in the Council which relegated it to the OAS could equally well have prevented any effective action from being taken by the Council itself. But at least if it had been obliged to take responsibility the Council might have been compelled to consider more seriously what action could or should be taken.

It could scarcely have failed to consider at least the possibility of despatching observers to establish the facts of the case, and to publicise the invasion to the world, as it had done in the case of Greece. It might even have been willing mildly to disapprove an attack on one country from the teritory of another to overturn its government (as the UN was to do without hesitation in the case of the attack, in similar circumstances and for the same purpose, against Hungary two years later). By failing even to do this, the Council revealed not merely how far it had become dominated by those favouring a particular political viewpoint. It had shown how far its effectiveness as a peace-keeping body was now inhibited by that fact.

16 Some Far Eastern Affairs

The UN never became directly concerned over the events of the Chinese civil war while it was being fought. It was regarded as the internal affair of China (even though both sides denounced the support allegedly being given to their opponents by outside sources). But the victory of the communist forces in China, together with the retention by their opponents of a precarious foothold in Taiwan and a few other territories, brought a number of problems in the years that followed.

Already in 1949, while the civil war still continued, the nationalist Chinese delegate had proposed in the Assembly a resolution deploring 'threats to the political independence and territorial integrity' of China and to the peace of the Far East through violations by the Soviet Union of the Treaty of Friendship between the two countries. During the civil war the Soviet Union, apart from allowing communist forces to take over Japanese weapons abandoned in Manchuria, gave, it is generally agreed, surprisingly little active support to the Chinese communists: perhaps because Stalin, when the civil war began, had no confidence in the ability of the communists to succeed and preferred meanwhile not to prejudice his relations with the government of Chiang Kai-shek. Undeterred by this, however, the Assembly passed a resolution calling on all states to respect the right of the Chinese people to choose a government independent of foreign control, and asking them to respect existing treaties relating to China and to refrain from seeking spheres of influence or special privileges there. This was universally understood to be directed against the Soviet Union.

In 1951, when the civil war was well over, nationalist China again proposed a similar resolution, once more accusing the Soviet Union of failing to carry out her Treaty of Friendship and Alliance with China in the period after 1945. This was supported by the United States and a number of other West-ern states. This time the Assembly adopted a stronger resolu-tion, categorically charging the Soviet Union with having failed to carry out its obligations under the treaty with China during the period since 1945.

This was a fairly typical cold-war move, once again reflect-ing the Western domination in the organisation at this period. A similar action took place two or three years later. When the Eisenhower administration came to power in the United States in 1952, it fulfilled its pre-election pledge to 'take the wraps off' Chiang Kai-shek. Henceforth the US Seventh Fleet, stationed in the China Sea, was used only to prevent attacks on Taiwan from the mainland, not to halt action in the opposite direction. The Nationalists thereupon undertook occasional, but mainly ineffectual, air raids, leaflet campaigns and forays by raiding parties in the coastal provinces of China off Taiwan. At the same time they continued to seek to maintain a blockade of the mainland. This frequently involved stopping on the high seas foreign shipping engaged in trade with China, seizing their cargo and detaining their crews for weeks, or even months, on end. Some Western states, including Britain and France, declared their anger at this practice, and Britain announced that she would provide merchant vessels with a naval escort which would resist any attempt to interfere with British ships.

In the autumn of 1954 the Soviet Union raised this issue in the Assembly. She denounced the nationalist action as a viola-tion of free navigation and asked the Assembly to condemn 'piratical raids' on merchant ships by naval vessels 'based on Formosa and controlled by the US authorities'. The United States denied that she had any control of the activities com-plained of or was 'occupying' Taiwan. The nationalist Chinese representative said that, since his country had been the main target of international communism in the period since the end of the Second World War, it was entitled to confiscate 'war contraband' being delivered to the communist regime in China, against which it was still at war. Most of the cargo seized was strategic material, on the delivery of which to China the General Assembly had recommended that an embargo should be placed during the Korean War. Most other members were unwilling to support the Soviet resolution of condemnation but in some cases expressed their own reservations about the activities of the nationalists. Eventually the Assembly decided to take no action on the Soviet complaint: it merely expressed the hope that the International Law Commission, which was at that time considering the law of the high seas, should take account of the Assembly discussions in its own deliberations. This refusal to pass any resolution even mildly criticising nationalist actions against shipping on the high seas, at a time when the civil war had been over for years, contrasted somewhat oddly with the strong criticism of the Soviet Union for a much less clear-cut violation of international rules a year or two before.

BURMESE COMPLAINTS

Another complaint resulting ultimately from the civil war was raised against the Nationalists. In 1953 Burma charged nationalist China in the Assembly with 'aggression' against Burmese territory. From the end of the civil war in China, a substantial contingent of nationalist Chinese forces had retreated south into Indo-China. Some of them had been disarmed and interned, but nearly 2000 had crossed into Burma. There they had lived off the countryside, preying on the local people, and were generally believed to make their living by cultivating opium and smuggling it to the outside world. The Burmese Government had demanded that they should leave Burmese territory or be disarmed and interned, but they had refused. Subsequently they had constructed an airfield by which they were receiving supplies from Taiwan and elsewhere. They had recruited further Chinese forces, partly refugees from southern China and partly from south-east Asia, so that the force had grown to about 12,000 strong, now led by the nationalist General Li Mi. The Burmese representative claimed that, besides repressing the local population with demands for food and other supplies, they had joined with other rebel forces in action against the Burmese Government. Attempts to solve the dispute by bilateral negotiations through the US Government had failed, so Burma now had to raise the question at the UN.

The nationalist Chinese representative said that the men in

question had mainly been recruited locally and had banded together to fight communism and for the liberation of their country. They were regarded as heroes by many Chinese all over the world, some of whom had contributed to maintaining the forces. But they were not under the control of the Government of the Republic of China, which had no responsibility for them. The forces were in the nature of guerrillas and their enemy was not the Government of Burma but the government ruling in China. The charge of aggression was thus unjustified. His government would however now give an assurance that it would no longer give clearance for any aircraft leaving Taiwan with supplies for these forces and would use its moral influence with the troops so as to get them to withdraw. Meanwhile Burma should not make matters more difficult by using force against them.

A number of Asian countries, as well as the communist states, supported the Burmese complaint, saying that, if the nationalist Chinese were serious in saying they did not wish to commit aggression against Burma, all they had to do was to give orders to Li Mi and his forces to leave. Others, including Britain, France and other Western powers, while sympathising with the Burmese complaint, doubted whether nationalist China could be held responsible for the troops, and therefore would not support the Burmese resolution (which asked the Assembly to 'condemn' the Kuomintang government in Taiwan for the aggression and to take all necessary steps to ensure the immediate cessation of its actions). The United States felt that the nationalist Chinese should agree in principle to withdraw the forces, which should anyway cease all hostile activity, and discussions should begin on the best way of achieving this. Eventually the Assembly adopted, instead of the somewhat intemperate Burmese resolution, a milder Mexican draft condeming the presence of the forces in Burma, declaring that they must be disarmed and interned or evacuated and asking for further negotiations for this purpose.

However, these were only partially successful. During the next six months over 6000 Chinese, including dependants, were evacuated voluntarily, but about the same number remained, with their arms. There were thus still 6000, camped near to the Burma-Thailand border, enriching themselves through the opium trade and, according to Burma, the forging of currency notes. They showed no desire to leave, and at the 1954 Assembly Burma therefore raised the question again, emphasising that the evacuation of the ramaining forces was still the responsibility of the nationalist authorities. The nationalist representative repeated that the forces were not under the control of his government; the affair was really a domestic Burmese question and not one for the Assembly at all. Eventually a compromise resolution was passed, with only China abstaining: this called on the remaining foreign forces to submit to disarmament and internment and asked all states to prevent any assistance which might enable them to remain in Burma.

This was the last that was heard of the matter at the UN. Burma abandoned the hope that the UN could assist her in the matter. But the Chinese forces remained for many years, becoming in effect outlaws and bandits, and remaining a continual source of trouble to the Burmese government.

THE OFFSHORE ISLANDS

A more significant after-effect of the Chinese civil war was the continuation of sporadic conflict between the communists and nationalists, especially over the so-called 'offshore islands'.

At the 1954 Assembly the Soviet Union raised a complaint of 'acts of aggression' against the People's Republic of China. For these the United States was held responsible: since the United States had recently concluded a mutual defence treaty with Taiwan, and as its fleet constantly patrolled the seas between Taiwan and the mainland, she must take responsibility for the raids which were constantly being undertaken from the island against the Chinese mainland. The Soviet delegate asked the Assembly to pass a resolution expressing concern at these unprovoked attacks by forces under the control of the United States, and asking the United States to take steps to end them.

The US representative said that the true aggressors in the Far East were the communist forces which had taken control of China, had launched the Korean War and despatched more than a million Chinese volunteers to Korea. The US presence in the China Seas was defensive only, designed to protect Taiwan from attacks from the mainland. The nationalist delegate said that there were only about 1200 Americans in Taiwan, who were there at the request of his government. Recent hostilities along the coasts of China had been started by the Chinese communists when they began to bombard the island of Quemoy from the mainland. Only communist speakers, therefore, supported the Soviet resolution. Others warned of the danger to peace in the area if the communist Chinese government were to seek to regain Taiwan by force. The Soviet resolution was then defeated by 44 votes to 5.

However, that autumn the bombardment of the offshore islands from the mainland suddenly intensified. There was growing concern that a large-scale assault might be launched and that the civil war might be rekindled. Early the following year New Zealand therefore asked the Security Council to consider the 'armed hostilities' around the offshore islands. Two days later, in retaliation, the Soviet Union asked for a meeting to discuss 'acts of aggression by the US against China in the area of Taiwan'.

When the Council met, the Soviet Union proposed that a representative of the Peking government should be invited to take part. The New Zealand president of the Council supported this idea, but suggested that the Council should first decide its agenda and therefore what item China would be invited to discuss. There was then a long altercation about the merits of the two rival proposals, with almost all delegates except the Soviet Union favouring priority for the New Zealand request: only nationalist China expressed reservations about this, since the proposal asked only for a ceasefire without making specific mention of 'communist aggression'.

Eventually it was decided that both items should be placed on the agenda, with the condition that discussion of the New Zealand item should be completed before the Soviet complaint was taken up. The Council then agreed, by 9 votes to 1, to invite a representative of the Peking government to attend the debate. However, on 3 February Chou En-lai rejected the invitation. The People's Republic of China would not take any part in discussions at the UN, nor take any account of its decisions, so long as the China seat in the UN was occupied by the Chiang Kai-shek clique. Only if the nationalist representative were evicted would China attend the discussions, and then only to debate the Soviet proposal (accusing the United States of aggression), not the item proposed by New Zealand.

In these circumstances a majority in the Council felt that discussion of the New Zealand item should be adjourned. The Soviet Union asked that the Council should therefore turn to her item. But the rest argued that the fact that discussion of the New Zealand item had been adjourned did not mean that it was completed. They thus rejected, by 10 votes to 1, the Soviet proposal that the Council should proceed to the Soviet item, declaring that, in the delicate situation in the area, it would be inappropriate to discuss the Soviet Union's accusations against the United States. This was an unusual move in UN terms, since normally any item proposed, however manifestly propagandist in intention, is at least debated.

So the matter was allowed to drop for the moment, without the Council's even passing a resolution on the offshore-islands question. The Chinese bombardment continued, and eventually the nationalists evacuated one of the disputed groups. There was clearly little that the UN could do on the question, especially given that China was not a member. The organisation did not attempt to take the matter up again.

THE CAPTURED US AIRMEN

There was one issue affecting China at this time, however, on which the UN was able to produce some results. This concerned fifteen US airmen who had been captured after being shot down by Chinese forces towards the end of 1952. According to the Chinese they had been shot down over Manchuria in northern China, and had been engaged in dropping supplies to US agents in China. According to the United States, the main plane involved, in which eleven of the airmen had been flying, had been shot down over North Korea fifteen miles south of the Yalu River, and were engaged in normal military duties during the Korean War. In November 1954 the men had been tried as spies and condemned to sentences of imprisonment ranging from four years to life. In addition five Chinese said to have been parachuted into China as spies had been sentenced to death for involvement in the affair.

In December 1954, Cabot Lodge, the US representative at the UN, sent a letter to the Secretary-General asking the UN to act 'promptly and decisively' to bring about the release of the airmen. Though the session was almost over, the sixteen countries which had had forces in Korea, including the United States, put down a resolution for the Assembly condemning the conviction of the airmen and declaring that their detention was a violation of the Korean armistice agreement. It asked the Secretary-General to seek their release and report to the next session of the Assembly. This was hurriedly added to the agenda and was then passed by the Assembly by a huge majority on 10 December. The idea was to mobilise world opinion behind the US demand for the release of the airmen.

This was one of the first occasions on which the Assembly adopted the technique of using the good offices and diplomatic skill of the new Secretary-General to sort out a contentious political issue; in other words, decided to 'leave it to Dag', as the method came to be known. This was in some ways a particularly appropriate issue for the use of the technique. The United States herself had no direct contact with China; and British intercession on her behalf in Peking had produced no results. A direct call by the UN would by itself have been almost equally valueless, given Peking's exclusion from the UN and her consequent rejection of UN authority. To ask the Secretary-General to act in a personal capacity invested the appeal with the moral weight of the world authority, yet removed some of the difficulty for Peking in dealing with the organisation at all.

Hammarskjöld immediately telegraphed the Chinese Government, proposing a meeting in Peking. This was at once accepted by Chou En-lai, the Chinese Prime Minister and Foreign Minister. 'In the interests of peace and relaxation of tension', he said, he was prepared to receive Hammarskjöld 'to discuss pertinent questions'. But the Chinese Government made it clear that it was hoping to discuss a number of other matters which had nothing to do with the question of the US airmen, especially Chinese representation at the UN. And it sent a further telegram insisting uncompromisingly on its own sovereign rights in the matter of the US airmen. 'No amount of clamour on the part of the US can shake China's just stand in exercising its own sovereign rights in convicting the US spies', this declared. And it favourably compared China's actions in prosecuting a few prisoners with that of the United States and the UN command in 'forcibly retaining 27,000 Korean and Chinese personnel captured by the Synghman Rhee clique'.

Hammarskjöld left New York for Peking on 30 December, stopping on the way for talks with the governments of Britain, France and India. He had four meetings with Chou En-lai between 6 and 10 January. It was again clear that the Chinese were anxious to use the occasion to discuss world affairs generally with the Secretary-General, and to be seen to be doing so by the world. The communiqué issued at the end of the talks said that they had included 'questions pertinent to the relaxation of world tension', and that it was hoped to 'continue the contacts established at these meetings'. This gained face for the Chinese Government in relation to the UN. But the communiqué said nothing at all about the US airmen and their fate.

A few days later it was announced by UN headquarters and the Peking Government that arrangements had been made to allow relatives from the US to visit the prisoners in Peking. Some of the relatives decided to take up this offer, and the US Red Cross agreed to help finance the visits. Dulles immediately announced, however, that the US Government had decided not to allow visits of this kind, because of the 'increasingly belligerent attitudes and actions of the Chinese communists in recent days'. So no visits took place.

None the less, contacts continued between Hammarskjöld and the Chinese Government over the next few months about the release of the airmen. In April the US Government announced it was allowing seventy Chinese students who had received technical training of various kinds in the United States to return to China. On 29 May the Chinese Government announced that it had decided to release four US airmen, who were not those about whom the US complaint had originally been made. But on 4 August it was announced that these eleven too had been released.

So Hammarskjöld's personal diplomacy brought results. Its success on this occasion undoubtedly encouraged the demand that he should be asked to act in the same capacity more frequently.

TIBET

Towards the end of the decade there was another question concerning China which was discussed several times at the UN. This concerned Tibet. Tibet had, from the eighteenth century to the beginning of the twentieth lived under a loose form of Chinese authority without any detailed day-to-day control. A Chinese resident had lived in Lhasa, but Tibet had in practice conducted its own affairs in its own way. From the early twentieth century, when Europeans first penetrated to the area, it had come to be held that Tibet enjoyed a form of 'autonomy' under ultimate Chinese 'suzerainty'.

After the Chinese revolution of 1911, Tibet had for a time become, in practice, totally independent. But she had taken no steps to establish an independent sovereignty; and Chinese nationalists and Chinese communists alike continued to regard the area as a part of China. In 1950 the communist government of China had, for the first time, asserted Chinese rights there by sending Chinese forces to establish control of the territory. Although still allowed some degree of local autonomy, at least in religious matters, the territory was increasingly brought within the political and social system prevailing in the rest of China. This led to growing friction with the religious authorities in Tibet (who had been in practice the secular authorities as well); and in 1959 the Dalai Lama had escaped, with several thousand followers, to India.

It was in these circumstances that, in September 1959, Malaya (this was before Malaysia had been formed) and Ireland asked that the Assembly should discuss the matter. They declared that there was *prima facie* evidence of an attempt to destroy the traditional way of life of the Tibetan people, as well as the religious and cultural autonomy which they had long enjoyed. The treatment they were now suffering represented a systematic disregard of the Universal Declaration of Human Rights, and the Assembly had a moral obligation and a legal right to discuss the situation and to seek to restore the religious and civil liberties of the Tibetan people. They proposed that the Assembly should pass a resolution demanding respect for the fundamental human rights of the Tibetan people and for their distinctive cultural and political life. The resolution also expressed grave concern at the reports that the Tibetan people were being forcibly denied fundamental human rights and freedoms and deplored the effect of these events in increasing international tension and 'embittering relations between peoples'.

This wording did not quite make clear whether Tibet was regarded as a part of China or not: the emphasis was primarily on the denial of rights rather than on any alleged threat to international peace. But the issue obviously raised immediately the question whether the UN had any right to discuss Tibet or whether it was a matter of domestic jurisdiction, barred under Article 2(7). Since the effective government of China was not present, and that purporting to represent China was only too glad to see its rival pilloried, this point had to be raised by other members. The Soviet Union and the communist states of Eastern Europe roundly asserted that Tibet was an integral part of China; any resolution on the question would thus be illegal and a complete violation of Article 2(7). They received some support on this point from Britain, France, Belgium, Ethiopia and Syria – mostly governments which had good grounds for being concerned to preserve inviolate the reservation contained in Article 2(7). These felt that the UN would not be justified in passing a resolution on the matter (even if, like Britain, they felt it could 'take cognizance' of the question on human-rights grounds). Against this, the United States, Australia and a number of others thought the UN was perfectly competent to pronounce on the matter: indeed, it would be failing in its duty if it failed to protest at the clear violation of human rights in Tibet.

There were, of course, equally wide differences on the merits of the question. The communist states declared that the religious beliefs, customs and habits of the Tibetans were being strictly respected by the Chinese Government and that there had in fact been huge social and economic reforms in Tibet over recent years. The chief Western countries and nationalist China declared, on the other hand, that there was ample evidence of serious violations of traditional religious and social beliefs by the Chinese authorities; and these should be condemned by the Assembly. Eventually, by a large majority, the Assembly passed with small amendments the resolution that had been proposed by Malaya and Ireland.

Very similar debates, discussing similar resolutions and using similar arguments, took place in the following two years. During the 1960 session, there was no time to debate the resolution in substance (though there was once more an angry debate about whether it should be discussed at all). In 1961 a resolution generally similar in tone to the earlier one was passed by an equally large majority (56–11, with 29 abstentions). In 1965, after a gap of three years, the matter was raised once more, and again a similar resolution passed, this time with a smaller majority. But there was now no real disposition to question that Tibet was a part of China. And the violations of human rights which occurred there, though undoubted, were scarcely worse than many which took place in many other parts of the world, without a word of protest from the Assembly. So, from this point, the matter was finally dropped.

CHINESE REPRESENTATION

There was one further question affecting China which was to affect the organisation over more than twenty years: who should represent that country in the UN? This was not a matter of membership, like the disputes we consider later (pp. 361–9). Everybody recognised that China was a member of the organisation, and had been from its foundation. The question was, which government should represent China in the UN?

In October 1949 the Chinese communists, having conquered most of the country, established the People's Republic of China, with its capital in Peking. In November, Chou En-lai, the Prime Minister and Foreign Minister, sent a telegram to the UN Secretary-General demanding that, 'according to the principles and spirit' of the Charter, the new government should take over the China seat in the UN. This caused some perplexity. The Charter said nothing about how problems of representation (as against admission) were to be decided where it was disputed, nor about who was to decide them. Such questions could therefore only be decided by each member according to its own conception of the 'principles and spirit' of the Charter.

Although later discussion of this matter took place almost entirely in the Assembly, at this point it was everywhere accepted that the matter was, in the first place, one for the Security Council. The assumption seemed to be that the procedure would be similar to that for admission: the basic decision would be by the Assembly but on the recommendation of the Security Council.

During the 1949 Assembly the matter was not discussed, despite Chou En-lai's telegram; and there was no disposition to challenge the nationalist delegate's credentials. The Soviet Union, then China's champion, was no doubt well aware that the voting balance in the Council would be far more favourable to the Peking government than that in the Assembly. Thus on 29 December the Soviet Union raised the question in the Council. It did not, however, press for immediate discussion, presumably knowing that several governments were on the point of transferring recognition.

Between 29 December and 6 January, after discussion between Commonwealth governments, India, Pakistan, Ceylon and Britain announced their recognition of the new regime. On 8 January Chou En-lai sent a further telegram, protesting once more at the failure of the Council to expel the nationalist delegate. The Soviet Union shortly afterwards formally proposed that the credentials of the nationalist delegate should be rejected (both powers apparently believed that there was a greater chance that the UN would agree, in the first place, to expel the nationalists than that it would accept the communists). The matter was then discussed during three meetings of the Council. The proposal to expel the nationalist delegate was finally rejected by 6 votes to 3, with 2 abstentions. Britain, though it had recognised the new government, was one of those that abstained.

The Soviet Union thereupon walked out of the Council and did not reappear until the end of July, after the Korean War had broken out. To some it began to appear as if the UN might break up altogether. Possibly for this reason Trygve Lie began a fervent personal campaign to persuade governments that the representative of Peking should be accepted in the UN.

He had a legal memorandum prepared, which suggested that only the government which effectively controlled the territory and population of the state concerned could fulfil that state's obligations as a member. And eventually he allowed this memorandum to be published, so, the nationalist delegate declared, seeking to influence the final outcome.

It was generally accepted that the initial Security Council decision on the matter was only an interim one; and that some of the governments represented in the Council might easily change their minds. It so happened that the representation at this time was unusually favourable to Peking. It included, besides the three countries which had supported China from the start (the Soviet Union, Yugoslavia and India), several others, including Britain, France, Egypt and Ecuador, that were thought to be wavering. Thus intensive lobbying continued throughout the summer. However, at a meeting between the governments of the United States, Britain and France in May, it was agreed to do nothing on the question until the end of August or early September. After that time it was thought that Britain at least would proceed to vote in favour of Peking (as she did). But the US Government, already under attack for 'selling out China to the communists', used all its influence with other member states to ensure that no change should be made in the near future which would give further ammunition to its critics.

The chances of a vote in favour of Peking were reduced by the start of the Korean War in June, and still further reduced after China became involved in October. The Assembly in that year passed no resolution specifically directed to the question, perhaps still awaiting a lead from the Council. It merely set up a committee to look into the matter, which eventually reached no conclusion. Meanwhile it did, however, pass a resolution recommending that whatever decision was finally taken by the Assembly on such matters should be 'taken into account' by other bodies within the UN family. This was an attempt to prevent the specialised agencies, which made independent decisions on membership, from accepting the representative of Peking while the UN still acknowledged the Nationalists (the UPU had already that year briefly acknowledged representatives of the Peking government).

The Security Council briefly considered the matter again in

November 1951, January 1955 and September 1955. But on each occasion it was decided that no action should be taken. Increasingly the lead on the matter passed to the Assembly. Every year from 1951 to 1960, the Soviet Union proposed that the Assembly should discuss the question of Chinese representation. Though this might not bring about a change, at least it could give considerable publicity to the case for giving the China seat to Peking.

However, for this very reason, the United States and her allies opposed any discussion of the question at all. Throughout this period they were able within the Assembly to secure a majority for the proposition, usually proposed by the United States, that the Assembly should 'postpone' or 'not consider' the question of Chinese representation: the so-called moratorium proposal. This was intensely debated, and in practice gave almost as much opportunity to discuss the merits of the matter as a substantive item would have done. The question was discussed and decided on strictly cold-war lines. Most Western countries, including nearly all Latin American states, voted that the question should not be discussed and that the government controlling Taiwan should therefore continue to be recognised in the organisation as the government controlling China. Even Britain, which had recognised Peking, now supported the moratorium. The communist states of course voted throughout to discuss the matter.

As in so many other things, it was the influx of new members which gradually brought about some change in attitude. Though not all of these voted for Peking, the number who supported some discussion of the question (in practice mainly those who wanted a change in representation) steadily increased. In 1952 there were only 7 in favour of the debate, with 42 against. In 1956 the figure in favour was 24 with 47 against; In 1960 it was 34 for and 42 against, with 22 abstentions. It began to look as if the dam would not hold much longer. Those who were opposed to the representation of the People's Republic began to seek new tactics for keeping it out of the organisation.

SOUTH EAST ASIAN QUESTIONS

A few other issues affecting Asia came up at this time, many of which (like those of the rest of the world) had cold-war overtones. They mainly resulted, directly or indirectly, from the thirty-year conflict in Indo-China, which was fought out, more or less fiercely, during the entire period between 1945 and 1975.

One such question was raised by Thailand in 1954. In May of that year, Thailand raised in the Security Council the disturbed situation in Indo-China, which, she claimed, represented a threat to her own security. This was at the very moment when the Geneva Conference, designed to bring peace to Indo-China, was meeting. Thailand claimed that despite this, Viet-Minh forces in Indo-China, with the support of outside powers (meaning China and the Soviet Union), remained in Laos and Cambodia, were seeking to overthrow the governments of those countries, and were spreading hostile propaganda throughout the area. Much of this propaganda was against Thailand, and represented a threat to her security. She asked that the Security Council should send a team of observers under the Peace Observation Commission set up in 1950, to examine the situation.

The Soviet Union at first opposed any discussion of the question at all, on the grounds that the whole Indo-China question was being considered in Geneva. When the item was none the less adopted on to the agenda, she claimed that there was no threat to Thailand and that a decision to send an observer team to that country would be an alarmist move which was not justified by events (and certainly, if every act of hostile propaganda was to be discussed in the Security Council, the Council would have had few spare moments). Finally, she therefore proceeded to veto Thailand's resolution calling for the despatch of observers. Thailand's immediate response was to ask that, since the Council had been able to do nothing, the General Assembly should take up the matter. But she later decided, after the Geneva agreements had been concluded, to withdraw this request. Nothing more was therefore heard of the matter.

A somewhat similar episode occurred five years later, in 1959. At this stage there existed in Laos a right-wing government under Phoi Sananikone, which had been formed at the demand of the strongly pro-Western, and anti-communist, Committee for the Defence of the National Interest. Towards the end of 1958, the US Government, alarmed at the increasing influence of the Pathet Lao in the national government formed the previous year, and at the success of the Pathet Lao in recent elections, had cut off all aid to Laos. It was this in part which had led to the formation of the new government, which excluded the Pathet Lao and which had taken power to rule without parliamentary support. In February 1959 the Government had repudiated its obligations under the Geneva agreements and announced it would accept no restrictions on the nation's freedom of action. The US Government had welcomed this statement and had agreed to establish a military mission in Laos. Shortly afterwards the Government declared that the Pathet Lao was now in open rebellion and that only a military solution was possible. Prince Souphannouvaoung and a number of other Pathet Lao leaders were placed under arrest.

At this point Laos applied to the UN, alleging incursions across the border from North Vietnam. The Security Council decided to establish a sub-committee, consisting of Argentina, Italy, Japan and Tunisia, to travel to the area to examine the situation on the spot and report to the Council. (On this occasion it managed to avoid the double veto and so to decide, as it had sometimes failed to do in the past, that the decision to set up such a sub-committee was a procedural one: the contrary vote cast by the Soviet Union therefore did not represent a veto.)

The sub-committee visited Laos between 15 September and 13 October 1959, at the invitation of the Laotian Government. Its report scarcely substantiated the charges which that government had made. It found that there was guerrilla activity in Laos and that there was evidence that the dissident forces were receiving various kinds of support from across the border. It seemed, from statements of the authorities in Laos and of some witnesses, that some of the hostile operations 'must have had a centralised coordination', but there was no evidence to support the accusation that North Vietnamese forces had invaded Laos.

In the following month the Government of Laos invited the Secretary-General himself to visit the country to acquaint himself with the situation there. He did not visit, but he finally decided to establish (as he had done in Jordan a year earlier) a representative, responsible to himself, who would be placed in Vientiane, the capital of the country. Although, formally, his mission would be to review the economic situation and make recommendations for development assistance, he would also be able to keep an eye on the political situation. Tuomioja, the executive secretary of the Economic Commission for Europe, accordingly went out to Laos to look at the situation. He issued a preliminary report and then returned. Subsequently Hammarskjöld sent the UN Commissioner for Technical Assistance, R. M. Heurgematt, to go to the country and discuss how the recommendations should be implemented.

These steps, especially because they were not endorsed by the Security Council itself, aroused the determined hostility of the Soviet Union. She regarded them as a further example of uncontrolled personal initiatives by the Secretary-General, initiatives which reflected political partisanship in favour of the West. In any case, at the end of the year the Laos Government was compelled to resign, and was replaced by a still more right-wing cabinet under Phoumi Nosavan. In the following year the escape of Prince Souphannouvaoung to the Pathet Lao area, and the revolt of a new neutralist faction under Kong Le, led eventually to a period of constitutional turmoil, a succession of coups and counter-coups, the division of Laos into three zones, communist-controlled, neutralist and pro-Western and, finally, to the Geneva Conference of 1961, which brought the 'neutralisation' of Laos. The UN took no further interest in these events.

Another question concerning South East Asia in which the UN did intervene was the longstanding frontier dispute between Thailand and Cambodia. A particular area under dispute was the Temple of Preah Vihear, which stood exactly on the border between the two states and was disputed between them, partly on religious grounds. In November 1958, Cambodia complained in a letter to the Secretary-General that Thailand had annexed the temple and was now concentrating troops on the border. Attempts to settle the question by negotiation had failed because of Thai intimidation, including violent demonstrations against the Cambodian Embassy in Bangkok, inspired by the Thai Government. Thailand was now threatening military action against Cambodia.

Thailand denied these charges and said that she would welcome a UN representative to come to observe the situation in the border area, to see the situation for himself. Thailand also said she would welcome the restoration of diplomatic negotiations between the two countries; but said that the release of thirty-two Thailand nationals who had been imprisoned in Cambodia was an essential precondition.

The Secretary-General explored the proposal that a UN representative should be sent to observe the situation. He believed that the representative should have a broader mandate, so that he could seek to resolve some of the other issues between the two countries. He managed to persuade the Thai Government to accept this. Both governments finally invited him to send a representative to help them 'find a solution to their difficulties': in other words, to act as a kind of mediator between them. In December he nominated the Swedish diplomat, J. Beck-Fries, as his representative for the purpose.

Beck-Fries visited both countries in January and February of the following year and inspected the contested frontier areas. He managed to secure the release of prisoners held on both sides and obtained pledges from both governments of their concern to see calm restored. On 6 February the two governments announced their intention to re-establish diplomatic relations with each other and returned their former ambassadors to their posts. So, for the moment, peaceful relations were restored. Shortly afterwards Cambodia submitted the question of the temple to the International Court. The Secretary-General was able to dispense with the services of his special representative.

On this relatively minor matter, at least – by promoting negotiation rather than passing ineffectual resolutions – the organisation had scored a significant success.

17 Disarmament

When great wars come to an end, there exists usually a widespread determination that such things shall never happen again. In recent times this has been expressed in the hope that the nations of the world could be persuaded, when peace was once restored, to divest themselves of the weapons with which wars are waged.

Thus the Covenant of the League of Nations had contained a pledge that national armaments would be reduced 'to the lowest point consistent with national safety', and the allied and associated powers pledged themselves to negotiate on general measures of disarmament to match those imposed on Germany. A series of negotiations and conferences on the subject were held in the 'twenties and 'thirties. But these did not arrive at any general understanding: the only disarmament agreements reached during this period covered naval vessels and these were reached outside the ambit of the League.

In 1945 the great powers never seriously thought of disarming themselves, and were not so rash as to commit themselves to do so. President Roosevelt, as we have seen, at one time hoped that the rest of the world could be disarmed, while the Big Four alone would maintain their military strength. But this unrealistic and discriminatory proposal was not pursued. Indeed, since the system for keeping the peace depended on the use of armed forces made available by members of the UN to the Security Council under special agreements, the UN system clearly presupposed that there should *not* be any general disarmament.

The original draft of the Charter contained no reference to the subject at all. Even in its final version the emphasis was on the 'regulation of armaments' rather than on disarmament as such. Responsibility, moreover, was divided somewhat uncertainly between different organs. The Security Council was made responsible, under Article 26, for 'formulating . . .

plans to be submitted to the members of the UN for the establishment of a system for the regulation of armaments' (something it has never done). The Military Staff Committee was, under Article 47, to advise and assist the Security Council on 'the regulation of armaments and possible disarmament' (and has been equally inactive on the question). Finally, the Assembly under Article 10 acquired at San Francisco the right to discuss 'general principles of cooperation', including 'the principles governing disarmament and the regulation of armaments'.

This somewhat cautious approach to the idea of disarmament at this time was understandable. There were many who believed that the previous conflict resulted from too much disarmament rather than too little. There was a feeling that the League had failed bacause it was not equipped to use force. And there was a general conviction that public-spirited states of the world should retain some arms in order to keep the peace in the age to come. It was only the villains – the defeated powers – that thus needed to be kept disarmed if peace was to be maintained.

All those proposals contained in the Charter were devised in the period before atomic weapons had been used, or were even known to exist by most governments. The first use of such weapons, against Japan in August 1945, though it brought an abrupt and welcome end to the conflict, also aroused in the minds of all an intense dread of the destructive power which had been unleashed. Whether or not disarmament in other fields was going to be possible, therefore, there was general concern to tame the genie now released from the bottle: to 'control' atomic energy. And it was to this subject that the first UN Assembly, meeting in January 1946, devoted the very first resolution which it passed.

The great powers themselves had invited the Assembly to consider the matter. The foreign ministers of the United States, the Soviet Union and Britain, meeting in December 1945, had agreed on a proposal (first discussed a month earlier between the United States, Britain and Canada) to set up a commission, to operate under the direction of the Security Council (the Soviet Union was insistent on this point), which would make proposals for the 'control of atomic energy to the extent necessary to ensure its use only for peaceful purposes' and for the elimination of atomic weapons from national armaments, with effective safeguards through inspection and other means of verification.

It was this proposal which was taken up by the Assembly in that first resolution passed on 24 January 1946. It agreed, without even debating the question, to act on the great powers' recommendation, and to establish an Atomic Energy Commission which would submit proposals to the Security Council for ensuring that atomic energy was used for peaceful purposes only, and for eliminating atomic weapons and other weapons of mass destruction through a system of inspection which would prevent evasion. The commission was to consist of the members of the Security Council plus Canada (since Canada had acquired some atomic capability in contributing to the development of the first US atomic bombs).

The new commission first met on 14 June 1946. The United States and the Soviet Union then each put forward their own proposals for dealing with the problem of 'atomic energy'.

The United States proposed the so-called Baruch Plan. Under this an international atomic authority was to be established which would take over direct control of all activities involving the use of atomic energy, whether for warlike or for peaceful purposes. The authority would control all raw materials used in the development of atomic energy and all the mines which produced them. It would itself take over ownership of all atomic-energy activities potentially dangerous to world security in every country of the world. It would assume powers to control, inspect and license all other atomic-energy activities. It would promote the beneficial uses of atomic energy and undertake its own research and development, so that the authority would remain in the forefront of atomic knowledge. Once the control system had been established, the manufacture of bombs would cease and existing bombs would be disposed of in any way which the treaty might specify. Penalties would be imposed for any violation of the treaty, including the illegal possession of any atomic weapons or the initiation of atomic projects without licence. Decisions on any such questions would be free of the veto of permanent members.

This was widely hailed as a generous and imaginative proposal. It was generally felt that the United States had shown itself willing to sacrifice its own lead in this field and to place its knowledge in international hands for the sake of removing the dangers such weapons could represent. In the eyes of the Soviet Union, however, there were a number of fundamental objections to the plan. First, there could be no cast-iron assurances, whatever the system of inspection, that every single atomic weapon at that time owned by the US could be detected and destroyed. Secondly, the Soviet Union herself would be prevented from acquiring the capacity to develop nuclear power and nuclear weapons (since production facilities could be detected far more easily than the weapons themselves.). Thirdly, even if all bombs were destroyed, the knowledge and technical capacity of the United States could not be undone: she would still retain the ability to resume manufacture at short notice, while the Soviet Union would require long years after a breakdown to acquire that ability. Fourthly, atomic materials and atomic production would be concentrated in the hands of a UN body – which, in Soviet eyes, meant a body under the control of its Western majority.[1] Fifthly, in consequence, the UN, by acquiring these powers, would be made into an organisation far more powerful and influential than the Soviet Union wished to see it become. Finally, not least significant, the scheme would involve a system of widespread inspection within the Soviet Union itself, of a kind that she most wished to avoid.

The interests of the Soviet Union were of course quite different. She wished, on the one hand, to be able to acquire the capacity to develop nuclear weapons for herself, the only ultimate answer to US power in this field. At the same time she wished to nullify, if possible, the superiority enjoyed by the United States until that took place. She therefore proposed to the Commission the so-called Gromyko plan. Under this the Security Council would approve an international convention under which the signatories would accept a general prohibition not only of the production but also of the use of atomic weapons, together with the destruction of the stockpiles of existing weapons within three months. The Commission would be responsible for securing observance of the convention. It would be given few powers for so doing, however, and in the final resort violations of the agreement would be punishable only under domestic legislation. Subsequently, the

Soviet Union agreed that the Security Council could take action against violations, but here of course the veto was to operate. The essential difference was that under the Soviet proposals the major emphasis was on the prohibition from the beginning of the use of atomic weapons, while the system of controls would only come into operation gradually and in any case would not include generally free inspection.

The Western powers complained that under the Soviet plan they would commit themselves to renouncing both production and use of atomic weapons, while never having any adequate assurance that production was effectively stopped within the Soviet Union. The Soviet Union complained that under the Western plan an elaborate system of controls would be introduced which would prevent Soviet production, but would not necessarily be followed by the subsequent abandonment by the United States of her own weapons. This fundamental difference between the position of East and West was not to be significantly altered for nearly ten years (when their strategic interests had in each case radically changed).

A few concessions were made. The Soviet Union agreed that the control organ should be able to take decisions by majority vote 'in appropriate cases'. In June 1947 she accepted the principle of international control over the mining of atomic materials and the production of atomic weapons, including regular inspection. But this would only be of declared installations. Moreover, peaceful uses of atomic energy would be excluded. Conversely, the West marginally relaxed its proposed system of controls. It accepted that installations for the peaceful use of atomic energy could be under national ownership and control, though only under licence from the atomic-energy authority, and under close inspection, and using materials made available by the authority.

But the key difference concerned the relative priority of the institution of controls and the prohibition of the use of the weapons. On this point the discussions in the Commission by 1948 reached an impasse. The three reports issued by the Commission reflected the disagreements. But they inevitably endorsed, by a large majority, the Western position. On these grounds the Soviet Union in June 1948 vetoed in the Security Council a US proposal to approve the findings and recommendations. But the 1948 Assembly, with its built-in Western majority, equally inevitably came out in favour of the US plan (on these grounds the plan came to be known in the West as the 'UN plan'). The Assembly brushed aside the compelling military reasons why the Soviet Union was almost bound to reject such a proposal (indeed, these may have commended it to some members). On disarmament, as on so much else at this time, the West was always able to rely on a majority vote in support of its own position.

The Assembly did, however, ask the Commission to re-examine the issues. But over the next year or two the Commission was still unable to resolve the basic differences. For a time, at the request of the Assembly, the permanent members conferred with each other separately, but this too brought no change in their positions. The Soviet Union did eventually accept that the institution of controls should be simultaneous with the prohibition of atomic weapons, but she was still evasive about the precise form those controls would take.

The worsening international climate did not improve the prospect for reaching agreement on this ultra-sensitive subject. Eventually, early in 1950, the Soviet Union walked out of the Atomic Energy Commission altogether (as she did from the Security Council), on the grounds that the Chinese seat should be awarded to the Peking government. Since quite obviously any nuclear disarmament must depend on Soviet agreement, the Commission was no longer able to do any useful work. In January 1952, it was dissolved altogether. So ended the first, wholly abortive, attempt to bring about nuclear disarmament.

CONVENTIONAL DISARMAMENT

Because of the general preoccupation with atomic weapons, conventional disarmament was relegated to a lower level of priority at first. Serious discussions did not begin in this sphere until 1948.

At the 1946 Assembly the Soviet Union had put forward a resolution calling for a general reduction of armaments, though this was linked with her recurrent demand for the prohibition of atomic weapons and other calls which were known to be unacceptable to the majority. The proposal was amended out of all recognition within the Assembly and eventually emerged as a 'set of principles governing the general regulation and reduction of armaments'. Among other things this called for the Security Council to formulate measures for the general regulation and reduction of armed forces.

Largely in consequence of this, the Security Council set up in February 1947 the Commission on Conventional Armaments, to discuss disarmament in that sphere. Even then the Commission did not begin serious work until the following year (it spent almost a year discussing its programme of work). When it did begin operation, all it could do was to reach agreement on a set of six principles of such vagueness and generality that they committed no government to anything of any substance whatever. Meanwhile the Soviet Union called for a reduction of a third in existing land, air and naval forces. Since the Soviet Union was herself at this time superior in all three arms, a proportionate reduction of this kind could of course offer no threat, and would preserve her existing superiority.

Moreover, while the size of the armed forces in the West was reasonably well known, there was no means of knowing the size of Soviet forces. The Western powers therefore demanded, as a first step, an attempt to establish the facts on this point. In the 1948 Assembly they proposed, and the Assembly agreed, to call for studies designed to publish and check information supplied by member states on the level of conventional arms. In the following year the Commission on Conventional Armaments adopted a French proposal, opposed by the communist states, for a census of all non-nuclear forces, including national police forces, through direct investigation by international inspection teams. This was rejected by the Soviet Union unless it was preceded by an agreement to ban all atomic arms and to reduce conventional weapons by a fixed proportion. As over atomic weapons, therefore, the same difference emerged: which came first, prohibition or control?

There were, however, a number of specific points which arose during these debates that were to remain at issue for many years. The Soviet Union consistently demanded the elimination of all 'foreign bases'. After the war the United States had retained military facilities in a number of areas which it had occupied, especially in the Pacific; and in the following years had acquired others in parts of Europe, North Africa, Pakistan, Turkey and elsewhere. In Soviet eyes these tipped the military balance against her, since they placed Soviet cities and other targets in the range of US bombers, while targets in the United States were, at this time, quite inaccessible to her own. By eliminating the bases she might have maximised the advantage of her own geographical situation, with short internal lines of communication and great concentration of power, while her smaller neighbours would have been made dependent exclusively on their own limited resources. Already in August 1946 Gromyko had asked the Security Council to study the question of foreign troops present in the territories of any states other than former enemy countries (where the Soviet Union herself had in many cases stationed troops). In November of the same year the Soviet Union proposed to the General Assembly that every member should provide information on the armed forces which they held in foreign countries.

The Western powers were concerned about a corresponding advantage enjoyed by the Soviet Union. This was the benefit she gained from the secrecy of her own system, which had the effect that there was great uncertainty about the level of effectiveness of her forces. It was on these grounds that they laid such stress on the need for inspection and adequate verification; and why, in the subsequent period, they proposed measures of area inspection and other means of acquiring better knowledge of the level of Soviet armed forces. There was of course no more progress on this point than on the other.

Thus, in the first six years after the war, in the bitter climate of ideological hostility prevailing, there was little agreement on the means of securing disarmament, in either conventional or nuclear weapons. Indeed, the effect of successive crises, including open conflict over Berlin and Korea, was that serious interest in disarmament declined sharply. The West, on the contrary, was busy rearming as hard as it could, to bring itself to some kind of parity with the Soviet Union.

The Soviet Union withdrew from the Commission on Conventional Armaments, as from the Atomic Energy Commission, in 1950. In the following year both commissions were abolished. There was then some discussion about the way negotiations could be got going again. In a speech to the Assembly in 1950, President Truman accepted that any useful disarmament proposals must secure the unanimous support of all parties; though a statement of the obvious, this did suggest that the West might be less inclined than before to seek to push through its own views by Assembly resolutions and was willing to search for a consensus. The Soviet Union, too, in accepting the need for a 'strict system of control' for enforcing a ban on nuclear weapons, moved a step nearer to the Western position that verification was an essential condition of disarmament. Slowly a willingness once more to attempt serious negotiations began to revive.

THE DISARMAMENT COMMISSION

In his speech to the Assembly in 1950, Truman had accepted that atomic and conventional disarmament were interdependent; and he had suggested the need for a 'new and consolidated disarmament commission' to be responsible for both subjects. The Assembly in that year set up a committee to examine this proposal.

This committee came out in favour of Truman's idea and the following seession of the Assembly implemented it, setting up a new disarmament commission. This was to have the same membership as the two earlier commissions: that is, the Security Council plus Canada. It was supposed to prepare proposals for the 'regulation, limitation and balanced reduction of all armed forces and all armaments, for the elimination of all major weapons capable of mass destruction, and for the effective international control of atomic energy to ensure the prohibition of atomic weapons'. It was provided that there should be 'progressive disclosure and verification of all armed forces, based on effective international inspection'. But this would be with 'a minimum degree of interference in the internal life of each country'. This form of words was carefully chosen to be as acceptable as possible to all states, including the Soviet Union.

But the basic question of priorities – should control precede a ban or *vice versa*? – was still not solved. There began now to be put forward by both sides a series of plans for phased disarmament, with disclosure and verification of a specific level of arms at each stage. This made the question of priorities not quite such an all-or-nothing matter, but the problem of timing remained.

Since the Soviet proposal for proportionate reductions of existing levels of arms was clearly unacceptable to the West, the West began to proposed *absolute* limits in the levels of arms to be allowed at each stage. In May 1952 the United States, the United Kingdom and France introduced a proposal providing for manpower levels of 1–1.5 million for the United States, the Soviet Union and China, 700,000 to 800,000 for the United Kingdom and France, and levels 'normally less than one percent of the population' for other powers. These reductions would be related to progress on other aspects of reducing forces and armaments. The ceilings could later be further reduced. The United States dropped the demand for international ownership of nuclear materials and international operation of nuclear facilities. In May 1954 she accepted the right of veto of permanent members in the proposed UN disarmament and atomic development authority.

In June 1954 a new sub-committee of the Disarmament Commission, consisting of potential nuclear powers only, was formed (the United States, the United Kingdom, France, Canada and the Soviet Union). Britain and France now for the first time made their own proposals, moving somewhat ahead of the United States. They accepted the Soviet demand for a prohibition of nuclear weapons, though with the proviso 'except in defence against aggression' (a rather crucial reservation), a step which was to occur halfway through the entire process. They also provided for the freezing of manpower and expenditure at 1953 levels, followed by interrelated reductions of conventional and nuclear weapons, with the progressive introduction of the controls necessary for each stage.

In 1954 the Soviet Union also began to make concessions. She accepted the new Anglo-French proposals as a basis for discussion. She accepted the idea of reductions to agreed target levels, rather than by proportion. She accepted that the initiation of reductions and the introduction of controls should be simultaneous. And she accepted that prohibition and control of nuclear weapons would occur only after half the other reductions were completed, as the Anglo-French plan had provided.

There was little doubt that this shift in the Soviet position partly reflected a big change in her strategic interests. Having exploded an atomic bomb in 1949, and a hydrogen bomb in 1953, she was beginning to move towards a position of technological parity with the United States, though at present her stocks of nuclear weapons were far lower. The demand for an absolute prohibition of atomic weapons was thus less essential for her. But at the same time the need to prevent German rearmament become overriding (this was also the period of settlements on Austria and Trieste and proposals for a united and disarmed Germany). Whatever the reason, in May 1955 the Soviet Union moved still further towards the Western position. She accepted the levels for force goals at the end of the first stage proposed by the West; she accepted the Anglo-French proposals for the elimination of nuclear weapons after 75 per cent of the reductions in other forces and a slower timetable for effecting the reductions; she accepted the idea of permanent control posts at large ports, railway junctions, aerodromes and main highways; and she even accepted that the control organ would have the right to require states to provide information about their armaments, and should have unimpeded access to 'all objects of control' and to budgetary records. This last was a crucial concession.

This was a dramatic change in the Soviet position – so much so that it seemed to take the West totally by surprise. Their response was certainly not a positive one. Britain and France continued to reaffirm their own proposals, which were now not so far from those of the Soviet Union. The United States, however, declared a 'reservation' on all earlier proposals: in effect this meant that they were withdrawn. Shortly afterwards, the Western powers raised the force levels demanded for the end of the first stage of disarmament sharply upwards (to 2.5 million against 1.5 million for the three major powers).

Thus, immediately the Soviet Union began to move nearer to the Western position, the West appeared to retreat. This probably reflected a reappraisal of the new strategic position produced by the development of Soviet nuclear weapons, similar to the reappraisal the Soviet Union herself had undertaken. Since this meant that the West no longer had a decisive superiority in that area, it needed to be able to match the Soviet Union in the conventional field too. Given the possibility of small-scale conventional wars all over the world, the West wished to retain the option of a higher force level than had previously been proposed. But, though the Soviet Union was catching up in technology, she still had not the same stockpile of weapons as the United States possessed. The US negotiations therefore now demanded above all a cut-off in production of fissionable material. This however, for obvious reasons, was unacceptable to the Soviet Union.

Britain and France began to adopt a position somewhat distinct from that of the United States: even to seek to mediate between the two sides. In 1956 they put forward a plan claimed to be a synthesis of earlier plans by both sides. It made no reference to eliminating nuclear stockpiles, nor to specific force levels. But it set out a new time table for a balanced reduction in arms, said to give no advantage to either side. In 1957, however, this was withdrawn when the three powers, together again, put forward a new plan. This incorporated the demand for higher force levels, the proposal for an early cut-off in the production of nuclear weapons and an extensive system of controls. Moreover, it was presented to the Soviet Union as a 'package'; in other words, it was not open to amendment or negotiation at all.

This was not exactly conducive to securing agreement. The Soviet Union in fact accepted the new and higher force levels now proposed by the West. She was not, however, willing to accept the cut-off of fissionable material, nor some other aspects of the Western plan. Eventually she proceeded to walk out of the disarmament sub-committee, claiming that the four other members were now ganging up on her; and she subsequently left the Disarmament Commission itself. She demanded the establishment of a new forum for disarmament discussions which was less heavily weighted against her views.

This was effectively the end of this phase of disarmament discussions. Over the next five years, to meet Soviet views, a number of new bodies were formed. The Disarmament Commission was first enlarged to twenty-five states, but was still regarded by the Soviet Union as unbalanced. The West then agreed to enlarge it yet again so that it had the same membership as the UN as a whole. But this was obviously far too cumbersome for serious negotiations, and eventually, in 1959, a body in which East and West were equally represented was set up. This was the Disarmament Committee,[2] which contained five members of NATO and five from the Warsaw Pact. None of these bodies, however, did much useful work to promote general disarmament. The most important disarmament proposals were now made in the General Assembly.

In September 1959, Selwyn Lloyd and Khrushchev both put forward proposals for 'general and complete disarmament'. And in 1960 the United States came out with a similar plan. These were each elaborate and complex scenarios, under which, by stages, all armaments, including nuclear weapons, would be progressively abandoned, leaving states with only the minimum requirements for internal security. It is not necessary to describe these immensely complicated plans here in any detail. As always, the crucial point was the order of the stages; and each plan reflected the strategic interest of the state or bloc which produced it. Under the US plan the cut-off of production of fissionable material and control of the launching of space vehicles would have been introduced at an early stage (so making it harder for the Soviet Union to complete the process of catching up). Under the Soviet plan the elimination of foreign bases came at an early stage, while, as always, inspection was reduced to a minimum. Under the British plan some nuclear weapons would be held until the final stage (so maximising the benefit to Britain of her own small nuclear force). France demanded that the means of delivery should be controlled at an early stage (since it was here that she was inferior). As before, the Soviet Union accused the West of demanding control without disarmament, while the West claimed the Soviet Union's plan provided for disarmament without control.

Thus each plan, as always, proposed the timetable most advantageous to the power presenting it. Disarmament proposals were formulated almost as a part of defence policy. Not surprisingly, since defence interests diverged, it was never possible to reach agreement on them. The complexity involved in seeking to devise, in advance, a precise and balanced timetable for the abolition of all arms all over the world was so formidable, and mutual suspicions so intense, that it was almost impossible that agreement should be reached on every detail of that long and precarious procedure. Most states preferred to rely on the uncertain security of arms rather than the still more uncertain security of a world without arms. Thus to a large extent the presentation of these plans, undertaken with the maximum publicity in highly visible forums such as the UN Assembly, was increasingly undertaken as a form of propaganda exercise rather than as a serious negotiating plan. It was directed at the general population rather than at opposing governments.

General disarmament was widely seen by most governments as a fanciful dream, to be held before the eye of the more naïve members of the public, not as a goal that anybody ever seriously expected to achieve.

LIMITED AGREEMENTS

Serious negotiations for these reasons now became concentrated far more on the conclusion of relatively limited agreements, confined to particular areas or weapons, which, while they would not remove the capacity to make war, might reduce particular dangers and, by increasing confidence, raise the general level of security among states.

Some plans of this kind had been discussed for several years. The three principal powers then involved all came out with different proposals during 1955. At the Geneva summit conference that year, President Eisenhower had put forward a proposal for 'open skies': that is, for permitted inspection from the air of the territory of one state by the aircraft of another. Since at this time the United states had far greater capability in long-range, high-altitude aircraft, and probably in photography as well, it is likely that the United States would have gained more by such a technique, especially since other types of intelligence were for her limited by the secrecy of Soviet society. For that very reason, however, the Soviet Union showed little enthusiasm for the idea. She did, somewhat surprisingly, accept the concept of aerial inspection in a zone covering an area of 500 miles on either side of the East–West border. Even then, however, there was disagreement about the exact areas to be covered. A number of proposals were exchanged in subsequent years for the inspection of areas of various sizes, in Europe, the United States and the Arctic. But agreement was never reached, and eventually the subject dropped out of disarmament negotiations. For a time the United States undertook aerial inspection unilaterally through clandestine U-2 flights. These came to an end, however, after the shooting down of Gary Powers in 1960. Soon afterwards the development of satellites and satellite photography made it possible for the same kind of information to be provided more reliably, without the use of aircraft or any specific intergovernmental agreement.

During these same years there was also discussion of proposals for control posts at communication centres and other places, to act as a check on any large-scale movement of forces. The Soviet disarmament plan of 10 May 1955 proposed that control posts of this kind at 'large ports and railway junctions, main highways and airports' should be set up at an early stage in the disarmament process. The idea was repeated in a subsequent Soviet plan of 18 March 1957. This was in turn taken up in the proposals put forward by the three Western countries in August 1957: this accepted the concept of 'ground observation posts at principal ports, railway junctions, main highways and important airfields'. The idea was discussed further at a conference on 'surprise attack' which took place in the autumn of 1958. No progress was made, however, and this idea too was gradually dropped.

A similar idea, however, increasingly discussed at this time, was the establishment of a zone between East and West in Europe in which arms would be limited, or even eliminated altogether. At the Geneva summit conference, Eden, the British Prime Minister, proposed the 'establishment of a system of joint inspection of the forces now confronting each other in Europe by joint inspection teams' in such a zone. This would lead to the establishment of a 'thinned-out zone' in which arms and manpower would be reduced. These proposals too were taken up, though somewhat amended, by the Soviet Union. The Soviet plan of March 1956 proposed a zone, to include Germany, in which armed forces of all states would be limited by agreement, and where atomic weapons would be banned. The following year the Western powers suggested a limited zone of inspection in Europe, on the understanding that this would include a significant part of the territory of the USSR as well as other East European countries. Finally, in October 1957, the Foreign Minister of Poland, Rapacki, brought forward his own plan for an atom-free zone in Germany, Poland and Czechoslovakia, a proposal which would have above all prevented any possibility of West Germany herself acquiring control of any atomic weapons. This idea too was discussed at the Conference on Surprise Attack at the end of 1958.

This conference began in Geneva in October 1958. It was intended to be a conference of 'experts', but there was a considerable difference of view on what this meant. The Western powers complained that the Soviet experts were officials of their foreign-office and defence departments and merely put forward an official view (it is difficult to imagine Soviet participants in such a conference doing anything else, wherever they came from). There were other disagreements about the purpose and scope of the Conference. The Soviet Union wanted recommendations that were in part political; this the Western states opposed. The Soviet Union wished to discuss the details of particular proposals, such as an inspected and thinned-out zone on the line dividing NATO and Warsaw Pact forces, control posts and aerial photography. The Western representatives said they were not empowered to consider proposals of this kind and wished to confine discussion to purely technical problems, such as the identification of the objects of control, the means of control, techniques of observation and inspection, and so on. As a result the Conference broke up in failure.

Thus, though proposals of this kind, for aerial inspection, control posts and thinned-out zones of inspection, seemed more realistic subjects of discussion than the vast plans for general and complete disarmament which were being negotiated at the same time, there was no greater success in securing agreement. The only subject on which there was agreement in this period, though outside the UN framework, was the somewhat marginal one of demilitarisation of the Antarctic, on which agreement was reached in 1959. But from

1958 there was increasingly intensive discussion of another subject, which was the focus of a much wider public concern: the establishment of a nuclear test-ban.

This proposal had first been raised by Indian Prime Minister Nehru in April 1954, when he proposed that all nuclear tests should be prohibited. The Soviet Union accepted the idea of such a ban in principle, but was unwilling to accept the verification measures which alone could give assurance it was being observed. At first the United States was, on these grounds, not prepared to accept any test ban, believing that evasion by the Soviet Union might have the effect that the United States lead in nuclear weapons would be reversed. During 1957, however, the United States proposed restrictions on the amount of nuclear weapons testing, leading eventually to a full prohibition under control. In June 1957 the Soviet Union seemed to go some way towards accepting such control in proposing that control posts which could monitor tests should be established in the territory of the USSR, the USA and United Kingdom and the Pacific Ocean. However, it was not made clear how much on-the-spot inspection would be permitted from these. In August 1957 the Western states proposed a twelve-month moratorium on testing, provided that agreement had been reached on the installation and maintenance of the necessary controls.

Much of this was propaganda, designed to go some way towards meeting the widespread alarm of world opinion over the dangerous amount of radioactivity released by the tests. As this concern built up, the nuclear powers, though still unwilling to abandon testing, began to negotiate more seriously for some agreement which might at least reduce the dangers to health. In August 1958 a conference of scientific experts from East and West met in Geneva. It was agreed that it was 'technially feasible' to monitor a test-ban agreement and to detect any nuclear explosions above the 5 kiloton range. It was suggested that, if 180 control posts could be set up in every continent of the world, all explosions of this kind could be detected, but there might be a percentage of seismological events, about 20–100 a year, where it would be impossible to determine whether they resulted from an explosion. For this purpose some on-site inspection would be necessary. It was agreed to hold another conference to discuss the details of the inspection system this would require. Such a conference was held that autumn but made little progress.

Meanwhile, however, the existing nuclear powers, first the Soviet Union, later the United States and Britain, had agreed to accept a moratorium on testing for a year. This was later extended for nearly three years till the summer of 1961. Discussion continued on the type of control system which would be necessary. The West did not believe that the evidence of seismological stations alone would be sufficient; and demanded a minimum number of on-site inspections a year. This was resisted by the Soviet Union, which eventually proposed instead the use of 'black boxes', technical devices which could be left in various areas to detect explosions even where there were no stations. There were differences on other points. At first the Western countries held that they would agree to a test-ban only as part of a general disarmament agreement. Early in 1959 the United States and Britian abandoned this condition, but at the same time raised their demands on the amount of inspection that would be required to police the ban. The Soviet Union for a time stated that she was willing to accept three on-site inspections a year, against which the West demanded a minimum of twelve a year. Finally, in 1960 the United States and Britain proposed that the ban should apply only to tests in the atmosphere, under water, and to those underground over a particular seismic threshold. While this would allow some tests to contine, it would at least put an end to contamination of the atmosphere. Another three years of negotiation were to take place on this proposal before agreement was finally reached on it in 1963.

Thus these negotiations on limited agreements, though apparently more practical and realistic, did not get very much further than the increasingly sterile discussions of comprehensive disarmament. They had, however, at least descended to a rather more down-to-earth level of discussion. They were concerned with matters on which, on the face of it, it should not be altogether impossible to find some mutual accommodation. And over the years to come it was increasingly, for that reason, on this type of measure that negotiations were to concentrate.

Agreement was at least reached on yet another change in the forum for discussion. Most of the limited agreements had been discussed on an *ad hoc* basis, outside the Disarmament Commission and the other bodies established in this period. In 1960 the Soviet Union and other communist members expressed dissatisfaction even with the Disarmament Committee, on which they had equal representation with the West, and walked out of it. There was increasing recognition that a place should be found in the talks for many third-world states, who were just as concerned over the question of disarmament but had interests different from both East and West. Eventually, therefore, in 1961, it was agreed to establish a new body, the eighteen-nation Disarmament Conference, including five Western, five communist and eight non-aligned members, which was to meet at Geneva. From 1962 onwards this was to become the main body for the discussion of disarmament questions. Within it general and complete disarmament increasingly faded into the background. But it had little greater success in securing agreement on more limited measures.

CONCLUSIONS

It is not certain how far any of those who took part in the protracted and intensive discussions about disarmament at this period seriously believed in them. No doubt there were some who would have been happy to see agreements reached, so long as it was on the terms they themselves proposed. But, as we have seen, those terms all closely reflected the interests of individual nations, and for that reason were most unlikely to be acceptable to their opponents. There existed nowhere, at this time of cold war, a sufficient sense of objectivity, the synoptic vision or world-view, which could take account of the genuine fears and interests of the opposing party, and might therefore formulate the type of compromise which would have satisfied both sides.

It was indeed particularly unlikely that agreement could be reached on such measures at this point in time. There is always some element of risk involved in undertaking disarmament agreements. A considerable measure of mutual trust is always likely to be necessary. Yet this was a period of maximum hostility, when little trust was to be found. Even the most limited measures of arms control, designed to *restrain* rather

than reduce armed power, would have been difficult enough
to attain at such a time. But in fact it was by no means limited
agreements which were at this period mainly attempted. The
negotiations were primarily aimed at the most ambitious goal
conceivable, and one that has eluded governments throughout history: the negotiation of an agreement by which
armaments of all kinds could be substantially, or even totally,
abolished. If any agreement at all was attainable in the tense
international atmosphere of these years, it was certainly
unlikely to be one of this far-reaching kind.

Further, if agreement was to be reached between the two
mutually suspicious blocs, it was only likely to occur with the
aid of the mediation and good offices of some middle group of
countries, less committed to the intensely partisan passions of
the main blocs themselves. Such a group might have been able
to induce a little of that sense of objectivity, that understanding of the opponent's viewpoint, that was at the time so sadly
lacking. Yet it was precisely at this period that no representatives of such a middle group took any part in the discussions at
all. The negotiations took the form, for most of the time, of a
direct confrontation between the Soviet Union on the one
hand and the Western powers (usually the United States,
Britain, France and Canada) on the other. Though Britain
and France once or twice claimed to be putting forward a
middle position as a compromise, they were in fact always
putting a position not too far from that of the United States,
and could certainly not be seriously regarded as mediators. It
was only in the period that followed, from 1962 onwards,
when the Disarmament Conference was established in
Geneva, that a group of third-world nations joined the
negotiations, and had some such mediating role to play. At
this time, when the East–West confrontation made their
presence most necessary, they were absent.

Thus, whatever the optimists might sometimes at the time
suggest, the two sides during this period were never really in
sight of agreement. It is sometimes suggested that, if the West
had responded more positively to the Soviet proposals of May
1955, some overall disarmament agreement might then have
been achieved. It is possibly true that the prospect of German
rearmament, the deepest of all Soviet fears, made the Soviet
Union at that particular point more willing to be accommodat-

ing than at any other. Yet the chances of securing an agreement then, even if the Western response had been less negative and ham-handed, were still remote in the extreme. On many of the basic issues – the type and amount of verification, the relative priority to be given to conventional and nuclear weapons, the control of the means of delivery, and, above all, the exact balance of arms to be attained at each point in the disarmament process – the negotiators were then, even after substantial Soviet concessions, little closer to agreement than at earlier times.

Indeed, the risks involved in any disarmament, in the eyes of cautious diplomats overseen by still more cautious generals and politicians; the degree of trust which is required (especially when one side is as resistant to inspection as the Soviet Union); the enormity of the consequences of any violations which occur; the delicacy of the balance to be achieved, between many different types of arms, among many different nations, which may at any time be regrouped in new and unpredictable alliances (for example, in calculating balances should China have been regarded at this time as an ally of the Soviet Union?) – all this makes the conclusion of a comprehensive disarmament agreement difficult enough at any time. At a period when distrust was as great as now, it made it virtually impossible to conceive.

Always, therefore, there seemed more hope for success in the discussion of limited agreements. It was to this that both sides increasingly turned from the late 'fifties onwards. The final outcome of these discussions – the conclusion of the test-ban treaty, of the non-proliferation treaty, of the hot-line agreement, and the initial SALT arrangement – all these belonged to a later era. During the time with which we are concerned, this type of discussion had barely begun, and even when they did take place the suspicions between the two sides, even in this field, were still so great that on none of the main proposals considered – air inspection, a thinned-out zone, measures against surprise attack, a test-ban – was any agreement forthcoming. The entire period was as barren of success in the field of arms control as in the field of disarmament.

The UN was throughout the umbrella organisation which formally promoted and organised these negotiations. But after the first two or three years the mass of the membership were little more than passive spectators, waiting on the great powers to reach agreement among themselves. Here at least the organisation did put into practice the sensible aim of promoting negotiation among the parties principally involved. Unfortunately there was not in this case sufficient motivation among them, alone and unassisted, to reach agreement. This was another case, therefore, where it was not enough simply to set negotiations in motion. There was a need for the organisation itself to remain actively involved; for the participation of members who, though not the most heavily armed, had an almost equal interest in the success of the discussions, to act as goad and mediator for the great powers themselves. Participation in this sense had to wait for a later era. At this time the negotiations merely took the form, like so many others, of a bilateral confrontation between the hostile and mistrustful forces of East and West.

18 The Secretary-General and the Secretariat

Trygve Lie took a more active view of his role than any of his successors. He was a politician by profession and by inclination. He was indeed chosen partly because of his political background. Roosevelt, and some others involved in the foundation of the UN, saw the Secretary-General as being a major and dynamic figure on the international scene who should be in a position to take personal initiatives to resolve world disputes. For this reason nearly all the candidates proposed at the first choice (p. 73) were people of political background.

Thus in following his own personal instinct to play an active and public role, Lie was only conforming with the image of the Secretary-General which was widely held at the time – at least, everywhere outside the Soviet bloc. He had no set design. He later claimed, 'I inclined, from the beginning, toward a middle way – a pragmatic and open-minded approach. I would listen to all my advisers and be directed by none. I had no calculated plan for developing the political powers of the office of Secretary-General, but I was determined that the Secretary-General should be a force for peace.'[1] He was not in fact unaware of the dangers of being too exposed. He recognised the need for some caution and discretion. But in practice his desire to be 'a force for peace' led him to feel that on many issues he must speak out, expressing his own views in the interest of the citizens of the world as a whole.

This was a major difference between himself and all his successors. Hammarskjöld would express firm views about the way the organisation should operate, and about his own personal role within it, but he almost never expressed publicly a strong view on any controversial issue in dispute (and if he did so it was in language so opaque as to be carefully non-

343

committal); and his successors did so still less. Lie, on the other hand, was ready to plunge into public discussion on every question, taking sometimes a highly personal line. His views were not crudely partisan – on some issues, such as the Iranian question and Chinese representation, he was closer to the Soviet viewpoint than that of the West – but they did something to erode his reputation for impartiality, and so reduced the authority that his office might otherwise have enjoyed. Eventually, on one major issue he took a viewpoint that was identical with that of the West, and diametrically opposed to that of the Soviet Union; and this led him into such difficulty that it may have made inevitable his ultimate resignation.

He revealed his desire to play a strong personal role early in his term of office. In April 1946 he insisted on presenting to the Security Council, unasked for, a statement of his views concerning the legal propriety of retaining the Iranian dispute (as the Western powers had demanded) on the agenda, even though both interested parties declared the question to be settled (p. 110 above). This action was one he was perfectly entitled to take, but it was immediately condemned by some Western powers as exceeding his authority. Soon afterwards he called for a revision of the draft rules of procedure of the Security Council to make clear that the Secretary-General had the right to intervene in debates without invitation. This proposal was strongly supported by the Soviet Union, which at that time saw Lie as a political ally.

On Palestine in the following year, Lie was an outspoken supporter of partition, even before the Assembly had adopted that course. He strongly advised delegates who consulted him to support the majority report of the Special Committee on Palestine containing this recommendation. After the Assembly had endorsed that solution, he became still more ardent in support of the cause of the Jewish state. He even prepared a report to the Security Council personally advocating the use of an international force to impose partition, though he never eventually delivered it. And, when the United States reversed its own policy in February 1948 (p. 178 above), and advocated abandoning a dictated partition, he was so appalled that he proposed to the US delegate, Warren Austin (who had originally been one of the strongest proponents of partition), that they should both resign over the issue, and he expressed a similar intention to Gromyko, the Soviet delegate. It is not clear how sincerely he intended this threat; when the Soviet Government, after some delay, advised against resignation, the proposal was withdrawn. The step was apparently an emotional gesture of disapproval. To this extent it exhibited a side of his nature which made him, in the eyes of some, less than perfectly qualified for the post he held, for which some believed a non-committal detachment to be better suited.

After full-scale war between Israel and the Arabs broke out on the end of the mandate, Lie was again active in seeking to stimulate the Security Council to action. He not only addressed notes to all five permanent members on the subject, but also sent personal emissaries to Washington and London to urge the governments there to action. Since he reasonably believed that the organisation faced on the issue its gravest threat since it had been founded – and since until that time all members of the Council had shown a masterly inactivity – such steps could be justified by the situation that confronted the UN. But they were more dramatic in style than some thought strictly necessary. And they were taken to confirm the personal commitment to Israel which had been manifested during the previous year (and for which he was denounced as pro-Zionist by the Arab states).

Later in 1948 (and partly as a consequence of the Palestine experience) Lie launched an initiative of his own in the Assembly: one of the very few individual proposals made by any Secretary-General in that body. When, earlier that year, he had strongly supported the view that the UN should seek to impose the partition solution it had adopted in Palestine, by force if necessary, no UN force had been available. So he now returned to the idea that the UN should dispose of some armed forces of its own, as envisaged in the Charter. Since the negotiation for a force to be contributed by members of the Security Council had broken down, he now envisaged a much smaller force, a UN guard, of perhaps 5000–10,000 men, which would be individually recruited. This might be useful in areas such as Jerusalem, Trieste and others where the UN was given special responsibilities. At Harvard University in June 1948 he declared, such a force could be recruited by the Secretary-General and placed at the disposal of the Security Council. Such a force would have been extremely valuable to it in the past and it would undoubtedly be very valuable in the future. . . . Such action would strengthen the United Nations, because it would add to the ability of the organisation to exert its authority.

The proposal was discussed at the 1948 Assembly. It was strongly opposed by the Soviet Union and her allies, on the grounds that it was not provided for in the Charter. But other states too opposed the idea, above all the suggestion that the force should be individually recruited. This attacked national sovereignty too frontally to be acceptable in an assembly of nation-states. Lie's suggestion was thus not accepted in the form proposed. But the Assembly did agree to set up a committee to study the question and report back to the next session. Lie then submitted new proposals, now somewhat reduced in scope. Even these were rejected as over-ambitious by the committee. All that finally emerged was the establishment, at the following session of the Assembly, of the UN Field Service. Though not an armed force, this was a small contingent, which has existed ever since, for servicing UN missions and activities abroad. It has its own uniform, and is concerned primarily with transportation, communications and logistics, as well as with providing security guards and other services. On a very small scale, therefore, this could possibly be regarded as the first hesitant step by the UN on the road towards the establishment of its own peace-keeping forces, and for this step at least Lie can take the lion's share of the credit.

All this personal activity inevitably involved him in criticism from many members. It was, as he pointed out, only to be expected that 'when he agrees with us governments tend to feel the Secretary-General is within his rights and is a good fellow besides; when his views differ from ours he clearly is exceeding his authority, his reasoning is bad, and even his motives may be suspect'.[2] Lie himself recognised that his influence was sometimes best exerted behind the scenes, rather than in public. On a number of occasions he proposed an adjournment of the public meetings of the Council, so that members might 'meet informally in the privacy of his office in an attempt to settle matters'.[3] But his effectiveness on such occasions was probably lessened by his frequent forays into the public arena.

The counter-productive character of some of his initiatives was seen over the Berlin dispute (p. 220 above). After the Soviet veto of the Western resolution on the matter in the Council, he made contacts with both the US and Soviet governments and proposed a confidential study, by senior Secretariat officials of US and Soviet nationality (Feller and Sobolev), of the currency problem. Each of these would be in close contact with his own government, to see if they could find a technical solution which would enable the blockade to be removed. This initiative, though perfectly sensible in itself, got hopelessly entangled with a parallel attempt at mediation being undertaken at the same time by the president of the Security Council and the 'neutrals' (p. 219 above). It was, moreover, resented by the Western powers as ignoring their repeated public declaration that there could be no negotiation while the blockade was maintained. Eventually he recognised these difficulties and was willing to wait until a more propitious chance for mediation arose.

Lie took another strong personal line over the question of Chinese representation (p. 313 above). His main concern over the deadlock was the effect of the Russian boycott on the organisation. He was understandably afraid that, if maintained, this could destroy its effectiveness. Thus, soon after the walkout in January 1950, he asked his legal department to prepare a memorandum on the legal position concerning Chinese representation. This concluded that, since Article 4 of the Charter demanded that a member should be 'able and willing' to carry out the obligations of membership, only a government which exercised effective authority within the territory of the state concerned and was habitually obeyed by the population could undertake this commitment, and so be eligible for membership. In other words, the implication was, the Peking government had the better claim to the China seat. Lie discussed this conclusion with other members of the Council and finally allowed the memorandum to be published. This aroused the intense anger of the Chinese Nationalist delegate, Dr Tsiang, who accused him of trying to influence the outcome. Parts of the US press, now increasingly shrill in its anti-communist sentiment, also denounced him for surrender to the Soviet Union. But this did not deter him. During journeys to Washington, London, Paris and Moscow, he declared his conviction that the China seat should be awarded to Peking and that some kind of UN trusteeship might be established over Taiwan.[4]

With the same excellent intentions, during the summer of 1950 Lie undertook a personal 'peace mission', travelling in turn to London, Washington, Paris and Moscow, to hold interviews with the heads of government in each place, and to make a plea for reconciliation. With him he bore a memorandum he had prepared setting out a twenty-year 'UN peace programme'. This included proposals for periodic meetings of the Security Council to be attended by foreign ministers or heads of governments and the development of other conciliation procedures; new efforts to solve the problem of the 'control of atomic energy', and of disarmament generally; a revival of the deadlocked negotiations for a Security Council force; acceptance of the principle of advancing as quickly as possible towards universality of membership; a development of the newly born technical assistance programme and other UN activities in the field of economic development, human rights and decolonisation; and an attempt to speed up the development of international law towards an 'eventual enforceable world law for a universal world society'.

This was not a very well-judged initiative. Many of the proposals concerned issues on which governments had been negotiating for years without success, and there was little real prospect that, because of a personal appeal by Lie, agreement on them would be suddenly produced out of a hat. All of the heads of state he approached were more or less sceptical. Truman, Attlee and Bidault were polite but somewhat noncommittal, declaring that everything depended on a more co-operative attitude by the Russians. The Russian reaction was even less cordial. Stalin and the other Soviet leaders listened carefully. But they resented particularly Lie's proposal for a review on the use of the veto (again misjudged, since in their eyes the veto was the essential safeguard which alone made UN membership acceptable to them), his references to the 'control' of atomic energy (the US demand) without mentioning 'prohibition' (at that time their own), and the demand for an active economic programme through the UN and the agencies (which they had always held to be outside UN competence).

Stalin and Molotov none the less agreed in principle to regular Security Council meetings, with foreign ministers attending if possible, using the memorandum as a basis for discussion. The Western governments were lukewarm about the value of such meetings, maintaining that they could scarcely resolve the basic differences between the governments on the other points raised in the memorandum. Thus eventually nothing came of the initiative. In June 1950 Lie published his memorandum without revealing the comments of the four governments. Three weeks later the Korean War broke out. And, though the following Assembly commended him for his initiative, and asked various UN organs to consider the proposals, in effect any chance of progress on his ideas was by then dead.

It was over the Korean War that Lie became most clearly committed to taking a public position on a controversial subject. As soon as the Security Council had decided to call for action to assist South Korea against the attack from the North, he became an outspoken advocate of the UN position in Korea. This was a perfectly reasonable position. He was supporting the viewpoint endorsed by a substantial majority, both in the Security Council and the Assembly. More important, he was, in his own eyes, supporting one of the basic principles on which the organisation was founded: that its members should join in the collective defence of a nation under attack. But the outspoken advocacy of his views won him the undying enmity of the Soviet bloc. It is arguable that he might have done better to leave the initiative more strictly in the hands of the Council, and have acted, as Hammarskjöld was to act over Suez, merely as the agent of the organisation, on the basis of the instructions he received from the political bodies.

In fact, he took a much more committed position. At the initial meeting of the Council which considered the matter, he said that it was 'plain that military actions had been undertaken by North Korean forces' and that it was 'the clear duty of the Security Council to take steps necessary to re-establish peace in that area'. He publicly stated that, if the ceasefire order were not obeyed by North Korea, the Council could properly use armed force on behalf of South Korea. He personally drafted a resolution, passed with little change, proposing that the US be given command of the UN force. He personally cabled all member-states, urging them to provide forces (using for this purpose a draft suggested by the US mission to the UN). He made many speeches calling for support for the UN action in Korea. Within his office in the Secretariat he established a specially composed unit, excluding all officials from communist states, to be responsible for Korean matters. He proposed his own terms for a settlement of the war (of a type certain to be unacceptable to North Korea, since they provided not only for withdrawal but also for elections in the North under the authority of the UN Commission). And he publicly supported the US initiative in introducing the Uniting for Peace procedure, which effectively amended the Charter in a way totally unacceptable to the communist states.

Although all these stands could be reasonably defended as designed to support or enhance the authority of the UN, in the eyes of the communists their effect was rather to support the Western conception of the UN's role and of UN policies. They increasingly regarded him as an overt ally of the West within the organisation. And he began to be denounced in the Moscow press as 'the abetter of American aggression ... humbly aiding Truman and Acheson to wreck the United Nations'.

This decisively affected his chance of remaining in office after his term expired early in 1951. Originally he himself had said that he did not wish for a second term: he had been, in his own words, a 'tired official, genuinely greateful for the chance to quit while the quitting was good'.[5] But, as the time grew nearer, he became willing at least to allow his name to go forward. And the fact that he came under public attack from the Soviet Union for his stand on Korea, he later said, made him more convinced that he could not allow himself 'to be pushed out of office in punishment for having done his duty'.[6] The United States, for the same reason, expressed strong support for his re-election. And Britain and France, though at first lukewarm, subsequently joined her in that attitude.

Until May 1950 the Soviet Union had said she would support Lie for a second term and had informed him accordingly. But after his Korean stand she announced that she could not accept him. And, when the proposal came up in the Security Council, she vetoed the proposal. This she had a perfect right to do: the whole point of the procedure for appointing the Secretary-General was that any person chosen had to be acceptable to all five permanent members. But the US Government was determined to make an issue of the question. It rejected an Indian plan designed to find a new candidate acceptable to all permanent members. And it announced that it in turn would veto any candidate other than Lie. Taunted by the Russians that the United States had said she would never use her veto, the US representative declared that in this case it was justifiable, since 'the Council is face to face with an attack on a moral principle, and the question is whether the unity of the free peoples will be maintained or broken up'.

There was a series of meetings to break the deadlock, but still the Council was unable to agree. The matter then went to the Assembly. Under the Charter the Assembly could not make an appointment except on the recommendation of the Security Council. But at US instigation, the Assembly eventually decided that Lie should 'continue in office' for a further three years after the end of his five-year term. This was a transparent device, designed to allow Lie to remain in office without going through the process of reappointment. It was manifestly contrary to the Charter provision which laid down that a Security Council 'recommendation' was required for appointment: expressly designed to ensure that the Secretary-General was acceptable to all five permanent members. It seems extremely doubtful if the International Court of Justice, had the question been put to it, would have held it to be legal. But it was what the Western powers demanded; and, since they controlled the organisation, it is what happened.[7]

The entire episode is a typical example of a gross abuse by the ruling majority of its voting strength. Either the Western powers should have insisted in 1945 that the appointment of a Secretary-General did not require a recommendation of the Security Council (that is should not be subject to veto); or, having accepted it, they should have recognised that the veto must apply in this case (even if denouncing its use for the partisan and malicious act that it was). But to seek a spurious means of evading the clear meaning of the Charter provisions was only to open the door to similar abuses, on similar questions, by any other majority which might finally come to power within the organisation.

The Soviet Union had announced that, if this procedure was used, she would refuse to recognise the legality of the reappointment, or to have any dealings with Lie thereafter. This commitment she fulfilled. During the next two years Soviet representatives consistently boycotted Lie on every occasion when he appeared. They refused every invitation from him to social occasions. They addressed all communications to the UN 'Secretariat', rather than to the Secretary-General himself. They even presented their credentials without referring to Lie or to his office.

Eventually, for this reason, Lie's position became increasingly untenable. Since his authority was totally rejected by a major power and its allies, his usefulness was almost at an end. In addition he was having increasing difficulties over Secretariat and budgetary matters. Eventually he himself decided not to see out his term of office. In November 1952, when less than two of the three years of his second term had elapsed, he announced his resignation. There were a few, rather half-hearted attempts to get him to change his mind. But it was soon recognised that he had reached a firm decision (though at a later stage he announced that he would be a candidate yet again if required) and the search began for a successor.

This did not prove easy. A number of names were suggested. Among these were Lester Pearson of Canada, Padillo Nervo of Mexico, Charles Malik of Lebanon, Sir Benegal Rau and Mrs Pandit of India. It was only in March that the Council began serious negotiations on the question. The United States finally supported Romulo of the Philippines. But Romulo did not secure enough votes to carry. Pearson obtained nine votes, but was vetoed by the Soviet Union. The Soviet nominee, the Polish Foreign Minister, secured only one vote. So the search went on.

Over the following three weeks the Security Council held a number of further meetings. Finally, quite unexpectedly, it was announced that it had reached agreement on a name not previously mentioned, and almost unknown to most people: Dag Hammarskjöld of Sweden. His name had first been proposed by Britain and France, and it was almost immediately accepted unanimously. The most curious feature of all was that he himself was never consulted in advance. He was merely informed of the recommendation, very much to his surprise, after it had already been agreed. Still somewhat bemused, he allowed his name to go forward. It was confirmed by the Assembly, without dissent, on 7 April. A new era in UN history had begun.

THE SECRETARIAT

Trgyve Lie had, as we saw, had the responsibility for building up the Secretariat almost from scratch. He accepted the basic organisational pattern which had been proposed to him by the Preparatory Committee (p. 70 above). He changed this hardly at all during his first term of office. He was beginning to consider more fundamental changes when he suddenly resigned in 1952. The question was then taken up by his successor. Hammarskjöld ultimately decided to make quite different changes.

By far the most important problem concerning the Secretariat which arose during Lie's term of office concerned the accusations which were made during the McCarthy campaign in the United States concerning the loyalty of US members of the staff. Lie had from the beginning bent over backwards to avoid employing US nationals against whom there might be accusations on security grounds. Indeed, he had in the eyes of many members of the UN staff risked the reputation of the Secretariat for impartiality in agreeing to check on the records of such employees. Already in 1948 he had submitted the names of 377 members of the staff to the US Government asking for 'the usual passport enquiries to be made, hoping to be notified of any case where a barrier to issuance of a passport existed'.[8] In June 1949, at his request, Byron Price, Assistant Secretary-General for Administrative and Financial Services (and a US national), asked a senior official of the FBI if the FBI could provide 'derogatory information' on US applicants for Secretariat posts; and in the autumn of that year the US State Department agreed to examine US records concerning such applicants. Later this was extended to all US nationals employed in the Secretariat, whose records were to be examined by the State Department to see if any security considerations (presumably considerations concerning US security) existed. Although Lie did not regard such reports as sufficient grounds in themselves for dismissing an employee, they could lead to a UN investigation which had the same outcome. Lie made it clear that he felt that he had a special obligation towards the host government to take account of its own security apprehensions, so that he would, for example, 'never knowingly have employed a member of the American communist party in the Secretariat'.[9]

During 1950 this policy led him into difficulty with the UN Administrative Tribunal, which had the specific task of looking into complaints of dismissals held to be in breach of contract by employees. Lie had earlier that year dismissed several staff members on temporary contracts on security grounds, believing that, in the case of temporary employees, this was justified even if he did not reveal the grounds on which action was taken. The Tribunal decided that, even for temporary employees, specific reasons for dismissal must be given. Lie accordingly secured an amendment in the staff regulations which would allow him to terminate the contracts of temporary members of the staff on the vague and untestable grounds that he believed 'such action would be in the interests of' the United Nations: this of course meant that he could dismiss whomever he liked without giving any information at all about the charges on which the dismissal was based. He then proceeded, during the following months, to dismiss a number of temporary employees on these grounds.

In 1952, however, he acted in a still more questionable way. In that year the McCarthy campaign began to turn part of its attention to the UN (which had been denounced for years in the United States as being a 'nest of communist subversives'). In October 1952 the Internal Security Sub-committee of the Senate Judiciary Committee, a key organ of the McCarthy witch-hunt, held a series of public hearings in New York partly devoted to the investigation of US citizens working in the UN Secretariat. During these hearings eighteen of the US citizens concerned pleaded the Fifth Amendment and declined to reply to questions. This they had a perfect constitutional right to do, and in itself it proved precisely nothing about the suitability of such people to hold posts within the UN Secretariat: the Amendment would of course have no meaning at all if a refusal to answer was taken as a confession of guilt. Yet Lie concluded that such staff members had 'gravely and irresponsibly transgressed the staff regulations. . . . They had not conducted themselves as international civil servants should.'[10]

Lie was apparently concerned not so much by what the refusals proved, but by the effect they had on opinion in the United States in 'discrediting' the Secretariat as a whole. He therefore decided to set up an international commission of jurists, selected by himself, to consider what action he would be justified in taking in these cases. He chose three members from the United States, Britain and Belgium (not exactly the most balanced group of nations that could be chosen) – members who were individually accused by some of the UN staff as being lacking in objectivity on such questions. On 13 November of that year, Abe Feller, the UN's legal counsel and almost the senior US member of the US staff, committed suicide by jumping from a third-floor window. This apparently resulted from his personal anguish at the course which the UN's policy on staff matters, in which he was heavily involved, was now taking.

At the end of November, the carefully selected team of jurists recommended, as Lie had hoped and expected, that a US member of the staff who pleaded the Fifth Amendment to avoid answering questions might be dismissed by the Secretary-General as being in breach of Article 1.4 of the staff regulations (which said that they should conduct themselves at all times in a manner 'befitting their status as international civil servants'). Lie subsequently endorsed this view, saying that staff members had a 'positive obligation to refrain from conduct which would draw upon themselves grave suspicion of being a danger to the security of a particular state'.[11] This was an extraordinary conclusion to draw on the basis of a single refusal, under an ancient constitutional safeguard, to answer questions, unaccompanied by the smallest evidence of subversive activity or other breach of duty. But nine US staff members – this time permanent staff members – who refused to withdraw their pleas were immediately dismissed.

Shortly afterwards, in January 1953, the US Government

introduced an executive order which provided for a full field investigation, to be undertaken by the FBI, of all US citizens belonging to the UN staff, as well as of future candidates for such posts. The results of these investigations were to be submitted to the Secretary-General and to be used by him in exercising his responsibility in selecting staff. Given the attitude so far adopted by Lie, they need have little doubt that he would act on the basis of any information so provided. This confidence was no doubt enhanced when he not merely announced his co-operation with the inquiry but also provided for the FBI full facilities in the UN building itself. So the FBI began, in the very headquarters of the organisation, the finger-printing and interviewing of US nationals. This was an abject submission by the Secretary-General to the demands of the US Government as host state; and it is an indication of the hysteria at that time prevailing in the United States that he should, despite the protests of very many UN officials, including many Americans, have permitted such a step.

This was the situation that Hammarskjöld, the new Secretary-General, inherited. During his relatively quiet first year Hammarskjöld had the time to sort out some of the problems which had arisen over the US security investigations. In November 1953 he demanded that FBI agents should no longer be allowed to carry out investigations on UN premises. He then sought to build up a clear body of procedures and rules for dealing with any accusations concerning loyalty. Before the end of 1953, he proposed amendments to the staff regulations which more explicitly defined activities which could be taken to reflect adversely on a staff member's 'integrity, independence and impartiality', but at the same time gave the Secretary-General greater power to terminate appointments under a system of safeguards. The Staff Committee representing UN employees, though thankful that the role of US investigators was reduced, believed that the safeguards provided were still insufficient: the Secretary-General could decide to dismiss an employee 'in the interest of good administration' or on the vague charge of 'lack of integrity', or on the basis of evidence provided by a particular government which the employee himself might have little chance to rebut.[12] None the less the rights of the staff were, as a result, considerably better protected under Hammarskjöld than they had been under Lie. And, as the McCarthy hysteria died down in the United States and Senate committees became less demanding, the anxieties among the secretariat staff began slowly to subside.

THE GROWTH OF THE SECRETARIAT

Under both Secretaries-General there was a steady expansion in the work of the Secretariat devoted to development assistance. Originally, as we saw, there were separate departments concerned with economic and with social affairs (corresponding to the different Assembly committees concerned with these two fields). Work in the economic area continually increased. Already in 1946 an Assembly resolution had called on the UN to grant 'expert advice' on economic questions to member states which required it. In 1948 the UN started its own technical-assistance programme, financed out of the regular budget. In the following year the much larger Expanded Programme of Technical Assistance, based on voluntary contributions, was inaugurated. This led to the establishment of the Technical Assistance Board, with its own staff concerned with organising the programme, run largely as a separate operation, under its own executive secretary (David Owen).[13]

Throughout the fifties this side of the UN's work continued to expand. For a number of years a proposal for a Special UN Fund for Economic Development was intensively discussed. In the end this never came to anything, owing to the hostility of the richer members, but some lesser programmes were instituted. In 1958 the Special Fund was set up, to undertake preinvestment projects in developing countries, and led to a further expansion of the UN's own economic work (in addition to that of the World Bank and other agencies).

Hammarskjöld personally promoted another innovation in this field: the establishment of the OPEX programme for despatching UN experts in an administrative rather than a technical role. The idea had first been proposed by Lester Pearson, and in 1956 Hammarskjöld took it up with enthusiasm, endorsing it to ECOSOC, and later presenting it as a formal proposal to the General Assembly. It was finally approved by the Assembly as an experiment in 1958, and became a permanent part of the technical-assistance programme in 1960. Under the programme, developing countries were provided with skilled administrators who, though despatched by the UN, acted when they arrived as an integral part of the administration of the country concerned, rather than as outside experts: in effect they were a more acceptable substitute for the expatriate colonial officials who had previously performed a similar role.

The growth of the economic and social work undertaken by the UN was accompanied by a development of its responsibilities for co-ordinating the UN system as a whole: the family of specialised agencies which were 'in relationship with' the UN but not a part of it. The Secretary-General acted as chairman of the Administrative Committee on Co-ordination (ACC), which was the official body responsible for co-ordination, and he began to develop a small staff in his own office responsible for co-ordination and for the affairs of the ACC. He and his staff had a never-ending struggle in seeking to contend with the somewhat autocratic attitude of the executive heads of the agencies, all of whom insisted strongly that they were responsible to their own inter-governmental councils, not to the UN and were determined to run their own affairs in their own way. Though there were innumerable attempts, in this as in later periods, to improve 'co-ordination', it was a struggle which never at this time secured any successes.[14]

CONCLUSIONS

The organisation of an international secretariat confronts many obvious problems. There is the difficulty of integrating people of many different nationalities, languages, cultures and political views, in a single integrated administration. There is the problem of selecting staff from a wide geographical distribution, as member-states (above all those which are under-represented) inevitably demand, without sacrificing efficiency. There is the problem of morale which arises in any large-scale organisation, especially one where the ultimate bosses (here the political bodies of the organisation) are so remote from the employees, who thus feel they have little chance of influencing policy, nor even of making their voices heard on their own conditions of service. There is the problem of deciding on what criteria staff shall be engaged or promoted, while paying due regard to the provisions of the Charter (p. 66). There is the question of whether staff should be engaged on permanent, lifelong contracts, so that they become generally 'international men', or should be seconded for shorter periods, so providing greater flexibility in recruitment and in the balance of nationalities engaged, but providing a lesser degree of commitment to the purposes of the organisation.

All of these were problems that the first two secretaries-general had to contend with at all times during their terms of office. Because they had wide-ranging responsibilities in the political field, neither of them, especially Lie, was able to devote as much attention to staff questions as would have been desirable, and at various times there was dissatisfaction among their subordinates about their conditions of work: especially manifest when Lie was succumbing to pressure from the US Government on the security issue. They were none the less able to supervise a massive expansion in the staff working for the organisation during their period of office, without encountering any insuperable problems. And they experienced none of the difficulties in securing contributions for the budgets needed to pay their staff which had continually plagued their predecessors in the League.

Lie and Hammarskjöld represented two alternative styles for playing the role of secretary-general. There was a case for attempting the more flamboyant and outspoken style adopted by Lie. If the Secretary-General is to be thought of as the voice of the common man, continually nudging and bullying governments into taking the actions ordinary men think necessary to maintain the peace, there is something to be said for playing the part in the way he adopted, despite the potential costs. If, on the other hand, the Secretary-General is to be thought of as the patient negotiator, the skilful mediator who may find the way for resolving differences among governments, or devise the procedure required to overcome a difficulty, then the style taken up by Hammarskjöld was the more appropriate. By the time Hammarskjöld was appointed, some of the difficulties created by the Lie approach had already become manifest (it is said that Britain and France were looking for somebody whose skills were more administrative and diplomatic when they proposed Hammarskjöld for the job). During the 'fifties the membership as a whole were also more willing to delegate responsibility to the Secretary-General for sorting out difficult issues, provided they could rely on his impartiality. It was on these grounds that Hammarskjöld was provided with the opportunity to exercise his supreme skills and so was able to assist the organisation for some of its more spectacular successes. Hammarskjöld too, however, for all his caution, was not to escape the problem that had destroyed Lie. He too was to find his work made almost impossible in the period that followed because of the opposition of a few individual members who became implacably opposed to the political positions that he adopted. Such is the peril that faces all those who undertake the precarious and lonely role of Secretary-General.

19 Membership Disputes

There had been a general hope when the UN was founded that it would be a virtually universal organisation. At San Francisco it was decided (p. 63 above) that it should be open to all 'peace-loving' states. But questions of admission were to be decided by the Assembly only 'on the recommendation' of the Security Council. It was generally accepted that the need for a Council recommendation meant that the veto applied over such questions (this had of course been the point of the provision). The use by the Soviet Union of this veto power – and the corresponding use by the Western powers of their majority vote – to exclude applicants from membership led during the first decade of the UN's history to a whole series of disputes.

The condition that a state should be 'peace-loving' was originally designed to exclude former enemy states. But it was obviously open to subjective interpretation. In theory, most members accepted that the organisation should be as nearly universal as possible: this should be one improvement over the League. But in practice they reserved the right to exclude any government they particularly disliked, on the grounds that it failed this qualification. Any member could use his vote for this purpose if he so wished. And in the case of the permanent members such a vote amounted to a veto.

The first major membership issue which arose concerned Spain. At San Francisco Mexico had proposed, and the Conference had agreed, to interpret the 'peace-loving' clause in a way that would prevent Spain's being accepted as a member. A resolution was passed that, under this provision, the organisation would not be open to the defeated Axis powers, nor to 'any regime installed with the help of the armed forces' of such powers. It was made clear by Mexico that this latter phrase referred to Spain; and France, supporting the resolution, expressed the hope that one day Spain would 'have a regime that will allow it to become a member of the UN'. In passing the resolution, therefore, the Conference seemed to accept that Spain, under her present government, was not eligible for UN membership. At Potsdam, the United States, the Soviet Union and Britain had reaffirmed that they would not support any application by Spain for membership. And at the first session of the General Assembly, in London early in 1946, a resolution was proposed by Panama calling on members to act in this respect according to the letter and the spirit of the San Francisco resolution and the Potsdam declaration. This was passed with little dissent.

In April of that year Poland proposed that the Security Council should in addition consider 'the situation arising from the existence and activities' of the Franco regime in Spain. She declared that the regime had not only been an active partner of the Axis powers during the war but had become a refuge for German war criminals and had caused international friction by massing troops on the borders of France, so compelling France to close the border. On these grounds the Council should declare that 'the existence and activities of the Franco regime' endangered international peace and security and that all members should be called on to sever diplomatic relations with Spain. The Council would also declare its hope that 'the people of Spain will regain the freedom of which they have been deprived with the aid and connivance of fascist Italy and nazi Germany'. This proposal was a more open interference in the domestic affairs of sovereign state than has perhaps ever been proposed before or since (it is interesting to consider how Poland, for example, would today regard a UN resolution expressing the hope that the people of Poland would soon regain their freedom). It was none the less supported by France, Mexico and the Soviet Union. The Netherlands, Britain, China and Brazil expressed doubt whether there existed any genuine threat to the peace which could justify Security Council action of this kind. A sub-committee was set up to look at the question and concluded that, while there was no present threat to the peace which would justify action under Article 39, there did exist in Spain a situation 'the continuation of which is likely to endanger the maintenance of international peace and security', which could thus be considered under Chapter VI of the Charter. It proposed that the Spanish question should be put to the Assembly, with a suggestion that, unless the situation in Spain was remedied, it should recommend that all members sever diplomatic relations with that country. This was a fairly tough recommendation. But the Soviet Union, regarding it as insufficiently strong, vetoed the proposal.

None the less the Assembly took up the matter in the autumn. There were some calls for a general severing of diplomatic relations. But a more limited step was finally adopted. A resolution was passed recommending that Spain should be barred from the specialised agencies of the UN (which took their own independent decisions on membership), as she already was from the UN itself; and that all members should immediately recall their ambassadors or ministers plenipotentiary from Madrid. If a democratic Spanish government was not established within a reasonable time, the Security Council should consider adequate measures to remedy the situation – another striking interference in domestic affairs (which might perhaps equally appropriately have been directed at a considerable proportion of non-democratic members at this time).

The withdrawal of heads of mission was symbolic rather than practical in effect. Of the fifty-two members, thirty states already had no diplomatic relations at this time and sixteen more had no ambassador or minister. Four states did recall their ambassador or minister; two others, which had them, did nothing. At the following session of the Assembly, in 1947, despite demands for much stronger action, including economic sanctions against Spain, the Assembly contented itself with expressing confidence that the Security Council would 'exercise its responsibilities under the Charter as soon as it considers that the situation in regard to Spain so requires'. But a paragraph reaffirming the previous year's resolution was not carried; and this was interpreted by some to mean that the demand for a recall of ambassadors was no longer valid.

In 1948 the Assembly rejected a Polish resolution calling for the suspension of all arms sales to Spain, and demanding a general refusal to enter into treaties or alliances with Spain. Instead it passed, by a simple majority, a Latin American resolution declaring that, because of what had happened the previous year, the General Assembly now permitted members full freedom of action in their relations with Spain. Because this did not have a two-thirds majority, as required for 'important decisions', it was without effect, but in 1950 the Assembly did pass a resolution, by a substantial majority, specifically revoking the 1946 recommendation. This said nothing about UN membership but declared that, since the specialised agencies were technical and 'largely non-political', they should decide for themselves whether to admit Spain. Though the recommendation to withdraw ambassadors and ministers was withdrawn, it was emphasised that any change made in this connection did not imply any judgement on the domestic policies of the Spanish Government. This was a typical piece of UN double-talk, enabling those countries which wished to do so to send back their ambassadors without implying any endorsement of the political character of the Spanish regime.

Thus, after making a bold, though quite ineffective, gesture of disapproval in 1946, the Assembly year by year retracted its steps until the gesture was totally annulled. In 1955 Spain submitted an application for membership of the UN. In the same year, in company with the considerable queue of applicants which had by then formed, she was admitted to membership with little recrimination or objection.

VETO AND COUNTER-VETO

Spain was a somewhat special case, because she was, at first at least, denounced impartially by East and West alike. There were, however, a considerable number of other potential members which became essentially the protegé of one group or the other. They were then blackballed by their opponents and became political footballs for the next decade.

A few countries which were well regarded by both camps managed to get in with little difficulty. Sweden, Thailand, Iceland and Afghanistan were all admitted during the course of 1946, as were Yemen and Pakistan in 1947, and Burma in 1948. But Albania, Mongolia, Jordan, Ireland and Portugal, which all applied in 1946, were less fortunate; the first two were blocked by the Western powers, the last three by the Soviet Union (which of course had to use her veto for the purpose). At this stage the United States, with other Western powers, was prepared to contemplate a package deal by which all would be admitted. The Soviet Union, however, rejected this, declaring that she had objections of principle to the blocked states which she could not overlook for the sake of a deal.

In 1946 the Security Council had set up the Committee on the Admission of New Members to consider questions of admission. This, in accordance with a request from the Assembly, examined each application individually. In August 1947, when the Council met to consider its report, Syria raised again the idea of a 'package': all the applicants should be admitted together. This was now roundly rejected by the majority, as conflicting with the principle that each application be considered on its merits. Nationalist China, particularly hostile to the admission of Mongolia, which she regarded as part of her own territory, was especially opposed to the idea. Thus individual votes were taken on each, and the result was as before: the communist candidates were not voted in, and the rest were vetoed.

During 1947 Austria, Bulgaria, Finland, Hungary, Italy and Romania joined the queue. The Assembly tried to impress its own preferences on the Council. It passed a resolution saying that 'in its judgement' the non-communist states (Austria, Finland, Ireland, Italy, Portugal and Trans-jordan) were qualified for admission; and asked that the last two in particular should be quickly reconsidered. But this produced no change. When the Western powers demanded a meeting especially to consider the case of Italy, immediately before important elections there in 1948 (a move widely held to be designed to influence the result of the election), the Soviet Union repeated her veto. But she now openly announced that, if the other former enemy states (those of Eastern Europe) were admitted, she would support Finland and Italy. And she was able to quote the Potsdam Declaration, in which the Western states had accepted that the conclusion of peace treaties with all those states would 'enable' them to support applications for UN membership from them.

Thus the initial positions had become transposed. The Soviet Union now made clear that she would not withdraw her veto of the non-communist states until she was assured that the five communist applicants would be admitted. The

Western powers, on the other hand, declared that any deal of this kind was unacceptable. Each applicant must be considered 'on its merits': what this implied was that they were justified in blocking the admission of the communist states – on the grounds of violations of human rights or because their governments had been imposed by the Soviet Union – while any corresponding action by the Soviet Union to block other applications was an irresponsible abuse of the veto power.

There began a long battle over the ever-growing list of applicants. These eventually became roughly twenty states: four in Eastern Europe, together with Mongolia, supported by the Soviet Union; and about fifteen other states supported by the West.

The battle soon became one not merely between East and West, but also between the Assembly and the Security Council. The Assembly, dominated by the West, supported the Western candidates. It too demanded that each application should be considered individually and 'on its merits'. And in particular it denounced the use of the veto over questions of admission: an understandable position, since what the abandonment of the veto would have meant was that the Western candidates would be admitted while the communist candidates, whose merits the majority opposed, would not.

There was thus a series of attempts by the Assembly to get the Security Council to think again. In 1947 it appointed a committee to negotiate with the Council on the whole procedure governing admission. As a result a few marginal changes in the rules of procedure of both the Council and the Assembly were made.[1] But the basic consitutional position was not altered: an applicant still had to be supported by the Council before being submitted to the Assembly. In other words, the veto still applied.

On these grounds the 1947 Assembly decided to ask for an advisory opinion of the International Court of Justice on the procedure for admitting new members, to see whether the veto could be avoided. In its opinion, issued in May 1948, the Court reaffirmed, by 9 votes to 6, that admissions must be subject to the Security Council's approval and therefore to veto (given the explicit wording of the Charter, it could hardly have found otherwise). But the Court did state that consent to the admission of a State could be withheld only on the grounds specifically set out in Article 4(1) of the Charter. Thus it could not be made conditional on the admission of another State. This did not really alter the position, since a member could always profess to be excluding a state on the grounds that it was not 'peace-loving' and change its opinion on the point only when some other state was admitted. But the 1948 Assembly asked the Council to reconsider the individual applications in the light of the opinion; and it again passed resolutions individually endorsing the applications of Portugal, Trans-jordan, Italy, Finland, Austria, Ireland and Ceylon. It also asked members of the Council to vote on the applications in accordance with the Court's opinion.

In November 1948 Israel applied. Her claim was vigorously opposed by Arab members on the grounds that she had been illegally created by force and was occupying Arab territory. The Committee on New Members decided that it had not sufficient information to reach a decision. In the Council itself several states, including Britain and France, abstained, so that the resolution recommending admission was not passed. But Israel at this time was in the fortunate position of having no permanent member strongly hostile to her. When the question was put again in March 1949, she received nine favourable votes and was not vetoed. In the Assembly she was called on to give undertakings about her policies on the protection of the holy places, the internationalisation of Jerusalem, Arab refugees, her borders and the assassination of Count Bernadotte, but her admission was none the less approved by a substantial majority.

In 1948 Ceylon also applied, but was blocked by the Soviet Union as being too Western-oriented and not genuinely independent from Britain. She was joined in the queue in 1949 by Nepal, and by two especially contentious cases, North and South Korea.

In June 1949 the idea of a package deal was again put before the Security Council. The Soviet Union proposed that all the twelve earlier applicants (that is, excluding the two Koreas) should be admitted together. The Western countries rejected this as incompatible with the Court's opinion and with Assembly resolutions. So once more separate votes were taken. Again the five communist states received only two or three votes in favour, the Western states declaring that they did not qualify for membership since their governments had been imposed and because of violations of human rights. And again the other countries were therefore vetoed by the Soviet Union. In the Assembly that year another Soviet proposal for a package deal was turned down; the non-communist applications, including Nepal and South Korea, were again endorsed; and once more an advisory opinion was requested of the International Court, now asked in particular whether an application might be approved by the Assembly alone if the Council had made no recommendation as a result of a veto.

This application had no more success than the last. The Court found, as it inevitably had to, that every admission required a recommendation from the Security Council as well as a decision by the Assembly. No admission could therefore be made by a decision of the General Assembly unless the Security Council had made such a recommendation first. All the Assembly could therefore do was to ask the Council to keep the applications under consideration in the light of its earlier resolutions.

There was virtually no progress on the question for the next five years. At the end of 1951 Libya and North and South Vietnam joined the list of applicants, and in 1952 Japan, Cambodia and Laos. Impatience at the impasse gradually built up, especially among the applicants themselves. In February 1952 the Assembly asked the permanent members to confer among themselves, but this produced no result. The 1952 Assembly set up another special committee to study the problem and consider various ways of overcoming the deadlock (for example, to consider whether votes on admission in the Council could be regarded as procedural questions). But the communist states refused to take part in this. Within the new committee, however, a number of members, including Egypt, the Philippines and Argentina, made clear their impatience at the existing situation, and now gave their clear support to the package concept. When the Committee's inconclusive report was debated in the Assembly, support for the package idea became still stronger. India, Sweden, Syria and Yugoslavia and some Latin Americans began to speak about the importance of the principle of 'universality'. And, when yet another committee, a committee of good offices, consisting of Egypt, the Netherlands and Peru, also failed to make any headway in discussions with the Soviet Union, it was eventually, in 1954, specifically asked to resume its labours in the light of the 'growing feeling in favour of the universality of the United Nations'. The deliberate inclusion of this phrase in the preamble of the resolution expressed a growing impatience with the rigid posture adopted by the United States and some other Western states and a growing feeling that the package formula represented the only means of resolving the dilemma.

The following September, in 1955, the Good Offices Committee, though it had made little progress, optimistically reported that 'in view of the current evolution of the international atmosphere' (this was the year of the Geneva summit conference), the positions taken up appeared to be 'not necessarily immutable'. Canada then proposed in the Assembly a resolution requesting the Security Council to consider all the applications except those of the divided countries (which were especially contentious) 'in the light of the general opinion in favour of the widest possible membership of the UN'. This was by implication another call for the package solution. Canada explicitly stated that she did not approve of the regimes of some of the applicants, but thought they would be likely to show greater tolerance and understanding within the organisation than outside it. Many other states supported this viewpoint.

Most important was a slight shift in the attitude of the United States. She now declared once again that 'she could not support' herself the applications of the East European states and of Mongolia, since they were 'not independent'; but she announced she would not use her veto in the Council to thwart the will of a qualified majority of either the Council or the Assembly. In other words, she would abstain in the votes on such countries so that their admission would depend on the number of votes they received alone. Only nationalist China now remained strongly opposed to the package principle, expressing once again her special distaste for the admission of Mongolia. None the less the Canadian resolution was passed, and the matter went back to the Council.

The Soviet Union was still somewhat suspicious. For, even if the United States and other Western states allowed through the communist applicants in the Council, there was in her eyes still a danger that the Western majority in the Assembly might be used to turn down the communist states at a later stage: having sold the pass in the Council, she would by then have no way to retrieve the situation. She therefore proposed that the Assembly should complete the procedure for admitting one applicant before the next one was considered in the Council. This would have been a highly cumbrous procedure. The West proposed instead that, to meet the point, the Council might recommend the applicants to the Assembly in a single resolution, which the Assembly would have to consider without amendment. This was accepted as a compromise by the Soviet Union.

The applications were then considered by the Council in turn. The East European states all got through. But Mongolia, as some had feared, was vetoed by China. The Soviet Union thereupon vetoed all the Western candidates. Since the paragraph taken as a whole now included recommendations only in favour of East European countries, it was then in turn vetoed by the Western permanent members.

This was an absurd and obviously unwanted outcome. There were frantic negotiations behind the scenes. A few days later, on 14 December, the Soviet Union asked for a further meeting of the Council. She agreed to withdraw her vetoes against all the Western countries except Japan, which would thus be made the hostage for Mongolia. She would allow the remaining twelve non-communist states to go through, together with the four East European states, and she tabled a resolution in this sense. The United States immediately put down an amendment to add once more the name of Japan. Since this would obviously have destroyed the basis of the compromise, it was probably meant as a gesture only. In any case it was predictably vetoed by the Soviet Union. The compromise proposed by the Soviet Union then went through without objection.

The Assembly too accepted this compromise without demur. As a matter of form each application was eventually considered and voted on separately (though as part of a single resolution). In practice every applicant received at least forty-eight votes in its favour, with only two or three contrary votes and a few abstentions. The whole resolution deciding to admit all the applicants together was then adopted without a vote, the president declaring that there was 'no objection'.

So the long saga finally came to an end. The obvious compromise settlement, which had been resisted for so long, to admit all alike, brought the whole affair to a close. To understand why the Western powers for so long strenuously resisted the obvious solution it is necessary to recall the atmosphere of this age. There was nothing in the Charter, nor in the conception of the UN, confining the organisation to democratic states. The West had accepted without demur membership for the Soviet Union, and had even allowed her three votes. Nor was there any alternative government claiming to represent the East European states which were applying. Still less would the Western voting majority in the organisation have been seriously eroded by letting them in. But the intensity of cold war feeling at this time, and the revulsion in the West against the takeover of the East European states by communist governments after 1945, as well as against the methods subsequently used by those governments, were such that any means seemed justified for denying recognition or legitimacy to such governments. Nor was this view confined to militant Western powers in North America and Western Europe. They were at first supported by many developing countries in other parts of the world, which at this time shared not only their political attitudes, but to some extent their conception of the UN as an organisation.

It was a somewhat difficult line to sustain in terms of the Charter. For the only real qualifications the Charter contained for membership was the demand that members should be 'peace-loving'. Whatever the defects of the regimes in Eastern Europe, it was not easy to show that they were less peace-loving than other states. In the case of Albania and Bulgaria the charge might have been made in the early years that they were supporting rebellion in Greece. But this was not in fact an argument that was widely used; it did not anyway apply to other applicants; and it ceased to have any real substance after 1949. The charge that the regimes were not representative, though undoubtedly true, could have been applied to many other member states, and indeed to some of the other applicants. The charge that their governments were imposed was equally true of some other countries (it might, for example, have been made against Jordan, where the Hashemite family was in practice installed by Britain). And the denial of human rights in those countries, even if more serious than in any of the other applicants, was no different from that in the Soviet Union, which was three times a member; and a clean bill in this regard was in any case never laid down in the Charter as a qualification for membership.

It was the fervour of the age which found it possible to regard these regimes as falling into a wholly separate category, to which membership of the organisation must at all costs be denied. And it was only when, with the 'spirit of Geneva', that fervour began marginally to subside that the obvious compromise could be used to resolve the dispute. That change symbolised not only a softening of the cold war but, in UN terms, something more significant. The West, though still in a majority, began to be more solicitous of third-world views.

20 Conclusions: the First Decade

The shape of the UN in its first ten years was inevitably largely dictated by the political environment in which it existed: an environment of bitter distrust and hostility between the two super-powers and the nations which surrounded them, of competition for hearts and minds all over the world, of fanatical faith among the members of each group that they, and the things they believed, were right, while their enemies were the embodiment of evil – in a word, an environment of cold war.

This had the effect that those who came to the organisation had little hope, and indeed little desire, to compromise, to come to terms, to do deals. If any bargaining was to take place at all, it would be outside the organisation: at meetings of foreign ministers, summit talks and other such occasions (and not all that often there). Within the organisation the need was to speak up for 'what was right' (that is, what was believed by the majority). The opportunity was provided there, and was used by the majority in the world body, to show that the world was on their side, to use the moral authority the organisation possessed to justify their own position. There is no reason to believe that the minority, had the positions been reversed, would have behaved any differently. They shared the same messianic belief in their own righteousness, and would undoubtedly equally have used the platform provided by a world organisation to spread their own message, and to prove, through the voting figures, the justice of their own cause. Being a minority, however, they denounced all such attempts to pass declaratory resolutions; and still more any attempt to increase the power and authority of the organisation – which would have the effect of increasing still further the political influence of the majority which controlled it. Conversely, the majority sought in every way to increase both the moral authority and the practical power of the organisation. In doing so, in their eyes, they were serving the purpose of mankind and of peace on earth. If a resolution was passed by a large majority of the members, it must clearly represent the view of mankind, and should thus be respected: the fact that it also happened to represent the view of leading Western states was merely coincidental.

There was another sense in which the immediate postwar environment affected the development of the organisation. A postwar age is an age of hope. The last war has always been fought to end all wars, and a new age will be one of perpetual peace, which will be preserved above all by whatever new international organisation has just been set up (Quadruple Alliance, League, UN). In such circumstances there is a natural disposition to invest that organisation with expectations beyond its capacity to fulfil. In the eyes of many, not only in the West but also elsewhere, the UN was the basis of world peace. It should need only to speak the word – to call for a ceasefire, to demand respect for human rights, to plead for a withdrawal – for every state immediately to respond, and all problems immediately be solved. This was a belief more easily held by the majority, against whom embarrassing demands were unlikely to be made, than by the minority, against whom those demands would most often be directed. But it was a belief held also by many in the third world, who widely felt that the UN was the one place where they could make their voice heard, despite their impotence and poverty; the one organisation which could be expected to speak up for their rights.

Such hopes, whatever their origin, inevitably aroused illusory expectations. They created a belief that the UN could be expected to act as God, to be called in to produce the answer to all problems. Above all, they created an irrational faith in the power of resolutions. Resolutions became for some in the nature of magic charms, which had only to be uttered to bring instantaneous cures. The effect was that, when the incantations sometimes failed to take effect – when the ceasefire did not happen, when human rights were not restored immediately, when withdrawal by a great power did not take place as soon as a resolution was passed – the hopes were replaced by exaggerated *disillusion*. From having been worshipped as the salvation of mankind, the organisation became denounced for its 'ineffectiveness'. Disenchantment followed inevitably from the fervour of the initial enchantment.

Faith in the power of resolutions was promoted by ultra-realists and ultra-idealists alike. The realists, seeing the UN merely as another instrument of propaganda, were happy with passing resolutions, however bitterly resisted by their opponents – indeed, all the happier if so resisted – since they served to demonstrate how wide was the support for their own side, and so to score a victory. The idealists were eager to pass resolutions, even against the will of protesting minorities, because they deluded themselves that this furthered the purposes of the organisation: the voice of mankind would have spoken, right sentiments would prevail and the minorities, seeing the resolutions, would surely suddenly change their minds, do the opposite of what they had previously declared and miraculously conform. Even the minority – at this time the communists – made little attempt to change the system. Since they were passionately opposed to strengthening the organisation, they would indeed have been against any reform which might give it greater effectiveness. So the Soviet Union too was perfectly content to put forward resolutions designed solely for propaganda effect (for total disarmament, for the abolition of all foreign bases, for the immediate ending of colonialism, and for other great causes). The West, on the other hand, professing concern to see a stronger and more effective organisation, had more reason to adopt means likely to bring this about. And, since it at this time controlled the majority, it alone had the ability to do so. If, throughout this period, the UN failed to become a forum for effective negotiation on world problems, or to find the means to solve them by consensus, and if it therefore failed to reach any decisions at all on many questions, it is the Western majority who must take the main share of the blame for it.

The reason lies largely in the psychology of the cold war. Paradoxically, a considerable proportion of the *issues* were not essentially cold war matters. The main cold war problems were dealt with outside the organisation, either because they were connected with the postwar settlement (which it was always accepted should be decided elsewhere) – the postwar treaties, Austria, German reunification – or because everybody knew the UN could do little about them. Again many of the issues that came to the UN were those that had already led to war, or could do so at any moment, and cold-war issues were usually not of this type (those which were, such as the Greek civil war, Berlin and Hungary, were discussed in the UN): for the most part, the mobilisation of most of the interested parties into two large military blocs of comparable military strength, the caution induced by terrible weapons, above all perhaps the absence of any powerful demands against the postwar territorial settlement (unlike in the interwar period), together proved sufficient to preserve the peace among cold-war antagonists. When cold-war issues, short of war, were brought to the organisation, the polarisation between the two blocs meant that there was little that it could do about them. Over Trieste, the Czech coup, human rights in Eastern Europe, all-German elections, it could pass resolutions (usually one-sided in effect), but it could achieve precisely nothing. Over Berlin alone, where for once a serious process of negotiations was put in hand, did the organisation achieve some success on a cold-war question.

The significance of the cold war was rather in determining attitudes towards the other questions which came up. For there was no shortage of issues of other kinds. The entire process of decolonisation – in the wider dimension of history far greater in consequence than the cold war – brought a good many. Indonesia was the first, somewhat before its time, since there the nationalist movement acquired a strong military and political position even before the colonial power was able to re-establish itself after the war. Palestine too was essentially a question of decolonisation, but again somewhat special in that the real problem concerned not whether independence was to be granted, but what form it should take given the coexistence of two hostile peoples in the territory concerned. During the early fifties some more typical cases of colonial disputes began to be taken up, first in the three French North African territories, and later in Cyprus. Finally, throughout this period there was continual discussion about the racial policies of South Africa,[1] a discussion which was to continue and indeed become fiercer during the following twenty years. On all these issues, with the possible exception of Palestine, the approach of the great powers was strongly influenced by their cold-war posture.

The Soviet Union's support for the anti-colonial struggle was influenced not merely by its own political viewpoint but also by its hostility to the chief colonial powers. The attitude of the United States, conversely, was influenced not only by its alliance with these colonial powers, but also by its need to compete with the Soviet Union in the appeal to developing countries. Because all discussion took place in public, the spillover effect of the underlying confrontation on the discussion of other issues was inevitably intensified: there could be little genuine objectivity, because there was greater concern over winning the battle of hearts and minds, before the watching eyes beyond the television cameras, than with the merits of each dispute.

The only major problem altogether outside these two categories was the series of continually erupting Middle East conflicts which emerged first at this time and confronted the organisation continuously throughout its subsequent history. Though originating from a semi-colonial situation, the Palestine mandate, and the large-scale Jewish immigration which accompanied it, it acquired a special character of its own. The establishment of a state inhabited largely by people of alien culture from outside the region, in a territory which the Arabs regarded as theirs, and at the cost of large numbers of refugees from that territory, left the Jewish state in a condition of continual insecurity. Nationalist sentiments and historic resentments among Arabs and Jews alike created the same threat to peaceful coexistence as national sentiments and historic resentments had created in Europe and elsewhere in earlier centuries. The conflict was to represent the most serious and longstanding single problem with which the UN was to be concerned, and was to tax much of its time and patience for three decades to come. And here too, though to a lesser extent, once the Soviet Union had sided clearly with the Arabs in the early 'fifties, discussion was often tinged with cold-war overtones.

It was the balance of the membership, rather than the nature of the issues, which caused the perception of almost everything, from membership disputes to distant colonies, in cold war terms. The leading members of the organisation at its foundation – the United States, the Soviet Union and the nations of Western Europe – were all heavily involved in the cold-war confrontation. Even among the third-world members at that time, the twenty or so Latin Americans were heavily committed to the Western cause, as were many of the relatively few representatives of other continents – the Philippines, Liberia, Ethiopia, Iran and so on. There were few members of the organisation in this early period which were not deeply engaged on one side or the other in the cold-war conflict. Thus inevitably the approach of all was influenced by the concern that was closest to their own hearts. What was nominally the discussion of other nations' disputes became more and more a discussion of their own.

For in the battle of hearts and minds, which the cold-war increasingly was seen to be, war was indivisible; and the UN could be an invaluable addition to the weapons available, above all to the winning side. It could be a justification, quantified in voting figures, for their own policies. It was a loudspeaker for sending a message to the world. It could even be used to alter the procedures and structure of the UN itself. The Western powers could not resist the temptation to use their majority in this way: in creating the Little Assembly in 1947, and in forcing through the Uniting for Peace resolution, which enabled the Assembly not only to discuss threats to peace and security, despite a veto in the Security Council, but also to call for the use of force in these circumstances if necessary (contrary to what the Charter had laid down). So, when Lie's first term came to an end, they used it to procure, manifestly contrary to the spirit as well as the words of the Charter, that he should remain in office for a further term against the will of a permanent member. So, over Guatemala, they used every device (including a refusal by the president to call a Council meeting and to place an item on the agenda) to prevent the organisation from taking any action on behalf of a member-state under attack. So, over the membership issue, they kept twenty states out of the organisation for nearly ten years, in order to prevent the admission of two states with communist governments of whose governments they disapproved. So they kept out of the organisation, for far longer, the government that controlled the entire Chinese mainland and 98 per cent of its population, keeping in its place, bearing its name, a defeated and rejected faction which controlled an island off its coast. And so on. In other words, on countless issues, the West used the power its majority bestowed on it to ensure that the organisation acted in ways favourable to its own political interests and contrary to the principle of great-power consensus – admittedly not easy to achieve at that time – on which the organisation was based.

No doubt, if they had been in a majority, the communist states would have behaved in much the same way. The conduct of the West was a response to the existing political environment; a confrontation in which political passions were mightily aroused and no holds barred. But it was none the less an abuse of power. And it was an abuse that those same members were likely to regret more than most when the balance of power changed again and a different majority assumed control of the organisation.

KEEPING THE PEACE

Given the unfavourable political background, the record of the organisation in seeking to maintain the peace during this period might well have been worse. Indeed, it could reasonably be maintained that more active steps were taken by it at this time, not only to preserve the peace when it was threatened but also to bring about settlements of the underlying conflict, than at any subsequent period.

On one or two occasions the cold-war environment probably even helped the organisation to adopt a more positive response to threats to the peace than would otherwise have been the case. As we saw earlier, the main problem in any collective security system is to induce among the member-states sufficient sense of commitment to be willing to take up arms to assist a state under attack, even though their own interests are not directly affected. In time of cold war it may be, for once, sometimes possible to arouse this sense. This was shown at the time of the Korean War. Here the cold-war atmosphere made it possible to secure a strong recommendation from the Security Council in favour of action on behalf of the state under attack (though such action would have been impossible but for the accident of the Soviet Union's absence). And in practice this was, as a result, perhaps the only occasion in history on which it can be said that an international organ-

isation successfully made use of armed force to defend a state
under attack. Indeed, in no other case, before or since, has
there even been an attempt to put the collective security principle into practice.

Against this there were other issues where the polarisation
of the organisation between East and West undoubtedly made
it harder for it to operate effectively. In the case of Guatemala,
the deep-rooted ideological hostility of the United States and
other Western states to the existing government in that country induced them to ensure, in the case of a direct attack on a
member-state, that the Security Council took no effective
action. Over the gun-battle for the offshore islands, discussion
in the UN took the form of sterile confrontation, without the
participation of one of the principal states concerned, of a
kind that could scarcely be expected to produce results. On
these and almost all other occasions the substantive discussion
was always in public, not in confidential negotiation. On such
questions, the objective was often to use the UN as a means of
subjecting the opponent to the pressure of hostile propaganda rather than to seek a settlement. It is thus scarcely to be
wondered at that settlements were not secured. Only where
the customary methods were abandoned and confidential
negotiations were effectively instituted were better results
sometimes had. Such private discussions as took place – for
example, under the auspices of the Secretary-General, over
Berlin – did bring results: on that matter the UN can take the
full credit for having set in motion the procedure which finally
brought about a solution (p. 220 above). Given the overwhelming evidence that this was the procedure most likely to
produce results, it is extraordinary that it is one which, then
and at all times since, has been so little used.

Even so, the organisation had its successes when breaches of
the peace occurred. In the Middle East in 1948, it called twice
for ceasefires when war broke out and was twice obeyed. In
Indonesia it called for two ceasefires, which were both fairly
rapidly heeded; even more strikingly, in that case it set in
motion a conciliation effort which finally succeeded in bringing about, in the Round Table Agreement, a settlement of the
underlying problem. It brought pressures for withdrawal of
the Soviet forces in Azerbaijan, and of French and British
forces from the Levant, which helped to resolve those prob-

lems. It sent an observation mission to observe the Greek civil war, which probably significantly deterred external involvement in that conflict. It sent observer teams which played an important part in maintaining the peace between Israel and her neighbours after 1948, and between India and Pakistan after 1949. And it played a significant role in promoting the negotiations which brought the Berlin blockade to an end in 1948. All this was achieved despite the antagonisms of the cold war, and quite often with agreement between East and West.

Over issues in the remoter parts of the world, especially, cold-war influences were not fatal in effect. On disputes between small states in which the great powers had little interest – as that between Thailand and Cambodia – it could sometimes win a success and even (as in that case) resolve the underlying conflict (p. 320 above). In such cases the task to be performed, the national resistances to be overcome, the concessions to be won, were not out of proportion to the limited influence at the UN's disposal. Similarly, where the function of the UN was simply to keep watch, to guard against external intervention, or to police a troubled border, it was often able to succeed, at this period as later. It was where overt conflict had already occurred, so that the role of governments was already heavily engaged, that the organisation's ability to exert influence was least. The UN normally can keep the peace only where there is already peace: once war has broken out, its sanctions are too feeble to have much power. Though there are still many people who believe that the UN has, or should have, some magic wand that has only to be waved to bring instant peace, in fact no such wondrous instrument exists, and it is futile to blame it for this deficiency. The experience of this period proved, as was to be proved later again and again, that if peace is to be secured it can only be through efforts made to resolve the underlying causes of conflict before war has broken out. It was here above all that the procedures of the organisation often proved inadequate.

For there was one reason above all others why the UN failed in this period – failed, that is, to act, as its founders had proposed, as a 'centre for harmonising the actions of nations', as the Concert of Europe often succeeded in doing among European states in the nineteenth century. What the Concert was able to do was to consider disputes before they led to war, and then to hammer out, in private negotiations among the great powers, settlements based on some degree of consensus – that is, solutions which were more or less acceptable to all the major powers (even those not directly concerned). It was in this above all that the UN failed; and it failed because it never even attempted to achieve it. It was not seen, even by most of its members, as a place where the major powers, or any others, negotiated settlements to their disputes. It was seen as a public forum where issues were publicly discussed, where opponents were publicly condemned, where resolutions were publicly carried, where public opinion could be mobilised for one's own cause. It was seen, therefore, rather as a battle-ground than as a peace chamber: as a means of scoring points rather than of securing settlements; as an instrument for confrontation rather than for conciliation.

Of course, there were other opportunities for negotiation outside the organisation; and these were sometimes used. But, if the UN was to be an instrument for peace-making as well as for peace-keeping, for prevention as well as cure, for resolving disputes and so preventing wars as well as picking up the pieces after them, then it should have more often promoted discussion between the parties. It is sometimes said that the negotiations that take place between UN delegations in the corridors are far more important than what takes place in the Council chamber itself: six-sevenths of the UN iceberg. It is true that there is sometimes hard bargaining in the corridors. But this is almost always only about the terms of a resolution: whether it should be more or less strong, whether it should say 'deplore' or 'condemn', whether one phrase, word or comma should be left out in return for a favourable vote. This is not negotiation on the *substance* of the issues, which is the type that is really required. For this to be possible it would probably be necessary for the Security Council to have more of its meetings in private, or at least to organise more often private discussions between member-states that are in dispute, perhaps under a mediator. It is unlikely that without such procedures it will become more effective in resolving underlying conflicts than it was during this period.

Certainly throughout these ten years it remained for many merely an instrument in the major battle of the day, the cold war. To the minority party it was a propaganda platform, where minority views could be aired in the full glare of the public eye. To the majority it was the means by which they could secure voting victories for themselves, and so evidence that the world was on their side.

What the ruling majority forgot was that they would not always remain a majority. They did not see that the example they set might be used, to their own disadvantage, in time to come when a new majority came to power. If the West had been tempted to use its votes to force through its own views with little thought of negotiation, to impose the tyranny of the majority, how much more would the third world, when it came to power, be tempted to do so? The West at least had possessed alternative means of securing the ends it cherished: overwhelming military power, widespread diplomatic opportunities, huge economic strength, unrivalled political leverage. The third, world had none of these assets. It had no military power, little diplomatic experience, negligible economic strength and insignificant political leverage. For these countries, it appeared, the one weapon at their disposal was the majority in the UN, which, not long after the end of this period, they knew to be permanently at their disposal. It is scarcely surprising that, armed with this weapon, and inspired by the example presented by their predecessors, they proceeded, over the coming decades, to exploit to the best of their ability the one asset at their disposal.

So in their decade of supremacy the Western powers had sown the dragon's teeth. They then thought little of the wild wind they were to reap in decades to come. Still less did they consider the damage which such methods might do to the long-term influence of an organisation which, only a few short years earlier, they had been so proud to bring to birth.

Notes

PREFACE

1. Descriptions of the UN economic and social activities, as well as of the principal specialised agencies, including brief histories, are included in the author's *International Agencies: The Emerging Framework of Interdependence* (1977).

CHAPTER 1: THE LESSONS OF THE LEAGUE

1. Even the commitment to undertake economic sanctions automatically was watered down by subsequent amendments. Similarly, the duty to provide armed forces, always a recommendation only, was made still less binding as time went on. In 1923 a resolution that it was for the 'constitutional authorities of each member' to decide in what form to respond to a call for collective measures received overwhelming support. Governments in the final resort, while willing to make general undertakings to come to the help of victims of aggression, reserved to themselves the right to decide what action they would take in individual cases. What this meant was that the Council could never have any assurance what forces would be available to it in any case where it recommended action against an aggressor.
2. There was an attempt in 1924–5 to fill this 'gap in the Covenant' – the right of a state to resort to war if the Council of the League disagreed. Under the Geneva protocol members would agree that in such a case they would accept the decision of arbitrators appointed by the Council to consider the dispute – another form of legal procedure which, however, in this case was not finally adopted.
3. Only when the League was dealing with a 'dispute' between two parties and had reached a judgement on the question were the interested parties prevented from using the veto to overturn that judgement. The Manchuria issue was dealt with under Article 11 of the Covenant, concerning action proposed by the League to 'safeguard the peace of nations', and the veto therefore still operated. See L. P. Walters, *A History of the League of Nations* (London, 1960) pp. 461–77.

CHAPTER 2: THE PLANNING OF THE CHARTER

1. Ruth Russell, *A History of the United Nations Charter* (Washington, DC, 1958) p. 21.

384

2. Lord Gladwyn, *Memoirs* (London, 1972) p. 121.
3. Russell, *History of UN Charter*, p. 96.
4. W. S. Churchill, *The Hinge of Fate* (London, 1940) pp. 802–3.
5. Ibid., p. 562.
6. Ibid., pp. 710–11.
7. Record of the Moscow Conference, Oct 1943.
8. R. E. Sherwood, *Roosevelt and Hopkins* (New York, 1948) pp. 781–7.
9. The United States envisaged a kind of division of labour. The system would require the stationing only of US naval and air forces in Europe, while Russia and Britain would provide the land forces. In the case of any major threat of aggression, the Four Policemen might be required to issue an ultimatum threatening that they would bomb or invade the aggressor country. Stalin, particularly concerned with the problem of controlling Germany, was anxious that there should be strong-points available to the enforcement authorities, on the borders of Germany, in the islands around Japan and elsewhere. This would require continuous occupation of such bases by the controlling powers. The United States was dubious about the need for bases. The two super-powers were to take up exactly opposite views on this later (see p. 100).
10. The Soviet Union originally wanted the Military Staff Committee to include representatives of the whole Security Council. She eventually accepted the British contention that it should be confined to the five permanent members only.
11. See p. 103.
12. E. R. Stettinius, *Roosevelt and the Russians: The Yalta Conference* (London, 1950) pp. 187–8.
13. Eden was personally willing to accept Lithuania as well as the other two republics as separate UN members (in itself surprising, since the British Government at that time had not accepted the Soviet annexation of the Baltic republics) but the Soviet Union subsequently reduced its demand to two extra seats: see Russell, *History of UN Charter*, p. 536.

CHAPTER 3: THE SAN FRANCISCO CONFERENCE

1. This was finally somewhat amended to read, 'until the Security Council has taken the measures necessary to maintain', etc.: this made still clearer that the right to use regional arrangements was a temporary one until the Security Council had effectively taken the matter under control.
2. But it is worth noting that it was not then intended that the reservation would apply to military alliances. When the Egyptian delegate raised the point, the United States delegate assured him that 'a naked offensive or defensive military alliance as such ... was obviously not a regional arrangement within the meaning of the Charter'.
3. Russell, *History of UN Charter*, p. 541.
4. This did not of course apply to South West Africa (Namibia), which South Africa never agreed to convert into a trust territory.
5. These arrangements only covered the normal trust territories. For the

strategic trust territories, the United States Government refused to accept any specific provision for petitions, for annual reports or for visits of inspection.

6. But the agreed commentary argued that members would not be 'bound to remain in the organisation if its rights and obligations as such were changed by Charter amendment in which it has not concurred or if an amendment duly accepted by the necessary majority in the assembly . . . fails to secure the ratification necessary to bring such an amendment into effect'.

CHAPTER 4: THE SETTING UP OF THE NEW ORGANISATION

1. Trygve Lie, *In the Cause of Peace* (New York, 1954) p. 18.
2. Lie intended later to appoint three or four deputies to take some of the burden off himself, but because of his resignation this was never put through.
3. Lie, *In the Cause of Peace*, p. 45.
4. This meant that five of the assistant secretary-generals, in addition to the Secretary-General, were Europeans. This was a distribution of posts which would have been quite unthinkable later, but at this time caused little comment (partly because the proportion of European states was greater than it is now, while the number of nationals of other countries with widespread experience of the League, was still small). The position was marginally rectified in 1947 when an Indian, Dr Lall, was appointed to take charge of conferences and general services. As time went on, the proportion of non-Western nationals appointed inevitably increased.
5. Lie, *In the Cause of Peace*, p. 54.
6. The possibility of using this site had been suggested much earlier by Robert Moses, New York Parks Commissioner. Trygve Lie claims in his memoirs that he was the first to suggest to Moses, and to the Mayor of New York City, the possibility of an approach to Rockefeller for cash to purchase the site.

CHAPTER 6: NEGOTIATIONS FOR A SECURITY COUNCIL FORCE

1. Security Council, 141st meeting, 16 June 1947. It will be recalled that Stalin had earlier raised with Roosevelt the danger that Russia would provide only land forces, while the United States provided the more decisive air forces and Britain and France sea forces (p. 28 above).
2. These and other quotations come from Annex A of the Military Staff Committee report 'General Principles of a Security Council Force'.

CHAPTER 7: AZERBAIJAN AND THE LEVANT

1. This was one of three occasions on which actions or statements by the Iranian delegate in the Council were almost immediately overruled by

his government. For this reason it was believed by some, including Trygve Lie, that he was personally more committed to using the Council to bring pressure on the Soviet Union than was his government.

CHAPTER 8: GREECE

1. The French representative signed neither report, considering both too political to contribute to a reconciliation between the four states.

CHAPTER 9: INDONESIA

1. Report of the Good Offices Committee, 26 Dec 1948 (S1156).
2. It retained a nominal existence until April 1956.

CHAPTER 10: PALESTINE

1. The only similar case was that of the Italian colonies of North Africa, whose future was to be discussed over the following two or three years.
2. UN Commission on Palestine, 'Special Report on the Problem of Security in Palestine' (S676), 16 Feb 1948.
3. This was a somewhat similar arrangement to that used a little earlier to secure a truce in Indonesia: here too it had the effect of preventing Soviet participation.

CHAPTER 11: ROUND ONE IN THE MIDDLE EAST

1. Two other French observers and the US member of the UN Truce Commission were also assassinated during this period. Altogether nine members of the observer force, along with the mediator, lost their lives during fourteen months in Palestine.
2. Besides the agreement itself, there was appended to it three annexes, and a number of letters to and from the acting mediator setting out understandings on particular points.
3. The mediator had been established by the Assembly, so he could not be retired by the Council alone.
4. In another resolution, the 1948 Assembly had set up a fund for the relief of Arab refugees and appointed a director of UN relief for Palestine refugees. In August 1949 the Commission established an economic survey mission which was designed to consider the economic development of the area as a whole, especially measures which would ease the suffering of the refugees. It recommended a programme of public works to supplement and even replace direct relief. This led, at the subsequent 1949 Assembly to the setting up of the UN Relief and Works Agency (UNRWA), with a budget of $34 million, of which $20 million was for direct relief and the rest for work programmes. This

organisation has provided the basis for relief work among Arab refugees ever since.

CHAPTER 12: TROUBLE SPOTS IN EUROPE

1. Some judges issued dissenting judgements, mainly based on the fact
   that there had been no proof that Albania had observed, or could
   observe, the mine-laying operation, still less that she herself was responsible for it.

CHAPTER 13: THE KOREAN WAR

1. H. S. Truman, *Memoirs* (New York, 1965) vol. II, p. 325.
2. Full diplomatic recognition, by the United States and other states, was
   withheld until the endorsement of the election by the General Assembly
   in January the next year.
3. A number of other countries offered to send small contributions, but
   these the UN command considered not worth accepting: a batallion was
   regarded as the minimum size worth incorporating in the UN force.
4. Consultations took place in Washington between the US Government
   and representatives of the sixteen nations providing forces. But these
   became something of a formality. All effective decision-making power
   was with the US Government. Certainly the UN had no control over
   military operations.
5. Speech to American Newspaper Guild, 29 June 1950.
6. This decision would have been vetoed by the Chinese nationalist representative on the Council, but Sir Gladwyn Jebb, the president, ruled,
   over his protests, that the decision was a procedural one which was not
   subject to veto.
7. This feeling was intensified after an ill-judged comment by President
   Truman at a press conference that in certain circumstances the United
   States might wish to use the atomic bomb in Korea: this brought a hasty
   flight by the British Prime Minister, Clement Attlee, to Washington and
   much critical comment throughout the world.
8. The Soviet delegates argued, with some justification, that embargo
   measures should be taken by the Security Council rather than the
   Assembly; the Soviet bloc therefore refused to vote at all on the question.
9. The only countries outside the Soviet group that refused altogether to
   be bound by it were India and Burma, and neither of these in any case
   had any trade with China in the embargoed items.
10. There had been earlier suspensions, of a week and two months respec-
    tively, the previous year because of alleged violations of the Kaeson
    neutral area.

CHAPTER 14: KASHMIR

1. Under this article the Council could 'recommend appropriate proce-

dures or measures of adjustment' for the peaceful settlement of disputes.

2. The Commission's mandate was subsequently, in a resolution of 21 April, extended to facilitate the restoration of peace and the holding of a plebiscite in Kashmir after this became the official policy adopted by the Council.

3. It appears that Nehru had already begun to feel that a continued partition might be preferable to a plebiscite that would deprive India of the whole territory. See J. Korbel, *Danger in Kashmir* (Princeton, NJ, 1954) p. 131.

4. The resolution originally contained references to the possibility of using a UN force to maintain law and order during the plebiscite and to holding separate plebiscites in different parts of Kashmir (the one vestigial outcome of the Dixon proposals). But these were later deleted in deference to the objections of India and Pakistan respectively.

CHAPTER 17: DISARMAMENT

1. As Gromyko said on 5 March 1947, 'The Soviet Union is aware that there will be a majority in the control organ which may take one-sided decisions, a majority on whose benevolent attitude toward the Soviet Union the Soviet people cannot count. Therefore the Soviet Union, and probably not only the Soviet Union, cannot allow that the fate of its national economy be handed over to this organ.'

2. This committee used UN premises but was not strictly a UN body.

CHAPTER 18: THE SECRETARY-GENERAL AND THE SECRETARIAT

1. Lie, *In the Cause of Peace*, p. 42.

2. Ibid., p. 76.

3. Ibid., p. 33.

4. In Moscow he suggested that a representative of the Peking government should be sent to Geneva, in the hope that he might be admitted as the Chinese representative to the WHO, which included no representative from Taiwan.

5. Lie, *In the Cause of Peace*, p. 367.

6. Ibid.

7. The legality of the action was not really affected by the fact that the Secretary-General's term of office was not laid down in the Charter, but by a subsequent decision of the Assembly (p. 65). A five-year term had been clearly laid down, and any extension of this period clearly represented a reappointment for the purpose of Article 97.

8. Lie, *In the Cause of Peace*, p. 389.

9. Ibid., p. 383.

10. Ibid., pp. 396–7.

11. The Secretary-General's report to the General Assembly, 'Personnel Policy', 30 Feb 1953.

12. Hammarskjöld refused to reinstate four UN employees who had been dismissed by Lie and subsequently cleared by the UN Administrative Tribunal (which recommended they should be restored to their posts): an act which aroused great disquiet among parts of the UN staff.
13. The problems of the Secretariat's organisation in this period are dealt with in volume 2.
14. For a more detailed examination of the problems of co-ordination in the US system, see Evan Luard, *International Agencies: The Emerging Framework of Interdependence* (London, 1977) ch. 17.

CHAPTER 19: MEMBERSHIP DISPUTES

1. It was made possible for applicants to subscribe formally to the obligations of the Charter in submitting their applications. And the Council was to give a statement of its reasons if an application was turned down.

CHAPTER 20: CONCLUSIONS: THE FIRST DECADE

1. The discussion of these questions is described in volume 2.

Index

Abdullah, King of Transjordan, 180
Abdullah, Sheikh Mohammad, 280, 284, 289
Acheson, Dean, 245, 247–8, 256, 261
Adenauer, Konrad, 226
Administration
  advisory committee (ACABQ), 70
  provision of experts, 357–8
Admission of New Members, Committee on, 365, 367
Advisory Committee on Administrative and Budgetary Questions (ACABQ), 70
Afghanistan, 301, 364
Agencies, see Specialised agencies
Air force, international, 28
Albania
  border dispute with Greece, 120
  Corfu Channel affair, 209–12
  membership application blocked, 364
  supplies to Greek guerrillas, 126–7
Amboina, 154–5
Antarctic, demilitarisation of, 336
Arab Higher Committee, 164
  boycott of Palestine Commission, 175
  non-co-operation with Special Committee, 165
  opposition to partition, 168–9
Arab–Israeli war (1948), 190–208
  armistice, 196–7, 198–200, 206–7
  ceasefire proposals, 191–2, 193, 195
  Conciliation Commission, 198, 200
  Lie's actions in Security Council, 345
  Paris Conference (1951), 205–6
  Tripartite Declaration, 203–4
  troop withdrawals, 196, 197
  truce periods, 192–4
Arabs
  case against Jewish immigration to Palestine, 160, 164
  expelled by Israelis, 204
  increasing hostility to Israel, 203
  Lausanne meeting, 200
  Palestine solution imposed by UN, 185

protest against special committee's terms of reference, 165
  see also Egypt; Israel; Jordan; Lebanon; Palestine; Syria
Arbenz, Guzman, 295
Argentina, 40–2
Armed forces, see Military forces
Arms limitation
  European zone proposal, 335–6
  later achievements of UN, 341
Atlantic Charter (1941), 17
Atomic energy
  peaceful uses, 325
  Soviet interests, 324–5
Atomic Energy Commission
  abolition, 328
  Baruch Plan, 323–4
  established, 74–5, 323
  Gromyko Plan, 324–5
  Soviet withdrawal, 326
Atomic weapons
  Anglo-French proposals, 330–1
  desire for control, 322, 324–5
  proposals on levels of armaments, 330, 331
  see also Arms limitation; Disarmament; Nuclear test ban
Attlee, Clement Richard, 1st Earl, 285, 348
Auchinleck, General Sir Claude, 284
Austin, Warren, 178, 344
Australia
  on use of veto, 48
  proposals on Assembly's powers, 55
  tables item on human rights, 221
  trusteeship proposals, 60
Austria, membership application, 365, 367
Ayyangai, Gopalaswamy, 280
Azerbaijan, 93, 106–12, 380
  analysis of UN actions, 115–17
  autonomy sought by Soviet Union, 108, 109

391